CHINA IN
LATIN AMERICA

CHINA IN LATIN AMERICA

The Whats and Wherefores

R. Evan Ellis

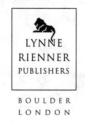

LYNNE
RIENNER
PUBLISHERS

BOULDER
LONDON

Published in the United States of America in 2009 by
Lynne Rienner Publishers, Inc.
1800 30th Street, Boulder, Colorado 80301
www.rienner.com

and in the United Kingdom by
Lynne Rienner Publishers, Inc.
3 Henrietta Street, Covent Garden, London WC2E 8LU

Library of Congress Cataloging-in-Publication Data
Ellis, Robert Evan.
  China in Latin America : the whats and wherefores / R. Evan Ellis.
    p. cm.
  Includes bibliographical references and index.
  ISBN 978-1-58826-650-7 (hardcover : alk. paper)
  ISBN 978-1-58826-675-0 (pbk. : alk. paper)
  1. Latin America—Relations—China. 2. China—Relations—Latin America.
I. Title.
  F1416.C6E55 2009
  382.098'051—dc22

                                                              2009002519

British Cataloguing in Publication Data
A Cataloguing in Publication record for this book
is available from the British Library.

Printed and bound in the United States of America

⊗   The paper used in this publication meets the requirements
       of the American National Standard for Permanence of
       Paper for Printed Library Materials Z39.48-1992.

    5   4   3   2   1

For Amelia, Brandon, Anthony,
Constantine, and Ian

Contents

Preface   ix

1 China's Expanding Ties with Latin America   1
The Scope and Character of China's Expanding Ties, 2
Key Considerations in the Dynamics of China's Relationships, 4
The Issue of Comparative Advantage, 5
Organization of the Book, 7

2 Why China Is Interested in Latin America   9
Latin America as a Source of Primary Products, 9
Latin America as a Market for Chinese Goods, 13
The Diplomatic Isolation of Taiwan, 14
Competition with the United States, 16
A New, More Confident Generation of PRC Leadership, 17

3 Why Latin America Is Interested in China   23
Hopes for Export-Led Growth, 24
Hopes for Investment in Fuel Development, 25
An Alternative to US Dominance, 28

4 The Southern Cone: Soy, Oil, Iron, and Customers   33
Chile, 34
Brazil, 49
Argentina, 62
Uruguay, 75
Paraguay, 81

5 The Andes: Fishmeal, Oil, and Tenuous Alliances   107
   Venezuela, *107*
   Ecuador, *122*
   Bolivia, *137*
   Peru, *147*
   Colombia, *157*

6 Mexico, Central America, and the Caribbean: 199
   Strategic Position and the Taiwan Card
   Mexico, *200*
   Costa Rica, *214*
   Panama, *224*
   Other Nations of Central America, *230*
   Cuba, *236*
   Other Nations of the Caribbean, *243*

7 Considering Latin America's Future   271
   Latin America's Economic Health Increasingly Tied to China, *273*
   The Importance of Chinese Communities and
       Entities in Latin American Politics, *275*
   Technology Partners, *277*
   The Transformation of Latin American Ports, *278*
   Pacific-Facing Countries as Hubs for Commerce with Asia, *281*
   New Patterns for Organized Crime, *281*
   Increasing Constraints for US Operations in the Hemisphere, *283*
   The Impact of China's Presence on US Agencies, *284*
   The Issue of Comparative Advantage Revisited, *286*
   Conclusion, *288*

Bibliography   297
Index   311
About the Book   329

Preface

I CAME TO STUDY THE PHENOMENON OF CHINA'S EXPANDING ties with Latin America largely by accident. In November 2004, I was in Talca, Chile, presenting a paper at a conference, when Chinese president Hu Jintao came to nearby Santiago to address the Asia-Pacific Economic Cooperation (APEC) forum summit. Although the boldness of the diplomatic initiative by President Hu and the quantities of investment being discussed took me by surprise, I was even more affected by the enthusiasm with which this was all received by the nations of the region. As I followed subsequent developments, I sensed that I was witnessing something terribly important—a growing series of initiatives and a flow of money that was, at that time, just a trickle, but with the potential to become far more.

As I have followed the expanding relationship between China and Latin America, I have come to understand how early computer enthusiasts must have felt following the expansion of the Internet: virtually every day in Latin America seems to bring news of a new project, event, or trip to China by someone, somewhere. Although this book seeks to provide a detailed account of China's growing relationship with Latin America, the rapidity of unfolding events also makes it a snapshot in time—an attempt to capture the shapes and patterns of something as it is exploding.

* * *

I could not have written this book without the assistance that I received from many people, at both personal and professional levels.

I would like to thank my children, who ultimately paid the price for the time I spent away researching, writing, and traveling. I would also like to thank Lynne Rienner, who put her faith in me to take on a project as ambitious as this one, as well as her staff, who patiently and diplomatically worked with me.

I am grateful to Mark Jacobsohn, Bill Thoet, and Mark Hermann at Booz Allen Hamilton; although I researched and wrote this book on my own time, their support and flexibility in allowing me to take personal leave for a significant number of research trips were critical to my ability to complete the project. I would also like to thank Susan Kaufmann Purcell, director of the Center for Hemispheric Policy at the University of Miami; Susan Davis, deputy director of the center; Bruce Bagley, head of the university's International Studies Program; and Brian Fonseca, of the Western Hemisphere Security Analysis Center at Florida International University, each of whom provided me with important contacts and academic forums to develop my thinking on the topic. I owe a debt of gratitude to Maria Velez de Berliner, president of Latin Intelligence Corporation, who was, at once, subject-matter expert, adviser, and good friend throughout my writing of this book.

As I worked on the book, I had the good fortune to travel to a number of countries both to conduct firsthand research and to present my work. I wish to thank the individuals in each country whose support was instrumental to my getting the story right.

In Chile, I thank Mario Ignacio Artaza, his nation's commercial attaché in Beijing, who went far beyond the call of duty to answer my many questions and to review numerous drafts of the section on Chile. I would also like to thank Patricio Navia, research director of the Asia-Pacific Program at Universidad Diego Portales, and Martin Schaffernicht at Universidad de Talca, as well as Alberto Sepúlveda Almarza and Ana Maria Cabello at Universidad Viña del Mar, each of whom helped me to understand the activities of their universities with respect to China and to the Chile-China relationship overall.

In Brazil, my thanks go to Rodrigo Tavares Maciel, executive secretary of the Brazil-China Business Council, for giving so generously of his time to answer my questions and review the Brazil portion of this book, as well as for putting me in touch with key colleagues to ensure that I got accurate answers to my countless questions. I thank Silio Bocannera, the distinguished journalist, who opened numerous doors for me in Brazil by allowing me the opportunity to discuss my research on his television program and who took the time to read my manuscript and provide feedback.

In Argentina, I thank Ernesto Fernández Taboada and Roberto Burgwardt, of the Sino-Argentine Chamber of Production, Industry, and Commerce, who—during my visit to the country and thereafter—helped me understand the details of China's commercial relationship with Argentina. I thank Julio Hang, director of Argentina's Institute of International Security and Strategic Affairs (CARI), as well as Jorge Triaca, executive director of Fundación Pensar, and his team, who provided me with a very important forum to present my ideas and interact with some of Argentina's leading strategic thinkers and businesspeople. I thank Joe Napoli, who was instrumental in opening many, many doors for me in Argentina, as well as Jaime Hulse, whose work on the Argentine telecom sector helped to orient me to the central role that such Chinese telecommunications firms as Huawei and ZTE are taking on today across the region.

In Venezuela, I owe a great debt of gratitude to Gustavo Coronel, who provided me with many key insights about Petroleos de Venezuela, Sociedad Anonima (PdVSA), and the politics of the country. I especially thank Makram Haluani and the Instituto de Altos Estudios de América Latina in Universidad Simón Bolívar, which hosted me during my research trip to Caracas in support of this book. I am indebted to Zhang Tuo, Venezuela's ambassador to China, who found time in his very busy schedule to meet with me and help me understand the emerging Venezuela-China relationship. I am similarly grateful for the time and assistance provided by Luis Davila, Anibal Romero, Tony Herrera, Adolfo Caste Jon, Eduardo Pocatello, Pascual Curcio, Alfredo Gruber, Richard Corrie, and Diego Gonzalez, as well as that given by Eugenio Hernandez, Fernando Fernandez, and Jesús Dávila of the Caracas office of the firm Baker McKinzie.

In Ecuador, I particularly thank Guido Zambrano, who humbled me with the amount of time that he spent helping me to understand the political and economic project represented by the Correa administration, making it possible for me to meet key figures in the Ecuadorian government and business community, and assisting me in getting accurate information about Ecuador's growing relationship with China. I thank Harry Sun Soria and Washington Hago, of the Ecuador-China Chamber of Commerce, who helped me understand the significance of the emerging business relationship between China and Ecuador and the unique place of the Chinese community within Ecuadorian society.

I am grateful to Cai Runguo, China's ambassador to Ecuador, for his time in speaking to me; and to Edison Guerrrero and Homero Zurita of the company Degso, who gave liberally of their time in supporting my research. I sincerely thank both Deborah Salgado Campaña and Paul Moreno in the Ministry of External Relations, as well as Ambassador Fernando Marco Samaniego and Fernando Guzman. I greatly appreciate the aid I received from Zheng Bingwen, director of the Chinese Institute of Latin American Studies, and from Susan Cabeza de Vaca, who helped me to set up contacts to travel to two of Ecuador's most distinguished universities, Escuela Superior Politécnica del Litoral (ESPOL) in Guayaquil and Facultad Latinoamericano de Ciencias Sociales (FLACSO) in Quito. Many thanks go also to Olaya Hanashiro and Adrian Bonilla for hosting me at FLACSO and to Gustavo Solórzano for hosting me at ESPOL.

In Bolivia, I thank Thomas Bonfiglio, who went far beyond the call of duty in helping me to organize a broad range of interviews and meetings with business and government leaders in Santa Cruz. I am grateful to Tom's colleagues at La Escuela de Altos Estudios Nacionales, who provided me with important insights for my research and made me feel that I was among family in Santa Cruz. I also thank Ambassador Gonzalo Montenegro; José Antonio de Chazal, executive director of Universidad Virtual; Carlos Vaca Guzmán, president of Electronorte; Luis Quiles, general manager of the firm Unicampo; David Suarez Nunez del Prado, principal executive of Economic Studies of the Chamber of Commerce, Industry, Services, and Tourism of Santa Cruz; and Jenny Ampuero Justiniano, head of the National and International Relations Department of Universidad Autónima Gabriel René Moreno, all of whom gave me important insights regarding the complex dynamics of Bolivia and its departments.

In Peru, I thank Chris Robertson, then a Fulbright fellow at Universidad de Lima, who created the opportunity for me to come to Lima to present my ideas and talk with his colleagues at the university. I also thank Luis Camacho Beas and Eduardo Morales Ortiz, who hosted me in my research and presentations at Universidad de Lima. I am grateful to Jimy Atunga Rios, whose expertise in logistics and transportation was indispensable to my understanding of the relationship between Peru and the rest of the region, as well as his family, who received me in their home multiple times, often at the last minute and under most unusual circumstances.

In Colombia, I owe a debt of gratitude to Isaac Dyner, who created the opportunity for me to come to the country to do research and present my work, and to Paula Escudero, who went far beyond the call of duty to take care of me while I was in Medellín and who helped me fall in love with the city and the warm and caring spirit of those who call themselves *paisas*. I also thank Pablo Echevarria Toro, former Colombian ambassador to China and director of the Asia-Pacific Studies Program at Universidad EAFIT, who dedicated a great deal of his time to me on a weekend, on very little notice, and in many follow-up conversations thereafter, to help me better understand China's emerging relationship with Colombia; I give many thanks as well to Nazly Munera Montoya, who provided me with a great deal of help in my dealings with the Asia-Pacific Studies Program.

In Mexico, my thanks go to Gloria Perez Salazar for making it possible for me to travel many times to her university, Instituto Tecnológico de Monterrey (ITESM), to further my research and present my ideas on the China-Mexico relationship; and to Raymundo TaMayo, who dedicated four days to taking care of me in Monterrey. My conversations with Ray during this time gave me a new appreciation for the personal and intellectual quality of the current generation of students at ITESM; I fully expect to find him someday among the senior leadership of Mexico and feel privileged to have made his acquaintance. I thank Jose Antonio Fernandez, executive director of Grupo FEMSA, and the leadership of his organization, including Luis Duran and Jose Mijares, who helped me understand the experience of FEMSA as a case study of an important Mexican firm positioning its product line in the Chinese market.

In Costa Rica, I am particularly grateful to Daniel Baldizón, who secured interviews for me with an incredible array of decisionmakers and business leaders. I especially thank Wang Xioyuan, ambassador from the People's Republic of China to Costa Rica, for his time in speaking with me. I am also particularly grateful to the following people for meeting with me and helping me with my research: Marco Vinicio Ruiz, minister of foreign trade; Francisco Morales, minister of work and social security; Ana Duran, vice minister of government and public security; Rowland Espinosa, assistant to the Costa Rican minister for interinstitutional coordination; and Alvaro Piedra, manager for international marketing, and Pedro Ramírez, coordinator of sectoral programs, of the Foreign Trade Corporation of Costa Rica. I would also like to thank Mónica Araya, president of the Costa Rican Chamber of Exporters; Carlos Sojo, director of FLACSO Costa Rica, and Manuel Rojas Bolanos of FLACSO; Ronald Peters Seevers, executive director of Costa Rica's Coffee Institute; Irving Soto, director of promotion and investment of the Costa Rican Investment Promotion Agency; and Rodrigo Vargas, general manager of Beneficiadora Sta. Eduviges. I also thank Mercedes Alonso and her family, who hosted me in their home during my stays in Costa Rica, and who convinced me of the power of character to make a difference in children's lives.

In Great Britain, I thank Monica Caro, who hosted me many times at Canning House, and whose knowledge of Latin America and connections in the business and diplomatic community were instrumental to me in writing this book. I thank Sir Geoffrey Bell, whose interest in hearing the analysis of one young and unknown scholar helped to open up many, many doors for me.

Finally, I sincerely thank Bob Melson, my senior professor and thesis adviser during my doctoral work at Purdue University many years ago. It was he, with great patience and kindness, who taught me everything that I can claim to know about the comparative method used in this book. I cannot suppose that my application of the methodology does justice to his teaching, but I want him to know that I have not forgotten.

In thanking these people, I wish to emphasize that any and all errors in interpreting what they told me are my own.

1

China's Expanding Ties with Latin America

THE RAPID EXPANSION OF COMMERCIAL AND POLITICAL TIES between the People's Republic of China (PRC) and Latin America has captured the imagination of a generation of business and political leaders throughout the Latin American region. For many, China represents an important market and a potential new source of investment capital. At the same time, many also look with concern at increasing volumes of competitively priced Chinese goods, both contraband and legitimate, that are beating out the goods of Latin American producers in their own countries and displacing them in their traditional export markets. From a political perspective, some in Latin America also see the increasing role of China in the region as a potential lever for asserting independence from the political influence of the United States and the economic dominance of Western institutions. Still others express concern about the long-term geopolitical ambitions of the PRC and worry about exchanging one form of dependency for another.

An increasing quantity of literature, both journalistic and academic, has begun to emerge in recent years documenting and analyzing the expanding ties between China and Latin America.[1] Many of these investigations document and characterize the growing trade ties between China and the region;[2] they include analyses of the positive and negative economic impacts of the growing ties,[3] of whether the net trade effect is more complementary or more competitive,[4] of whether China has diverted global investment capital away from Latin America,[5] and of various other themes at the sectoral level.[6] Various Chinese political figures and scholars have provided their perspectives on China's relationship with Latin America.[7] Such authors as Joseph Cheng and He Li address dimensions of China's interest in Latin

America that go beyond economic interests; as, for instance, the struggle for diplomatic recognition between the two Chinas that is playing out in Central America and the Caribbean.[8] Some analyze the possibilities of an alliance between the PRC and Latin America,[9] or point to potential threats that the new relationships pose to US interests,[10] while some argue that concerns over such threats are overblown.[11]

Beyond such works, there is a rapidly growing business-oriented literature on China's economy and trade ties in general, including political and cultural drivers.[12] Although these works are not focused on China's relationship with Latin America, they are instructive in understanding the experience that Latin American producers have had doing business in China and competing economically with the PRC in their own countries and in traditional export markets.

While each of these studies makes a valuable contribution to the literature, in late 2008, there were no books describing in detail the emerging relationship between China and Latin America. This book is designed to fill that void, painting a picture of the complex dynamics produced as businessmen, politicians, and social forces interact across the two regions.

■ The Scope and Character of China's Expanding Ties

The expansion of China's relationship with Latin America has affected each of the countries of the region. As other studies have noted, China's engagement has created winners and losers at both national and sectoral levels.[13] On the economic spectrum, the PRC has significantly expanded its exports across a broad range of sectors, from such labor-intensive, low-end manufactures as toys, textiles, and footwear to more sophisticated products, such as motorcycles, automobiles, telephones, and computers. At the same time, many Latin American countries have also significantly increased their exports—particularly with respect to primary products (fishing and agricultural products, petroleum, metals, minerals, and so on), and also with respect to internationally recognized consumer goods and premium products catering to the cosmopolitan tastes of a growing new Chinese middle class. Whereas not all Latin American countries have been equally successful in exporting to China, the hope of doing so is virtually ubiquitous in the region. Such hope is reflected in a proliferation of China-oriented business programs and Chinese-language offerings in institutes and universities across Latin America, in increasing opportunities to attend trade fairs in China, and in new service companies to help producers place their products in the Chinese market.

Chinese investment is also on the rise in the region. Although, in many countries, the expectation of funds from the PRC has far outstripped the reality, Chinese corporations, banks, and state enterprises are investing increasing quantities of capital in Latin America to establish reliable sources of supply for the primary products that China needs to sustain its economic growth. Such investments include acquisitions and joint ventures in petroleum and mining, as well as infrastructure investments to facilitate the import and export of goods between Latin America and China. Many, but not all, of these projects have taken place in countries with relatively anti-US foreign policy positions, such as Venezuela and Ecuador, or countries that have changed their diplomatic posture on Taiwan, such as Costa Rica, reflecting the complex mixture of economic and strategic considerations that drive Chinese investments in the region.

In addition to expanding economic ties, China is establishing an array of new political, social, and cultural links with Latin America. In the political realm, as Shixue Jiang notes, in the past decade, seventy-four Latin American heads of state and members of the legislature have visited China, while Chinese leaders have visited nineteen Latin American countries.[14] Exchanges are increasingly occurring at all levels; they include trips by parliamentary and party delegations and by military officers; the establishment of cultural programs such as the Confucius Institutes, which promote the spread of Chinese language and traditions in the region; and almost one hundred sister-city relationships.[15] China has also been involved with such multilateral and supernational institutions in the region as the Inter-American Development Bank (IADB),[16] the Caribbean Development Bank (CDB),[17] the Organization of American States (OAS), the Latin American Parliament, and the Corporación Andino de Fomento.

The issue of ties with China plays an increasing role in the politics and policy debates of individual Latin American nations. In virtually all countries of the region, expanding commerce with the PRC, including the promotion of exports and the attraction of Chinese investment, has become an important objective of national policy. Although some countries—for example, Venezuela, Bolivia, and Ecuador—have adopted very different approaches than the more traditional market-oriented policies of others—like Chile, Colombia, and Peru—each has sought to attract Chinese investment in one way or another.

Engagement with the PRC is also profoundly impacting the performance and structure of Latin American economies. As Carol Wise and Cinthia Quiliconi note in "China's Surge in Latin American Markets," China's expanding demand for such primary products as copper, petroleum, and soy has generated a commodity-led export boom that has affected virtually all countries of the region. At the same time, Chinese manufactured goods are increasingly gaining market share in individual countries, as well as displacing Latin American producers from their traditional export markets.[18] As a result, increasing trade with the PRC has begun to move Latin

America away from its development of manufacturing industries, and "back" toward greater reliance on export-oriented primary product sectors. Although Latin America is currently experiencing a period of unprecedented growth, this structural shift will have important long-term implications for both the development and the political stability of the region.

■ Key Considerations in the Dynamics of China's Relationships

I argue that China's relationship with Latin America is an evolving, multidimensional phenomenon, and that the dominant characteristics of China's ties with individual countries of the region vary greatly as functions of both the economic attributes and the political orientation of each particular country. The PRC has been very effective in building individual relationships with the region's countries by engaging each according to its unique political circumstances and by basing ties on what each country offers in terms of resources, markets, and strategic advantage.

In understanding the dynamic of China's relationship in each country, it is useful to look at a number of factors.

• The historical context in which the relationship between that country and China has evolved—including the legacy of alignment on international issues—shapes the political landscape by which the PRC relates to the country in the modern context.

• The size and characteristics of a country's ethnic Chinese community, including its economic and social position, influence both the commercial opportunities presented by the PRC to that country, and the socioeconomic tensions resulting from the expanding relationship. As Sergio Cesarin notes, the ethnic Chinese in Latin American countries play roles as traders and link-builders between both sides.[19]

• The products that each country has available to export, in combination with China's needs, shape the pattern of China's imports and investments with each country. In some cases, Chinese activities are devoted not simply to establishing supplier relationships and importing goods, but also to creating a local presence in the country and/or an infrastructure to ensure a reliable future supply of products.

• The volume and type of sales by China to each country of Latin America depend on the level of personal income in the country, the structure of the local market, and attitudes of the population toward Chinese products. The level of personal income and the structure of the market are important in determining whether Chinese sales are concentrated in light manufactures or extend to more sophisticated goods, such as autos and

computers, as well as whether they are concentrated in the formal or informal sector. The existence of an infrastructure to import and sell Chinese
products in the country is also key, as is the existence of regulatory and
other mechanisms to protect local producers.

• The ability of Latin American companies to do business with China
on favorable terms is a function of the legal, financial, and logistics infrastructures that support this commerce. The capability of placing products in
the Chinese market in a sustainable fashion, or of establishing other successful commercial relationships, is facilitated by such factors as knowledge of the language, culture, and transactions required. Such knowledge—
leveraged either from within the company itself or through consulting
firms—is important to establish and maintain long-term supply relationships in a geographically and culturally distant market. At the country level,
the viability of an arrangement, and thus ultimately of the pattern of trade,
is conditioned by the availability of a supporting logistics infrastructure
(such as efficient Pacific ports and the ability to transport products to those
ports), including effective support by the Latin American government.[20]

• China's relationship with each Latin American country includes, and
is shaped by, its interactions with each country in the political and military
spheres. Initiatives in this category include a myriad of items, from visits
between heads of state to legislative exchanges to donations for projects
meant to advance goodwill. In the military realm, Chinese cooperation with
Latin America is generally limited to the construction of personal relationships through officer exchanges and military visits, although China does
sell or donate military goods—generally of the nonlethal variety—to various Latin American countries, from Venezuela and Bolivia to Argentina and
Colombia.

Each of the themes presented in the analytical framework above is
touched upon in subsequent chapters of this book.

■ The Issue of Comparative Advantage

The new commercial relationship emerging between the PRC and the countries of Latin America calls attention to the traditional question of comparative advantage in the modern global economy, including whether and under
what conditions an economic approach based on comparative advantage in
the production of primary products can serve the long-term development
goals of the country. On one side of the question, Raul Prebisch,[21] Andre
Gunder Frank,[22] and others have argued that Latin America's participation
in the system of global economic relations is actually prejudicial to its
development. Urging a different view, some contemporary literature—rep-

resented by authors (e.g., Franko)[23] and studies by such institutions as the World Bank[24] and the International Monetary Fund—emphasizes that pursuing economic activity in areas in which a country has a comparative advantage, under the right conditions and with effective management by the state, can contribute to development of the country.

In the economic interactions between China and Latin America examined by this book, evidence suggests that patterns of trade specialization are indeed emerging, with each partner tending to export those goods in which it has comparative advantage. In general, as Robert Devlin and others have noted, the PRC leverages its advantages in manufacturing, including inexpensive labor, to sell products to Latin America and other global markets.[25] Reciprocally, as noted by Francisco González, Latin American countries have capitalized on abundant natural resources, including petroleum, iron, and copper, as well as available land for export-oriented agricultural crops such as soy.[26]

Despite the general pattern of specialization, the countries of Latin America vary greatly with respect to their primary-product endowments, industrial and technological bases, infrastructures, political and regulatory environments, and other factors. For this reason, the economic interaction between China and Latin America provides insight on the ability of comparative advantage to promote mutual development of trading partners over the long term.

The China–Latin America interface also includes many situations in which the PRC is competing head to head with Latin American exporters in markets like the United States, where gains by Chinese companies come at the expense of Latin American producers.[27] Such cases serve as a reminder that the economic and social dislocations produced by generating "winners" and "losers," and the policies to address the economic and social consequences of those outcomes, are significant components of pursuing comparative advantage in the modern global age.[28]

The examination of China's interactions with each country in the region puts such questions of comparative advantage in a dynamic context, which includes the effects from, and consequences for, economic and political structures and political actors. Free-trade agreements, political orientation, and government and business infrastructures help to shape in what sectors and in what form the dynamics of comparative advantage are realized. The fact that the Chinese are actively seeking to move up the manufacturing value-added chain into such sectors as computers, cars, and aircraft[29] while Latin America undergoes a process of progressive "deindustrialization"[30] illustrates that comparative advantage is a dynamic process, whose evolution is shaped by policymakers and individual economic actors.

This book also highlights the importance of intangible considerations with a bearing on comparative advantage (such as differential access to intellectual property) that complement production costs. It suggests the manner in which new infrastructure investments—generated by the pursuit of that comparative advantage—potentially create long-term benefits for the region's development, even if the activity in which the region's comparative advantage is concentrated is not associated with high salaries or the diversification of the economic base. The analysis also touches on the interaction between the economic dynamics of comparative advantage and its social and political consequences, asking the question whether pursuing an activity that generates significant profit at a macro level but ultimately destabilizes the society is the most economically rational course of action.

■ Organization of the Book

Chapters 2 and 3 explore the motives driving China's interests in Latin America and, reciprocally, Latin America's interest in China. This establishes the context for the regional and country-specific analyses in Chapters 4–6, which are organized to facilitate comparisons among the cases. Chapter 4 focuses on the relationship between China and countries of the Southern Cone: Argentina, Brazil, Chile, Paraguay, and Uruguay. Chapter 5 examines China's relationship with the countries of the Andean region: Bolivia, Colombia, Ecuador, Peru, and Venezuela. Chapter 6 turns to China's relations in Mexico, Central America, and the Caribbean. Chapter 7, the final chapter, marshals evidence from the previous chapters to identify and discuss the key implications of Latin America's growing relationship with China.

■ Notes

1. See, for example, Domínguez, 2006; Cesarin, 2008; Kurlantzick, 2006; Dunbaugh and Sullivan, 2005; Li, 2007; Montalva and Navia, 2007; Dreyer, 2006a; Dreyer, 2006b; and Oppenheimer, 2005.
2. Maciel, 2008; ECLAC, 2005; Mesquita-Moreira, 2007; Loser, 2006; Devlin, Estevadeordal, and Rodríguez-Clare, 2006; Blázquez-Lidoy et al., 2006; Jenkins and Dussel Peters, 2006.
3. Lederman et al., August 2007a; Lederman et al., August 2007b; and Colburn, 2008.
4. See, for example, Gallagher and Porzecanski, 2008; González, 2008; Lora, 2007; Trinh et al., 2006; Blázquez-Lidoy et al., 2006; López-Córdova et al., 2008; Castro, Olarreaga, and Saslavsky, 2007.
5. Cravino, Lederman, and Olarreaga, 2007a; Cravino, Lederman, and Olarreaga, 2007b.
6. See, for example, Palacios, 2008; Loser, 2005; CEPAL, 2007; Hulse, 2007; and Agostin, Martini, and Saavedra-Rivanro, 2004.

7. See, for example, Shixue Jiang, 2008a; Xiang Lanxin, 2008; Cheng Siwei, 2005.

8. He Li, 2005; He Li, 2008; Cheng, 2006.

9. Stallings, 2008.

10. See Kenny, 2006; Lafargue, 2006; Kurlantzick, 2006; Ellis, 2005; Dreyer, 2006a; and Erikson, 2006.

11. See Tokatlian, 2008.

12. See, for example, Naughton, 2007; Chi Lo, 2007; Rongxing Guo, 2007; Xueyuan Zhang and Reinmoeller, 2007; Dutta, 2006; Guthrie, 2006; McGregor, 2005; Mastel, 1997.

13. See, for example, Jenkins, Dussel Peters, and Mesquita-Moreira, 2008.

14. Shixue Jiang, 2008b, p. 43.

15. Ibid.

16. In October 2008, the PRC was officially accepted as a member of the Inter-American Development Bank, contributing a modest $350 million in capital to the institution, and culminating a long process that began with its formal application to join the bank in 1993. The success to date of the PRC bid for membership reflects a number of factors. From within the bank itself, the new IADB president, Luis Alberto Moreno, lobbied for inclusion of China as a vehicle for attracting more capital and attention to the institution. The United States, which had previously opposed Chinese membership, dropped its objections as part of a broader agreement with China to support the nation's expanded integration into international institutions. Japan, which was, for a time, the only Asian member of the bank, had also previously opposed the PRC bid, but was persuaded by the United States to drop its objections.

17. In May 1997, China was admitted into the Caribbean Development Bank. He Li, 2005, p. 87.

18. Wise and Quiliconi, 2007.

19. Cesarin, 2008, p. 24.

20. The latter includes such considerations as commercial enabling agreements, activities by embassies and trade promotion organizations, etc.

21. Prebisch, 1981.

22. Frank, 1971.

23. Franko, 2007.

24. Lederman and Maloney, 2007.

25. Devlin, 2008; Mesquita-Moreira, 2007.

26. González, 2008.

27. Gallagher and Porzecanski, 2008. See also López-Córdova et al., 2008.

28. See González, 2008.

29. Naughton (2007, p. 394) notes that the rapid surge in China's export of high-technology goods is "truly impressive."

30. See, for example, González, 2008, p. 160.

2

Why China Is Interested in Latin America

AS NOTED IN CHAPTER 1, CHINA'S ENGAGEMENT WITH LATIN America is driven by a number of different interests, although the specific manner in which Chinese government, corporate, and social actors relate to individual countries in the region is also affected by situational factors.

China's interests in Latin America can be divided into four areas: (1) acquiring primary products, (2) obtaining markets for Chinese exports, (3) gaining international isolation of Taiwan, and (4) securing strategic alliances as part of China's global positioning as it emerges as a superpower. This chapter analyzes each of these interests.

■ Latin America as a Source of Primary Products

China's interest in Latin America as a source of primary products is based in the rapid and sustained growth of the former's economy and the industrial character of that growth. Since China initiated its economic opening in 1978,[1] its gross national product (GNP) has grown at an average annual rate of over 10 percent per year. Indeed, prior to the global financial crisis of 2008, China's GNP growth had accelerated to exceed 11 percent per year. In 2007, according to China's Ministry of Commerce, China's economy grew by 11.9 percent.[2] Even as the global recession deepened in late 2008, China was still expected to grow by 7 to 8 percent. With such sustained growth, the Chinese economy has expanded dramatically. In 1978, the PRC accounted for approximately 1 percent of global gross domestic product (GDP), but by 2008 this share had expanded to 14 percent.[3]

Although some speculate that China's slowing growth will culminate in

9

crisis,[4] the Chinese have arguably proven themselves as capable as their Western counterparts in recognizing their demographic vulnerabilities and the contradictions in their economic system, and in working to address them.

The sustained nature of Chinese growth has combined with two additional factors to convince Chinese planners that the ample natural resources of their own country, and of Asia more broadly, will not be sufficient to meet the nation's needs over the long term.[5] First, because Chinese economic expansion has been based primarily around the production of industrial goods for sale abroad, the expansion of the nation's consumption of primary-product factor inputs has been even more dramatic than the expansion of the economy as a whole.[6] Second, due to a combination of factors that are exacerbated by China's rapid industrial growth, the nation's agriculture is increasingly in a state of crisis, requiring the nation to import ever greater quantities of foodstuffs to feed its people.

As a consequence of strong Chinese encouragement of exports as a path to development, the economic sectors that have emerged in the last thirty years are strongly connected to foreign markets.[7] In 2007, China surpassed Germany to become the nation with the largest volume of international trade.[8] The export orientation of China's growth is also evident in its persistent, enormous trade surpluses with most of the rest of the world. In 2007, for example, China had a net trade surplus of $262.2 billion, reflecting an increase of 48 percent over the prior year.[9]

China is a great consumer of primary products not only because its economy is oriented to produce for sale abroad, but also because its manufacturing sector is concentrated on goods that use large quantities of primary-product factor inputs. As Barry Naughton notes, the share of China's GDP represented by industrial production is extremely high for a large economy, as reflected in the country's reputation as the "factory floor of the world."[10] Certainly, the expansion of China's manufacturing capacity, in itself, requires a significant quantity of primary products, including cement, steel, and wood for the construction of new buildings, and various types of metals for the construction of production machinery. The concentration on manufacturing and capital formation is reinforced by relatively low consumption of goods by the Chinese population. Due to a range of both cultural and economic factors, including the lack of a reliable and universally available pension system, the Chinese save a remarkable 40 to 45 percent of their income. As a consequence, income that would be directed toward the purchase of consumer goods in other societies is channeled back into investment pools, where it is often used to purchase capital goods. Overall, the combination of such factors helps to explain that, although the PRC still only accounts for approximately 7 percent of the world's GDP, in 2007 it consumed 31 percent of the world's coal, 30 percent of its iron, 27 percent of its rolled steel, and 40 percent of its cement.[11]

Although the PRC is a nation relatively rich in natural resources,[12] the sheer volume of goods needed and the rate of industrial expansion have overwhelmed its ability to acquire the required capital goods and factor inputs domestically, or among its Asian neighbors, where logistical costs and cultural challenges are arguably fewer for China than reaching out to other regions of the world for the needed materials.[13] A case in point is petroleum. Chinese consumption of oil is expected to jump from 4.8 million barrels a day in 2000 to 12.8 million barrels a day in 2025.[14] Because of such increasing oil consumption without a corresponding increase in oil production within the PRC itself, the percentage of oil that the nation imports is expected to rise from its current 48 percent to 60 percent by 2020,[15] and perhaps 70 percent by 2030.[16] Such needs exceed what China can expect to obtain from its traditional petroleum suppliers, including Oman, Iran, and Indonesia, particularly in light of declining Indonesian reserves.[17] Such difficulties are, however, in no way limited to petroleum. In 2007, overall Chinese imports of primary-product imports increased by 25.4 percent.[18]

China's increase in imports is one element of a strategy crafted in recognition of the trend in the nation's resource needs. In its tenth five-year plan (2001–2005), the Chinese Communist Party recognized China's inability, over the long term, to produce and acquire solely within China the materials it needs to sustain its industrially based economic growth. In that plan, the government promoted a strategy of "going out" *(zouchuqu),* in which it encouraged major Chinese enterprises to seek out relationships abroad in order to construct global supply chains to ensure adequate material inputs to sustain Chinese economic activity.[19] With this guidance, major Chinese entities such as China Minmetals and China National Petroleum Corporation (CNPC) have actively pursued cooperative relationships, joint ventures, and acquisitions throughout the world. One result has been a number of high-profile deals, including the $4.2 billion acquisition of PetroKazakhstan by CNPC in 2005.[20]

As a complement to its needs for primary products for manufacturing and capital formation, China also increasingly needs to import food products. Demand is growing significantly as a product of rising prosperity in China, which fuels consumption of meat and other proteins.[21] At the same time, China's agricultural sector is in an escalating state of crisis. As Naughton notes in his overview of the Chinese economy, China's hilly and complex terrain means that relatively little of the land is suitable for cultivation;[22] only 13 percent of the land is usable for agricultural purposes.[23] Moreover, the ability to use productively the agricultural land available to grow foodstuffs is undercut by a number of factors. There is a rising deficit of traditional farmers as peasants leave rural areas in the interior of the country in search of better-paying jobs in the cities.[24] Complicating this shortage, as Naughton notes, the growth of cities is leading to encroachment into previously productive farmland and to disputes over property rights.[25] In January 2006, then Chinese prime minister Wen Jiabao publicly noted that conflicts between peasants and land speculators in rural areas were putting at risk China's ability to feed its population.[26]

Industrialization of agricultural areas undercuts agricultural productivity in other ways as well. Industry consumes significant quantities of water—an increasingly scarce resource in many parts of China—competing with the availability of water for agricultural use. The projected growth in water demand will make it increasingly difficult for the agricultural sector to irrigate crops and maintain livestock.[27] Periodic serious droughts in China in recent years have only served to punctuate the shortage of water and its adverse impact on agriculture production.[28]

Chinese agriculture is also adversely impacted by growing quantities of industrial waste. One Chinese study estimates that 10 percent of the farmland in the country is contaminated by by-products of industry.[29] If the levels of regulation and enforcement—now relatively low—are not raised, the ongoing, rapid expansion of industry into the interior provinces will increasingly undermine the productivity of the land that remains available for agricultural purposes.

As a consequence of these challenges, China is importing greater than ever quantities of its food from abroad. Between 2000 and 2005, Chinese agricultural imports more than doubled. By 2005, for example, 40 percent of the world's soybean exports went to the PRC.[30]

As the PRC looks abroad for the products that it needs to feed its people and its industry, it has found significant quantities of those goods available in Latin America. Venezuela, Brazil, and Ecuador, for example, are positioned to export progressively more oil to the PRC. When the heavy petroleum deposits of Venezuela's Orinoco region are counted, for example, that nation has the world's largest oil reserves—larger than even Saudi Arabia's—although China's ability to exploit this oil is fraught with logistical, technical, and political challenges. With respect to minerals, Latin America has an estimated 25 percent of the world's reserves of silver, 30 percent of its tin reserves, and 45 percent of its copper reserves.[31] Chile is one of the world's largest copper exporters, while Brazil is a major iron supplier. The iron deposits in neighboring Bolivia may ultimately eclipse even those of Brazil, while Peru exports a range of metals and minerals to China.

With respect to agriculture, Chile and Peru account for an estimated 80 percent of Chinese fishmeal imports.[32] Similarly, Brazil and Argentina have emerged as major suppliers of soybeans and associated vegetable oils to the PRC. One-third of all soy exported by Brazil and Argentina goes to the PRC.[33]

Growing Chinese prosperity and the development of more cosmopolitan tastes among its new middle class have also expanded interest in Latin

American food products. The Chilean wine industry, for example, is bene-fiting tremendously from the emergence of a newly prosperous middle class in the PRC with an interest in foreign wines. Similarly, Mexican beer pro-ducers, such as Grupo FEMSA and Grupo Modelo, are profiting from a growing Chinese interest in "authentic" Mexican beer—as Colombian and Costa Rican producers are from the growing Chinese taste for coffee.

At the same time, it is important to recognize that China's search for secure supplies of agricultural goods, capital goods, and industrial factor inputs is global in its scope. Indeed, in some ways, Chinese diplomacy and commercial actions to secure access to primary products in Africa parallel its activities in Latin America. Moreover, the emphases that China places on different parts of the world may shift over time as it encounters success in one region relative to another. Chinese frustrations in securing its objectives in Latin America, for example, could lead it to place more weight on other areas, such as Africa. Over the long run, however, the expansion of Chinese demand for a broad range of primary products will lead it to do business in every part of the world.

■ Latin America as a Market for Chinese Goods

Although much attention is given to Chinese interest in Latin America as a supplier of primary products, the region is also increasingly important to China as a market. Indeed, in 2007, according to the PRC Ministry of Commerce, China sold $51.5 billion in goods to Latin America, an amount slightly greater than the $51.1 billion that it purchased from the region dur-ing that year.[34]

Although Chinese companies seek to sell their products wherever they can, there are a number of reasons that Latin America represents a particu-larly important market. The economic growth of the developed countries that have traditionally been the primary customers for China's export prod-ucts has slowed during recent years. Indeed, with the global economic crisis of 2008, the economies of the United States and Europe began to contract. The PRC has recognized the need to diversify away from its declining tradi-tional markets in order to maintain its growth. As Jiang Shixue, chair of the Latin American Studies Department at the Graduate School of the Chinese Academy of Social Sciences and a leading Chinese scholar, argues, "[E]xpanding its market share in Latin America has been part of China's objective to reduce its dependence upon the United States, Japan, and Europe."[35] Moreover, in each of these countries, the rapid growth in Chinese imports has damaged domestic manufacturers, giving rise to politi-cal pressures to restrict, or to impose renewed tariff barriers on, Chinese imports. To cite one instance, in April 2007, the United States officially brought a complaint against China in the World Trade Organization for a range of unfair practices, including insufficient protection of intellectual property. As Jiang notes, "China views the United States as a country that uses its economic leverage to exert political pressure on China, which is one reason that China seeks to diversify its economic relationships."[36]

As the PRC seeks new markets for its export products, Latin America represents an attractive and logical customer base. Most of the nations of Latin America fall into the "middle income" category in terms of per capita GNP. In other words, Latin American countries generally have a significant number of consumers with sufficient income to purchase Chinese export products. As Jiang states, "Latin America, with a population of more than 500 million and an economy of nearly $3 trillion, is an attractive market for Chinese products."[37]

With the exception of a small elite, Latin American consumers are generally very responsive to the low prices offered by Chinese goods. Although some are willing to pay a premium for designer clothing, many are not—and Chinese products look similar to, but are significantly cheaper than, the corresponding alternatives. Regarding the market for more expensive products, such as computers, motorcycles, and cars, the "value" orientation of the Latin American consumer is an even more powerful factor. In South America, for example, a new Chinese motorcycle can be purchased for approximately $1,000, versus $5,000 for a similar Japanese motorcycle. While the quality of the Chinese motorcycle may not be perceived as equivalent to that of its competitor, the difference in price is so great that the real choice for the consumer may be between buying the Chinese product and not buying the product at all.

Beyond the factors that make Latin America attractive as a formal market for Chinese goods, the region also presents a range of opportunities for China to sell its products through the informal sector. Because of income levels and cultural factors, there exists a substantial base of consumers in many Latin American societies willing to purchase contraband products—pirated music CDs, DVDs, imitations of designer clothing and footwear, and similar items. In many Latin American countries, customs and other enforcement authorities are not able effectively to block either the entry of such products into the country or their sale, because enforcement organizations are underresourced, corrupt, or simply overwhelmed by the volume of contraband products involved.[38]

■ The Diplomatic Isolation of Taiwan

The nature of China's interests in Latin America varies significantly by region. Central America and the Caribbean, for example, do not have significant quantities of oil, metals, or minerals for sale to China. Although Central America does export some agricultural goods, it has not yet developed the connections and logistics to export large quantities of its products to the PRC on a sustained basis. Reciprocally, although countries in Central America and the Caribbean purchase modest quantities of Chinese products, the small size of their economies, and the relatively small middle class in each, limit these nations' potential as markets for Chinese export products.

Despite their modest footprint in economic relations with China, Central America and the Caribbean play an important role in the long-term global strategy of the PRC to internationally isolate its rival, the Republic of China (ROC), which it officially regards as a renegade province. Indeed, He Li argues that China's quest to isolate and reincorporate Taiwan is one of the top issues on its foreign policy agenda.[39]

Currently, twelve of the twenty-three countries in the world that recognize Taiwan as the legitimate government of China are concentrated in Central America and the Caribbean.[40] Jiang writes, "[T]he issue of Taiwan remains a sticking point for China's policy in the region."[41] Six of the countries that recognize Taiwan are located in Central America: Panama, Nicaragua, El Salvador, Honduras, Guatemala, and Belize. The other five are in the Caribbean: the Dominican Republic, Haiti, St. Kitts and Nevis, St. Vincent and the Grenadines, and St. Lucia. In South America, only Paraguay continues to recognize Taiwan.

For China, the countries of Latin America that recognize Taiwan are high-value strategic targets. Because the contest for recognition is fundamentally a diplomatic one, played out in international organizations in which each nation generally has one vote, the position of tiny St. Lucia, for example, technically carries the same weight as that of Brazil.[42] As He Li writes, "Fearing Taiwan's push for international recognition will lead to its declaration of independence, Beijing is determined to contain Taiwan in every corner of the world, especially in Central America and the Caribbean."[43]

The small size of the countries that recognize Taiwan also suggests that they can be tempted by relatively modest aid packages, or the promise of preferential trade access to the vast Chinese market. In 2004, for example, the ROC declined to give the Commonwealth of Dominica a requested $58 million aid package. This dispute was one of the reasons that Dominica switched its diplomatic recognition to the PRC in 2005.[44] In return for this action, the PRC gave the island nation $11 million in immediate aid, plus an additional $100 million in grant aid over six years. Although modest in absolute terms, the aid package was enormous in relative terms, representing more than a third of the government's normal revenue during this period, and amounting to $1,750 for each of the island's 70,000 inhabitants in per capita terms.[45]

■ Competition with the United States

In his paper "An Alternative Chinese View," Xiang Lanxin disputes the common opinion that China's entry into Latin America is simply a consequence of a "going global" strategy. He argues, by contrast, that, for China, traditional geopolitic factors "are still the primary drivers of Chinese policy toward Latin America, albeit in a new context."[46]

As is the rest of the world, China is conscious that its rapid economic growth, if sustained, will make it the world's largest economy within the next generation, and possibly as soon as 2027.[47] Although the position of China in the world system in the twentieth century was relatively weak, in previous centuries, China, as the Middle Kingdom, was often a dominant regional power, sending emissaries and traders to all parts of the world and receiving tributes from lesser powers. Indeed, some studies suggest that Chinese explorers may have been the first to discover the Americas, with the visit of Chinese monks to Mexico in the fifth century AD.[48] Similarly, British scholar Gavin Menzies claims that Chinese admiral Zheng He, with a fleet of 300 ships, discovered America in 1421 and later sold his maps to European navigators.[49]

In the context of hundreds of years of history linking the China of today to a tradition of geopolitical dominance and empire, it is relatively natural for the PRC to interpret the current period as merely the nation's return to its traditionally dominant role in the world system after a brief period of weakness. In "resuming" its customary place in the international system, China is almost certainly aware of the concern that its actions generate in the United States, currently the dominant power in that system. Thus, one of China's goals is to manage the transition well, which includes the avoidance of a situation whereby the United States is motivated to block the process or—better yet, by its lights—is able to do so.[50]

Part of China's campaign to avoid provoking the United States during this transition has been to refer to the dynamic as China's "peaceful rising,"[51] a process that Xiang characterizes as an attempt to mitigate the "reactions of alarm and preoccupation about the potential long-term impact of China's expansion into the region."[52]

China's management of its rise as a global power also involves its promotion of multilateralism and a multipolar world, to avoid a world order dominated by the United States not only politically and militarily, but also with respect to global institutions.[53] Jiang asserts, "Politically speaking, Latin America could be a partner for China . . . in their efforts to oppose hegemony, establish a just world order and a harmonious world."[54] While China may not seek to use these institutions in a proactive fashion in the near term, its presence in them helps to ensure that they will not be used as a multilateral instrument to "lock China out" of the region, either politically or financially.

Many of the Latin America–related organizations in which China has a role (such as its observer status in the Organization of American States, or its membership in the Inter-American Development Bank) would appear to fit within this strategic framework.[55] As Monica Hirst has noted, this also includes global organizations that put China and Latin American countries together in a common "South-South" framework, like the Group of Seventy-Seven (G-77) and the United Nations Conference on Trade and Development (UNCTAD).[56]

China's recognition of the governments of Mexico, Brazil, Venezuela, and Argentina as "strategic partners"[57] is consistent with this logic. Strategic partner status not only bestows recognition, but also establishes mechanisms for coordination and resolution of disputes, both economic and otherwise. Each nation that China recognizes as a strategic partner has current or potential influence over other nations of the region. Brazil and Argentina have traditionally been the dominant economic and political powers in South America; as such, they have significant leverage over other countries in the continent. Similarly, Mexico is influential with respect to the states of Central America. Venezuela has a degree of economic and political leverage over the nations of the Caribbean, and seeks to use its oil wealth to expand its influence in that region through such partnerships as Petrosur, Petrocaribbe, Bancosur, and the Alternativa Boliviariana de las Americas (ALBA). Thus, the "special treatment" that the PRC gives to these four key powerbrokers as strategic partners may be seen as a vehicle for China to increase its influence by working through the current political power dynamics of the region.

Finally, China's support for populist regimes in the region, including those of Venezuela, Ecuador, and Bolivia, may also be regarded as a type of strategic positioning. While it is doubtful that China wishes to establish client states in Latin America in the near term, as the Soviet Union did with Cuba and Nicaragua during the Cold War, supporting states in the region that verbally and materially oppose the US presence there ultimately serve the interests of the PRC because it prevents the United States from establishing unquestioned control over the region's financial and political institutions.[58] Xiang Lanxin, for example, argues that China sees the "Bolivarian revolution" of Hugo Chávez as a potential vehicle to move countries in the region away from the Monroe Doctrine and reduce the region's dependence on the North American market.[59]

▓ A New, More Confident
Generation of PRC Leadership

Although the logic behind the growing Chinese engagement in Latin America is clear, China's decision to expand its political, cultural, and economic ties with the region at this particular time, and at such speed, must be understood in terms of the leaders who made those decisions, as well as their interpretations of, and responses to, the opportunities and threats presented by the international system.

Hu Jintao and the group that is currently in power in Beijing, and to some extent his predecessor, Jiang Zemin, represent a generation that has come of age in a China no longer struggling merely to survive in the international system.[60] Mao Zedong and the leadership who consolidated power following the communist revolution of 1949 inherited a China that was relatively weak in military and economic terms. In the early years following the revolution, China was struggling to feed its people, while trying to define the meaning of Chinese communism domestically and to position itself between two powerful geopolitical rivals—the United States and the Soviet Union. Although Mao's successor, Deng Xiaoping, began to situate China once again as a great power in the world system, it was the China inherited by Jiang Zemin and his successor, Hu Jintao, that finally had begun to accumulate the economic weight and liberty in the international arena to focus on the challenges of growth rather than on the imperatives of survival. Although the collapse of the Soviet Union in 1989 was paralleled by a political crisis in China that ultimately led to the events of Tiananmen Square and an associated series of crackdowns across the country, the disappearance of the Soviet Union also redefined the position of China in the international sphere as the last contender among a group of communist countries that had fought against the capitalist world order during the Cold War.

Although the People's Republic of China inherited by Hu Jintao was communist only in terms of its political structure, the ability of the regime to survive Tiananmen Square allowed China to lay claim to being the only remaining great-power alternative to a US-dominated world order. This position, and the economic strength of the China inherited by Hu and his leadership team, allowed China to build a new type of relationship with Latin America. Now China must decide, as Xiang Lanxin puts it, what role, if any, it wants to play in the death of the Monroe Doctrine, in which Latin America falls within an exclusive US sphere of influence, "off limits" to foreign powers.[61]

At the time of this book's research, preliminary indications were emerging of the leaders who may ultimately replace Hu Jintao. The retirements and promotions that took place in conjunction with the Seventeenth Congress of the Chinese Communist Party in October 2007, for instance, provided hints of who may become the leadership when the Eighteenth Communist Party Congress is convened in 2012. China experts speculate that Xi Jinping, the party boss of powerful Shanghai Province, could succeed Hu Jintao as the next president.[62] Xi Jinping is a protégé of Hu, and was one of the four members newly appointed to the Politburo. Similarly, experts speculate that another newly elected Politburo member, party boss of Liaoning Province, Li Kequiang, could become the next prime minister.[63]

Whoever are the next leaders of China, and however their personal styles interact with the unfolding domestic and international environment, they will decide how China will relate to particular Latin American countries as it responds to the situational imperatives for resources and markets and positions itself globally—while avoiding crises that could create an unwanted, or premature, conflict with the United States.[64]

▣ Notes

1. "China, la révolución galáctica." *Nacion*. San José, Costa Rica. http://www.nacion.com/proa. June 24, 2007.

2. "BM: China crecerá el 9,8 en el 2008." *El Universal*. Caracas, Venezuela. http://www.el-universal.com. June 19, 2008. See also, "China restringe préstamos en intento de desacelerar su economía." *Diario Financiero*. Santiago, Chile. http://www.df.cl. July 30, 2007.

3. "China acelera el paso para consolidarse como la primera potencia mundial." *Diario Financiero*. Santiago, Chile. http://www.df.cl. July 9, 2008.

4. See, for example, Wolf, Yeh, and Zycher, 2003.

5. Arguably, obtaining the needed resources within Asia would be more attractive, if it were a viable strategy, insofar as it would involve shorter supply lines, with relatively greater cultural familiarity.

6. The development and growth strategy pursued by the Chinese state has emphasized industrialization and export sales of manufactured goods as vehicles for development. China has pursued a number of strategies to attract foreign investment to set up export-oriented manufacturing operations in China. Until Chinese tax laws were reformed in 2007, for example, profits from foreign capital investment were taxed at roughly half the rate of that imposed on domestic investments. "Acuerdos del congreso popular de China revelan las prioridades del gobierno." *Diario Financiero*. Santiago, Chile. http://www.df.cl. April 2, 2007.

7. The ratio of China's bilateral trade volume to its GDP is 70 percent, significantly higher than the ratio for other industrialized economies. O'Quinn, 2005.

8. Namur, 2007. See also, "China sera el mayor exportador mundial." *La Nacion*. Buenos Aires, Argentina. http://www.lanacion.com.ar. July 24, 2007.

9. "Main Indicators of Foreign Trade and Economy (2007/01–12)." *Ministry of Commerce. People's Republic of China*. http://english.mofcom.gov.cn/aarticle/statistic/iein-dicators/200802/20080205371703.html. February 4, 2007.

10. Naughton, 2007, p. 156. Indeed, 93 percent of Chinese exports in 2006 were manufactured goods. César Ferrari, "China, Colombia y Perú: Impactos sobre crecimiento e Ingreso." *Latin American Trade Network*, no. 25. April 2007.

11. Guthrie and Preston, 2007. See also Díaz, 2005.

12. Scholars such as Jiang Shixue note, however, that China's endowment of resources is relatively lower than the world average by some standards. Shixue Jiang, 2008b, p. 44.

13. In some cases, such as the consumption of coal for the generation of electricity, the challenge is not simply a lack of material or a lack of capacity to extract and process it, but also a logistics infrastructure that is inadequate to transport the materials to their needed markets in a timely fashion and at reasonable cost.

14. Although China has attempted to reduce its petroleum consumption, conservation goals have not been met, and Chinese oil consumption continues to rise in relation to the expansion of China's GDP.

15. "China importará el 50% de su consumo de crudo en el 2010." *Nacion.* San José, Costa Rica. http://www.nacion.com. June 25, 2007.

16. Palacios, 2008, p. 171.

17. Lafargue, 2006, p. 80.

18. Indeed, by contrast to the United States and other developed nations, very little of China's imports are consumer goods. According to the PRC Ministry of Commerce, in 2006, 21.2 percent of Chinese imports were capital goods, used to expand manufacturing capacity; 75.6 percent of imports were interim products, and only 3.1 percent of imports were consumer goods. "Imports by Major Categories (2007/01–12)." *Ministry of Commerce of the People's Republic of China.* http://english.mofcom.gov.cn/aarticle/statistic/ie/200802/-20080205372493.html. February 4, 2008.

19. Cheng Siwei, 2005.

20. "Compañía Petrolera China CNPC compra Petrokazakhstan." *El Universal.* Caracas, Venezuela. http://www.eluniversal.com. August 22, 2005. See also, "Analistas detectan sed asiática por energía foránea." *El Universal.* Caracas, Venezuela. http://www.eluniversal.com. August 24, 2005. In addition, a number of Chinese initiatives have been blocked because of the fears and concerns they provoked in the host countries, including the attempt by China Minmetals to acquire the Canadian mining firm Noranda in 2004 (Jubany and Poon, 2006, p. 32), and the attempt by CNPC to purchase UNOCAL in 2005. "Chinese Firm Abandons UNOCAL Bid." *BBC News.* http://news.bbc.co.uk/2/low/business/4738939.stm. August 2, 2005.

21. According to a survey done in 2008, for example, annual Chinese meat consumption in the western part of the country was expected to rise by 20 percent, while consumption of dairy products was expected to double. "La carnivore revolución de la mesa China." *El Universal.* Caracas, Venezuela. July 4, 2008. Similarly, according to a different study, Chinese demand for fish is expected to rise 40 percent between 2007 and 2020. "Consumo de pescado en China crecerá 40% a 2020." *Diario Financiero.* Santiago, Chile. http://www.df.cl. November 6, 2007.

22. Naughton, 2007, p. 20.

23. "China modernizará sistema agrícola y concederá pensiones rurales." *Nacion.* San José, Costa Rica. December 24, 2007. To view the problem in relative terms, China, with 21 percent of the world's population, only has 9 percent of the world's arable cropland. US Department of Agriculture, 2000.

24. Although migration in China is officially limited by the requirement of residence permits to move to and work in an area, substantial numbers of Chinese have migrated without permission, creating enormous floating populations and a substantial informal sector around urban areas. Thus, rural areas are left with large numbers of people still registered there as workers, but no longer available to work the land.

25. Anecdotal evidence suggests that town and village party officials, who have substantial amounts of autonomy in rural areas, often grant permits for industry to use agricultural land without being constrained by the long-term impacts on the agricultural productivity of the region. Naughton, 2007, p. 121.

26. "Alarma en China por situación en el campo." *El Tiempo.* Bogotá, Colombia. http://www.eltiempo.com. January 20, 2006.

27. Demand for water in China, estimated to be 52 billion cubic meters for the year 2005, is expected to increase by a factor of 5 to 269 billion cubic meters by

2030. "China está amenazada por una fatal crisis hídrica." *El Comercio.* Quito, Ecuador. http://www.elcomercio.com. November 5, 2006.

28. In 2007, for example, wide areas of southwestern China were affected by a drought that led to limitations on drinking water. "Drought Affects 5.5 Million People in SW China." *China Daily.* Beijing, China. http://english.people.com.cn. March 23, 2007.

29. "Más del 10 por ciento de la tierra arable de China está contaminada." *El Sol de Toluca.* Toluca, Mexico. http://www.oem.com.mx.elsoldetoluca/notas/n249781.htm. April 22, 2007.

30. Trinh et al., 2006, p. 4.

31. Lafargue, 2006.

32. "Cepal: América Latina debe aprovechar potencial de China e India." *El Universal.* Caracas, Venezuela. http://www.eluniversal.com. September 14, 2006.

33. Alexandre Rocha. "Brazil and Argentina Unite to Counter US Soy Prices." *Brazzil Magazine.* São Paulo, Brazil. http://www.brazzilmag.com. October 24, 2004.

34. "Total Import and Export Value by Country (Region) (2007/01–12)." *Ministry of Commerce.* People's Republic of China. http://english.mofcom.gov.cn. aarticle/-statistic/ie/200802/20080205371690.html. February 4, 2008.

35. Shixue Jiang, 2008b, p. 46.

36. Shixue Jiang, 2008a, p. 34.

37. Ibid.

38. It is difficult to establish whether Chinese authorities knowingly promote contraband activities. In some cases, products shipped legitimately from China are diverted from their official destinations, and the government has little knowledge of where such exports ultimately end up. The indirect result of the dynamics of contraband, however, is to elevate the official number of exports to Latin America above the tally of exports achieved through official channels alone—thus increasing the apparent importance of Latin America as an export market for Chinese goods.

39. He Li, 2008, p. 53.

40. Peter Enav, "Taiwán anuncia medidas diplomáticas tras ruptura con Costa Rica." *Nacion.* San José, Costa Rica. http://www.nacion.com. June 7, 20007.

41. Shixue Jiang, 2008a, p. 37. See also Stallings, 2008, p. 247.

42. In the World Trade Organization, for example, where a supermajority is required to bring certain classes of trade actions, the alignment of countries with the PRC can be decisive in the PRC's achieving its commercial, as well as its diplomatic, objectives.

43. He Li, 2008, p. 53.

44. He Li, 2005, p. 88.

45. Ibid. See also Mosher, 2006.

46. Xiang Lanxin, 2008a, p. 45.

47. A study by Goldman Sachs, for example, estimates that China will become the world's largest economy as soon as 2027. See, "China acelera el paso para consolidarse como la primera potencia mundial."

48. "Discurso del Ministro de Relaciones Exteriores Qian Qichen en la Academia Diplomática del Ecuador." Transcript translated from Chinese into Spanish. *El Comercio.* Quito, Ecuador. http://www.elcomercio.com. June 5, 1989.

49. "Panamanian Researcher: Chinese Admiral Discovered America." *People's Daily Online.* Beijing, China. http://english.people.com.cn. October 14, 2007.

50. While the Chinese are likely aware that they are in the midst of a "power transition" in which the nation is attaining, and may ultimately surpass, the economic and political influence wielded by the United States, it is not clear whether a plu-

rality of the Chinese leadership believes that such a transition makes military conflict with the United States inevitable.

51. Indeed, some within the Chinese leadership have even been concerned that the use of the term "rising" could be interpreted as overly aggressive. See Suisheng Zhao, 2005–2006, p. 139.

52. Xiang Lanxin, 2008a, p. 44.

53. See, for example, Suisheng Zhao, 2006; Trinh et al., 2006, p. 11.

54. Shixue Jiang, 2008b, p. 45.

55. At the same time, Xiang Lanxin (2008a) argues that China's desire to relate to Latin American regional bodies is made more difficult, to some degree, by the relative weakness of its multilateral institutions.

56. Hirst, 2008, p. 91.

57. Cheng Siwei, 2005.

58. On the other hand, Xiang Lanxin (2008b, p. 62) argues that China is reluctant to maintain too close a relationship with anti-American leaders such as Hugo Chávez in Venezuela for fear of provoking the United States.

59. Xiang Lanxin, 2008a, p. 54.

60. The current leadership consolidated its power during the 16th Communist Party Congress in November 2002. Scobell and Wortzel, 2004, p. 1.

61. Xiang Lanxin, 2008b, p. 63. See also, Watson, 2008; Hawksley, 2006.

62. "China revela posibiles sucesores de sus líderes." *Nacion*. San José, Costa Rica. http://www.nacion.com. October 23, 2007.

63. "Hu Jintao sale reforzando a la cabeza de un nuevo equipo dirigente chino." *Nacion*. San José, Costa Rica. October 22, 2007.

64. Palacios (2008, p. 181), for example, argues that the anti-US campaign of the Venezuelan government of Hugo Chávez puts China in a difficult position, because the latter does not wish its strategic partnership with Venezuela to involve the PRC in actions that alienate the United States.

3

Why Latin America
Is Interested in China

———————■———————

AS A COMPLEMENT TO THE DISCUSSION OF CHINA'S INTEREST IN Latin America presented in Chapter 2, the reciprocal question is equally important: Why is Latin America interested in China? From a Latin American perspective, China is a culturally and geographically distant nation. Pursuing business, social, or political relationships with the PRC involves a considerable number of costs and barriers. Developing a distribution network and selling products in the PRC, for example, entails personnel familiar with Chinese culture, business practices, and language.[1] Until recently, Latin America had relatively few people with such capabilities; those in Latin America who spoke a second language generally learned English,[2] with the more affluent sending their children to English-language schools from a relatively young age. In addition, significant differences exist between the legal systems and business practices of the two regions. Even surmounting such differences, doing business in China is still largely dependent on personal relationships, implying the expenditure of a significant amount of time to develop contacts and build associations involving personal trust.

Even if the difficulties described above are set aside, other hurdles impede a China–Latin America connection. Latin American political history includes multiple rebellions against trade relationships with the United States and Western corporations that involved both selling primary products with relatively low added value and buying manufactured goods.[3] Now, in the early years of the twenty-first century, both leftist populist governments and neoliberal governments appear to be embracing a trade relationship with China that looks surprisingly similar to that criticized so arduously a half century ago; the question remains open as to why these governments are doing so.

Although the motivations are complex, they may be divided into three main thrusts. First, many in the region hold hopes that export sales to the PRC will fuel export-led growth that will benefit their organization, their sector, or the development of their country. Second, many hope that investment by the PRC will compensate for both the relative dearth of investment that Latin America has received in recent years from Western lending institutions and the difficult conditions attached to that aid. Third, some in Latin America see China as a vehicle by which the region can offset the traditional political, economic, and institutional dominance of the United States.

■ Hopes for Export-Led Growth

Although the opportunities represented by China attract different actors and social sectors in Latin America for different reasons, it is arguably the lure of China's 1.3 billion–person market that captures the imagination of the Latin American public. By 2011, according to a widely cited study by McKinzie, some 290 million Chinese are projected to belong to the middle class, with household earnings of at least $12,500 per year,[4] representing a significant and growing market for Latin American products.

Whatever the precise number of consumers, with its 1.3 billion people, China is simply the most populous nation on earth. Moreover, when measured over the long term, China is also the country experiencing the highest sustained rate of growth. Such figures create a sense that the Chinese market is one of virtually limitless possibility. Although other populous, rapidly growing countries such as India also generate significant interest, China's population and growth put it first among equals.[5]

The possibilities afforded by China as a market are real, although difficult to predict with precision. In 2006, China surpassed Great Britain to become the world's fourth-largest economy, and in 2007 it surpassed Germany to become the world's third largest, behind only Japan and the United States.[6] Moreover, as Chinese prosperity increases, demand for consumer products is expected to grow substantially. According to a study by the investment bank Credit Suisse, for example, by 2015, China will become the world's second-largest consumer market, behind only the United States.[7] The impact of market size and sustained growth, together, on the calculations of Latin American governments and businesspeople is significant. In discussing Costa Rica's July 2007 action to recognize the People's Republic of China, its minister of foreign trade, Marco Vinicio Ruiz, emphasized that one of the most important results of his nation's action was that Costa Rica would have access to the economy that is becoming the new engine of world economic growth.[8]

Even in the near term, China's commodity purchases have impacted the economies of virtually all nations. In 2007, according to China's Ministry of Commerce, the PRC purchased $243 billion worth of primary products.[9] These purchases not only directly benefited the countries that sold China the goods, but also helped to sustain high prices for those items in international markets, significantly increasing returns for producers. A World Bank study looking at the impact on Latin American markets from the emergence of both China and India concluded that these countries' growth has created opportunities that are only beginning to be realized.[10]

The countries of Latin America could look at such aggregate demand and price data, as well as the pattern of Chinese commodity purchases, and find reason to believe that they would be major beneficiaries of the new trade. By the first quarter of 2007, for example, China surpassed the United States to become Chile's number one export customer.[11]

Despite the progress implied by such numbers, the items that Latin America wishes to sell to China are not always aligned with those that China wishes to buy. The Chinese government is often most interested in purchasing Latin American primary products at the very bottom of the value-added chain—iron ore, rather than steel, for example. China's principal agricultural purchases from the region are typically simple, low value–added commodities. China purchases much more fishmeal from Peru and Chile (to feed poultry and livestock) than meat from the region. It purchases soybeans and sunflower oil from Argentina and Brazil, rather than the products that these commodities are used to make. However, whereas mining and agro-export firms in Latin America continue to sell ever greater quantities of goods to the PRC, trade fairs in China are frequented by Latin American vendors of consumer products and manufactured goods, arguably reflecting those items that the region hopes to sell to the PRC.

One factor in Latin America's favor with respect to the new pattern of trade is that China is not the only emerging purchaser for Latin American products. Indeed, while the United States remains important for many exporters, and while the European Union is also making inroads, yet another Asian giant is emerging on the scene: India. Although India's economy remains smaller than China's and is not growing as rapidly, its 9 percent rate of growth in 2007[12] was far greater than that of any of the "developed" countries. India also devotes more of its GDP to consumption than does China, and thus could ultimately emerge as an important market for certain categories of goods that Latin America is looking to sell.[13]

■ Hopes for Investment in Fuel Development

In addition to China's appeal as a market for its goods, Latin America looks to the PRC as a potential new source of investment. During much of the twentieth century, the United States was Latin America's primary source of investment capital. US and other Western companies invested considerable capital in the region and contributed significantly to key sectors, including extractive industries and export-oriented agriculture. A combination of events in the late 1980s and 1990s—including a series of debt crises and mediocre economic performance in Latin America, coupled with strong economic performances in Asian economies—led investors to move capital to Asia that previously had been directed, in part, toward Latin America. Events—such as the implosion of the Internet bubble, which reverberated through the Latin American telecommunications industry; the 2001 collapse of the Argentine economy; increasing street crime and kidnappings, from São Paulo to San Salvador—reinforced the trend away from Latin America. The economies of Asia appeared as increasingly attractive destinations for global investment capital in both relative and absolute terms, and in this "contest," Latin America was on the losing end. In 2003, foreign direct investment (FDI) in the region hit a low of $36 billion.[14]

It was within this context of falling Western investment in Latin America and an apparent loss of Western political interest in that region that Chinese president Hu Jintao, in November 2004, made a five-nation tour of Latin America in conjunction with his trip to the Asia-Pacific Economic Cooperation (APEC) forum in Santiago, Chile. The press covering the trip widely reported a statement by President Hu that the PRC would invest a total of $100 billion in Latin America over the next ten years.[15] For a region feeling abandoned by both Western capital and decisionmakers in Washington, Hu's promises, including an array of potential, multibillion-dollar projects for specific countries, generated hope that China could step into the role of Latin America's benefactor and driver of development, which the West had seemingly abdicated.[16]

For Latin America, the anticipated Chinese investment was not simply seen as a replacement for or supplement to Western investment, but also as possibly different in character from the assistance provided by the West. Part of this hope—particularly among those who were not intimately familiar with the details of the proposed projects and their terms—was that "communist" China would provide significant infusions of new capital for infrastructure and social development projects not funded by Western organizations. Moreover, since China was not "the West," hope existed at the popular level that the PRC's money would be free of the types of oversight and political conditions imposed by Western lending institutions.[17]

As analysts like Robert Devlin have noted, the quantity of Chinese investment realized in Latin America prior to recent years has been very modest.[18] According to the Chinese Ministry of Commerce, total Chinese nonfinancial FDI to Latin America in 2005 was only $659 million, out of a total of $41 billion received by the region from all sources as investment.[19]

The portion of PRC investment going to Latin America overall, as an indication of China's relative interest in the region, has also been highly variable. Although it rose from 36 percent in 2003 to 49 percent in 2004, it fell to 16 percent in 2005.[20] Moreover, as Rodrigo Maciel points out, China invests in infrastructure projects in order to control commodities and natural resources—an approach that does not always align with the interests of recipient countries.[21]

At the same time, Chinese investments in strategically important sectors of Latin American economies have been growing. According to the PRC Ministry of Commerce, cumulative Chinese investment in Latin America rose from $10 billion in 2000 to approximately $22 billion by 2006, with more than 30,000 Chinese projects registered in the region.[22] As Luisa Palacios notes, looking at one example, despite relatively low overall levels of investment in the region, China has become an increasingly important investor in its energy sector, as part of its worldwide quest for energy sources.[23] Similarly, in some countries (for instance, Mexico), China has shown a willingness to invest in final-assembly facilities oriented toward selling products to the United States or to other countries in the region.[24]

Preliminary evidence suggests that Chinese investment ending up in Latin America is increasing significantly. Specific individual projects that have been publicly announced, such as investment in the Toromocho and Rio Blanco mines in Peru, participation in oil fields in Venezuela and Ecuador, automobile manufacturing in the Mexican maquiladora sector, and the establishment of telecommunications networks by the Chinese firms Huawei and ZTE, collectively amount to tens of billions of dollars. In September 2007, during a visit to Honduras, Wang Jinzhen, vice president of the Chinese Council for the Promotion of International Trade (CCPIT), announced that China had $30 billion worth of planned investment projects in Latin America, although he did not specify the timeframe.[25]

Perhaps the most significant new conduit channeling Chinese investment into Latin America is a commodity fund, first announced in March 2007 by Chinese prime minister Wen Jiabao.[26] The fund is a Chinese initiative to make more effective use of the massive foreign currency reserves generated by its ongoing trade surpluses with most of the rest of the world. As of late 2008, those reserves had reached a level of $1.9 trillion, although they had begun to fall because of the global recession.[27]

In September 2007, the PRC established the China Investment Corporation (CIC), with an unprecedented capitalization of $200 billion and the objective to identify opportunities for investment.[28] The PRC has said that it will use a small portion of its reserves to purchase greater control of primary products critical to the functioning of its economy, as well as the means to produce them.[29] Although such reserves traditionally are put in very safe assets, the implications of such a fund for Latin America would be dramatic if any significant part of it were used by the Chinese to acquire or invest in Latin American mines, refineries, agricultural lands, and related assets, bringing an enormous new infusion of capital to the area. Although the manner in which China will use its foreign currency reserves and other sources of capital remains unclear, by the end of 2008 the global financial crisis was causing investment capital from Western banks to become more limited, thus increasing the potential importance of the China–Latin America relationship even further.

An Alternative to US Dominance

In addition to "purely" economic interests, Latin America is interested in China because of the possibility that the Asian giant will help the region to offset the traditional political, economic, and institutional dominance of the United States, giving it greater freedom of action to pursue a more autonomous course politically.[30]

China's ability to transform itself, within the span of a generation, from a relatively impoverished nation to a rising power that challenges the United States in the global economy is a source of inspiration for many Latin Americans. Although different elites and social sectors within the region interpret the lessons of China differently, in general the rapid, sustained growth of the PRC suggests an alternate development model in which progress and prosperity can be achieved through the use of mercantilist trade policies and without giving up state control of strategic sectors.

The term "Beijing consensus," referring to the example of China, is a derisory allusion to the "Washington consensus" and policies pursued during the 1990s that failed to address—and, in the eyes of some, may have deepened—Latin America's deep-rooted problems of inequality, corruption, and stagnant growth. By contrast, the example of China is of great interest for Latin America. Thirty years ago, China was far poorer than the vast majority of Latin American countries. Since that time, rapid growth has taken hundreds of millions of Chinese out of poverty,[31] while preserving the role of the state in important sectors of the economy and without opening up the society to disruptive political discourse or permitting widespread debates about issues such as human rights.[32] In other words, whatever the lessons of the Chinese experience that can be applied realistically in Latin America, the "Chinese model" is a convenient rhetorical tool for regimes in search of development, but who do not want to follow a path of transparency, accountability, and institutional reforms that could result in the ouster of the existing leadership—and, potentially, even their criminal prosecution.

Beyond serving as a model for an ambiguously defined set of policies that present an alternative to the US agenda, China also contributes directly and indirectly to the viability of regimes opposed to US interests in the region. While such an argument does not, in any way, imply that China directly promotes anti-US activities in the hemisphere, the PRC helps to support anti-US regimes in at least three ways.

First, China is a major purchaser of commodities, such as petroleum, that represent important revenue streams for the strongly anti-US, populist regimes currently in power in Latin America. China's purchase of these commodities, such as petroleum, is generally not, however, a deliberate strategy to prop up the regime; rather, PRC interest in the commodity drives it to build a relationship that allows it to acquire the commodity. However, it is not entirely a coincidence that countries with economies centered on production of commodities in which the PRC is interested have populist regimes, since the very lack of both economic diversity and a middle class in these countries makes them more susceptible to populism.[33]

Second, China has served as an important investment partner for populist governments, helping to compensate for regime policies that have pushed out Western investment, although other nations such as Russia and Iran are also moving to fill this void. The ability of the Chávez government in Venezuela to nationalize petroleum operations in the strategically important Orinoco belt, for example, is arguably related to the availability of foreign state–owned firms, such as the China National Petroleum Corporation (CNPC), to continue or broaden their participation after Western multinationationals left. Similarly, $8 billion of the $12 billion Venezuelan Heavy Investment Fund are loans from China Development Bank, and play an increasingly important role in funding capital projects because so much of Venezuela's revenue stream is earmarked for social programs and international commitments. In Ecuador, the regime of Rafael Correa has convinced such state-owned enterprises as CNPC to invest in the country's oil fields, including not only existing oil fields such as Tarapoa, but also a potential role in future oil fields such as Ishpingo Tambococha Tiputini (ITT),[34] and possible help in funding a new $6 billion refinery in the department of Manabí.[35]

Third, China has also provided technology to newly elected populist administrations. Such help has included selling Venezuela a Zhongxing-22A telecommunications satellite (launched in November 2008 and operated jointly with Venezuela), which uses a ground station and tracking facilities also purchased from the Chinese.[36] Similarly, the Chinese firm Lang Chao has formed a mixed company with the Venezuelan government and has invested $16 million in a facility in the Venezuelan state of Falcon to assemble computers from Chinese components, for sale to Venezuelan government agencies, and potentially to interested private parties.[37] Although the technological benefits of such projects may be ephemeral, they allow newly elected populist governments to represent to their followers that, under their leadership, their nations are developing economically.

Finally, in addition to the concrete benefits that the PRC has provided to a limited set of Latin American governments, China has important symbolic appeal to a group of Latin American leaders on the left side of the political spectrum, through what may be termed "nostalgic radicalism." While the China of the early twenty-first century manifests few recognizable features of communism as an economic system, the new PRC is the sole heir of the legacy of Mao Zedong's China, which acted as a revisionist power on the world stage and as a source of inspiration for leaders such as Hugo Chávez of Venezuela and Evo Morales of Bolivia. These ties help to explain otherwise curious statements, such as that by Evo Morales, who, during his January 2006 visit to the PRC, proclaimed himself to be a "great admirer of Mao"—a sentiment probably not forcefully shared by the members of the current Chinese Politburo whom he was addressing.[38] Similarly, Hugo Chávez, during a trip of his own to China, proclaimed that Simón Bolívar and Mao would have been great friends[39]—although Simón Bolívar, as a member of the landed gentry of Latin America, would have been horrified by what Mao represented. Even Colombia's conservative and generally pro-US president, Alvaro Uribe, could not resist paying homage to Mao, referring to the Chinese leader during a visit to the country as a "great revolutionary" and "the practical philosopher with the clearest message in recent decades."[40]

■ Notes

1. Capability in the Mandarin language is becoming increasingly important for doing business in China. The Chinese government now requires, for example, that senior executives in financial enterprises pass oral and written tests for competency in the language. See, "Para hacer negocios en China es obligado hablar mandarin." *El Universal.* Caracas, Venezuela. http://www.eluniversal.com. September 2, 2007.

2. Moreover, the differences in the language base and script between Mandarin and Spanish or Portuguese make learning Mandarin a considerable investment of time.

3. Such trade relationships were perceived to inhibit the development and economic diversification of the region over the long term. Indeed, the political economy of Latin America in the 1960s, including the politics of import substitution industrialization, was an attempt to escape such relationships.

4. As cited in Farrell, Gersch, and Stephenson, 2006.

5. As Naughton (2007:3) notes, since the 1980s, China has been the fastest-growing economy on earth.

6. "China ya superó a Alemania como la tercera economía." *El Deber.* Santa Cruz, Bolivia. http://www.el-deber.com. July 22, 2007.

7. "Credit Suisse: Chinese Consumer Goods Market to Rank Second by

2015." China Council for the Promotion of International Trade, China Chamber of International Commerce. http://english.ccpit.org/Contents/Chanel_413/2007/0326/30531/content_-30531.htm. March 26, 2007. See also, "Chinese Consumer Goods Market to Rank Second Behind U.S. by 2015: Credit Suisse." *People's Daily Online*. Beijing, China. http://english.people.com.cn. March 24, 2007.

8. Author interview with Marco Vinicio Ruiz, minister of foreign commerce. San Jose, Costa Rica. January 24, 2008.

9. "Imports by Major Categories (2007/01–12)." *Ministry of Commerce of the People's Republic of China*. http://english.mofcom.gov.cn/aarticle/statistic/ie/200802/-20080205372493.html. February 4, 2008.

10. Lederman, Olarreaga, and Soloaga, 2007a.

11. Eduardo Olivares C., "China es mayor destino de exportaciones tras el TLC." *El Mercurio*. Santiago, Chile. http://diario.elmercurio.com. April 18, 2007. In the first ten months of 2007, according to the Chilean national customs service, exports to China reached $8.1 billion, in comparison to $3.9 million during the previous year. See "Exportaciones por paises y bloques." *Servicio Nacional de Aduanas*. http://www.aduana.cl/prontus_aduana/site/artic/20070416/pags/20070416165951.html. Accessed December 7, 2007.

12. "FMI revisa al alza crecimiento mundial, deja a Latinoamérica a distancia." *Nacion*. San José, Costa Rica. July 25, 2007.

13. Ironically, the danger for Latin America with progress toward an Asian free-trade area is that China will beat out Latin America in supplying goods to the closer Indian market.

14. ECLAC, 2004, p. 13.

15. See Stallings, 2008, p. 250.

16. In absolute terms, the quantity of FDI entering Latin America has rebounded somewhat since 2003, reaching a level of $72.4 billion in 2006. Nonetheless, in percentage terms, Latin America continues to receive an ever smaller share of global FDI. In the 1970s, Latin America received 17 percent of world investment. In the 1990s, the figure was still approximately 16 percent, but by 2006, only 8 percent of global investment was going to Latin America. "Señal de alerta para la región." *La Nacion*. Buenos Aires, Argentina. http://www.lanacion.com.ar. May 8, 2007.

17. Logan and Bain, 2005.

18. Devlin, 2008, p. 115.

19. "China Makes More Overseas Investment in 2005, Mainly in Asia." *People's Daily Online*. Beijing, China. http://english.people.com.cn. February 10, 2006.

20. Ibid.

21. Maciel, 2008, p. 29. Moreover, the extent to which such funds are productive investment, as well as their ultimate destination, remains unclear. According to the Chinese Ministry of Commerce, for example, the three primary destinations for Chinese FDI within Latin America in 2005 were the British Virgin Islands, the Cayman Islands, and Venezuela—the first two of these enjoying the reputation as tax-shelter destinations, rather than the likely final destination of the investment. See, "China Makes More Overseas Investment in 2005, Mainly in Asia."

22. "25% of China's Investments Abroad Received by L. America." Official website of the Chinese government. http://www.gov.cn/misc/2008-04/16/content_946321.htm. April 16, 2008.

23. Palacios, 2008. p. 187.

24. Shixue Jiang calls this type of operation, which relies on Chinese components assembled in other countries for export, "processing with our own materials." 2008b, p. 45.

25. "Misión comercial de China busca contactos en Honduras." *El Comercio.* Quito, Ecuador. http://www.elcomercio.com. August 29, 2007.

26. Chris Zappone, "China poised for global shopping spree." *CNN.* http://www.cnn.com. March 30, 2007.

27. "La reserva de divisas china, la mayor del mundo, cae por primera vez en cinco años." *El Comercio.* Lima, Peru. http://www.elcomercio.com.pe. December 22, 2008.

28. "China reducirá reservas en dólares y tambalea la divisa estadounidense." *Diario Financiero.* Santiago, Chile. http://www.df.cl. November 8, 2007.

29. Although the PRC originally invested its reserves primarily in dollar-denominated assets, the enormous US governmental and commercial debt has increasingly undermined the world's confidence in the dollar. The PRC has begun a slow process of diversifying out of dollar-denominated investments, while simultaneously taking steps to leverage more fully the economic and political weight represented by its reserves.

30. June Teufel Dreyer (2006b: 96) notes, "The PRC could potentially provide a source of leverage against the U.S. for Latin America and Caribbean countries, but it has not yet done so."

31. Poverty in China fell from 63.8 percent in 1981 to 16.6 percent in 2001. Ferrari, 2007.

32. See Hawksley, 2006.

33. The lack of a diverse economic base in these countries generally means the lack of a sizeable independent middle class with resources independent of the state. As the state has moved to seize control of the revenues from the nation's strategic industries, such as hydrocarbons and mining, the benefits from expanded Chinese purchases of these commodities have increasingly flowed to the populist state, helping the newly elected elite to pay off its support base. Because these products are generally fungible commodities, Chinese demand has also helped to increase revenues worldwide for these products, enlarging margins realized by the populist regimes in selling their goods. For a more extensive presentation of this argument, see Ellis, 2007.

34. "PdVSA estudia asociaciones con Ecuador en yacimientos de ITT." *El Universal.* Caracas, Venezuela. http://www.eluniversal.com. April 17, 2007.

35. "Sinopec y Petroecuador firman acuerdo para explotar el yacimiento Ishpingo-Tambococha-Tiputini." *El Comercio.* Quito, Ecuador. http://www.elcomercio.com. March 26, 2007.

36. See, "Satélite blindará comunicaciones de la FAN." *El Universal.* Caracas, Venezuela. http://www.eluniversal.com. August 27, 2008. See also, Eduardo Camel Anderson, "Tecnología china apoyará las telecomunicaciones locales." *El Universal.* Caracas, Venezuela. http://www.eluniversal.com. February 20, 2007.

37. Distribution of the computers began at the end of 2006. "El gobierno active la entrega de las PC bolivarianas." *El Universal.* Caracas, Venezuela. http://www.eluniversal.com. June 12, 2007.

38. "Is the Chinese Model Gaining Political and Economic Influence in Latin America?" White Paper. Washington, DC: Hudson Institute. March 2007.

39. Schiller, 2006b.

40. Doctorado Honoris Causa cierra la visita del presidente Uribe a China." *Caracol Radio.* http://www.caracol.com.co/noticias/166103.asp?id=166103. April 8, 2005.

4

The Southern Cone: Soy, Oil, Iron, and Customers

CHINA'S INTERACTION WITH THE NATIONS OF THE SOUTHERN Cone has been dominated by economic considerations. With the exception of Paraguay, these nations are generally middle-income economies that provide value to the PRC both as purchasers of Chinese manufactured goods and as increasingly important suppliers of agricultural goods and metals. Indeed, in some ways, the region is rapidly becoming the "breadbasket" of China, with Argentina and Brazil alone supplying some 29 percent of all Chinese food imports—principally soy products.[1]

The existence of significant and established manufacturing sectors in countries like Argentina and Brazil has fueled domestic political resistance to the expansion of trade with China. At the same time, this economic diversification, and the existence of mature, technology-intensive industries, have translated into opportunities for corporate partnerships and technology collaboration.

The Andes mountain range is an important consideration in the logistics of the growing commerce with China. The Andes creates a physical divide that separates Chile and its Pacific ports from the rest of the Southern Cone nations, whose ports and infrastructures are oriented primarily toward the Atlantic. Because of this divide, in general, the logistics costs and delay times for Chinese exports to and imports from Chile are significantly lower than those faced by the other Southern Cone countries, which must either export their goods via Atlantic ports—with significantly longer maritime transits—or ship their goods over the Andes for embarkation from the Pacific ports of other Latin American nations.

Although the relationships that the Southern Cone nations have with China are dominated by economics, they differ significantly in terms of the dominant products involved, the relative role of imports versus exports, the logistical and infrastructure considerations, the dynamics of domestic politics within which the hopes and fears generated by China are played out, and the technology partnerships and other noneconomic dimensions of each relationship.

This chapter examines the individual dynamics, points of commonality, and differences in the relationships between individual Southern Cone nations and the PRC.

■ Chile

Chile is both a leader among nations of the region in building a commercial relationship with the PRC and an exemplar of the challenges that such a relationship can create.

If any nation should be able to benefit from a relationship with China, it is Chile. Within the region, Chile has among the best commercial and bureaucratic infrastructure for doing business with Asia. Its geographic position along South America's Pacific coastline makes its ports the logical points of entry for Chinese products bound for Argentina, Brazil, Bolivia, Paraguay, and Uruguay, and logical routes of egress for South American products bound for Asia. Chile is one of only three nations in Latin America that are members of the Asia Pacific Economic Cooperation (APEC) forum, and was the first nation in both the region and the world to sign a free-trade accord (FTA) with the PRC with respect to goods.[2] For Chile, this agreement complemented numerous other such accords with the United States and nations of Latin America and Asia, leveraging Chile's other advantages to position itself as a commercial nexus between Asia, Latin America, and the United States.[3]

In general terms, Chile's is one of the economies that has most benefited by the expansion of China.[4] In 2006, the first year in which the Sino-Chilean FTA was in effect,[5] Chilean exports to the PRC jumped by 140 percent, making China Chile's number one export customer.[6] At the same time, however, a remarkable portion of this trade is concentrated in copper and a handful of other export products. Indeed, 98 percent of Chilean exports come from nine primary-product sectors.[7] Beyond these products, Chile's success in selling key agricultural commodities to China has been relatively limited compared to Chilean exports to other markets. Although such business leaders as Ricardo Claro,[8] Andronico Luksic, and Enrique Ponce Lerou have taken important steps to build a Chilean commercial relationship with China,[9] the number of mainstream Chilean businesses establishing a long-term presence in China is still relatively small.

Historical Context

Chile was the first nation in South America to establish formal diplomatic relations with China, doing so in January 1971. The watershed event actually had its antecedents in the formation of Latin America's first bilateral cultural friendship association, between Chile and China in 1952. Some people who later became influential in the government of Chile's first socialist president, Salvador Allende, played important roles in this association; they include author Pablo Neruda, who was one of its first presidents, and the painter Jose Venturelli.

Although the socialist orientation of Allende's government was a key factor in Chile's recognition of the PRC, the subsequent military government of General Augusto Pinochet, which overthrew Allende in a military coup, chose to continue diplomatic ties with China. Indeed, the ability of the Chinese government to develop an effective working relationship with both the Allende government and Pinochet's military dictatorship is a testimony to the pragmatism that the Chinese have historically used in their diplomatic relations with the region's countries.[10]

Although Chile has avoided vocal support for Chinese positions in international bodies, the two nations have nonetheless enjoyed a consistent history of positive relations and mutual support in the international sphere. In 1999, for example, Chile supported China's membership in the World Trade Organization (WTO), and China returned the favor, supporting Chile's bid for a nonpermanent seat on the United Nations (UN) Security Council in 2003–2004.[11] Beyond such diplomatic alignments, however, Sino-Chilean ties prior to 2000 were relatively limited. In the political realm, the visit by Chinese president Jiang Zemin to Chile in April 2001 was the first PRC visit of this level to the country.

Since the 1990s, Sino-Chilean economic relations have expanded rapidly, accelerating in recent years. Between 1997 and 2006, bilateral trade between China and Chile expanded by 641 percent.[12] The visit by Chinese president Hu Jintao to Santiago in conjunction with his presentation to the annual APEC summit was, in many senses, a watershed event, reflecting and calling attention to the emerging economic relationship between China and Chile.[13] The PRC became Chile's number one export customer by the middle of 2007[14] and its number two trading partner overall. As of late 2008, China had become Chile's number one overall partner in bilateral trade and Chile was China's second-largest trading partner in Latin America, after Brazil.[15]

The Chinese Community in Chile

The Chinese community in Chile is estimated to be approximately 7,000 people, principally from the southern provinces of China, including

Guangzhou and Fuzhou, as well as from Taiwan.[16] In reality, however, it makes more sense to speak of two Chinese communities, with relatively separate histories. One community, concentrated in the northern part of the country, was originally part of the larger group of Chinese immigrants (predominantly from Guangzhou) who immigrated to Peru during the late nineteenth century, fleeing political unrest and economic hardship in their home country. Newly arriving Chinese were principally employed under very harsh conditions on the railroads and in the nitrate mines of northern Peru.[17] Later, these Chinese and their descendants established themselves in northern cities, such as Arica and Iquique, opening restaurants and other shops as towns grew up around the nitrate industry.[18] When Peru lost these territories in the War of the Pacific, the Chinese who had been living there found themselves part of Chile.[19] Today, the Chinese community in this area, in combination with more recently arrived Chinese businesspeople, plays an important role in the Iquique free-trade zone (ZOFRI), which supplies products to much of the rest of the region.

A second Chinese Chilean community lives in the vicinity of Santiago. A lot like the Chinese community in Buenos Aires, Argentina, this Chinese community is much more recently arrived. Many of the latter group have immigrated to Argentina in recent years from poorer regions of southeastern China, such as Fushien, in search of economic opportunity, and thus have very little connection to the more established Chinese population to the north.

China's Interest in Chilean Mining Products

Chilean exports of copper and other mining-sector products to the PRC have consistently been a key part of the commercial interaction between the two countries, although the volume of trade has expanded considerably in recent years. Indeed, copper accounted for over 83 percent of Chile's exports to China during the first half of 2007.[20]

Chilean copper exports to China are of great significance to both countries. Chile has an estimated 17 percent of the world's proven reserves of copper and is one of the world's largest exporters of the metal.[21] In 2005, some 30 to 35 percent of all Chilean copper exports went to the PRC.[22] For the Chilean national copper company, CODELCO, China is also an increasingly important customer. In 1994, China accounted for only 2 percent of CODELCO's copper sales by volume, but by 2006, the figure had risen to 12 percent.[23]

Chilean exports of copper to China illustrate not only China's interest in the primary-product sectors of Latin America, but also the manner in which Chinese investment in Latin America has been instrumentally focused on gaining or improving access to those products. In February

2006, CODELCO finalized an agreement by which China committed to purchase Chilean copper at a fixed price, providing money in advance to help the Chileans increase output to keep up with expanding Chinese demand. The agreement, with an estimated potential value of up to $2 billion, involved an initial infusion of $550 million to CODELCO by the PRC,[24] and a fixed, preferential price.[25]

As in other countries in Latin America, the development of Chile's primary-product export relationship with the PRC has come into conflict with internal political imperatives that have complicated the relationship. One of the more controversial provisions of the accord between CODELCO and China Minmetals, for example, was an option for the latter to buy up to a 49 percent interest in the new Chilean mine, Gabriela Mistral (Gaby).[26,27] Although the agreement did not guarantee China Minmetals the right to acquire Gaby over other bidders, the provision was sensitive because metals and minerals are considered part of Chile's national patrimony. In March 2007, these sensitivities came to the fore when China Minmetals indicated its intent to exercise its option to purchase interest in Gaby (for $838 million),[28] prompting protests by CODELCO workers.[29] Sharply declining production in Chuquicamata, one of CODELCO's leading mines, made the Chilean government even more reluctant to sell off part of Gaby and the significant new production that it represents. The Chilean government declined to sell interest in Gaby to China Minmetals, and although the latter initially sought to take the matter to arbitration, by late 2008, China Minmetals had effectively abandoned efforts to acquire the mine.[30] The controversy highlights the fact that—in contrast to Chinese ownership of mines in Peru—even when engaging in relatively large agreements such as the CODELCO deal, Chinese companies have not yet become significant owners or operators of mines in Chile.

Beyond the relationship between China Minmetals and CODELCO, Chinese companies have made a limited number of advances in the Chilean mining sector. In November 2007, the Chilean national mining federation signed an agreement with a Chinese firm to construct a copper-processing plant in the Antofagasta region of Chile.[31] The plant, in the vicinity of a number of mines, will create a market through which the output of small and medium-sized producers in Chile can be processed and sold to the PRC.[32] In the same month, industry sources also reported that China Minmetals was negotiating with the mining group Antofagasta Minerals, of the Luksic group, to provide $1.5 billion in funding to develop a new mine, called Esperanza, in the same region.[33]

China's purchase of Chilean copper evidences its interest in Latin America's primary-product sectors; it also demonstrates the emergence both of global partnerships between Chinese and Latin American companies and of new, integrated supply chains connecting China to the region. In

November 2006, CODELCO announced that it was contemplating the construction of a foundry in China, in partnership with the Chinese company Yunnan Copper.[34] Reciprocally, within Chile, CODELCO has turned to Chinese suppliers, such as Minmetals and Sinochem, to obtain explosives and other inputs that it requires for its mining operations.[35]

Although copper and molybdenum receive a great deal of attention in the press as Chile's principal mining exports to China, Chile has also become the main supplier of potassium nitrate to the PRC, a water-soluble fertilizer used by China's tobacco farmers.[36] As with other Chilean initiatives, Chilean nitrate exports are the product of a single company, Sociedad Química y Minera de Chile (SQM), whose president is Enrique Ponce Lerou. SQM established itself as a potassium nitrate supplier to China in the early 1980s; it currently supplies some 250,000 tons of the product, from the Maria Elena mine in the north. In July 2008, SQM strengthened this relationship, entering into a joint venture with the Chinese firm Migao to build and supply a plant in China that would produce 40,000 tons of refined potassium nitrate per year.[37]

China's Interest in Chilean Agriculture and Fishing

Although China's involvement in Chile's fishing sector is not widely recognized, the products of this industry are one of the most important Chilean exports to the PRC. Chile, together with Peru, supplies 80 percent of all of the PRC's imports of fishmeal, a major staple of the Chinese diet.[38]

Chile's ability to sell other types of fish to China besides fishmeal, such as salmon, has been extremely limited in comparison to the quantity that the former sells to other nations.[39] The fishing industry has also been a subject of dispute between the two nations, with Chile banning Chinese fishing boats from the use of its ports in 2005 over allegations of overfishing. Indeed, the Chilean prohibition has been a key factor blocking the Chinese from acquiring Chilean fishing fleets and shore facilities to support their operations, as they have done in Peru.

Chile also has a substantial and growing agro-industrial sector that is a logical supplier to Chinese markets. To date, Chile's agricultural sales to the PRC have been almost insignificant compared to the volume of its agricultural sales to the rest of the world. In part, this reflects slow progress in reaching agreement with the Chinese in negotiating the individual protocols required for each type of agricultural product to enter China. Of the hundreds of kinds of agricultural products exported by Chile, the nation has been able to establish protocols with the PRC on only six: grapes, apples, plums, chicken products, cheese, and cherries. Nonetheless, Chile's combination of efficient deepwater Pacific ports, good transport infrastructure, effective government support to exporters, and its free-trade agreement with the PRC[40] affords the nation's agriculture sector a number of potential advantages over Brazilian and Argentine producers if the inherent restrictions imposed by agricultural protocols can be overcome.[41]

One of the leading agricultural success stories for Chile is its sale of wine to the PRC.[42] Indeed, in 2005, according to the Economic Commission for Latin America and the Caribbean, 45 percent of Chinese imports of wines and grapes came from Chile.[43] As in the case of Mexican beer, the success of Chilean wines reflects effective branding and international reputation, in combination with an increasingly affluent Chinese middle class who has purchasing power and a taste for such goods.[44] In addition, at least one Chilean company is producing wine in China: the Chilean investor Andronico Luksic invested in land in the Xinjiang province of China to produce a Chinese wine with Chilean technology under the brand "1421."[45] While Chilean wine represents a large percentage of Chinese wine imports, it is notable that the $28 million in wine that Chile sold to the PRC in the first half of 2007[46] was less than 5 percent of Chile's wine sales worldwide that year.

Chile as a Market for Chinese Goods

Chile, like other middle-income countries of Latin America, is a relatively attractive market for Chinese manufactured goods. Indeed, outside of a handful of small Caribbean nations, Chile is the wealthiest nation in Latin America in per capita income.[47] Due, in part, to its wealth, Chile has been a leading market for the PRC as it seeks to diversify its exports to ever more sophisticated, higher value–added products, such as motorcycles and computers. In 2006, companies in Chile began to expand sales of Chinese cars, taking advantage of the fact that Chinese autos cost, on average, 30 percent less than those of the competition.[48] Santiago, for example, was one of the first points of sale in Latin America for the Chinese automaker Great Wall Motors, which introduced the Chinese brand into the Chilean market through local distributor Derco.[49] By June 2008, six different Chinese car brands were present in Chile—representing 4.7 percent of the market—with the expectation that ten Chinese brands would be there within a year.[50] The car brand Chery is reportedly so popular that the entire supply to Chile for 2007 was sold out, and sellers had an extensive waiting list in 2008.

Even before the introduction of Chinese cars, Chile has been a strong market for Chinese motorcycles, including such brands as Takasaki, Jianshe, Lifán, and Kinlon. In 2003, 4,000 Chinese motorcycles were sold in Chile; by 2007, this figure had jumped to 70,000, representing 70 to 80 percent of the entire Chilean market.[51]

Chinese trucks have also entered the Chilean market. A September 2006 article in *El Sur*, the major newspaper serving Chile's Eighth Region, highlighted the positive experience of Chilean distributor Mariano Ebensperger in selling the Chinese truck brand YueJin in the city of Concepcion.[52]

Beyond motor vehicles, as in other parts of Latin America, Chile has provided a strong market for the expansion of Chinese telecommunications companies. Both Chinese telecom giants Huawei[53] and ZTE[54] have offices in Santiago, and both have won major contracts in the country. In December 2004, for example, ZTE was awarded a contract to build a network in Santiago for the local telecom provider Transam, using the (then–new technology) global system for mobile communications (GSM).[55] With respect to Huawei, according to the company's Web site, its products have been used across Chile in a range of applications, from fixed lines to fiber-optic and wireless networks, including the construction of network backbones for three Chilean telecom operators and a transmission network in Santiago.[56]

Lower-end Chinese products have also increasingly penetrated Chilean markets, as well as markets throughout Latin America. An estimated 80 percent of the clothing sold in Chile, for example, comes from China.[57] Despite this penetration, Chilean manufacturers have been less prone to respond with calls for protection than have their counterparts in other Latin American countries. In part, this may reflect the relatively small size of the Chilean manufacturing sector; it may also reflect the generally protrade Chilean political culture, in which the nation is seen as relatively small and in need of external ties to prosper.

Potential Cooperation in the Nuclear Industry

One wildcard in Chile's relationship with China is the possibility of collaboration with the Chinese in developing Chile's potential for nuclear power generation.

Energy security, and the vulnerability of the Chilean economy to cutoffs in energy supply, are increasing concerns for the Chileans. The nation has very few gas and oil resources of its own, relying principally on neighboring Argentina for imports of natural gas. In recent years, however, Chile has repeatedly had problems with Argentina as a supplier, including times in which Argentina cut off gas supplies to Chile when it had problems with its own gas supply.[58] Such difficulties, and their economic and human impacts, have given urgency to Chilean efforts to achieve energy self-sufficiency, including its reevaluation of strategies previously ruled out, such as the development of nuclear power. Although Chilean president Michelle Bachelet promised during her campaign that Chile would not develop nuclear power–generation capability under her administration, she announced publicly in September 2007 that Chile was exploring options for doing so in the more distant future.[59] Indeed, some analysts have suggested that Chile could begin to pursue a nuclear power option as soon as 2010, following a change of political administration.[60]

In the event that the Chileans do pursue this option, they will likely collaborate with other countries and nuclear power suppliers to do so. Although those knowledgeable about the industry believe that the current Chilean focus is on US and European partners, this could change in a future Chilean administration. The Chinese are among the world's leaders in the active employment of nuclear power. In addition to their existing nuclear capabilities, they announced in 2005 that they would build up to forty-two new nuclear reactors in their country over the next twenty years.[61] China's practical experience with nuclear power makes it a logical partner in helping Chile develop its own nuclear power industry.[62] Moreover, the Chileans have demonstrated—as in their talks with the China International Trust and Investment Corporation (CITIC) about providing electric power to mining interests in Antofagasta[63]—they they are willing to talk with the Chinese regarding other forms of power generation.

Chile as a Commercial Nexus

Chile has effectively positioned itself at the commercial nexus between Asia, Latin America, and the United States. Although other nations in Latin America, such as Peru, Ecuador, and Costa Rica, are seeking to play such a role, Chile is currently situated to make the strongest claim for this position: it has effectively leveraged a combination of geographic location, good physical infrastructure, government and business infrastructure, and an interlocking network of free-trade agreements.

Chile dominates the Pacific coastline of South America, giving the nation strategically valuable real estate in commerce between the continent and the nations of Asia. Chilean ports are important to Brazil and Argentina's commerce with China, and several major, ongoing infrastructure projects connect other South American countries to the Pacific through Chilean ports and thus will augment Chile's role in the continent's growing commerce with Asia. These projects include the intercoastal highway, announced in December 2007, running from the Brazilian port of Santos, through Bolivia, to the Chilean ports of Arica and Iquique.[64] Other connections have been discussed, including improved highways between the Mendoza region of central Argentina and the Chilean port of Valparaiso, and between Salta, in the north of Argentina, and the Chilean ports of Antofagasta and Iquique.[65]

Beyond these infrastructure projects, Chile's position is bolstered by the relative capacity and efficiency of its ports, which include Iquique, Valparaiso, Antofagasta, and Arica. The ZOFRI free-trade zone, which is the largest in South America, includes 1,650 businesses. With an annual trade throughput of $4.7 billion,[66] ZOFRI has become a hub for importing a wide range of products from China and elsewhere in Asia to markets throughout the Southern Cone.

In general, the Chilean customs administration has a reputation for reasonable efficiency and lack of corruption, contributing to the desire of shipping companies to use Chilean ports, rather than other alternatives, to minimize delays and associated costs. As discussed in the next section, this physical and governmental infrastructure is reinforced by a business infrastructure that provides numerous options and effective support for commercial transactions between Latin America and Asia, augmenting the business case for using Chile as a logistics hub.

Finally, the role of Chile as a commercial nexus connecting Latin America and Asia is bolstered by the network of free-trade agreements linking Asia to the markets of Latin America and the United States through Chile.[67] Perhaps the most important such accord is the free-trade agreement signed between Chile and the PRC in November 2005 at the APEC forum, which went into effect in October 2006.[68] The accord was the first such agreement signed between China and a Latin American country; it has become a model for similar deals currently being pursued with China by Peru and Costa Rica.[69] The Sino-Chilean free-trade agreement had a significant impact on commerce between the two nations, bringing about a jump of more than 100 percent in bilateral trade volume within the first year of its implementation,[70] even though only a portion of trade between the two nations has been subject to its provisions.[71] In 2008, China and Chile expanded the agreement with provisions that applied to services and investment, as well as a bilateral cooperation agreement in the area of small and medium enterprises.

Although important in its own right, the Sino-Chilean accord also complements a series of agreements in place between Chile and other countries in both Latin America and Asia. In Latin America, Chile has signed agreements granting it preferential access to Panama, Peru, and Colombia.[72] With respect to Asia, Chile has signed free-trade agreements with Japan[73] and South Korea; strategic commercial association agreements with New Zealand, Singapore, and Brunei; and a partial accord with India.[74] As of early 2009, Chile was also negotiating accords with Australia and Malaysia.[75]

Even at the local level, Chilean regional authorities are engaged in negotiating trade promotion accords with their Chinese counterparts. Examples include accords between the Santiago metropolitan region and Beijing, between the Fifth Region (Valparaíso) and the province of Guangdong,[76] and between the Eighth Region and Chengdu, as well as sister-city agreements between Pingxiang and Copiapó and between Qingdao and Puerto Montt.[77] By mid-2007, at least a dozen Chilean cities and provinces had such arrangements with their Chinese counterparts.[78] The combination of such contracts with free-trade accords between the United States and Latin America positions Chile to act as an intermediate production hub, importing components from low-cost Asian producers for further value-added production in Chile and final export to markets in the United States and Latin America.

Government and Business Infrastructures

As a leader in South America in commerce with Asia, Chile has relatively well-developed and effective government and business infrastructures.

On the government side, the system that Chile has put in place to promote its exports and to support its companies in their commercial transactions with China is one of the most mature and extensive in Latin America. In general terms, the competency and technical depth of this bureaucracy were demonstrated through its successful negotiation of the continent's first free-trade accord with the PRC, which has come to complement, and to serve as a model for, free-trade accords with other Asian nations. It was also demonstrated by the integration of some one hundred businesspeople into the delegation of Chilean president Michelle Bachelet, which traveled to China in April 2008.[79]

The infrastructure that Chile has in place for supporting companies doing business in China compares favorably to that of other Latin American countries. Given the size of China and the diversity of the regions within it, it is important that the Chilean Ministry of Foreign Affairs maintain not only an embassy in Beijing, but also representative offices in both Shanghai and Hong Kong.[80] Moreover, the official Chilean trade promotion organization, ProChile, has offices in each of the ministry's bureaus in China, integrated with the activities of the ministry, in order to support the dealings of Chilean businesses in China.[81] Although the resources and staffing of these offices are relatively modest, they do provide basic orientation, information, and services to visiting Chilean businesspeople, including telephone and computer access, meeting rooms, logistical support, and other business services.[82] In 2007, ProChile invested some $250,000 in an image campaign in China, targeted on Shanghai, including an arrangement with the Chinese Shenzhou-7 media center, through which Chile became the first country in Latin America to be promoted on the video entertainment system for Air China flights across all of China.[83] ProChile also facilitates participation by Chilean businesses in numerous trade fairs in China[84] and helps small and medium-sized Chilean businesses transform themselves into export-oriented concerns, whether directed toward China or other markets.[85] In addition, the resources of the Chilean state copper firm, CODELCO, and its presence in China are important in advancing Chilean interests in the PRC. In

January 2008, CODELCO upgraded its representative office in China, strategically located in Shanghai, in order to interact more directly with China concerning potential acquisitions of capital goods to be used in mining ventures in Chile.[86]

Chile's infrastructure for doing business with China is supported by a network of agreements, including the accord signed in October 2005 eliminating tariffs over the course of ten years in the trade of most commodities between the two nations. In March 2008, during her state visit to China, President Michelle Bachelet also signed an agreement governing investment in a series of sectors, including computing, mining, and ecologically oriented industries,[87] and in 2008 completed a supplementary agreement governing free trade in the exchange of services.

The maturity of Chile's commercial infrastructure for doing business with China is further reflected in the activities of established professional organizations (such as the Chile-China Business Committee[88] and the Chile-China Chamber of Commerce, Industry, and Tourism) and in the number of China-oriented business activities. Ties between Chinese and Chilean organizations were sufficient, for example, to put together the region's first Latin American–Chinese business summit, in Santiago, Chile, in November 2007.[89] The event attracted 400 businesspeople, mostly from China, but also from across Latin America. The organizers were able to secure the active participation of Michelle Bachelet, in addition to the involvement of the Chile-China Chamber of Commerce, the Chile-China Business Committee, and ProChile.[90] Concurrent with the business summit in Santiago, a business roundtable sponsored by ProChile took place in Arica, in the north of the country, bringing together Chilean exporters from the agricultural, fishing, and mining industries with Asian importers.[91] During the same month, Chile led a significant delegation to the first Latin America and Europe commodities trade fair, in Beijing in 2007, which included a number of booths representing the country.[92] Just three months prior to this, Chile's Society for the Promotion of Industry (SOFOFA) was host to the Second Shanghai Federation of Commerce and Industry Business Encounter.[93] In December 2006, Santiago hosted the trade fair Expo China, featuring more than 100 Chinese firms interested in doing business with the country.[94] And in September 2006, the Chile-China Economic Cooperation forum was held, which included 350 businesses, as well as representatives from both countries' governments.[95] These events may not prove that the Chilean business community is oriented toward China to any significant extent, but Chile's ability to conduct the events and draw local businesspeople compares favorably to that of other Latin American countries, suggesting that Chile's ability to transact business with the PRC is, in relative terms, ahead of that of many of its neighbors. Chilean leadership is also suggested by the number of Chilean firms that have exported to China. According to Chile's commercial attaché in Beijing, during the first quarter of 2007, 398 Chilean companies exported to China some type of goods that they produced.[96]

Ironically, behind the successes registered in Chile's trade with the PRC are the activities of a relatively small number of companies and their leaders. These include Andronico Luksic, who has been instrumental in the entry of Banco de Chile in China and in establishing Chilean wines in China,[97] and Enrique Ponce Lerou, whose company, SQM, exports potassium nitrate to the Chinese agricultural industry. One of the early milestones in the development of Chilean business ties with China was the purchase of the Hong Kong–based shipping company Norasia in 2001 by Ricardo Claro's enterprise, Compañia Sudamericana de Vapores,[98] creating a powerful Sino-Chilean logistics connection. Claro's companies also play a large role in Chilean mining exports to China.

Mirroring the limited number of Chilean corporate actors, the presence of Chilean businesspeople in China is also relatively limited. According to one estimate, as of 2007 there were only 140 Chileans in China, including a combination of students, traders, businesspeople, and embassy personnel. Nonetheless, this relatively small number of Chileans is greater than the number of people in China from most other Latin American countries.

Finally, the banking sector is a key component of the business infrastructure supporting Sino-Chilean commerce. Major Chilean institutions, such as Banco de Chile, have led Latin America in establishing a presence in China through representative offices, which provide services to their commercial customers wishing to do business there, following the December 2006 "equalization" of Chinese banking laws to facilitate greater foreign participation.[99] Banco de Chile has also played a proactive role in China-oriented trade-promotion events such as the November 2007 Latin America–China Business Summit.[100] The involvement of Banco de Chile reflects its owners' commitment to China as an emerging market, and establishes important financial and service links to China for Chilean businesses—links that do not exist in many other Latin American countries. Reciprocally, in May 2008, China Development Bank announced plans to open a representative office in Chile as a first step in establishing a presence in the Chilean market.[101]

Intellectual Infrastructure

In addition to the capabilities within the government and private sector to support commerce with the PRC, Chilean universities and other institutions are creating an impressive facility to support commerce with China, by providing courses in Mandarin and business-oriented China studies. In the words of Chilean columnist Ximena Pérez Villamil, the fever has been unleashed in Chile with the force of a tsunami: "Institutes, universities, and colleges are responding to the demand of the Chileans with courses, workshops, university minors, and intensive summers in China."[102]

With respect to the Mandarin language—a key element for conducting business on an equal footing in Chinese markets—Chile has significantly increased the number of students studying the language. In 2004, Chilean minister of education Sergio Bitar signed an accord with his Chinese counterpart to promote the teaching of Mandarin in Chile, helping to bring about a 500 percent increase in enrollment in Mandarin Chinese programs within the first year.[103] Chile has also seen a significant increase in Mandarin offerings both within Chilean universities and in private institutes, with many of the programs that previously had concentrated on English beginning to include Mandarin.[104] As early as November 2005, Chilean universities that had added Mandarin-language instruction included Universidad Católica, Escuela Militar, Universidad Bernardo O'Higgins, Universidad del Pacífico, and Universidad de Santiago de Chile (Usach).[105]

Chile does not yet have a Confucius Institute, a program sanctioned by and coordinated with the Chinese government to provide instruction in Mandarin, as well as other forms of information about Chinese history and culture. Nonetheless, plans for two such institutes in Chile are in the works. The biggest impediment reportedly is the lack of funding from the Chilean government: Confucius Institutes operate like business franchises, with the expectation that the host nation will supply virtually all of the financial support.

In addition to Mandarin-language training, a number of Chilean universities have created or expanded Asian studies programs. In the months following events of the November 2004 APEC summit in Santiago, for example, Universidad Diego Portales, one of Chile's most prestigious private universities, established a new Asia-Pacific program to support the training of future Chilean businesspeople.[106]

Chilean exchange programs with China, previously almost nonexistent, are also expanding. Prior to 2007, the only significant exchange program was between Tsinghua University in Beijing and Chile's Pontificia Universidad Católica,[107] reflecting, among other considerations, an absence of funding from both governments for such programs.

The first program after Católica's was one by Universidad Viña del Mar, in which, for three weeks, a group of fourteen students went to Zhejiang Gongshang University for a unique curriculum combining English-language work study with coursework focused on doing business with China.[108] By the end of 2007, Universidad Viña del Mar was offering a six-month exchange program, and had developed its own Mandarin offering in response to student requests.[109] In January 2008, the university sent its third delegation (forty students) to Zhejiang Gongshang University,[110] including not only its own students, but also ones from Pontificia Universidad Católica de Valparaíso, Universidad de Valparaíso, Universidad Aconcagua, Universidad Central, Universidad Católica del Norte, Universidad Técnica Federico Santa María, and Pontificia Universidad Católica.[111]

A number of important Chilean educational institutions still do not have Mandarin or China studies programs, including FLACSO Chile, Universidad Arcis, and Universidad de Chile.[112] However, many have plans in the works to start them, such as Universidad de Talca,[113] Universidad de Santo Tomas, and Pontificia Universidad Católica de Santiago.[114]

Political and Military Relations

Growing Sino-Chilean political and military contacts reflect the importance that each nation gives to the other as a trading partner. In April 2008, Chilean president Michelle Bachelet made a state visit to China, celebrating thirty-eight years of diplomatic relations between the two countries and the status of Chile as the first nation in South America to have granted diplomatic recognition to the PRC. She exuberantly declared, "Here is Chile and its people, and this president is aware of what that means."[115] Her visit was the first presidential-level visit by the Bachelet administration to China; however, it was the November 2004 visit to Chile by Chinese president Hu Jintao that helped set in motion many of the political and commercial activities oriented toward China currently unfolding in the country.

In addition to state visits, the two nations have conducted diplomatic exchanges on a regular basis, including the January 2007 visit by Wu Bangguo, chairman of the Standing Committee of China's National People's Congress (NPC), to the Chilean Congress.[116] The visit came shortly after a delegation of the Chilean political party Partido Por la Democracia (PPD) came to China in October 2006, and a delegation from the Chilean Senate, headed by Senate president Eduardo Frei, came in September 2006. In the same month, NPC Standing Committee chairman Wu Bangguo made his own visit to Chile, which included signing various agreements with President Bachelet.[117]

The Sino-Chilean bilateral relationship has been relatively positive, based on opportunities for mutual benefits in trade and an open agenda. The only major outstanding issue between the two countries is a dispute over Chilean allegations of Chinese overfishing in the waters outside the Chilean 200-mile limit in the South Pacific, which led the Chilean Ministry of Fisheries to limit the use of Chilean ports by Chinese fishing vessels.

In the military realm, the relationship between Chile and China reflects the shared interests of both countries, as maritime nations, in the Pacific sea routes that carry increasing volumes of trade between them, although Chile continues to privilege its strategic relationship with the United States. Sino-Chilean contacts include an increasing number of military-to-military visits, training activities, and visits by military ships to each other's ports.

The Chinese and Chilean militaries have a number of points of logical interaction. Both nations, for example, have a presence in Antarctica, with the Chinese base located next to the Chilean base. Chinese military and supply ships supporting its presence in Antarctica regularly visit Chilean ports to acquire supplies and perform other activities, as do the ships of other nations operating in the Antarctic. Chilean and Chinese military units operate together in the Brazilian-led UN Stabilization Mission in Haiti (MINUS-TAH);[118] China contributes approximately 125 military police and Chile approximately 400 soldiers, including air force engineers, medical personnel, and helicopters, plus marines and army personnel. In addition to these contacts, a Chinese navy flotilla is expected to make a port call in Chile in 2009 and to conduct joint exercises in the South Pacific with its Chilean counterparts. If the joint exercise occurs as planned, it will be only the second time in recent history that the two nations have conducted joint exercises, the other occasion being in 1998.[119]

Such interactions require regular meetings between high-level military officials of the two countries. In September 2003, for example, the Chinese defense minister met with then–commander-in-chief of the Chilean navy Angel Vergara.[120] Several months later, in May 2004, PRC defense minister Cao Gangchuan met with then–Chilean defense minister Michelle Bachelet in Beijing.[121] Subsequently, in October 2004, Liang Guanglie, the chief of staff of the People's Liberation Army, had a meeting in Beijing with his counterpart, the commander-in-chief of the Chilean army, General Juan Cheyre;[122] and, in October 2005, Cao Gangchuan met with the commander-in-chief of the Chilean air force, Aldo Sarabia Vilches, in Beijing.[123] In June 2006, the commander-in-chief of the Chilean navy, Rodolfo Codina, visited Beijing; Commander-in-Chief Oscar Izurieta of the Chilean army also paid a visit to Beijing in 2006.[124] In September 2008, the head of the People's Liberation Army Air Force, Xu Qiliang, visited the country to meet with Chilean defense officials.

Although the Chilean armed forces have been more restrained than their counterparts in Argentina in purchasing Chinese military equipment, the Chileans have bought a range of nonlethal goods from the PRC, including uniforms, personal gear for soldiers, and medical supplies.[125]

Sino-Chilean military ties also include officer exchanges, albeit at low levels:[126] officials from the Chilean War College study Mandarin in the PRC and, in 2006, two military officers from the PRC went to Chile for a two-year assignment to teach Mandarin to Chilean military officers.[127]

■ Brazil

Brazil occupies a dominant position among China's commercial partners in Latin America: it is simultaneously the region's largest exporter to China and the region's second-largest customer for Chinese products,[128] meriting its recognition by the PRC as a "strategic partner." Indeed, Cynthia Watson argues that the PRC's ties with Brazil are among the most significant, yet overlooked, components of China's expanding relationship with the region.[129]

In 2007, according to the Chinese Ministry of Commerce, Brazil accounted for more than 36 percent of all Latin American exports to China.[130] The majority of these exports are primary products, with three commodities accounting for 70 percent of Brazilian exports to the PRC: soy products, iron, and petroleum.[131] China is currently Brazil's third-largest trading partner;[132] Brazil aspires to make it number one by tripling its exports to the PRC by 2010.[133] The diversity of the Brazilian economy and the technical sophistication of its leading sectors create opportunities for unique China-Brazil partnerships in industries from petroleum, iron, and steel to aerospace.[134]

It should be noted that similarities in the structure of exports have also made Brazil and China competitors, producing tension in Brazil as Chinese products replace those of Brazilian manufacturers in such markets as the United States and the European Union.[135]

Beyond trade and economic issues, as authors such as Monica Hirst have argued, Brazil's traditional leadership role in the region also earns it special recognition by the PRC, including the role that it plays in important international forums, such as the G-8, the World Trade Organization, and the United Nations.[136]

Historical Context

Brazil is one of China's oldest trading partners in Latin America, with Chinese-Brazilian commerce dating back to the 1800s. Brazil has historically been at the forefront of the region with respect to the establishment and expansion of associations with China. It was one of the first nations in the continent to establish formal diplomatic relations with the PRC, doing so in 1974. Similarly, it became a strategic partner with China in 1993, making it the first country in Latin America to achieve this status.[137]

The Chinese Community in Brazil

Brazil has the largest Chinese community in Latin America, estimated in 2005 at 300,000 people. Relative to other groups in this large and varied country, however, the number of Chinese is small. Brazil's ethnic Chinese are primarily concentrated in the state of São Paulo and, in particular, in the district of Liberdale,[138] although there is a smaller Chinese community in Rio de Janeiro.[139]

The Chinese communities of Brazil, in general, are somewhat more recently arrived than those of Mexico and Peru, yet more established than those of Argentina. As is true in some other South American countries, the first waves of Chinese immigration to Brazil took place in the late nineteenth century from the province today called Guangzhou;[140] a significant wave also arrived in 1949, following the communist revolution, so that many of Brazil's Chinese residents today speak Chinese as well as Portuguese. As with the Chinese in Ecuador, and in contrast to the Chinese in Mexico and Peru, Brazil's Chinese citizens have had relatively few problems in their relations with other members of the nation's multicultural society.[141]

China's Interest in Brazilian Soy

As in Argentina, agricultural products are Brazil's primary export to China.[142] The availability of fertile farmland in Brazil for producing soy and other agricultural crops complements China's increasing need to import foodstuffs.

Brazil exports corn and wheat to China, but its agricultural exports to the PRC are dominated by soybeans and soy oil.[143] Indeed, soy products account for an estimated $2 billion of the $12 billion in *total* Brazilian exports to China.[144] Brazilian soy exports to the PRC have also been growing substantially. In 2006, Brazil exported eleven million tons of soybeans to China, representing a 100 percent increase over the volume that it had exported to China just two years earlier.[145] These exports are significant from the Chinese perspective, as well, with Brazil single-handedly supplying approximately 45 percent of all PRC soy imports, roughly double that of the next-largest supplier, Argentina.[146]

Although soy is traditionally bought and sold as a commodity in markets like the Chicago Board of Trade, the significant and growing volume of Chinese soy purchases from Brazil has led Chinese agricultural entities to explore purchasing soy products directly from Brazilian farmers through long-term contracts, rather than from major agro-exporters—e.g., Archer-Daniels Midland, Cargill, Bunge, and Dreyfus.[147] In 2004, for example, the PRC indicated that it would encourage private investors to buy land in Brazil for soybean farming.[148] Since that time, Chinese investors have made some minor land purchases,[149] but these have been concentrated principally in land in the Amazon known for its timber, and such activity has been relatively limited.[150]

Although the expansion of Brazil's soy exports to China may be regarded as a success story, it has also exposed serious deficiencies in the ability of the nation's infrastructure to support such commerce. Exporting soy products to China involves transporting them over poor-quality roads across Brazil, then loading them onto ships in Atlantic ports for an equally lengthy maritime journey. According to one estimate, because of the poor Brazilian infrastructure, moving soybeans from farms to ports in Brazil is more than four times as expensive as doing so in the United States.[151] Although the Brazilian government has made commitments for a number of major transportation infrastructure projects to address such deficiencies, very little of the promised investment has actually taken place.[152]

China's Interest in Brazilian Iron and Steel

As with the Chilean copper industry, the Brazilian iron and steel industry has been a major supplier for Chinese companies as well as an important partner and, in some cases, a competitor. Brazil is the world's largest iron ore exporter; in 2005, it was the third-largest exporter of iron ore to the PRC, behind the geographically closer nations of India and Australia.[153] Such Brazilian companies as Comphania Vale do Rio Doce (CVRD) and Gerdau have played significant roles as iron ore suppliers to Chinese steel producers, particularly prior to the 2008 global recession, when China was rapidly increasing its consumption of steel for capital formation and other uses.[154] Reciprocally, when Chinese demand for steel declined sharply in the second half of 2008, Brazilian suppliers were badly hurt. CVRD, for example, cited the falloff in demand from China as the driving factor in having to lay off 1,300 workers in December 2008.[155]

Prior to the decrease in steel demand that accompanied the global recession of 2008, Chinese steelmakers had been working closely with their suppliers in Brazil to help these companies expand production, in a fashion that resembles the collaboration between China's Minmetals and Chile's CODELCO. In February 2006, for example, China Minmetals and China Metallurgical Construction group provided a loan package of $236.5 million to the Brazilian firm Gerdau to assist it with a new plant and equipment purchases.[156] Similarly, in 2006, the Chinese steelmaker Baosteel entered into a $1.4 billion joint venture with CVRD to build a new steel plant in the Brazilian state of Maranhao,[157] and, in August 2007, CVRD and Baosteel announced plans to build yet another steel plant, in Ahchieta, in the Brazilian state of Espirito Santo.[158]

Chinese companies in the iron and steel sector—similarly to those involved with the Chilean copper industry—are evolving from purchasers of Brazilian iron and steel to partners in joint production endeavors. In January 2007, the Chinese firm Shougang announced that it was entering into a partnership with CVRD to supply iron to a new plant in the Hebei province of China.[159] In a similar fashion, in September 2006, CVRD entered into a joint venture to build a steel plant in Guangdong.[160] When CVRD bought the nickel producer Inco in 2007, it acquired, with the purchase, a number of plants in China.[161] Prior to the 2008 global recession, CVRD had announced plans to invest a total of $6.5 billion to increase its operations in China, including the expansion of supply arrangements with Chinese steel producers.[162]

China's Interest in Brazilian Petroleum

The PRC has a growing interest in Brazilian petroleum. The most tangible signs of this interest are the agreements that it has made with the Brazilian state oil company, Petrobras, for the exploration and development of oil fields in Brazil and offshore.[163] In July 2006, Petrobras signed its first export contract with a Chinese counterpart, Sinopec, estimated to be worth up to $1 billion in annual sales by 2012.[164] In 2007, according to Brazilian figures, petroleum exports to the PRC amounted to $791 million.[165] In July 2008, in the wake of major new petroleum finds announced by Brazil in the oil fields of Tupi, Jupiter, and Carioca, Sinopec signed a new memorandum of understanding with Petrobras, agreeing to increase the business links between the two companies.[166] In December 2008, China offered to extend Petrobras a $10 billion loan to support the development of its new petroleum reserves,[167] representing a quantity greater than the total of loans that it had provided to Venezuela during the previous two years.

Although the relative importance of Brazil to the PRC as an oil supplier has increased significantly with the discovery of significant quantities of oil off the Brazilian coast beginning in late 2007,[168] a number of impediments restrain the growth of this relationship. First, the dramatic fall in oil prices during the course of 2008 and the decrease in oil demand accompanying the global recession that began the same year have caused delays in virtually all major investments in the sector. In addition, as with Venezuelan oil shipments to the PRC, the Brazilian oil partnership with China is restrained by the relatively high logistical costs of shipping Brazilian oil to China.[169] The oil consumption needs of the growing Brazilian market also create uncertainty about the quantity of petroleum available to the PRC in the future.[170]

Despite such hurdles, Brazil is an important partner for the Chinese in the petroleum sector for three reasons. First, although Brazil's oil reserves are not as big as Venezuela's, they are composed of a mixture of crude that is generally lighter, and both easier and cheaper to process, than the Venezuelan. Second, the amount of petroleum that Brazil has available to export is likely to increase greatly as newly discovered oil deposits are exploited. Third, Petrobras, as China's associate in Brazil, has a reputation as a reliable partner, operating in a politically stable country with a relatively solid legal and juridical framework. For the PRC, such stability and reliability are important counterweights to the relative unpredictability of Venezuela and Ecuador as petroleum suppliers—particularly since security of supply is a principal factor driving China to build new petroleum partnerships in the Americas.

In addition to its petroleum, Petrobras has a number of capabilities and technologies that Chinese companies are interested in to support their oil exploration and development efforts worldwide. For example, negotiations between Petrobras and the Chinese firms Sinopec, China National Offshore Development Corporation (CNODC), and Petrochina in September 2006 were driven in part by China's desire to leverage and learn from the advanced technologies that Petrobras has in this area.[171]

China's Interest in Other Brazilian Products

In addition to soy products, iron, and petroleum, Brazil has a range of other products of interest to the PRC. As with other countries in Latin America, Brazil has a substantial wood and wood products industry, which has been a source of exports to China. According to one report, some 30 percent of the wood exported from Brazil's Amazon region goes to the PRC, where it is used in furniture and flooring, among other applications.[172] China is also a significant purchaser of Brazilian pulp and paper, which account for 3.7 percent of Brazil's exports to China.[173] From the Chinese perspective, Brazilian wood pulp and paper products accounted for 8 percent of Chinese imports of such products in 2004.[174] PRC interest in Brazilian wood products has also prompted Chinese investors to buy timberland in the Brazilian Amazon, although such purchases have become a matter of controversy among indigenous peoples and other residents of the region.[175]

Brazil exports relatively substantial amounts of meat and meat products to the PRC. Indeed, Brazil accounted for 11 percent of all Chinese meat imports in 2004, with the expectation that these imports will increase with growing Chinese prosperity and corresponding improvements in the national diet.[176] However, Brazil's direct export of meat products to the PRC is limited by the difficulties in the trade infrastructure between the two countries, including the lack of phytosanitary agreements between the two countries. As a result, virtually all Brazilian meat destined for China is first sold to Hong Kong, from where it is reexported to the mainland by middlemen.[177] (In December 2007, for example, the group JBS/Friboi was approved to export Brazilian beef to China; yet the news report indicated that the approval's impact would be on the flow of products through Hong Kong.[178]) Despite such hurdles, by the end of 2008, progress by the Brazilian government in opening up the Chinese market to Brazilian poultry gave Brazilian producers reason to believe that they would continue to expand sales to the Chinese market.[179]

Brazil as a Market for Chinese Goods

Brazil is an increasingly key market for Chinese exports. Indeed, the $11.37 billion of goods that Brazil purchased from China in 2007, according to the PRC Ministry of Commerce, was exceeded only by the $11.71 billion of goods that Mexico purchased from the region.[180] Furthermore, since roughly 2003, China's sales to Brazil have been increasing more rapidly than its purchases from the country:[181] 2007 saw a 54 percent increase in Chinese exports to Brazil, versus a 42 percent increase in Brazilian exports to China during the same period.[182] Because of these trends, in 2007, for the first time in recent years, Brazil incurred an annual trade deficit with the PRC.[183] Reflecting, in part, concern arising from such increases, a delegation from the Brazilian government traveled to China in July 2008; it met with the Chinese Ministry of Commerce to negotiate a "voluntary agreement" to reduce exports to Brazil of Chinese toys and textiles.[184]

Chinese products entering Brazil include not only low value–added products such as textiles and footwear, but also industrial products and high-end consumer goods. Indeed, thanks in part to Brazil's growing industrial partnership with China, 73 percent of Brazil's imports from China are capital goods and raw materials used as factor inputs in Brazilian production.[185]

China is increasingly exporting more sophisticated consumer goods to Brazil, such as cars, motorcycles, and consumer appliances. By late 2007, the Chinese car brand Chery was being sold in Brazil, with the expectation that a new Chery assembly plant being constructed in Montevideo, Uruguay, would sell even more cars in the Brazilian market under free-trade provisions of Mercosur (Southern Common Market).[186] The Chinese motorcycle manufacturer Jialing is also present in the Brazilian market; additionally, the Chinese appliance maker Haier and the electronics manufacturer Gre have facilities in Brazil's free-trade zone, where they assemble products from Chinese components for sale in Brazil and other Mercosur markets.[187]

Besides exporting consumer goods to Brazil, Chinese companies increasingly provide components and services in the Brazilian telecommunications market. Indeed, Brazil is both an important market and the regional base of operations for the two Chinese telecommunications companies with a strong presence in Latin America: Huawei and ZTE.

Huawei has been remarkably successful in penetrating the Brazilian market since choosing São Paulo as the site of its first Latin American office in 1999.[188] Virtually all of the providers of fixed (nonwireless) network services in Brazil use Huawei's version of the core Digital Subscriber Line Access Multiplexer (DSLAM) technology, and a third of all DSLAM subscribers in Brazil use Huawei's equipment.[189] In 2005, Huawei was expected to double its sales in Brazil to some $200 billion,[190] and, in 2006, the company reached the landmark of selling one million Abstract-Type and Scheme-Definition Language–type (ASDL) ports.[191] The company's biggest break in Brazil, however, came in 2007, when it won a contract with Vivo, the country's major wireless service provider, to switch the company's infrastructure from the older Time Division Multiple Access (TDMA) technology to Global System for Mobile Communications (GSM) lines.[192]

China's ZTE has also had considerable success in the Brazilian market, with a focus in the south. Like Huawei, ZTE has located its Latin American regional office in São Paulo.[193] In August 2005, the company won major contracts to supply Direct Subscriber Line (DSL) modems to the Brazilian fixed-telecommunications provider Telefónica. Separately, in the same month, it was awarded a contract by the major Brazilian telephone and wireless company Telmar to provide DSL Access Multiplexor (DSLAM) equipment.[194]

Infrastructure Projects

As mentioned earlier, Brazil's ability to sell primary products to China and to act as a market for Chinese goods is restricted by the Brazilian infrastructure, including inadequacies in the nation's highways and railroad system that make it time-consuming and expensive to transport goods to market. In acknowledgment of such deficiencies, the government of Luiz Inácio Lula da Silva has presented a number of projects for improving this infrastructure, although budget shortfalls have slowed progress.

As a key trading partner, the PRC has a vested interest in helping Brazil resolve its infrastructure challenges—particularly those that facilitate transportation of Chinese goods to Brazilian markets and the export of Brazilian products to China.[195] Several major projects with potential backing from the Chinese have been discussed that would improve and extend highway and rail routes crossing the Andes, better connecting Brazilian suppliers and markets to Pacific ports, such as those of Ecuador, Peru, and Chile. Perhaps the most ambitious project currently under discussion is a proposed interoceanic corridor from the Brazilian port city of Manaus to the Ecuadorian port city of Manta.[196] The proposed corridor would involve an estimated $800 million in initial investment and would include both highway and rail links between the two modern deepwater ports, saving an estimated ten to fourteen days in transit time.[197] An important part of the value of the project is that it supports the development of the interior of Brazil. Given that Brazil established a free-trade zone in Manaus and seeks to promote the development of industry in the city, the proposed corridor makes it more economically viable to import factor inputs from Asia to producers located in the city, and export their finished goods via Pacific ports.

In addition to the Manta-Manaus corridor, a second project, included as part of the South American Regional Infrastructure Integration Initiative

(IIRSA), involves the construction of highway and rail connections from the Brazilian Atlantic port of Santos to the Chilean Pacific ports of Arica and Iquique.[198] In December 2007, Brazil, Chile, and Bolivia signed an agreement to invest $600 million in the highway portion of this route by the first quarter of 2009[199]—of this, Brazil committed to fund $162 million.[200] Other highway improvements are currently under way, creating new routes from the Peruvian port cities of Paita and Ilo, across the Andes, linking up with waterways in the Brazilian Amazon; as well, new highways and rail lines are contemplated that would extend from the Peruvian port of Tacna through the Bolivian cities of La Paz and Santa Cruz, ultimately connecting to the Brazilian state of Mato Grosso.

In addition to transportation projects to connect Brazil to the Pacific, Chinese companies have been exploring a number of projects to bolster the Brazilian energy infrastructure. One of the most advanced of these initiatives is the construction of the 1,400-mile Gasene natural gas pipeline by the Chinese firm Sinopec.[201] The pipeline is designed to link the northern and the southern Brazilian gas infrastructures in order to facilitate the supply of natural gas to Brazilian iron producers, helping them more reliably and inexpensively supply the metal to Chinese consumers. Although the project experienced a number of delays due to sharp increases in the cost of the metals used for the pipeline itself,[202] by late 2008, construction of the first leg represented a Brazilian investment of $239 million.[203]

The PRC has also committed to a number of other projects in the energy sector, reflecting the relationship between Brazil's energy production and the nation's ability to export goods of interest to the PRC. One project is a 350-megawatt coal-burning thermoelectric plant in Rio Grande do Sul.[204] In total, the PRC has committed to invest $1.1 billion in Brazilian energy projects, although how many projects will actually be brought to fruition is less than clear.

One of the reasons that so little of the anticipated Chinese investment in Brazilian infrastructure projects has come about is that the Chinese often attempt to use their own companies and laborers to do the work. This requirement, in combination with the fact that the funds provided are frequently low-interest loans that have to be repaid, raises serious objections among key stakeholders on the Brazilian side. Part of the arrangement involving Chinese investment in the thermoelectric plant in Rio Grande do Sul, for example, was that the work would be done by the Chinese Yanguang Group. Similarly, when the German firm ThyssenKrupp sought to build a new factory in Rio de Janeiro in partnership with the Chinese, the PRC originally sought to bring in some 4,000 Chinese laborers to work on the project. In the end, the PRC compromised, settling for permission to bring in 600 workers from China, and hiring the rest from the local labor market.[205]

Technology Cooperation

As China scholar Barry Naughton has noted, Chinese firms are increasingly using international networks as paths to acquire needed technologies.[206] Because of Brazil's status as a relatively large and diversified economy, the country has a number of advanced industries with technologies and processes of interest to the Chinese.

As noted previously, China's partnering with Petrobras and other leading Brazilian companies indicates not only China's interest in Brazilian products per se, but also its interest in the technology used to produce or acquire them—such as deepwater exploration and drilling technology, in the case of the oil sector.[207] It can be seen that the use of Brazilian companies in major Chinese infrastructure projects, such as the construction of the Three Gorges Dam,[208] is, in part, another reflection of China's interest in the technology that these firms bring to the table.

In the manufacturing sector, a number of Brazilian companies have located important portions of their production and operations in the PRC. One of the earliest to do so was the Brazilian compressor manufacturer Embraco, which established a factory in China in 1994; by 2007, it had captured 30 percent of the Chinese compressor market, with an operation that involved 1,500 employees.[209] More recently, Weg, an $8 billion company and the biggest machinery manufacturer in Brazil, decided to set up operations in China.[210] Other examples include the consumer electronics producer Gradiente, which was doing 40 percent of its manufacturing operations in Shenzen by 2007,[211] and Azaléia, which moved an 800-person factory from Rio Grande do Sol to China in 2006 to produce 30 of its shoe brands.[212]

In the aircraft industry, the Brazilian manufacturer Embraer has an ongoing joint venture with the Second Chinese Aircraft Industry Corporation (CAICII) to manufacture midsized business jets in the province of Harbin, for sale to the Chinese market.[213] In addition to supplying the Chinese demand for commercial aircraft, the joint project arguably fills a Chinese national strategic goal to develop a capability for the manufacture of "large aircraft."[214] The success of this joint venture led the two partners to broaden the relationship, with the regional Chinese Hainan Airlines placing a $2.7 billion order, announced in August 2006, for 100 aircraft, with part of the production taking place in Brazil for the first time.[215] The relationship has also been troubled, however, with uncertainty about the volume of orders from the Chinese domestic market, and other issues.[216]

In the domain of space technology, Brazil is arguably China's leading partner in the region. Brazil is one of two countries in South America with whom China has signed a space cooperation agreement in recent years, the other being Argentina.[217] The principal collaborative project between Brazil and China in this sector is the joint China-Brazil Earth Research Satellite (CBERS) effort. The first of the CBERS satellites was launched in 1999, the second in 2003,[218] and the third in 2007.[219] The initial satellites involved the use of Brazilian photo-imaging technology, and was believed by some analysts to have helped the Chinese improve their military over-the-horizon targeting capability.[220] At least two more satellites remain to be launched as part of the CBERS program, with one scheduled for launch in 2010 and the other in 2012.[221]

Brazil is also of interest to China over the long term as a technology partner and as a resource provider in the nuclear industry. In November 2003, a delegation from the Chinese Science and Technology Commission for Industry and National Defense met with Eduardo Campos, the Brazilian minister of science and technology, and expressed an interest in collaborating with Brazil across a range of nuclear energy issues, from security at nuclear installations to medical and agricultural uses of radioisotopes. However, in subsequent public statements Campos denied that any decision had been taken to move forward on such cooperation.[222] Nonetheless, both nations are looking again at the possibility of expanding their nuclear power–generation capabilities. China is completing new nuclear reactors at the unprecedented rate of two per year, and requires increasing quantities of uranium to fuel them. Although it currently plans to acquire the uranium from Australia,[223] Brazil also has significant reserves of the metal that could be of interest to the PRC. While other nations in Latin America, such as Colombia and Ecuador, have potential uranium deposits as well, Brazil has the ability to enrich its uranium in-country; indeed, Brazil announced in 2004 that it would begin to use its centrifuge technology to enrich and export uranium. China is one of the natural markets for this product.[224]

In addition to the sale of uranium itself, given the relative global shortage of experienced nuclear engineers and technicians, potential exists for China and Brazil to collaborate in the design and development of new reactors, as well as in the modification or improvement of existing facilities. In short, Brazil and China could emerge as either natural partners or competitors in selling nuclear reactors to other Latin American nations and in helping other countries in the region develop their own capabilities.

Government and Business Infrastructure

Brazil has a series of permanent coordinating mechanisms and a relatively well-developed government bureaucracy for supporting its commerce with the PRC. In March 2006 in Beijing, Brazil and China held a meeting of the High Level Commission, the principal coordinating body at the senior levels of government, to manage the strategic relationship between the two nations.[225] As a complement to the High Level Commission, in November 2007 in São Paulo, the two nations held what was called the first Sino-Brazilian "strategic dialogue," including representatives from both countries' governments and private sectors.[226] Despite the promise of such vehicles, however, Brazilian businessmen have noted off the record that the level of official attention given to the High Level Commission has been limited, and that its working-level groups have not met on a regular basis.

In addition to official coordination mechanisms, the Brazilian government has good capability to support companies seeking to do business with the PRC. The Brazilian Ministry of Foreign Relations, for example, has trade-promotion offices in both Beijing and Shanghai, with the express purpose of "gathering and disseminating data on business and investment opportunities"; organizing trade fairs, missions to China, and other events; developing market and product surveys; performing analyses of competitiveness and competitors; and providing other forms of assistance to Brazilian firms looking to export to China.[227] As with virtually all of the Latin American embassies and national trade-promotion offices in the PRC, however, experts in the field suggest that the personnel and resources available through the Brazilian government in China are not adequate to meet the demand for services by Brazilian companies wishing to do business in China or Chinese companies seeking to establish contacts in Brazil.[228]

In addition to the Ministry of Foreign Relations, Brazil has an official organization for the promotion of exports: the Brazilian Agency for Investment and Export Promotion (APEX). It is interesting to note that prior to 2007 this organization had almost no resources focused on the PRC.[229] In that year, however, a new president was appointed to APEX—Alessandro Teixeira—who focused on a narrower range of target markets,[230] opening an office in China, and using a considerable portion of the agency's resources to promote Brazilian exports to that country.[231] Under this new leadership, APEX participated in the strategic dialogue in São Paulo in November 2007, which included an agreement with its counterpart, the Chinese Council for the Promotion of International Trade (CCPIT), to promote bilateral commerce.[232]

In addition to capabilities at the government level, as a relatively advanced and diversified economy, Brazil has a well-developed commercial infrastructure, with large corporations, service companies, and banking institutions with international reach to support the conduct of commerce with the PRC. In the private sector, Brazil has numerous public and private companies with the resources, sophistication, and worldwide contacts to do business with China, including firms such as Embraer and Petrobras.

In the banking sector, Brazilian institutions are increasingly becoming involved in China, even as Chinese banks set up a presence in Brazil. As an example, the parent company of Brazil's leading bank, Itaú, has established a commercial office in Shanghai,[233] as has Banco do Brasil.[234] Reciprocally,

China Development Bank has an office in São Paulo,[235] and, in late 2007, Bank of China announced plans to open an office there as well.[236]

As with Chile, Costa Rica, and a growing list of other Latin American countries, Brazil conducts and participates in various trade fairs and promotional events involving commerce with China. In August 2007, to take one instance, Brazil hosted the third Latin America–East Asia Cooperation forum (FOCALAE).[237] However, although Brazil has also been one of the major national exhibitors at the Canton trade fair,[238] it surprisingly has no official representation there.[239]

In promoting trade with China more broadly, as of 2007 Brazil had thirty-seven different China-oriented chambers of commerce.[240] The Brazil-China Chamber of Commerce and Industry, formed in 1986 and located in São Paulo, is one of the oldest such organizations in Latin America. In addition to these organizations, the Brazil-China Business Council likewise acts to promote the interests of its member companies with respect to advancing their commercial activities in China.[241]

Reflecting the growing commerce with China, Brazil has been a leader in Latin America with respect to logistics services and, in particular, air transportation, which is not significantly hampered by the country's lack of a Pacific port. In December 2006, for example, Air China launched its first flight to São Paulo,[242] hoping to capture the patronage of some of the 53,000 passengers who traveled from China to Brazil during the previous year—a figure representing an increase of 24 percent over the year prior.[243]

Intellectual Infrastructure

Despite the size and economic diversity of the country, the intellectual infrastructure in Brazil to support business with China is relatively modest. Surprisingly, there is not a single university in the country with a program of dedicated China studies.[244] Although some institutes and universities have Mandarin-language programs, the offerings among the country's major universities are inconsistent at best. For instance, while Universidad de Brasilia has a Chinese program, the reputable FLACSO Brazil does not. The Universidade Estadual Paulista system also does not have an official Mandarin program, although it was looking to initiate one in late 2008.[245]

In addition to this relatively modest number of Chinese-language programs in Brazil's universities, the Chinese community in Brazil provides a "natural infrastructure" of people with the linguistic and cultural knowledge to support the expansion of Sino-Brazilian commerce. To the extent it is used, through official channels or private-sector initiative, this community stands to play an increasingly important role in a new generation of Brazilian businesses that do business with China—providing logistics, information, and other services to Chinese corporations and visitors coming to Brazil.[246]

Political and Military Relations

Reflecting its status as China's strategic partner, Brazil has regular contact with the PRC, at the working level and at senior levels, in both the political and military arenas.

Brazil's contacts with China in the political realm are characterized by regular, bilateral, working-level visits, punctuated by an occasional high-level state visit. In 2004, Chinese president Hu Jintao traveled to Brazil to meet with his Brazilian counterpart, Luiz Inácio Lula da Silva. Lula subsequently went to China to meet again with President Hu.[247] Although these were the last visits between Brazilian and Chinese heads of state as of 2008, there has been a series of lower-level contacts between the two nations. In March 2006, for example, Chinese vice president Zeng Quinghong traveled to Brazil to meet with his counterpart, José Alencar. The visit also represented the first session of a new coordinating body that had been set up to strengthen China-Brazil relations: the China-Brazil High-Level Committee on Consultation and Cooperation.[248] That September, Wu Bangguo, chairman of the Standing Committee of the Chinese National People's Congress, made a six-day visit to Brazil in which he met with President Lula and leaders of both houses of the Brazilian Congress.[249] In April 2007, PRC foreign minister Yang Jiechi met with a Brazilian delegation headed by Vice President José Alencar during the Fourteenth Brazil-China Political Consultation Conference.[250] In September of the same year, the Chinese assistant foreign minister received a delegation from the politically important Workers' Party (PT) of Brazil.[251] Finally, as noted previously, in November 2007, China and Brazil held their first strategic dialogue to discuss how to advance the partnership between the two countries, featuring a meeting between Chinese foreign minister Yang Jiechi and Brazilian deputy foreign minister Roberto Jaguaribe Gomes de Mattos.[252]

As with China's relationship with Chile, Mexico, and other Latin American countries, one of the more interesting developments in the Sino-Brazilian relationship is that of ties at the subnational level. In August 2007, for example, the governor of the Brazilian state of São Paulo, José Serra, visited the Chinese province of Guangdong, leading to the signing of a friendship agreement between São Paulo and Guangdong.[253] Similarly, when Chairman Wu Bangguo of the Standing Committee traveled to Brazil in September 2006, he made a point to visit the Brazilian states of Amazonas and São Paulo, holding meetings with their governors and talking about China's relationship with each state.[254]

In the military arena, as in the political sphere, China and Brazil conduct regular interactions, exchanges, and official visits. In March 2006, José Alencar went to Beijing, and included a visit with his counterpart, Chinese defense minister Cao Gangchuan.[255] The visit came a year and a half after the October 2004 meeting in Brazil between Cao Gangchuan and José

Alencar's predecessor, José Viegas Filho,[256] and, prior to that, the November 2003 meeting between Cao Gangchuan and Viegas in Beijing.[257]

Brazil and China have conducted a series of officer exchanges, including the hosting of Brazilian students by the Chinese National Defense University. Furthermore, Brazilian representatives are included as observers in major Chinese military exercises. In September 2005, for example, Brazilians were among forty officers among twenty-four invited to observe the People's Liberation Army (PLA) exercise ("North Sword") in Inner Mongolia.[258]

◼ Argentina

In some senses, the Argentina-China relationship has been overshadowed by others that are either more controversial, such as the PRC's relationship with Venezuela, or larger in economic terms, such as the PRC's relationship with Brazil. Nonetheless—and largely unnoticed beyond Latin America— Argentina has amassed a significant economic, political, technological, and military relationship with China, consistent with the strategic partner status that it currently enjoys with its Asian counterpart.[259]

Argentina's economic relationship with the PRC is dominated by its exports of soy products and sunflower oil. Not only has Argentina benefited from selling increasing quantities of these goods to the PRC, but also it has profited from the global increase in commodity prices that Chinese demand helped to fuel prior to the 2008 global recession, including a 40 percent rise in the price of soy over the course of 2007.[260] At the same time, Argentina also is a large and growing market for Chinese manufactured goods and has great potential as a supplier of metals and mineral products to China, although this potential is yet to be fully realized.

Although Argentina's bilateral trade with China in absolute terms is less than that between China and Brazil, Argentina nonetheless accounted for an impressive 12.4 percent of all Latin American exports to the PRC in 2007.[261]

The expansion of Sino-Argentine trade, though beneficial for many sectors, has also created problems. In 2007, rising imports from the PRC threatened to turn Argentina's net trade position into a deficit. Companies, organized labor, and other interests in Argentina have pointed to such facts as evidence that the country's manufacturing sector is being damaged by commerce with China, although econometric studies dispute this.[262] The Argentine relationship with China has also been soured somewhat by disappointed expectations of Chinese investment, and by the 2008 Argentine agricultural strike, which forced the PRC to scramble to find alternative suppliers for its soy products. In addition to these tensions, Argentina faces a growing logistics challenge as its trade with the PRC expands: goods bound for or coming from China must either go through Atlantic ports, implying a long ocean transit, or cross a number of Andes mountain passes, which are frequently rendered unusable in the heart of winter.

Argentina is engaged not only in trade with the PRC, but also in important technological and military collaboration with it. The Chinese telecom companies ZTE and Huawei are rapidly expanding their presence in Argentina, as they are elsewhere in Latin America. The Argentine military continues to lead most of the region in deepening its China connection, including the purchase—from the PRC—of uniforms and trucks, an abandoned deal to buy military helicopters, the contemplated acquisition of advanced radar systems, and the expansion of training programs and officer exchanges.

Historical Context

Argentina was part of the first group of Latin American countries to follow the lead of Chile and extend diplomatic recognition to the PRC,[263] doing so in February 1972.[264] As with Sino-Chilean ties, however, the relationship between Argentina and China remained relatively limited until the end of the 1990s.

Like Chile, Argentina is able to maintain a positive relationship with China, despite ideological differences, thanks in part to each nation's silence concerning the domestic politics of the other. During the early years of their relationship, China avoided adding its voice to the growing international community of states and groups criticizing the human rights practices of the then–Argentine military dictatorship. Reciprocally, Argentina was the first nation to send a presidential-level delegation to China following the diplomatic ostracism of the PRC after China's 1989 crackdown on protesters in Tiananmen Square and other parts of the country.[265]

Expanding political contacts between Argentina and China have paralleled the growing economic ties between the two countries. In April 2001, Jiang Zemin visited Argentina—the first time a Chinese president had ever done so. In 2004, President Hu Jintao went to Argentina in conjunction with his trip to the APEC forum, committing to explore a number of specific investment deals in the country, and highlighting the emerging importance of Argentina to China as a customer and as a supplier of primary products.[266]

The Chinese Community in Argentina

Argentina currently has a modest-sized Chinese community, with 65,000 to 70,000 ethnic Chinese, concentrated primarily in major urban areas of the country. This community is unique in that the majority of these immigrants have arrived within the past thirty to forty years, providing a wealth of people who still speak Mandarin and who have lived in China in their own life-times. The linguistic abilities and cultural knowledge of this group are potential competitive advantages for Argentina as it endeavors to deepen its commercial relationship with the PRC.

Although some Chinese arrived in Argentina in the late nineteenth century, the most significant wave of immigration from China occurred from the 1970s to the 1990s. Chinese immigrants arriving in Argentina during the first part of this period came principally from Shanghai, while those arriving later came from the less prosperous Fushien province.[267] Newly arriving Chinese immigrants joined a larger, more established Asian community, which had arrived from Japan and Korea during the previous century.

Currently, Argentina's ethnic Chinese are principally found in the nation's major urban areas, including Córdoba, Mendoza, Rosario, Salta, and Mar del Plata.[268] An important Chinese community is found in the Buenos Aires suburb of Belgrano.[269] This community, which generally traces its origins to Taiwan, is different from most other Chinese communities in the region in that it has been active in Argentine politics, forming a small but important current within the Argentine Peronist party during the 1990s, called the Unión de Residentes Taiwaneses Justicialistas.[270]

As Sergio Cesarin notes, Chinese immigrants have come to play an important role in the small grocery stores that are a tradition in urban neighborhoods across Argentina.[271] The Chinese moved into this economic niche at the same time that Spanish merchants were being displaced from this market by competition with larger supermarkets,[272] but ran their businesses in ways that allowed them to survive where their Spanish predecessors had not been able to do so. By 2007, the small Sino-Argentine community accounted for an estimated 30 percent of all small grocery store sales across Argentina.[273]

Despite such success, the proliferation of Chinese-run small grocery stores in Argentine neighborhoods has caused some resentment. Some in the community, unhappy with the new Chinese merchants, grumbled that Chinese merchants band together to buy wholesale goods at lower prices, while others allege that Chinese merchants are involved with the Chinese mafia or sell contraband or stolen goods.[274] In June 2006, ongoing tensions between Chinese shopkeepers and the surrounding community manifested themselves when a union of Argentine truck drivers launched a boycott of Chinese-owned shops in protest of alleged mistreatment by Chinese store owners.[275]

Despite some tensions with other members of Argentine society, the Chinese community represents a potential, largely unexploited resource as Argentina expands its commerce with the PRC. The development of commercial relationships with China and the growth of tourism will fuel demand for people with an understanding of Chinese culture and the ability to speak Mandarin—including not only professionals in consulting firms, logistics operations, and major corporations, but also tour guides and service personnel in banks, hotels, restaurants, and businesses. The linguistic abilities and cultural connections of the Chinese Argentine community may well play an important role in meeting this demand.

China's Interest in Argentine Agriculture

Although Argentina is a relatively developed and economically diverse country, it is Argentine agriculture that dominates the nation's relationship with the PRC in terms of sales volume. The northern part of Argentina has a relatively temperate climate and vast quantities of land suitable for crops. Like the midwestern part of the United States, the relatively flat grasslands in the center of Argentina, known as the "pampas," are a major agricultural belt, producing soy, sunflowers, wheat, corn, and a range of other products, as well as grazing land for cattle and other livestock. This production of agricultural products is complemented by Argentina's relatively small population, making a logical case for the country to serve as the breadbasket of China.[276]

Argentina is a major exporter of soy products to the PRC. Although the size of its soy exports to China is only half that of neighboring Brazil, Argentina nonetheless supplies an impressive 23 percent of PRC soy imports;[277] approximately 87 percent of Argentina's exports to China involve soy and soy products.[278] As of 2006, the export of soy products was a $40 billion–per–year industry for Argentina, and has been called the "star sector" of the Argentine economy.[279] Argentina's role as an exporter of soy products to China was damaged to some extent by the 2008 agricultural strike, which forced Chinese purchasers to scramble for other sources of supply. Nonetheless, the nation's exports to China recovered and increased significantly during 2008, despite the deepening global recession.[280]

In addition to soy, Argentina supplies the PRC with sunflower products[281] and a range of other agricultural goods.[282] Overall Argentine and Brazilian exports to the PRC have been so significant that Chinese companies have reportedly explored the possibility of entering into direct, long-term contracts with individual growers. Efforts to enter into such relationships, however, are difficult because of the fragmentation of the Argentine agricultural market into a large number of small producers.[283] Currently, such agricultural companies as Monsanto or Cargill provide the service of buying up the production of Argentine farmers and making it available to export markets.[284]

Moving from grains to meat products, although Argentine beef has a very positive international reputation, exports to the PRC from this sector have been limited.[285] In part, this is because Argentina has a significant internal market for its meat, in contrast to its soy products and sunflower oil, and it prioritizes this internal market. Meat that is not used in the internal market, in turn, typically goes to fulfill the nation's allotted quantity of beef exports to the European Union, known as the "Hilton quota."[286] Although the product remaining after meeting internal demand and the Hilton quota is potentially available for export, Argentine producers have experienced difficulties getting the PRC to certify their slaughterhouses and other facilities to comply with phytosanitary regulations. During a 2004 review, for example, PRC inspectors certified only five of the twenty-two Argentine facilities inspected as meeting the standards required to permit export to China.[287] Some progress has been made in this area, however, with Argentina and the PRC signing an accord in January 2005 that would make it easier for Argentine beef to enter the Chinese market.[288]

Despite the difficulties experienced in exporting Argentine beef to China, the nation has been successful in expanding its exports to the PRC in certain niche markets in the meat industry. As an example, up to 70 percent of the exports of Argentine chicken subproducts, such as feet and wings, are destined for China.[289]

Argentina also exports a modest quantity of timber and wood products to the PRC, as do its Andean neighbors. These exports generally come from the northern part of the country[290] and, together with leather goods and wools, account for another 6.6 percent of Argentine exports to the PRC.[291]

China's Interest in Argentine Petroleum

Although Argentina is a country that possesses petroleum reserves,[292] it is not a "petroleum exporting country" in the sense that this term might be applied to Venezuela.[293] Nonetheless, Argentina sells modest amounts of oil and natural gas to China, accounting for 7.7 percent of total Argentine exports to the PRC in 2004—roughly a tenth of the value of its sales of soy and sunflower oils to China.[294]

Chinese companies have been involved in several large investment deals in the Argentine petroleum sector, but these have not yet come to fruition. When Hu Jintao, China's then-president, traveled to Argentina as part of his five-nation trip to Latin America in November 2004, he outlined a series of potential Chinese investments in Argentina totaling $19 billion— and signed a memorandum of understanding that committed his government to investigate a partnership between China Sonangol and the Argentine state oil firm Enarsa[295] encompassing $5 billion in investment projects, such as the joint exploration for oil off the Argentine coast.[296] Although nothing ever came of the contemplated partnership, talks of a new deal surfaced a year later, in November 2005, with the Chinese petroleum company CNPC reportedly interested in acquiring the assets of the Argentine oil company

Bridas, valued at approximately $5 billion.[297] Like the Enarsa-China Sonangol project, however, the Bridas deal never materialized. Several months later, reports surfaced that the Spanish firm Repsol YPF was engaged in talks with the China National Oil and Gas Exploration and Development Corporation (CNODC) regarding a partnership involving its Latin American assets, although Repsol quickly denied the rumors.[298] In July 2007, rumors again emerged that CNPC was considering acquiring the Latin American assets of Repsol, although this time it was CNPC that denied the rumors.[299] Since then, the Argentine state energy firm, Energía Argentina Sociedad Anónima (ENARSA), has indicated an interest in collaborating with Chinese firms to explore for oil offshore in the south of the country, although no significant activity has taken place on this front.[300]

China's Interest in the Argentine Mining Sector
The Argentine metals and minerals sector has significant, but as yet unrealized, potential with respect to the nation's commercial relationship with the PRC. While the products of this sector are Argentina's number one commodity export, only approximately 3 percent of these exports go to the PRC.[301]

A modest yet symbolically important PRC foray into the Argentine mining sector occurred in 2005, with a Chinese company's purchase of the Sierra Grande mine in the province of Rio Negro[302] for the modest sum of $6.4 million.[303] The mine is believed to have limited quantities of iron, as well as cobalt and other minerals. It had formerly been the property of Hiparsa, a firm of the Argentine state, and had been exploited partially before being closed down. Although the quantity of minerals in Sierra Grande may be modest, the deal represents the first initiative by the PRC to purchase a mining operation outright in the country, and puts Argentina in the company of neighboring Peru, where the PRC owns and operates a series of mines.[304]

China's Interest in Other Argentine Products
As with other Latin American economies, such as those of Mexico, Brazil, and Chile, some of Argentina's greatest commercial successes in the Chinese market have involved larger Argentine companies with internationally recognized brands, selling to the growing Chinese upper class in the luxury segment of the market. The Argentine candy maker Arcor, for example, has enjoyed some success in selling its cookies, caramels, and chocolates in the PRC through a distribution office in Shanghai.[305] Similarly, Argentine lingerie manufacturers have reportedly had positive results, capitalizing on the image and creative resources of the Argentine fashion industry to enter China, following the lead of other brands like Victoria's

Secret.[306] Argentina's winemakers have also been successful in China, although not to the same extent as their Chilean counterparts. Argentine vineyards—San Hubierto and Bodegas Norton, for example—have built a successful business exporting bulk wines to the PRC to be repackaged and bottled there, with Argentine wine exports to China tripling in 2007.[307]

Argentina as a Market for Chinese Goods

Like many of its counterparts in Latin America, Argentina, as a middle-income country, is an attractive potential market for Chinese goods. Not only does the nation's mean annual per capita income of $6,992 in 2006 put it on a par with other nations of the Southern Cone, but it is also a large economy in absolute terms.[308] In 2007, the nation imported over $3.6 billion of goods from the PRC, making it the fifth-largest market for Chinese products in Latin America, behind Mexico, Brazil, Chile, and Panama.[309] Argentine purchases of Chinese goods have grown significantly in recent years. According to a study by the Argentine firm Techint, Argentine purchases of manufactured goods from China tripled between 2001 and 2006.[310] In 2007, imports from China increased by 78 percent;[311] in December 2007, according to a report by Argentina's Industry Economy Institute, the PRC replaced Brazil as Argentina's leading supplier of textiles.[312]

Argentine purchases of Chinese goods include not only simple manufactured items (low-quality textiles, toys, footwear, and the like), but also an increasingly broad selection of higher value–added products (cars, motorcycles, electronic goods, even small aircraft and trains, and so on).[313] In the automotive sector, the Chinese manufacturer Chery has taken the lead in introducing its products into the Argentine market.[314] Such sales are expected to expand with the opening of a plant to produce Chery cars in nearby Montevideo, Uruguay;[315] these cars will be able to enter the Argentine market without significant tariffs, by means of Uruguay's previously unused Mercosur auto export quota.[316] In addition, Grupo Socoma, Chery's partner in Argentina, announced plans in July 2008 to invest potentially $500 million in Argentina to build a second Chery production facility, which could possibly be producing cars by 2010.[317]

With respect to electronics, plans are under way for three Chinese firms to manufacture televisions in the Argentine free-trade zone in Tierra del Fuego, at the southern tip of the country, with the expectation that much of this production will eventually be destined for Argentina or other Mercosur markets.[318]

China has also entered the Argentine railroad and aircraft industries. In 2007, the PRC sold the Argentine government some 25 locomotive engines and 100 passenger cars in a deal valued at $120 million, in support of rail operations on the 70-kilometer route from Buenos Aires to the nearby city of Pilar.[319] In 2006, the Chinese manufacturer Xi'an Phoenix Aircraft Corporation sold some 150 aircraft for use in Argentina's general aviation industry.[320]

As they have in other countries in the region, Chinese firms have been making significant advances as service and component providers in the Argentine telecommunications sector. Chinese firms such as Huawei and ZTE have established a presence in both fixed telephony and the cellular market.[321] In the case of fixed telephony, the market is dominated by two providers: the French firm Telcom and the Spanish firm Telefónica. Both currently purchase significant quantities of their infrastructure and associated services from Huawei and, secondarily, from ZTE.[322] A similar situation exists in the cellular market, where the principal suppliers depend heavily on Huawei and ZTE.[323]

Huawei has established an office in Buenos Aires and a factory in La Plata, where it has an operation for manufacturing up to 400,000 cellular telephones per year.[324] ZTE is playing a major role in the construction of infrastructure for a wireless Internet corridor between the cities of Calafate and Perito Moreno, in the southern Argentine province of Patagonia.[325] In a demonstration of the synergy that often exists between actions by the Chinese government and the penetration of Latin America by local firms, an important part of the infrastructure for the Calafate project was reportedly donated by the Chinese government as part of the package of agreements and aid resulting from Argentine president Nestor Kirchner's trip to China in 2004.[326]

As in other industrialized countries of the region, such as Brazil, as Sergio Cesarin notes, the growth of Chinese imports and service providers in Argentina, and the sense that such imports are forcing local producers out of the market, are fueling domestic pressures to erect new trade barriers to protect local manufacturers against competition from Chinese goods.[327] In December 2006, for example, the Argentine government had 19 pending requests from various companies and organizations to open antidumping investigations against the PRC.[328] A number of lobbying groups (for instance, the 150-member textile industry foundation, ProTejer) have been active in lobbying for protection against Chinese competition.[329] Reflecting such sentiment, Argentine minister of the economy Miguel Peirano made several strong statements regarding such imports, including promising to make control of Chinese imports a focus of his administration.[330] Adding to such pressures, by late 2007, on the eve of Argentine elections, the trade position of the country with the PRC threatened to change from a net surplus to a deficit,[331] leading the Argentine government to impose new customs restrictions against a range of Chinese products, from tires to textiles, toys, and leather products.[332]

The political sensitivity in Argentina to Chinese imports has also been augmented by disappointment over the failure of expected Chinese investments in the country to materialize. During his trip to Argentina in connection with the November 2004 APEC summit, Chinese president Hu Jintao discussed a series of potential Chinese investments in Argentina totaling more than $19 billion, according to calculations made at the time by journalists.[333] Although a great deal of ambiguity was associated with the promised investments, the expectations that such talk generated played an important role in the Argentine Congress's decision to recognize the PRC officially as a "market economy"—making it substantially more difficult for the country to bring antidumping charges against the PRC in the World Trade Organization.[334] Since this recognition, however, almost none of the hoped-for Chinese investments in Argentina have come about,[335] fostering disillusionment in a substantial segment of the Argentine population toward China.[336]

Infrastructure Projects

The transportation of goods between Argentina and China is a long-standing problem, given the elevation of the Andes mountain range that forms the border between Argentina and Chile, separating the former from the Pacific coast ports of the latter. As commerce between Argentina and the PRC expands, improving transportation options is becoming an increasingly important issue for both countries.

Traditionally, Argentina has moved goods to and from Asia in one of four ways:

1. Shipping goods out through Atlantic ports, then via a westerly maritime route that circumnavigates the tip of South America, and, from there, across the Pacific Ocean to China
2. Shipping goods out through Atlantic ports, then via an easterly maritime route that circumnavigates the Horn of Africa, and, from there, to China
3. Transporting goods west, overland across the Andes, to Chilean ports on the Pacific coast (such as Valparaiso), then across the Pacific Ocean to China
4. Moving goods north, overland around the tallest elevations in the Andes, and, from there, to a Pacific coast port (such as Antofagasta, Iquique, or Arica), then across the Pacific Ocean to China

Each of these four routes imposes significant costs and delays on the shipment of goods between Argentina and China.

In the case of agricultural goods, many of Argentina's soy products and related exports are transported to ports along the Rio Parna, such as Rosario and Valle Blanca, where they are then loaded onto ships for transport across the Atlantic Ocean. In the case of many Chinese goods entering the country, the process is reversed. Goods that arrive via the Atlantic are offloaded at the port of Buenos Aires, where the Chinese firm Hutchison Port Holdings currently operates a major container terminal,[337] or at an upstream port.[338]

With respect to the shipment of goods across the Andes to Chilean ports, the principal challenge is that harsh winter weather conditions occasionally close key mountain passes in these routes for weeks at a time, causing significant delays in shipments. The Argentine government has indicated an interest in winterizing key routes through the Andes, such as the Cristo Redentor and Aguas Negras passes, and the Chinese have reportedly expressed interest in being a silent partner in such work.[339] In addition, the development of alternative routes has been discussed, including a route connecting the Mendoza region of central Argentina to the Chilean port of Valparaiso, as well as routes connecting Salta, in the north of Argentina, to the Chilean ports of Antofagasta and Iquique. To date, however, no work has been done to take such projects beyond the discussion stage.[340]

It is worth noting that in addition to such national-level infrastructure projects, Chinese companies are interested in participating in local infrastructure projects funded by the Argentine government or by local governments. In July 2008, for example, the Chinese holding company Citic Group indicated interest in bidding for a project to extend the Argentine subway system.[341]

Technology Cooperation

In addition to the telecommunications sector, Argentina, as a relatively developed economy, has a number of strategic industries and sectors of interest to the Chinese, including space, nuclear, and biotechnology.

Sino-Argentine collaboration in the space industry includes a number of agreements, among which is a November 2004 accord for cooperation between the two countries in the use of space.[342] The agreement makes Argentina the only nation in South America other than Brazil with whom the PRC has signed a space cooperation accord in the past five years.[343]

The potential for Sino-Argentine space cooperation has deepened with the emergence of difficulties in an Argentine program for developing and launching a satellite into a high Earth orbit. In May 2005, Argentina and the PRC signed an agreement creating the framework by which the Chinese government may supply technical assistance and components to the Argentine firm Investigaciones Aplicadas Sociedad del Estado (INVAP), which is developing and manufacturing the satellite.[344] The Chinese have also reportedly spoken with the Argentine government about the possibility of providing launch services to the Argentine national space corporation, ARSAT, in exchange for obtaining stock in the company.[345]

Beyond cooperation on the Argentine satellite,[346] the PRC has also worked with Argentina to install a satellite laser rangefinder at San Juan University. The project is a joint effort between San Juan University and the China National Astronomical Observatories (NAOC),[347] and is characterized in China as the "largest international astronomical cooperation project ever launched by China in South America."[348]

Argentina has also explored collaboration with the PRC in the nuclear arena. In November 2004, for example, President Hu Jintao toured the Argentine nuclear facility in Rio Negro and reportedly agreed in principle to purchase Argentine nuclear reactors.[349] According to an article that year in the newspaper *La Nacion*, the Argentine nuclear agency Comisión Nacional de Energía Atómica–Argentina (CONEA) was reportedly exploring a project with the PRC to develop a 27-megawatt prototype nuclear reactor, as the initial step in developing a 300-megawatt fourth-generation reactor, which could ultimately be sold to countries with medium-sized power-generation needs—such as Latin America countries.[350]

Finally, China has also given some attention to Argentina's biotechnology sector. The Argentine pharmaceutical company Bio Sidus, to take one instance, apparently has interested the PRC in its technologies (interferon and growth hormones, among others) and has established a representative office in China through the entity United Company.[351]

Government and Business Infrastructures

Compared to other countries in Latin America, Argentina has relatively well-developed infrastructures for doing business with the PRC, both at the governmental level and in private industry.

At the governmental level, the mechanisms supporting the relationship between Argentina and China as strategic partners provide an important framework that benefits both political and commercial interactions. This framework includes a permanent committee, which has periodic meetings to address commercial, regulatory, and other issues. Argentina and China have also made relatively good progress in signing accords that provide a legal and regulatory framework for their commerce. The Argentine Ministry of Foreign Relations has registered sixteen such agreements since November 2004, in areas from tourism to health to space exploration—although many of these are memorandums of understanding, rather than formal treaties.[352] The number of agreements that Argentina has been able to put into place, however—such as phytosanitary agreements easing access by specific agricultural products and other goods to the Chinese market—has been limited.

In addition to having a framework to manage the strategic relationship between the two countries, the Argentine government provides a relatively effective capability to assist commerce at the working level, through its diplomatic facilities and government offices. Besides the Argentine embassy in Beijing, the Ministry of Foreign Relations maintains a facility in Shanghai, opened in 2001 to accommodate demand stemming principally from business, and which includes a trade promotion office. As of the end of 2008, the Argentine government had plans to open a third office in Guangzhou, also focused on trade promotion.[353]

There exist important limitations, however, to trade-promotion activities by the Argentine government in Beijing. The government's resources in China have been predominantly focused on agriculture, as reflected by the fact that the embassy in Beijing does not have a commercial attaché but, rather, an agricultural attaché.[354]

The Argentine government also promotes its exports through a quasi-public industry organization, Fundación Exportar. As with similar organizations in other countries—ProChile, APEX in Brazil, PROCOMER in Costa Rica, and the export and investment promotion corporation of Ecuador, Fundación Exportar provides information and services to Argentine companies seeking to export their products abroad and also conducts various educational and promotional activities, including participation in trade fairs, like the China Education Expo held in Beijing in October 2007.[355]

Argentina's local and provincial governments are also involved in individual deals and in the promotion of Argentine products for export to the PRC. In July 2008, the governor of Buenos Aires, Mauricio Macri, made a trip to China, during which, among other activities, he signed an agreement with the Chinese telecom company Huawei to work together to help convert Buenos Aires into a center of technology and software development. The deal included Huawei's donation of $500,000 in equipment to the local government.[356] Local initiatives include a trip to China in 2005 by the governor of the Argentine province of Santa Fe, and one in April 2007 by the governor of Córdoba.[357]

Argentina's governmental infrastructure for doing business with China, like those of Chile and Brazil, is complemented by various private-sector institutions. The Sino-Argentine Chamber of Commerce, for example, provides information, facilitation, and other services supporting commerce with China, including classes in Mandarin Chinese.[358] As of late 2007, for example, the Argentine Chamber of Commerce was working with the Chinese organization CCPIT to develop a mechanism for the arbitration of disputes involving private Argentine investors entering into commercial deals in China.[359]

With respect to financial-sector infrastructure to support Sino-Argentine commerce, by late 2008, no Argentine bank had a representative office or other presence in the PRC. However, there were two Chinese financial institutions in Argentina, the Industry and Commerce Bank of China (ICBC) and the China Development Bank (CDB), each with a single individual in Buenos Aires serving as its representative.[360] Both have further taken steps to expand their ability to work with clients in Argentina. In August 2007, CDB signed an accord with its Argentine counterpart, Banco de Inversión y Comercio Exterior (BICE), including a line of credit from the former to the latter so that Argentine clients could more easily obtain loans to support routine commercial transactions with China.[361] Similarly, in October 2007, ICBC purchased a 20 percent share of the Standard Bank Group, an African bank with a strong presence in Argentina.[362]

Intellectual Infrastructure

Argentina's geographic location on the Atlantic side of South America has contributed to an orientation toward Europe and North America in its universities and other intellectual institutions. Despite this historic bias, Argentina has proven remarkably adaptable in shifting its focus to prepare the next generation for the opportunities represented by China and other Asian trade partners.[363] Argentina was the first nation in the Southern Cone to establish a Confucius Institute for the study of Chinese language and culture, signing an agreement in May 2008 to establish a program at the Instituto Technologico de Buenos Aires.[364] Another example of China-oriented educational programs in Argentine universities is the Universidad del Salvador in Buenos Aires, which has a series of undergraduate and graduate degree programs in Asian studies, including Chinese-language programs. Another example is the social sciences–oriented FLACSO Argentina, which is the only member within the FLACSO university system to offer a formal Chinese program.[365] Several prestigious regional institutions (one example is Universidad Nacional de Cuyo, in Mendoza) offer limited programs in Mandarin.[366] In total, twenty universities in Argentina had some form of Chinese-language instruction as of late 2008.[367]

Despite these forward-looking programs, substantial room for growth remains. As of 2008, a number of important Argentine universities, such as Universidad Torcuato di Tella, for example—do not yet offer Chinese-language instruction as part of a degree program, or international business programs with a focus on China.[368] Others, such as Universidad de Córdoba, offer optional Mandarin courses, but without integration into a degree program.[369]

Political and Military Relations

As noted previously, Argentina is one of only four countries in Latin America that the PRC deems a strategic partner, having upgraded the relationship to this level in 2004.[370] In part, this status reflects China's recognition of the technological sophistication and diversity of the Argentine economy, as much as its sheer potential as an agricultural exporter and a market for Chinese goods. The Sino-Argentine political relationship has been hampered somewhat by domestic resistance to Chinese imports; however, a continuing positive relationship with the PRC not only benefits the nation's export performance, but also supports the goals of the left-of-center, independent foreign policy being pursued by the governments of both Nestor Kirchner and Cristina Fernández de Kirchner.

The positive political relationship between Argentina and China is indicated by the attention given to the relationship by the leaders of both countries. Nestor Kirchner visited China in 2004,[371] with Hu Jintao returning the favor in November of that year, including Argentina as one of the five nations he visited during his historic trip to Latin America. In October 2006, Argentine vice president Osvaldo Scioli visited Beijing to meet with his counterpart, Zeng Quinghong,[372] and, the following month, Argentine foreign minister Jorge Taina traveled to China.[373]

In the military realm, despite historically strong ties between the US and Argentinean militaries, Argentina has emerged as one of China's closest partners in the region. In May 2007, Defense Minister Nilda Garré traveled to the PRC and signed a cooperation agreement with her Chinese counterpart, Cao Gangchuan, to facilitate the interchange of military personnel and the development of logistical capabilities, including a declaration of intent to evaluate the purchase of PRC helicopters and transport vehicles.[374] The purchase of the Chinese X-11 helicopter would have been the first acquisition of a major Chinese combat platform by a Latin American government;[375] the deal became sidetracked, however, when the French complained that the helicopter had been illegally copied from a Eurocopter design. Additionally, the Chinese participated in the $50 million competitive procurement of a new air-defense radar to provide coverage to Argentina's northern frontier.[376] Although the Chinese radar was not regarded as a serious contender in the procurement, the PRC was regarded as having a realistic chance to sell Argentina a new fleet of military trucks, also included in the procurement.[377]

In addition to serious Argentine interest in procuring Chinese military goods, progress in the military relationship is reflected in officer exchanges and in regular bilateral visits, which include not only the Garré trip, but also the trip to Argentina in October 2005 by the chief of staff of the People's Liberation Army, Liang Guanglie.[378]

■ Uruguay

Like Argentina's, Uruguay's principal relationship with the PRC is as an exporter of agricultural products and as a purchaser of Chinese consumer

and industrial goods. Also like Argentina's, Uruguay's commercial relationship with the PRC is impeded by the nation's geographic position on the
Atlantic side of the continent.

Despite such obstacles, the government of Uruguayan prime minister
Tabaré Vásquez has made considerable efforts to attract investment and
expand commerce with the PRC, including the expression of interest in
negotiating a free-trade accord with China independent of the Mercosur
trade block. In December 2007, Uruguayan economic minister Daniel
Astori proclaimed that China and India would be the principal foci of commerce for the country in 2008,[379] and that Vásquez would lead a delegation
to the PRC in that year.[380]

Historical Context

Uruguay decided to recognize China in 1988, making it the last country in
South America to do so, with the exception of Paraguay, which still has not
done so.[381] Since establishing diplomatic relations, Uruguay and China
have exchanged a number of high-level delegations, including trips to
China by President Julio Maria Sanguinetti in 1988 and 1997, and by
President Luis Alberto de Lacalle in 1993. Reciprocally, Chinese president
Yang Shangkun visited Uruguay in 1990 and Jiang Zemin visited the coun-
try in 2001.

As is true for other nations in Latin America, Uruguay's trade with the
PRC has expanded in recent years. What is particularly striking, however, is
that for the period in which data are available, virtually all of that growth
has come from Uruguayan imports from the PRC, which have grown by a
factor of thirteen: from $27 million in 1994 to $351 million in 2006.[382] By
contrast, Uruguayan exports to the PRC during the same period rose from
$115 million in 1994 to $159 million in 2006.[383]

The Chinese Community in Uruguay

Relatively little information exists concerning the Chinese community in
Uruguay. According to the national census institute, only approximately 1.8
percent of Uruguayans trace their origins to Asia.[384] The Chinese embassy
in Uruguay registers a total of only 400 Chinese citizens living in the country.[385]

According to anecdotal reports, the Chinese in Uruguay principally
arrived in the country during the second half of the twentieth century, later
than other immigrant groups. The Chinese population is principally concentrated in the center of Montevideo and in its old town district, near the Plaza
Independencia—although the city does not have an officially designated
"Chinatown" district.[386]

With respect to commercial activity, the Chinese Uruguayan community is known for operating restaurants and small shops, although it is also engaged in the fishing industry.[387] Perhaps the distinguishing characteristic of the community is its small size, by contrast to the much larger one in neighboring Argentina. According to a news account of the yearly traditional Chinese New Year celebration put on by the Chinese embassy in Montevideo, the dinner served for the entire community and its guests involves, in total, fewer than 700 people.[388]

China's Interest in Uruguayan Agriculture

Although Uruguay is smaller in economic and geographic terms than Argentina, the country has a similarly well-developed agricultural sector. However, Uruguay's modest exports to the PRC have centered on wool, leather goods, and frozen fish.[389] In the case of wool, over 40 percent of Uruguayan exports go to China, with Italy, Germany, and Turkey being other major export destinations.[390] This mirrors Uruguay's export pattern in general, in which almost a third of its exports in 2006 were wools, meats, and similar products.[391] In addition, the nation is developing cattle exports to China.[392]

Although the climate and terrain of Uruguay potentially could allow it to follow in the footsteps of Argentina and Brazil—exporting soy and grain products to China—Uruguay has not yet built an export-oriented agricultural sector for these products.[393] Indeed, in 2006, cereals and vegetable oils accounted for a scant $53 million—less than 1.4 percent—of the nation's total exports.[394] Similarly, although Uruguay has a wine industry that exports modest quantities of its product, none of the wine exported by Uruguay in 2006 went to China, in contrast to that exported by Argentina and Chile, according to Uruguayan government figures.[395]

China's Interest in Other Uruguayan Goods

Like its neighbors Brazil and Argentina, Uruguay has a substantial manufacturing sector. Although this sector generally competes with manufactures from the PRC, its output is of interest to China in certain niche areas. In one high-profile case, China is purchasing a portion of the output of the new Uruguayan paper mill in Frey Bentos, opened in November 2007 amid strong objections by environmental groups.[396]

Uruguay as a Market for Chinese Goods

Uruguay has one of the highest per capita incomes in Latin America, making it a potential market for a range of Chinese goods, including not only textiles and footwear, but also more sophisticated goods and services, such as cars and motorcycles.[397] However, although Uruguay's purchases from the PRC have expanded significantly over the past decade, the nation and its population are small, limiting Uruguay's overall potential as a market. Indeed, because of its small size, the nation's purchases in dollar terms are on par with the countries of Central America. Among its Latin American neighbors, only Belize, Bolivia, Honduras, Guyana, Nicaragua, and Paraguay purchased less from the PRC.[398]

Historically, the products that Uruguay has imported from China have been concentrated in textiles and other light manufactured goods.[399] In addition to the (relatively) low value–added goods noted above, Chinese companies are selling limited quantities of very sophisticated machinery and other goods to Uruguay. As an example, the Montevideo port authority purchased a sophisticated $3 million scanner from the Chinese company Nuctech. (The public became aware of this transaction primarily because the scanner was damaged when it was dropped at the dock during unloading and had to be returned to the PRC for repairs.)[400] Similarly, when the Uruguayan government decided to launch a major new public-security project, including cameras in streets and a public-security command center, it bought the technology from China, at an initial investment of $14 million.[401]

As in other Latin American countries, a substantial quantity of contraband goods from the PRC are sold in the Uruguayan market, with at least some of these goods believed to enter the country through the free-trade zones in Palmira and Libertad.[402]

In addition to purchasing Chinese goods, Uruguay is a market for the growth of Chinese telecommunication companies in the region. Both Chinese telecom giants, Huawei[403] and ZTE,[404] have offices in Montevideo, and both have expanded sales in Uruguay in recent years,[405] including a significant win by Huawei in September 2006, when Uruguay's state-owned cellular telephone company, ANTEL, selected it to build a Universal Mobile Telecomunication System (UMTS) network in the country.[406]

As has occurred in other Latin American countries with an established manufacturing sector, the entry of Chinese goods into Uruguay is generating resistance among local producers concerned about their own survival. In August 2007, as one indication of this apprehension, Uruguayan manufacturers banded together with their Mexican counterparts in the Latin American Footwear Industry Forum in Buenos Aires to call for increased tariffs on Chinese shoes.[407]

Uruguay as a Production and Distribution Hub

Although the market for Chinese goods in Uruguay is relatively modest, the country has the potential to play an important role in the expansion of the sale of Chinese products throughout South America. Because Uruguay is a member of Mercosur, qualifying products produced in Uruguay are able to enter other Mercosur countries virtually tariff-free. Moreover, compared to Argentina and Brazil, Uruguay is a relatively inexpensive country with respect to labor and other factors of production. Capitalizing on such considerations, in July 2007, the Chinese auto manufacturer Chery announced that it would invest $100 million to build a production facility in Uruguay.[408]

The incentives for Chery and other manufacturers[409] to locate production facilities in Uruguay are similar to those driving Chinese manufacturers to establish such facilities in Mexico as part of a global supply chain to serve the US market. These Uruguayan Chinese facilities allow Chinese manufacturers to serve the sizable and geographically proximate middle-income markets of Brazil and Argentina, which are Mercosur countries: Chinese manufacturers are able to hold down costs, while simultaneously meeting domestic-content requirements under Mercosur, which enables their products to enter those markets without tariffs. Although the use of Uruguay by China as a point of entry for supplying other Mercosur nations is in its infancy, it appears to be an initiative with significant potential.

Government and Business Infrastructures

Despite its small size and Atlantic orientation, Uruguay's government has a respectable infrastructure for promoting trade with the PRC. As do its larger neighbors, the Uruguayan government not only maintains an embassy in Beijing, but also has delegate offices in Shanghai and Hong Kong capable of providing limited services to Uruguayan companies interested in doing commerce with the PRC, as well as to Chinese companies looking to export to Uruguay.[410] The government also has established the initial legal framework for commercial transactions with the PRC in the agricultural sector, including a number of phytosanitary agreements signed in 2002.[411]

In the private sector, Uruguay's corporations are also expanding the resources and associated capabilities dedicated to the Asian market, including the sending of delegations to the international trade fair in Xiamen.[412] Within Uruguay itself, Alliance Securities put on a China-oriented foreign commerce forum in October 2007.[413] The country also has a small but growing number of companies with experience doing business with China. Perhaps one of the leading examples is the women's apparel chain Lolitas, with roots in Uruguay, which has set up manufacturing operations in China for 80 percent of its production, even while continuing to use Uruguayan wool.[414]

Intellectual Infrastructure

The intellectual infrastructure in Uruguay to support trade with China is relatively limited. As noted previously, the community of ethnic Chinese in the country is virtually nonexistent,[415] providing very little basis to form a China-oriented business service sector, although the recognition of the country as an official tourist destination is likely to bring additional Chinese visitors and broaden awareness of China within the society as a whole.[416]

Beyond the Chinese Uruguayan community, for the small size of the country, its universities and institutions have a respectable and growing capability with respect to both Mandarin and China studies. Ort University of Uruguay, as one example, has a Mandarin program associated with its school of business administration.[417] Plans are also under way to establish a Confucius Institute in Uruguay, in coordination with the Chinese government.[418] On the other hand, significant room for growth remains: major Uruguayan universities, such as La Católica, Universidad de la República de Uruguay, and FLACSO Uruguay, have neither a formal program of Chinese-language instruction nor a China-oriented course of business studies.[419]

Political and Military Relations

Political and military contacts between Uruguay and the PRC have been modest, but have the potential to expand significantly, including a possible visit by President Tabaré Vásquez to China in 2009.[420]

In the political realm, prior to the announced presidential visit, contacts between the two countries have occurred on a regular basis, but not at the most senior levels of leadership. In September 2006, the chairman of the Standing Committee of the National People's Congress, Wu Bangguo, made an official visit to Uruguay. Reciprocally, in January 2007, an Uruguayan parliamentary contingent traveled to the PRC to meet with their counterparts in the Chinese Communist Party.[421] Prior to these two visits, in December 2005, then–Uruguayan president Tabaré Vásquez and members of the newly elected Frente Amplio coalition met with members of the Chinese Communist Party Political Bureau at the Mercosur summit, affording an opportunity for the president-elect to exchange opinions with the Chinese—but without qualifying their meeting as an official state visit.

In the military realm, as well, contacts between Uruguay and the PRC have been regular, yet limited. The two governments first established military attaché offices in each other's countries in 1997, with periodic exchanges of senior and midlevel military officials thereafter. Uruguayan defense ministers paid visits to the PRC in 1994, 1997, and 1999,[422] and, in September 2004, the commander of the Uruguayan air force, General Enrique Bonelli, met in Beijing with his counterpart, People's Liberation Army air force commander Qiao Qingchen.[423] In November 2005, the chief of staff of the People's Liberation Army, Liang Guanglie, met with President Vásquez in Montevideo;[424] in September 2006, Liang Guanglie met with Alejo Diaz, commander of the Uruguayan army, and Heber Fernandez, commander of the Uruguayan navy in China.[425]

■ Paraguay

Paraguay's relationship with China is dominated by the consequences of its ongoing recognition of the Republic of China, rather than the PRC. The corresponding absence of diplomatic relations with the PRC has reinforced Paraguay's relative isolation as a conservative, landlocked country, restricting the growth of Sino-Paraguayan political and economic ties.

Paraguayan-Chinese commercial contacts, where they have existed, have included the entry of Chinese products into the modest Paraguayan consumer goods market, indirect exports of Paraguayan soy to China through intermediaries, and participation by some Paraguayan businesspeople in trade delegations to the PRC.[426] While Paraguay seeks to expand its exports to China, it has achieved very limited success in doing so. Paraguay, like Uruguay, has also expressed an interest in pursuing a free-trade agreement with the PRC outside of the boundaries of Mercosur,[427] although few developments have occurred in this area.[428]

Historical Context

Under the military dictatorship of Alfredo Stroessner and the succession of Colorado Party governments that have dominated the nation's politics since Stroessner, Paraguay has pursued a foreign policy that has been both conservative and relatively isolationist. The combination of this foreign policy with Paraguay's nonrecognition of the PRC, plus the nation's lack of access to a seacoast that would facilitate the development of commerce beyond trade with its immediate neighbors, has restricted Paraguay's interactions with mainland China.

Interactions between China and Paraguay have been limited to relatively low-level contacts and nongovernmental groups such as the China-Paraguay Friendship Society and the China-Paraguay Chamber of Commerce. At the governmental level, the limited set of interactions between Paraguay and the PRC has included the reception of a Paraguayan legislative delegation by representatives of the Chinese National People's Congress in 2001.[429] In April 2002, a technical delegation from the PRC visited Paraguay to explore prospects for forming diplomatic relations, but without result.[430] In 2007, a Paraguayan delegation participated in the Central America–China Friendship Federation.[431]

The Chinese Community in Paraguay

By contrast to many other states in Latin America, a significant portion of the ethnic Chinese currently living in Paraguay arrived in the 1970s and 1980s, settling into urban areas of the country.[432] It is important to note that because of the history of diplomatic relations between Paraguay and

Taiwan, and the associated difficulty for Chinese from the mainland to obtain a Paraguayan visa, virtually all ethnic Chinese in Paraguay are officially from Taiwan, with fewer than thirty families in the country tracing their origin to mainland China.

Although the capital city of Asunción hosts a small Chinese community, the numerically more significant community of Chinese in Paraguay lives in the vicinity of Ciudad del Este, where the nation shares a border with Argentina and Brazil.[433] Approximately 4,000 people of Chinese origin live in the area, while a smaller community is found in the city of Pedro Juan Caballero, which borders Brazil in the northeast of the country. Ciudad del Este has a reputation for illicit commerce, and Chinese and Taiwanese mafias are believed to have a presence there.[434] Similarly, Pedro Juan Caballero has a reputation as a transit point for drug trafficking.

Paraguay's Nonrecognition of the PRC

When Uruguay officially extended diplomatic recognition to the People's Republic of China in 1988, Paraguay became the last nation in South America that continues to recognize Taiwan, rather than the PRC, as the legitimate government of China.[435] For Taiwan, maintaining its relationship with Paraguay is part of its struggle for national survival. In May 2006, as a manifestation of the importance that it places on Paraguay's diplomatic recognition, Taiwan announced a $250 million package of investments in electronics, plastics, and information technology in Paraguay.[436] The decision by Costa Rica in June 2007 to extend diplomatic recognition to the PRC prompted some analysts to speculate that Paraguay might be convinced by the Costa Rican example to change its own diplomatic posture. Whether or not Paraguay was considering following in Costa Rica's footsteps, within days of Costa Rica's announcement, Taiwanese vice president Annette Lu announced that she would travel to Paraguay to celebrate fifty years of diplomatic relations between the two countries.[437]

When Ferdinand Lugo was elected president of Paraguay in April 2008, statements that he had made during his campaign and following his election raised the prospect that he would change the country's diplomatic posture upon taking office.[438] However, his election coincided with the return of the Kuomingtang party to power in Taiwan, and a diplomatic reapproachment between the new Taiwanese president Ma Jing-jeou and PRC president Hu Jintao. Part of this reapproachment between Taiwan and the PRC was an agreement that the two nations would suspend "checkbook diplomacy," the process of seeking to convince nations to change their diplomatic posture by offering them packages of financial aid more generous than that being received by their present partner. As a consequence, despite statements by Paraguayan officials indicating a receptiveness to changing the country's diplomatic posture, an official change never materialized.[439]

Although Paraguay receives tangible benefits from its diplomatic recognition of Taiwan, its diplomatic posture has significantly limited its ability to export its products to the PRC. In 2006, these exports were a modest $20 million, having fallen 63 percent from the previous year,[440] while nearby Uruguay, whose economy is comparable in size, but which diplomatically recognizes the PRC, exported $342 million to the PRC during the same period.[441] Indeed, Paraguay's exports to China during this period actually fell 63 percent from 2006 to 2007, representing the worst change in export performance with China for any country in South America; Paraguay is the only nation in the region, other than Suriname, whose exports to China did not grow during the period.[442]

If Paraguayan exports to the PRC have been limited by the government's diplomatic posture, participation by PRC companies in Paraguay have been limited as well. In June 2007, for example, the Chinese telecom firm Huawei sought to take part in a public auction by the Paraguayan communications company Copaco to construct a wireless network in Paraguay, but was ruled ineligible because of the lack of a commercial relationship between Paraguay and the PRC.[443]

Despite the lack of official relations between Paraguay and the PRC, some possibilities for significant investment were beginning to emerge at the end of 2008, including a group of Chinese and US investors representing the Crown American Investment Corporation that traveled to Asunción in December 2008 to talk about a series of projects in the city that could eventually receive up to $20 billion in investment.[444]

China's Interest in Paraguayan Products

Paraguay's principal export of interest to the PRC is soy. Indeed, Paraguay currently exports significant quantities of soy to the PRC, but does so through intermediaries. Paraguay has a livestock industry centered in the western portion of the country that could possibly export meat and leather goods to the PRC. Modest potential reserves of natural gas have been identified in the Chaco region, and the Paraguayan government has been seeking to attract investors to explore and develop them.[445] Furthermore, the nation has a pharmaceutical industry, which announced in December 2007 that it would seek to enter the Chinese market in 2009.[446]

Paraguay as a Market for Chinese Goods

Like other Latin American countries, Paraguay purchases a variety of Chinese products. Although the Paraguayan consumer market is relatively modest in size, Chinese cars made their debut in the country in June 2006 with the arrival of vehicles from the automaker Chery.[447] Several producers in Paraguay also manufacture motorcycles in the city of Luque from

Chinese components,[448] and there was talk in 2008 of establishing a production facility in Paraguay for the Chinese truck manufacturer Tayo.[449]

In the domain of technology, Paraguay was also one of two Latin American countries to participate in the "one laptop per child" initiative,[450] a program aimed at providing inexpensive technology for children in marginalized areas, but which ultimately involved government-subsidized purchases of thousands of Chinese-made computers.

Military and Political Relations

Paraguay's diplomatic relationship with Taiwan, in combination with its relatively close relationship with the United States, has limited its development of political and military ties with the PRC. Indeed, following Costa Rica's change in diplomatic posture in June 2008 to diplomatically recognize the PRC rather than Taiwan,[451] Paraguay acted to dispel any doubts concerning its own position and firmly reavowed its commitment to Taiwan. Nonetheless, statements made by Paraguayan president Fernando Lugo prior to and following his election in 2008[452] suggest that the new Paraguayan regime could diplomaticly recognize the PRC if the PRC government presents it with an attractive reason for doing so.[453]

▨ Notes

1. "China, fundamental para desarrollo de AL." *El Economista*. Mexico City, Mexico. http://www.eleconomista.com.mx. July 6, 2006.

2. China has signed a free-trade agreement with the Association of Southeast Asian Nations (ASEAN). In addition, other nations have signed agreements with China regarding trade, but not a comprehensive accord for the elimination of tariffs with respect to goods. See Artaza, 2007b.

3. Chile also hopes to leverage the FTA with China, in combination with its other FTAs, to motivate the Chinese to add Chilean content to their manufactured goods, so as to facilitate entry of these goods into the European Free Trade Area, Canada, and Mexico, under the system of preferences embodied in these agreements. Correspondence with Mario Ignacio Artaza, commercial attaché of the government of Chile to the People's Republic of China. January 28, 2008.

4. "Chile es una de las economías más beneficiadas por expansión de China." *Diario Financiero*. Santiago, Chile. http://www.df.cl. April 27, 2007.

5. The China-Chile Free Trade Agreement was signed in October 2005, and came into effect in October 2006, targeting commodities and reducing or eliminating tariffs on 97 percent of goods traded between the two countries over a span of ten years. Deng Quingfen, "China, Chile Start New FTA Talks as One Goes into Effect." *China Daily*. Beijing, China. http://www.chinadaily.com.cn/bizchina/2006-11/30/content_746607_2.htm. November 30, 2006.

6. Andrés Rebolledo, "TLC Chile-China: Exitoso primer año." *Diario Financiero*. Santiago, Chile. http://www.df.cl. October 3, 2007.

7. "Comercio con China creció 641% en una década." *Diario Financiero*. Santiago, Chile. http://www.df.cl. June 25, 2007.

8. Ricardo Claro passed away in November 2008. His companies, including Compañía Sudamericana de Vapores S.A., were among the leaders in developing Chile's commercial relationship with the PRC.

9. Mario Ignacio Artaza notes that many of the greatest accomplishments of the Chilean relationship with China have been driven by the actions of exceptional individuals, rather than being a broad-based, systematic advance. See Artaza, 2007d.

10. In fact, some scholars have suggested that Latin American military regimes, such as that of Pinochet in Chile, found the relationship with China to be a useful counterweight to the United States, particularly in resisting US pressure over human rights issues. See Dreyer, 2006b.

11. "Bilateral Political Relations." *The Ministry of Foreign Affairs of the People's Republic of China.* Official website. http://www.fmprc.gov.cn/eng/wjb/zzjg/ldmzs/gjlb-/3478/default.htm. September 26, 2003.

12. "Comercio con China creció 641% en una década."

13. The importance of China as a commercial partner to Chile is relatively new. In 1991, for example, the PRC occupied the twenty-first position in bilateral trade with Chile. From *1995 International Trade Statistics Yearbook.* Volume 1. New York: United Nations, 1996. p. 191.

14. Olivares, 2007.

15. In 2007, trade between Chile and China increased 75 percent, from $8.4 billion to $14.5 billion. Correspondence with Mario Ignacio Artaza, commercial attaché of the government of Chile to the People's Republic of China. January 14, 2008.

16. Correspondence with Mario Ignacio Artaza, commercial attaché of the government of Chile to the People's Republic of China. January 12, 2008.

17. Ibid.

18. "Riqueza floral de Huara estará presente en feria china." *Chasquis.* Arica, Chile. http://www.chasquis.cl/actualidad05102106.htm. October 21, 2005.

19. Indeed, during the war, part of the Chilean campaign was an effort by a British-trained, Mandarin-speaking Chilean officer, Patricio Lynch, to organize the Chinese who had been working in harsh conditions in the nitrate and guano industries in Peruvian territories to rise up against the Peruvians. A contingent of Chinese also served in the Chilean army as cooks and medical personnel.

20. "Primer semestre 2007 principales productos de Chile a China." *China Customs.* Commercial Office. Beijing, China. August 2007.

21. "China Minmetals hará uso de su opción por mina Gaby." *Portal Minero.* http://www.portalminero.com. March 30, 2007.

22. Patricia Pérez-Cejuela, "China busca conquistar el mercado latino." *Univision.* http://www.univision.com. April 10, 2006.

23. Daniel Barria, "Los desafios de CODELCO." Presentation to the 4th Encuentro Coldelco y Provedores Tica. *CODELCO.* http://www.codelco.cl. December 14, 2007.

24. "Codelco y China Minmetals firman contrato por 15 años." *Portal Minero.* http://www.portalminero.com. December 21, 2005.

25. The price was reported in the press to be $1.40 per pound through 2012. "China Minmetals hará uso de su opción por mina Gaby."

26. The name of the mine was changed in April 2007 to give it a more "local" flavor. "Codelco cambia nombre a Gaby por Gabriela Mistral." *El Mercurio.* Santiago, Chile. http://diario.elmercurio.com. April 25, 2007.

27. Under the deal, China was given the option to purchase 25 percent of the Gaby mine in 2008, with the option of later acquiring another 24 percent. "China Minmetals hará uso de su opción por mina Gaby."

28. The $838 million that the Chinese would pay to acquire an initial 25 percent stake in Gaby is considered by industry analysts to be significantly less than the value of the mine, particularly given that the estimate of reserves believed to exist in the mine has increased considerably since the initial terms of the deal were established. Ibid.

29. "Férrea oposición a la venta de ex mina Gaby." *El Mercurio.* Santiago, Chile. http://diario.elmercurio.com. April 26, 2007.

30. "Codelco y Minmetals podrían acudir a arbitraje por Gaby." *Diario Financiero.* Santiago, Chile. http://www.df.cl. July 16, 2008.

31. "Fenami firma acuerdo con empresa China." *Portal Minero.* http://www.portal-minero.com. November 29, 2007.

32. "Mineras pequeños y medianos se unen y dan salto a China." *Minería Chilena.* Santiago, Chile. http://www.mch.cl/noticias/index.php?id=8378. December 11, 2007.

33. "Luksic negocia sociedad con China Minmetals para ingresar a esperanza." *Portal Minero.* http://www.portalminero.com. November 28, 2007.

34. "Codelco estudia fundición en China." *Diario Financiero.* Santiago, Chile. http://www.df.cl. November 17, 2006. See also "Codelco planea construir una fundición de cobre en China." *El Mercurio.* Santiago, Chile. http://diario.elmercurio.com. November 17, 2006.

35. Codelco held a suppliers' meeting in Shanghai in 2006, atended by China Minmetals, Sinochem Internacional, China Ordins, and others. In the previous year, it held a similar conference for suppliers to its steel operations, which was attended by some forty Chinese executives. "Codelco busca proveedores en Asia." *Diario Financiero.* Santiago, Chile. http://www.df.cl. October 1, 2007.

36. Correspondence with Mario Ignacio Artaza, commercial attaché of the government of Chile to the People's Republic of China. January 12, 2008.

37. "SQM firma acuerdo con China Migao para producir nitrato de potasio." *Diario Financiero.* Santiago, Chile. http://www.df.cl. July 16, 2008.

38. "Primer semestre 2007 principales productos de Chile a China." Fishmeal is less important for Chile than for Peru, however, accounting for only 2.5 percent of all Chilean exports to the PRC in the first half of 2007.

39. Chile sold approximately $8.3 million worth of salmon to the PRC in the first half of 2007. Ibid.

40. Olivares, 2007.

41. Given the perishability of agricultural goods in general, Chile's infrastructure and Pacific ports allow it to get goods to Chinese markets comparatively quickly. The shorter distances and transit times, in combination with the lack of tariffs, also make some Chilean goods cheaper than corresponding goods from countries on the Atlantic side of South America, such as Argentina and Brazil.

42. Although Chile traditionally has been an exporter of grapes to China, the export of significant quantities of wine to the PRC is a relatively new phenomenon.

43. "Cepal: América Latina debe aprovechar potencial de China e India." *El Universal.* Caracas, Venezuela. http://www.eluniversal.com. September 14, 2006.

44. As of 2007, the PRC was the tenth-largest consumer of wine in the world. "China, un nuevo gran mercado para el vino." *ABC Digital.* Asunción, Paraguay. http://www.abc.com.py. June 17, 2007. Indeed, the PRC wine market itself has grown by 10 percent per year during recent years. In January 2007, the Hong Kong retailer Top Cellar opened the first three specialty wine stores in the Beijing financial district, to take advantage of the growing "culture of wine" in China. "Los chinos comienzan a apreciar las bondades de un buen vino." *El Mercurio.* Santiago, Chile. http://diario.elmercurio.com. January 29, 2007.

45. The wine is currently available for sale in China. Correspondence with Mario Ignacio Artaza, commercial attaché of the government of Chile to the People's Republic of China. January 12, 2008.

46. "Primer semestre 2007 principales productos de Chile a China."

47. "Gross Domestic Product per Capita, Current Prices (U.S. Dollars)." *International Monetary Fund.* World Economic Outloook Database. http://www.imf.org/external/pubs/ft/weo/2007/01/data/index.aspx. April 2007.

48. Soledad Miranda, "El coqueto con el auto chino." *El Mercurio.* Santiago, Chile. http://diario.elmercurio.com. April 14, 2006.

49. "Se inicia la venta de auto de marca china." *El Mercurio.* Santiago, Chile. http://diario.elmercurio.com. February 24, 2007.

50. "Ventas de vehículos crecen 8,7% a mayo y llegarán cuatro nuevas marcas chinas." *Diario Financiero.* Santiago, Chile. http://www.df.cl. June 24, 2008.

51. "Sales of Chinese Motorcycles Booming in Chile." *China Daily.* Beijing, China. www.chinadaily.com.cn. June 17, 2008.

52. "Chile y China, más que arroz con palitos." *El Sur.* Concepción, Chile. http://www.elsur.cl/edicion_hoy/secciones/ver_rep.php?id=2887&dia=1159502400. September 29, 2006.

53. "Contact Us." *Huawei.* Official website. http://www.huawei.com/about/officeList.do#Chile. Accessed December 30, 2007.

54. "Regional Offices." *ZTE Telecom.* Official website. http://wwwen.zte.com.cn. Accessed December 30, 2007.

55. "ZTE Strengthens South American Market Position in Santiago Chile." *Wi-Fi Technology Forum.* http://www.wi-fitechnology.com/displayarticle1688.html. December 7, 2004.

56. "Chile." *Huawei.* Official website. http://www.huawei.com/es/catalog.do?id=324. Accessed December 30, 2007.

57. Artaza, 2007b.

58. When Argentina's principal gas supplier, Bolivia, increased the price of gas, Argentina sought to pass the entire price increase on to Chile. On repeated occasions when disruptions in Argentine gas production, or gas supplies from Bolivia, have threatened to create domestic shortages, the Argentine reaction has been to suspend gas sales to Chile. Such cuts are particularly critical, because gas is used in electricity production by the mining industry in the north of Chile.

59. Henriquez, 2007. See also "REFILE-Chile's Nuclear Decision to Take Years." *Reuters.* http://www.alertnet.org/thenews/newsdesk/N25388579.htm. September 25, 2007.

60. Interview with Patricio Navia, research director, Asia-Pacific Program, Universidad Diego Portales. Miami, Florida. October 11, 2007.

61. "La hora de la revancha nuclear." *La Nacion.* Buenos Aires, Argentina. http://www.lanacion.com.ar. March 5, 2006.

62. Over the long run, China is a current test bed for a variety of new nuclear reactor designs; at about the time that Chile is reentering the nuclear energy business, China will be well positioned to sell its reactors as proven designs. See Dune Lawrence and Alan Katz, "China se posiciona para ser potencia mundial en el uso de energía nuclear." *El País.* Montevideo, Uruguay. http://www.elpais.com.uy. December 10, 2007. However, although a partnership with the PRC is a possibility, if the Chileans pursue the nuclear option, they are likely to contract commercially for the construction of a plant. The domestic political sensitivity associated with Chile's return to nuclear power is likely to lead the government to avoid entering into a partnership perceived as excessively bold or risky. Despite the Chinese experience with nuclear power, thus, politics may dictate that the Chilean government

contract with a French or Japanese firm to build its nuclear power–generation capability. Interview with Patricio Navia, research director, Asia-Pacific Program, Universidad Diego Portales. Miami, Florida. October 11, 2007.

63. Mario Ignacio Artaza, "No estamos de brazoas cruzados con China." *Portal Chile Asia-Pacifico.* http://asiapacifico.bcn.cl/columnas/no-estamos-de-brazos-cruzados-con-china. December 28, 2007.

64. "Brazil Gets Port on Pacific Coast and China Becomes Much Closer." *Brazzil Magazine.* http://www.brazzilmag.com. December 17, 2007. The portion of the project crossing the Andes is extremely challenging from an engineering perspective, and costs may rise significantly beyond initial estimates. Despite public commitments, there is no guarantee that the project will be realized, or how long it will take to be completed.

65. Interview with Ernesto Fernandez Taboda, executive director of the Sino-Argentine Chamber of Production, Industry, and Commerce. Buenos Aires. November 7, 2007.

66. Zona Franca de Iquique. Official website. http://www.zofri.cl/. Accessed January 1, 2009.

67. See, for example, Nicolás Ossa, "China y China." *Diario Financiero.* Santiago, Chile. http://www.df.cl. June 22, 2007.

68. Olivares, 2007.

69. Colombia has also raised the possibility of such an agreement, but had not taken any concrete steps down this path as of late 2008.

70. "TLC con China cumple un año con un aumento de 100% en las exportaciones." *Diario Financiero.* Santiago, Chile. http://www.df.cl. October 1, 2007. See also Olivares, 2007.

71. According to one estimate, approximately 40 percent of exports from the PRC to Chile applied the preferential treatment and only 50 percent of Chilean exports to China applied preferential treatment. Correspondence with Mario Ignacio Artaza, commercial attaché of the government of Chile to the People's Republic of China. January 25, 2008.

72. Alejandro Foxley, "Chile: El próximo paso." *El Mercurio.* Santiago, Chile. http://diario.elmercurio.com. January 2, 2007.

73. "Entra en vigor TLC entre Japón y Chile que elimina arancel a 92% comercio." *El Universal.* Caracas, Venezuela. http://www.eluniversal.com. September 3, 2007.

74. Soler, 2007.

75. Sandra Novoa. "Los mercados que se abrieron." *El Mercurio.* Santiago, Chile. http://diario.elmercurio.com. December 31, 2006.

76. Reyes, 2007.

77. Artaza, 2007d.

78. Artaza, 2007a.

79. "Bachelet prepara aterrizaje en China con nutrida delegación empresarial." *Diario Financiero.* Santiago, Chile. http://www.df.cl. March 18, 2008.

80. "Missiones in Asia." *Ministerio de Relaciones Exteriores, Republica de Chile.* Official website. http://www.minrel.gov.cl/webMinRel/home.do?sitio=1. Accessed December 30, 2007.

81. "ProChile en el Mundo." *ProChile.* Official website. http://www.prochile. cl/servicios/red_internacional/red_internacional.php. Accessed December 30, 2007.

82. See, for example, "Centro de negocios ProChile de Shanghai." *ProChile.* Official website. http://www.-prochile.cl/servicios/red_internacional/red_ internacional.php. Accessed December 30, 2007.

83. Correspondence with Mario Ignacio Artaza, commercial attaché of the government of Chile to the People's Republic of China. January 12, 2008.

84. Trade fairs in China advertised by ProChile for 2008, for example, include Sial China (May, Shanghai), Vinexpo (May, Hong Kong), and China Fisheries (November, China). "Ferias Internacionales." *ProChile.* Official website. http://www.prochile.cl/servicios/ferias/2008/alimentos_2008.php. Accessed December 30, 2007.

85. "¿Que es ProChile?" *ProChile.* Official website. http://www.prochile.cl/quienes_s-omos/que_es_prochile.php. Accessed December 30, 2007.

86. The CODELCO office in Shanghai will also help to facilitate technology transfer from Chile to Chinese mining activities. Correspondence with Mario Ignacio Artaza, commercial attaché of the government of Chile to the People's Republic of China. January 14, 2007.

87. "Firman China y Chile acuerdo commercial." *Portal Minero.* http://www.portal-minero.com. July 15, 2008.

88. The organization, created in 2005, has not yet undertaken significant activity to promote Sino-Chilean business. As of late 2008, it had met only twice, and has not yet set forth an agenda of activities to promote. Nonetheless, the existence of the council, and its potential to coordinate the activities of Chilean companies seeking to conduct business with China at a senior level, help to put Chile's infrastructure ahead of that of many of its Latin American counterparts.

89. "Chinese, Latin American Business Leaders Discuss Trade, Investment." *People's Daily Online.* Beijing, China. http://english.people.com.cn. November 28, 2007.

90. "Bachelet inaugura primera Cumbre Empresarial China–América Latina." *Xinhua News.* Beijing, China. http://www.spanish.xinhuanet.com/spanish/2007-11/28/content_532647.htm. November 28, 2007.

91. "Realizarán rueda de negocios con países asiáticos en el norte de Chile." *Chasquis.* Arica, Chile. http://www.chasquis.cl/actualidad07101101.htm. October 11, 2007.

92. Artaza, 2007c.

93. "Juan Claro llamó a promover inversion y comercio con China." *Diario Financiero.* Santiago, Chile. http://www.df.cl. August 31, 2007.

94. "Embajador chino: 'El proceso de reformas no se ha detenido.'" *El Mercurio.* Santiago, Chile. http://diario.elmercurio.com. December 19, 2006.

95. "China fortalece lazos con Chile." *El Sur.* Concepción, Chile. http://www.elsur.cl/-edicion_hoy/secciones/articulo.php?id=76889&dia=1157515200. September 6, 2006.

96. Correspondence with Mario Ignacio Artaza, commercial attaché of the government of Chile to the People's Republic of China. January 28, 2008.

97. Artaza, 2007b.

98. Artaza, 2007b.

99. "China abre su mercado bancario." *El Comercio.* Quito, Ecuador. http://www.el-comercio.terra.com.ec. December 25, 2006.

100. "Bachelet inaugura primera Cumbre Empresarial China–América Latina."

101. Nicolás E. Cáceres, "Gigante chino prepara su arribo al mercado bancario chileno." *Diario Financiero.* Santiago, Chile. http://www.df.cl. July 16, 2008.

102. "El chino mandarín está de moda." *El Mercurio.* Santiago, Chile. http://diario.elmercurio.com. April 15, 2006.

103. "Ministro Bitar recibe a profesores chinos que imparten idioma mandarin en escuelas chilenas." *Universidad Arturo Prat.* Santiago, Chile. http://www.unap.

cl/p4_santiago/site/artic/20051028/pags/20051028104620.html. October 28, 2005.

104. "Crece interés por aprender chino mandarín." *El Mercurio*. Santiago, Chile. http://diario.elmercurio.com. January 23, 2006.

105. Paulina Hidalgo, "La fiebre del chino mandarín." *La Nacion*. Santiago, Chile. http://www.lanacion.cl/prontus_noticias/site/artic/20051116/pags/20051116184049.html. November 17, 2005.

106. Interview with Patricio Navia, research director, Asia-Pacific Program, Universidad Diego Portales. Miami, Florida. October 11, 2007.

107. Artaza, 2007b.

108. Correspondence with Ms. Ana Maria Cabello, coordinator for Inter/National Cooperation Networks, International Office, Universidad de Viña del Mar. December 30, 2007.

109. "Curso de China Mandarin." *Universidad Viña del Mar*. Official website. http://www.uvm.cl/oiie/noticias.shtml?cmd%5B97%5D=i-97-ea8e855864c8d11e7f19d9-dcc568039e. September 4, 2007.

110. "Tercera delegacion Chilena Universitaria viaja a China." *Spoken English Promotion Project. Universidad Viña del Mar*. Official website. http://www.uvm.cl/oiie/noticiassepp/deleg.shtml?cmd[139]=i-139-2c3f5288cd7cd829b577307d07fb0fd5. January 3, 2008.

111. Correspondence with Ms. Ana Maria Cabello, coordinator for Inter/National Cooperation Networks, International Office, Universidad de Viña del Mar. December 30, 2007.

112. Based on a personal survey of conference attendees at the Congreso Latinoamericano y Caribeño de Ciencias Sociales, FLACSO Ecuador. Quito, Ecuador. October 29–31, 2007.

113. Interview with Martin Schaffernicht, Universidad de Talca. Interview in Buenos Aires, Argentina. November 7, 2007.

114. Correspondence with Ms. Ana Maria Cabello, coordinator for Inter/National Cooperation Networks, International Office, Universidad de Viña del Mar. December 30, 2007.

115. Exequiel Pino, "Bachelet concluye gira realzando la nueva etapa en las relaciones con China." *Diario Financiero*. Santiago, Chile. http://www.df.cl. April 16, 2008.

116. "Senior Chinese Official Meets with Chilean House President." *People's Daily Online*. Beijing, China. http://english.people.com.cn. January 23, 2007.

117. "Roundup: Top Chinese Legislator's Latin America Visit Fruitful." *People's Daily Online*. Beijing, China. http://english.people.com.cn. September 11, 2006. See also "China Enhances Int'l Cooperation via Parliamentary Exchanges." *People's Daily Online*. Beijing, China. http://english.people.com.cn. March 17, 2007.

118. Artaza, 2007b.

119. Correspondence with Mario Ignacio Artaza, commercial attaché of the government of Chile to the People's Republic of China. January 28, 2008.

120. "Chinese Defense Minister Meets Chilean Navy Chief." *People's Daily Online*. Beijing, China. http://english.people.com.cn. September 2, 2003.

121. "Chinese Defense Minister Holds Talks with Chilean Counterpart." *People's Daily Online*. Beijing, China. http://english.people.com.cn. May 25, 2004.

122. "Liang Guanglie Meets Commander-in-Chief of Chilean Army." *People's Daily Online*. Beijing, China. http://english.people.com.cn. October 12, 2004.

123. "China-Chile Military Relations Good: Chinese DM." *People's Daily Online*. Beijing, China. http://english.people.com.cn. October 21, 2005.

124. Correspondence with Mario Ignacio Artaza, commercial attaché of the government of Chile to the People's Republic of China. January 12, 2008.

125. The last is reported to have saved the Chilean navy a significant amount of money compared to what they previously had been spending for the same medical supplies from Europe or North America—allowing Chilean naval hospitals to examine the possibility of offering medical care to a broader group of people. See Artaza, 2007d.

126. The Chilean military has traditionally had good ties with that of the United States; the increase in Chile's military interactions with China can be traced back to the suspension of US International Military Education and Training (IMET) programs under provisions of the 2002 American Serviceman's Protection Act. Gertz, 2006. As in other countries in Latin America, this suspension, in combination with the growing importance of the commercial ties between Chile and China, prompted the Chilean military to turn increasingly to China for the "foreign military education" experience that is an important part of the career of the most promising officers in many Latin American militaries. Although cooperation between US and Chilean militaries resumed in 2006 following the act's suspension, the institutional ties between the Chilean and Chinese militaries continue under their own momentum.

127. The presence of the officers is arguably more important for their role in strengthening ties between the two militaries than for their attendance at the language program per se, since only ten Chilean officers were to receive the training.

128. "Total Import and Export Value by Country (Region) (2007/01–12)." *Ministry of Commerce.* People's Republic of China. http://english.mofcom.gov.cn. aarticle/-statistic/ie/200802/20080205371690.html. February 4, 2008.

129. Watson, 2008, p. 67.

130. Calculated from "Total Import and Export Value by Country (Region) (2007/01–12)."

131. Telephone interview with Rodrigo Tavares Maciel, executive secretary, Brazil-China Business Council. December 20, 2007.

132. "Brasil planea convertir a China en su principal socio commercial." *Xinhua.* Beijing, China. http://www.spanish.xinhuanet.com. July 10, 2008.

133. "China Forecast to Be Brazil's Top Trade Partner." *China Daily.* Beijing, China. www.chinadaily.com.cn. July 10, 2008.

134. Some 77 Chinese companies were registered in Brazil by the end of 2005. For its part, Brazil had 348 investment products in China, worth an estimated $120 million. "Backgrounder: China, Brazil Strengthen Relations." *People's Daily Online.* Beijing, China. http://english.people.com.cn. August 30, 2006.

135. According to one study, China is responsible for more than 30 percent of Brazil's losses in exports to markets in Chile and the United States. Maciel, 2008, p. 29.

136. Hirst, 2008, p. 97.

137. "Chinese Top Legislator Lauds China-Brazil Strategic Partnership." *People's Daily Online.* Beijing, China. http://english.people.com.cn. September 1, 2006.

138. Despite the size of the Chinese community in São Paulo, the city lacks a formal "Chinatown" district, such as those found in other Latin American capitals. Telephone interview with Rodrigo Tavares Maciel, executive secretary, Brazil-China Business Council. December 20, 2007.

139. Ibid.

140. Ibid.

141. Ibid.

142. Ironically, soy is relatively new as a major agro-export crop in Brazil. The industry took off during the 1980s when the United States initiated a grain embargo against the Soviet Union, and nations of South America (e.g., Brazil and Argentina) expanded their production to meet the demand. After the demise of the Soviet Union, the expansion of China as a market for Brazilian agricultural products helped to rescue the industry. Barrionuevo, 2007.

143. The vast majority of Chinese purchases are soybeans, rather than soy oil, reflecting a Chinese preference for realizing the value-added processing operations in China rather than in Brazil. Telephone interview with Rodrigo Tavares Maciel, executive secretary, Brazil-China Business Council. December 20, 2007.

144. "Empresas chinas quieren invertir en corredor bioceánico Chile-Brasil." *Diario Financiero*. Santiago, Chile. http://www.df.cl. November 6, 2006.

145. Barrionuevo, 2007.

146. "Chinese Soybean Farmers Battered by Low Import Prices." *People's Daily Online*. Beijing, China. http://english.people.com.cn. December 1, 2006.

147. Telephone interview with Rodrigo Tavares Maciel, executive secretary, Brazil-China Business Council. December 20, 2007.

148. "Brazil: Lula's Great China Trip." *Brazzil Magazine*. http://www.brazzil. com. May 2004.

149. Barrionuevo, 2007.

150. At least one expert in Brazil indicates that this has not yet become a significant phenomenon. Telephone interview with Rodrigo Tavares Maciel, executive secretary, Brazil-China Business Council. December 20, 2007.

151. Barrionuevo, 2007.

152. Telephone interview with Rodrigo Tavares Maciel, executive secretary, Brazil-China Business Council. December 20, 2007.

153. Trinh, Voss, and Dyck, 2006, p. 7.

154. According to Brazilian figures, iron exports to the PRC in 2007 amounted to $3.4 billion, a 40 percent increase over 2006. Telephone interview with Rodrigo Tavares Maciel, executive secretary, Brazil-China Business Council. December 20, 2007.

155. Riomar Trindade. "Brazil's Vale Fires 1,300 and Halts Operations Due to Crisis." *Brazzil Magazine*. http://www.brazzil.com. December 9, 2008.

156. "Brazil Steel Company Eyes China Deal." *China Economic Net*. Beijing, China. http://en.ce.cn. February 15, 2006.

157. Stewart, 2006. See also Jubany and Poon, 2006, p. 32.

158. The latter would have a capacity to produce 5 million tons of steel per year, and would be 80 percent owned by Baosteel, with 20 percent participation by CVRD. "CVRD construirá una planta de acero con China Baosteel." *Portal Minero*. http://www.portalminero.com/noti/noticias_ver_ch.php?codigo=3466. August 24, 2007.

159. "Brazil's CVRD, China's Shougang Plan Joint Venture: Report." *Yahoo*. http://sg.biz.yahoo.com. January 4, 2007.

160. "Brazil's Mining Giant CVRD to Start Joint-Venture Steel Plant in China." *People's Daily Online*. Beijing, China. http://english.people.com.cn. September 29, 2006.

161. The plants included Jinco Nonferrous Metals in Kunshan, Inco Advanced Technology Materials in the coastal city of Dailan, and Inco Advanced Technology Materials in Shenyang. See "Asian Joint Ventures." *Vale Inco*. Official website. http://www.inco.com/global/jointventure/default.aspx. Accessed December 20, 2007. See also Alan Clendenning, "CVRD to offer $15.3 billion for Inco." *CBS News*. http://www.cbsnews.com/stories/2006/08/11/ap/business/mainD8JEEL681.

shtml. August 11, 2006. See also Telephone interview with Rodrigo Tavares Maciel, executive secretary, Brazil-China Business Council. December 20, 2007.

162. "Brazilian Iron Ore Giant to Boost Investment in China." *People's Daily Online.* http://english.people.com.cn. March 8, 2007.

163. "Brazil's Petrobras Eyes Partnerships with Chinese Oil Firms." *Xinhua.* http://www.uofaweb.ualberta.ca/chinainstitute/. September 10, 2006.

164. "Brazil Signs $600-MM Oil Contract with China." *Alexander's Gas and Oil Connection* 11(15). August 15, 2006. See also Logan and Bain, 2005.

165. Telephone interview with Rodrigo Tavares Maciel, executive secretary, Brazil-China Business Council. December 20, 2007.

166. "Brazil Petrobras, Chinese Sinopec Sign MoU." *Latin America News Digest.* http://www.uofaweb.ualberta.ca. July 2, 2008.

167. "China Offers Brazil US$10 Billion for Oil Exploration." *Brazzil Magazine.* http://www.brazzil.com. December 10, 2008.

168. Major new oil discoveries announced in November 2007 could raise Brazilian petroleum reserves as much as 40 percent. See "Oil Discovery Rocks Brazil." *CNN.* http://www.cnn.com/2007/WORLD/americas/11/08/brazil.oil.ap/index.html. November 8, 2007.

169. Currently, the oil must be loaded onto tankers at Atlantic ports. From here, the typical route is to load the oil onto Very Large Crude Carriers (VLCCs) and ship it to China via a long eastward transit around the Horn of Africa. The alternative is to use smaller tankers and send the oil through the Panama Canal, incurring expenses and delays.

170. "Country Analysis Brief: Brazil." *Energy Information Administration.* http://www.eia.doe.gov. September 2007.

171. Jubany and Poon, 2006. In the end, however, Sinopec decided to develop the technology in-house, so as to avoid dependence on Brazil with respect to its future use. Telephone interview with Rodrigo Tavares Maciel, executive secretary, Brazil-China Business Council. December 20, 2007.

172. "China's Influence Now Extends from Australia to Africa." *CNN.* http://www.cnn.com. September 3, 2007.

173. Telephone interview with Rodrigo Tavares Maciel, executive secretary, Brazil-China Business Council. December 20, 2007.

174. Trinh et al., 2006, p. 9.

175. Telephone interview with Rodrigo Tavares Maciel, executive secretary, Brazil-China Business Council. December 20, 2007.

176. Trinh et al., 2006, p. 10.

177. Telephone interview with Rodrigo Tavares Maciel, executive secretary, Brazil-China Business Council. December 20, 2007.

178. "Brasileños venderán carne bovina a China." *El País.* Montevideo, Uruguay. http://www.elpais.com.uy. December 10, 2007.

179. Danelo Macido. "China Gives Green Light to Brazilian Chicken." *Brazzil Magazine.* http://www.brazzilmag.com. December 5, 2008.

180. "Total Import and Export Value by Country (Region) (2007/01–12)."

181. Maciel, 2008, p. 27.

182. "Total Import and Export Value by Country (Region) (2007/01–12)."

183. "China Forecast to Be Brazil's Top Trade Partner."

184. Correspondence with Rodrigo Tavares Maciel, executive secretary, Brazil-China Business Council. July 17, 2008.

185. Calculated from the *China-Brazil Trade Report* 1(2). *Conselho Empresarial Brasil-China.* www.cebc.org.br. June 26, 2008.

186. Under the provisions of Mercosur, for example, Uruguay is able to export

up to 2,000 autos to Brazil tariff-free. It is expected that Chery will leverage this quota in exporting its cars to Brazil. Telephone interview with Rodrigo Tavares Maciel, executive secretary, Brazil-China Business Council. December 20, 2007.

187. Ibid.

188. The role of Huawei in Brazil has not been without its problems, however. In December 2007, Brazilian police raided its offices in São Paulo and detained seventy staff on charges that visiting overseas staff were working in the country without obtaining the proper work visas from the Brazilian government. "Police Raid Huawei Offices in Brazil." *Light Reading.* http://www.lightreading.com/document.asp?doc_id=140867. December 7, 2007.

189. "Huawei Successfully Deploys 1 Million ADSL Lines in Brazil." *AMEInfo.* United Arab Emirates. http://www.ameinfo.com/84077.html. April 25, 2006. See also "Huawei's 1 Million ASDL Lines in Brazil." *SOFT32. com.* http://news.soft32.com/huaweis-1-million-adsl-lines-in-brazil_1311.html. April 22, 2006.

190. "Huawei to Double Brazil Telecom Equip Sales." *China.org.cn.* Beijing, China. http://china.org.cn/english/BAT/117836.htm. January 14, 2005.

191. "Huawei Successfully Deploys 1 Million ADSL Lines in Brazil."

192. Telephone interview with Rodrigo Tavares Maciel, executive secretary, Brazil-China Business Council. December 20, 2007.

193. "Regional Offices." *ZTE Telecom.* Official website. http://www.en.zte.com.cn. Accessed December 10, 2007.

194. "ZTE Wins in Brazil." *Light Reading.* http://www.lightreading.com/document.asp?doc_id=79250. August 29, 2005.

195. A substantial portion of prospective Chinese investment in Brazil mentioned by Hu Jintao during his November 2004 trip to Brazil involved highway and rail infrastructure investment. In 2005, Chinese companies continued to talk about potential investments of $5 billion in the Brazilian highway and port infrastructure. "El impacto chino en América Latina." *El Diario.* La Paz, Bolivia. http://eldiario.net. March 14, 2005. After more detailed examination, however, it was clear that many of the projects involved loans and terms that the Brazilian government could not meet. Because of such complications, in combination with funding shortfalls in the Brazilian budget, very few of the contemplated projects have come to fruition.

196. "Eje Manta-Manaos, alternativa al Canal de Panamá para desarrollo de Amazonía." *El Comercio.* Quito, Ecuador. http://www.elcomercio.com. May 6, 2007.

197. The Corporación Andina de Fomento (CAF) has been mentioned as one possible source of financing for the project, which would significantly improve Brazil's ability to export soy and other products to China, as well as China's ability to get its manufactured goods to Brazilian markets. "Eje Manta-Manaos, alternativa al Canal de Panamá para desarrollo de Amazonía."

198. "Empresas chinas quieren invertir en corredor bioceánico Chile-Brasil."

199. Vaca, 2007.

200. The public commitment was made jointly by the presidents of Brazil, Bolivia, and Chile on December 16, 2007, in La Paz. "Brazil Gets Port on Pacific Coast and China Becomes Much Closer."

201. "Petrobras Delays Pipeline Construction as Sinopec Raises Cost." *Alexander's Gas and Oil Connections* 10(14). http://www.gasandoil.com/. July 20, 2005.

202. "Petrobras Delays Pipeline Construction as Sinopec Raises Cost."

203. Telephone interview with Rodrigo Tavares Maciel, executive secretary,

Brazil-China Business Council. December 20, 2007. See also "Petrobras Hires Sinopec to Build 300 km Stretch of Gasene Pipeline." *Alexander's Gas and Oil Connections* 11(9). http://www.gasandoil.com/. May 4, 2006. See also "Brazil: Petrobras otorga contracto a Sinopec, de China." *Voice of America.* http://voanews.com/spanish. April 18, 2006.

204. Gerald Jeffris, "China Offers BRL 2.5B Financing for Brazil Energy Projects." *Dow Jones Chinese Financial Wire.* http://www.uofaweb.ualberta.ca/chinainstitute/. June 14, 2006.

205. "Rio Industries Agree to Hire Chinese Workers." *People's Daily Online.* Beijing, China. http://english.people.com.cn. December 21, 2006.

206. Naughton, 2007, p. 270.

207. "Brazil's Petrobras Eyes Partnerships with Chinese Oil Firms."

208. "Top Chinese Legislator Hails China-Brazil Economic Relations." *People's Daily Online.* Beijing, China. http://english.people.com.cn. September 1, 2006.

209. Telephone interview with Rodrigo Tavares Maciel, executive secretary, Brazil-China Business Council. December 20, 2007.

210. Ibid.

211. *Gradiente.* Official website. http://www.gradiente.com/site/home/index.asp. Accessed December 21, 2007. See also "The Economy of Heat." *The Economist.* http://www.economist.com/specialreports/displaystory.cfm?story_id=89-52496. April 12, 2007.

212. Fernando Scheller, "Azaléia vai fabricar na China e deixa de ser 100% brasileira." *O Estado do S. Paulo.* http://www.estado.com.br/editorias/2006/03/06/eco54692.xml. March 6, 2006. See also "The Economy of Heat." *The Economist.*

213. "Chinese Military Company Delivers 144 Planes in 2005." *People's Daily Online.* Beijing, China. http://english.people.com.cn. January 11, 2006.

214. "China to Manufacture Large Aircraft." *People's Daily Online.* Beijing, China. http://english.people.com.cn. February 1, 2007.

215. The order included 50 ERJ-145 50-seat aircraft to be produced by the Embraer facility in China, and another 50 E-190 106-seat aircraft to be produced in the Embraer facility in Brazil. "Brasileña Embraer y canadiense Bombardier producirán más en China." *Los Tiempos.* Cochabamba, Bolivia. http://www.lostiempos.com. August 11, 2006.

216. Gregory Polek. "Optimistic Embraer Tempers Its View of China with Caution." *AINOnline.* http://www.ainonline.com. February 19, 2008.

217. "China Signs 16 Int'l Space Cooperation Agreements, Memorandums in Five Years." *People's Daily Online.* Beijing, China. http://english.people.com.cn. October 12, 2006.

218. "Full Text: China's Space Activities in 2006." *People's Daily Online.* Beijing, China. http://english.people.com.cn. October 12, 2006.

219. "Satélite chino-brasileño es una super herramienta de control de la Amazonía." *Nacion.* San José, Costa Rica. http://www.nacion.com. September 27, 2007.

220. Ellis, 2005.

221. "Brazil and China to Distribute Free Satellite Images to Africa." Ministry of External Relations. Press Release No. 570. http://www.mre.gov.br/ingles/imprensa/nota_detalhe3.asp?ID_RELEASE=4953. November 28, 2007. See also "Satélite chino-brasileño es una super herramienta de control de la Amazonía."

222. Edla Lula, "Minister: Brazil's Uranium Not for Sale." *Brazzil Magazine.* http://www.brazzil.com. May 1, 2004.

223. "Australia venderá uranio a China." *BBC Mundo*. http://bbcmundo.com. April 3, 2006. See also "Camberra y Pekín firman acuerdo sobre energía nuclear." *Nacion*. San José, Costa Rica. http://www.nacion.com. April 2, 2006.

224. "China in Latin America: Trade, Not Military Involvement." *Latin America–Asia Review*. July 2006, p. 5.

225. Telephone interview with Rodrigo Tavares Maciel, executive secretary, Brazil-China Business Council. December 20, 2007.

226. The dialogue included a week of events in São Paulo and was attended by business representatives and government officials up to the vice-minister level. "Foreign Minister Yang Jiechi Meets with Brazilian Deputy Foreign Minister Roberto Jaguaribe Gomes de Mattos." *Ministry of Foreign Affairs of the People's Republic of China*. Official website. http://www.fmprc.gov.cn/eng/wjb/zzjg/ldmzs/gjlb/3473/3475/default.htm. November 30, 2007.

227. "BrazilTradeNet." *Brazilian Ministry of Foreign Relations*. Official website. http://www.mre.gov.br. Accessed December 11, 2007.

228. Telephone interview with Rodrigo Tavares Maciel, executive secretary, Brazil-China Business Council. December 20, 2007.

229. It was, for example, the Brazilian Ministry of Industry and Commerce that played a role in the entrepreneurial committee sent to the PRC in March 2007. "Brazil to Send Business Delegation to China." *People's Daily Online*. Beijing, China. http://www.english.people.com.cn. March 13, 2007.

230. Geovana Pagel, "Red Tape Prevents Brazil from Becoming Global Industrial Giant." *Brazzil Magazine*. http://www.brazzilmag.com/content/view/8910/54/. November 24, 2007.

231. Telephone interview with Rodrigo Tavares Maciel, executive secretary, Brazil-China Business Council. December 20, 2007.

232. "Brasil y China firman protocolo para la promoción del comercio internacional." *Empresa Exterior*. http://www.empresaexterior.com. December 2, 2007.

233. *Banco Itaú Holding Financiera S.A.* Official website. http://www.itau.com.br/portalri/index.aspx?idioma=ing&AspxAutoDetectCookieSupport=1.

234. Telephone interview with Rodrigo Tavares Maciel, executive secretary, Brazil-China Business Council. December 20, 2007.

235. Ibid.

236. Bank of China announced in September 2007 that it was seeking permission to open the branch. See "Bank of China Plans to Open Branch in São Paulo." *MacauHub*. http://www.macauhub.com.mo/en/news.php?ID=4088. September 21, 2007. See also "Overseas Branches." *Bank of China*. Official website. http://www.boc.cn/en/-common/third.jsp?category=ROOT>en>Information%20Center>BOC%20Network>Overseas%20Branches&pages=3. Accessed December 14, 2007.

237. "Brasilia será sede del tercer Foro América Latina–Asia del Este." *El Comercio*. Quito, Ecuador. http://www.elcomercio.com. August 2, 2007.

238. See, for example, "Canton Fair Sets Up Booths for Foreign Commodities." *People's Daily Online*. Beijing, China. http://english.people.com.cn. March 30, 2007.

239. Telephone interview with Rodrigo Tavares Maciel, executive secretary, Brazil-China Business Council. December 20, 2007.

240. Ibid.

241. See *Conselho Empresarial Brasil-China*. Official website. http://www.cebc.com.br.

242. In subsequent months, Air China increased the number of flights, as well

as the size of the aircraft used for the route. "Air China Increases Frequency of Flights to Brazil." *People's Daily Online.* Beijing, China. http://english.people. com.cn. November 30, 2007.

243. "Air China to Launch First Flight to South America." *People's Daily Online.* Beijing, China. http://english.people.com.cn. December 10, 2006.

244. Telephone interview with Rodrigo Tavares Maciel, executive secretary, Brazil-China Business Council. December 20, 2007.

245. Based on a personal survey of conference attendees at the Congreso Latinoamericano y Caribeño de Ciencias Sociales, FLACSO Ecuador. Quito, Ecuador. October 29–31, 2007.

246. "China's NPC Consolidates Strategic Alliance with Brazil." *People's Daily Online.* Beijing, China. http://english.people.com.cn. September 4, 2006.

247. "China's NPC Consolidates Strategic Alliance with Brazil." *People's Daily Online.* Beijing, China. http://english.people.com.cn. September 4, 2006.

248. "China, Brazil Pledge to Strengthen Relations." *China View.* http://www.chinaview.cn. March 23, 2006.

249. "China's NPC Consolidates Strategic Alliance with Brazil."

250. "China Appreciates Strategic Association with Brazil: Official." *People's Daily Online.* Beijing, China. http://english.people.com.cn. April 12, 2007.

251. "Assistant Foreign Minister He Yafei Meets with President of Workers' Party of Brazil Berzoini." *Ministry of Foreign Affairs of the People's Republic of China.* Official website. http://ww.fmprc.gov.cn. September 12, 2006.

252. "China, Brazil Hold First Strategic Dialogue." *People's Daily Online.* Beijing, China. http://english.people.com.cn. November 30, 2007.

253. "Chinese Province Guangdong, Brazil State São Paulo Sign Friendship Agreement." *People's Daily Online.* Beijing, China. http://english.people.com.cn. August 30, 2007.

254. See "Wu Bangguo Meets with Governor of Brazil's Amazonas State." *People's Republic of China Ministry of Foreign Affairs.* Official website. http:www.fmprc.gov.cn. September 3, 2006. See also "Wu Bangguo Meets with Governor of São Paulo State." *People's Republic of China Ministry of Foreign Affairs.* Official website. http://www.fmprc.gov.cn. September 2, 2006.

255. "Chinese Defense Minister Meets Brazilian Counterpart." *People's Daily Online.* Beijing, China. http://english.people.com.cn. March 25, 2006.

256. "Brazilian President Meets with Chinese Defense Minister." *People's Daily Online.* Beijing, China. http://english.people.com.cn. October 24, 2004.

257. "Chinese Defense Minister Meets Brazilian Guests." *People's Daily Online.* Beijing, China. http://english.people.com.cn. November 24, 2003. Lower-level Brazilian defense leaders have also gone to Beijing. In April 2005, for example, Brazilian army commander Francisco Roberto de Albuquerque went to Beijing for a series of meetings that included an audience with Cao Gangchuan. "China, Brazil to Enhance Cooperation Between Armed Forces." *People's Daily Online.* Beijing, China. http://english.people.com.cn. April 5, 2005.

258. "China Launches 'North Sword 2005' Military Exercise." *People's Daily Online.* Beijing, China. http://english.people.com.cn. September 27, 2005.

259. "Chinese, Argentine Vice Presidents Hold Talks." *People's Daily Online.* Beijing, China. http://english.people.com.cn. October 26, 2006.

260. Matías Longoni, "Otra record para la soya y el trigo: La cosecha vale US$20,000." *Clarín.* Buenos Aires, Argentina. http://www.clarin.com. August 31, 2007.

261. Calculated from "Total Import and Export Value by Country (Region) (2007/01–12)."

262. Castro, Olarreaga, and Saslavsky, 2007.

263. Peru and Mexico also established diplomatic relations with China in approximately this period—Peru in November 1971, and Mexico in February 1972.

264. "Bilateral Relations." *Ministry of Foreign Affairs of the People's Republic of China.* Official website. http://www.fmprc.gov.cn/eng/wjb/zzjg/ldmzs/gjlb/3453/default.htm. September 26, 2003.

265. Cardozo, 2007.

266. "China promete negocios por casi US$20 mil millones en diez años." *Clarín.* Buenos Aires, Argentina. http://www.clarin.com. November 17, 2004.

267. Interview with Ernesto Fernandez Taboda, November 7, 2007.

268. Ibid.

269. "El barrio que cambió el exotismo asiático por el glamour porteño." *La Nacion.* Buenos Aires, Argentina. http://www.lanacion.com.ar. March 5, 2006.

270. The office of the party was later closed. Interview with Ernesto Fernandez Taboda, November 7, 2007. See also Sofia Butler, Charlotte Rault, and Maria Urioste, "Colectividades y elecciones." *University of British Colombia.* http://www.argentinaelections.com/2007/10/colectividades_y_elecciones.php. October 25, 2007.

271. Cesarin, 2008, p. 25.

272. Interview with Ernesto Fernandez Taboda, November 7, 2007.

273. Ibid.

274. Such comments were offered to this author by multiple sources in frank, off-the-record conversations during my research in Argentina.

275. "Los camioneros ratifican el boicot a los súper y autoservicios chinos." *Clarín.* Buenos Aires, Argentina. http://www.clarin.com. June 26, 2006.

276. While emphasizing Chinese interest in Argentine agriculture, it is also important to note that other Asian nations, such as India, are likewise expanding their purchases of Argentine agricultural commodities—e.g., soy. Indeed, significant increases in sales to India over 2006–2007 helped Argentina compensate for a temporary decline in Chinese imports of Argentine soy products. "Más ventas argentinas a la India." *La Nacion.* Buenos Aires, Argentina. http://www.lanacion.com.ar. May 11, 2007.

277. "Chinese Soybean Farmers Battered by Low Import Prices." See also "El impacto chino en América Latina."

278. According to 2004 trade data, $2 billion out of a total of $2.6 billion in Argentine exports to the PRC came from oils and oil seeds. "Exportaciones Argentinas hacia China por grandes rubros (en miles de dolares)." Table 4. *Fundacion Exportar.* http://www.exportar.org.ar/web2006/index.php?modulo=fichapais&s=4. May 2005.

279. Luis Fracchia, "El desafío de las exportaciones argentinas." *La Nacion.* Buenos Aires, Argentina. http://www.lanacion.com.ar. March 7, 2006.

280. "Brazil Expecting a 10% Drop in Grain Crop." *Brazzil Magazine.* http://www.brazzilmag.com. December 28, 2008.

281. Carlos Marín Moreno, "El girasol está de nuevo en carrera." *La Nacion.* Buenos Aires, Argentina. http://www.lanacion.com.ar. May 12, 2007.

282. Argentina also grows significant quantities of such other products as wheat and corn, although these are not destined for the Chinese market. Interview with Ernesto Fernández Taboda, November 7, 2007.

283. Moreover, by contrast to Brazil, where the Chinese have purchased some land for both timber and agricultural production, Chinese investors have not yet bought significant quantities of Argentine agricultural real estate.

284. Interview with Ernesto Fernández Taboda, November 7, 2007.

285. "Ganadería cada vez más eficiente." *La Nacion.* Buenos Aires, Argentina. http://www.lanacion.com.ar. August 20, 2005.

286. Interview with Ernesto Fernández Taboda, November 7, 2007.

287. In addition, the Chinese want Argentine beef and other livestock to be free from the disease Aftosa without the need for vaccination, known as "zero risk." Interview with Ernesto Fernández Taboda, November 7, 2007.

288. "China abre su mercado para las carnes argentinas." *Clarín.* Buenos Aires, Argentina. http://www.clarin.com. February 1, 2005.

289. Interview with Ernesto Fernández Taboda, November 7, 2007.

290. Ibid.

291. See note 278, above.

292. Argentina's reserves are concentrated throughout the country, along the eastern front of the Andes mountains, although the geography is such that the oil in the south of Argentina is much closer to the surface and cheaper to access. Interview with Ernesto Fernández Taboda, November 7, 2007.

293. This distinction was made by Ernesto Fernández Taboda, ibid.

294. See note 278, above.

295. See "Tratados bilaterales: Republica Popular de China." *Ministerio de Relaciones Exteriores.* República Argentina. http://www.mrecic.gov.ar/. Accessed January 1, 2008.

296. "Argentine Petroleum Firm Seeks Foreign Help for Oil Exploration." September 20, 2005. *People's Daily Online.* Beijing, China. http://english.people. com.cn. September 20, 2005. See also Pino Solanas, "Enarsa a la angoleña?" *Página/12.* Buenos Aires, Argentina. http://www.pagina12.com; and "China-Argentina Oil Investment Deal Gives Angola Key Role." *Alexander's Gas and Oil Connection* 9(24). http://www.gasandoil.com/. December 9, 2004.

297. Jon Nones, "China National Petroleum Looks to Argentina." *Resource Investor.* http://www.resourceinvestor.com. November 29, 2005.

298. "Repsol YPF negó que tuviera en venta sus activos en el pais." *La Nacion.* Buenos Aires, Argentina. http://www.lanacion.com.ar. March 4, 2006.

299. "Rumores de nuevas ofertas a Repsol por YPF." *La Nacion.* Buenos Aires, Argentina. http://www.lanacion.com.ar. July 23, 2007.

300. Interview with Ernesto Fernández Taboda, November 7, 2007.

301. A much larger portion of Argentine mining exports is currently destined for South Korea. Ibid.

302. Harvey Beltrán, "Sinosteel, A Grade Trading Mull Joint Hiparsa Investments: Argentina." *Business News Americas.* http://www.bnamericas.com. February 27, 2006.

303. "Regimen Chino invierte US$6.4 milliones en la mina de hierro más grande de sudamérica." *La Gran Época.* http://www.lagranepoca.com/. October 24, 2006.

304. The purchase of Sierra Grande also illustrates some of the commercial practices by the Chinese that have generated controversy in the region. The Chinese company that bought the mine wanted to not only bring in its own heavy mining equipment from the PRC, but also use Chinese laborers to do much of the actual mining work. In the end, however, the Argentine government refused the petition by the company to bring in its own workers, and the project has remained stalled. Interview with Ernesto Fernández Taboda, November 7, 2007.

305. Ibid.

306. Ibid.

307. "China bebe vino latino." *BBC Mundo*. http://www.bbcmundo.com. June 25, 2008.

308. "Gross Domestic Product per Capita, Current Prices (U.S. Dollars)."

309. "Total Import and Export Value by Country (Region) (2007/01–12)."

310. "Techint advierte por las importaciones." *La Nacion*. Buenos Aires, Argentina. http://www.lanacion.com.ar. December 15, 2006.

311. "Total Import and Export Value by Country (Region) (2007/01–12)."

312. "China Becomes Argentina's Top Source of Garment Imports." *People's Daily Online*. Beijing, China. http://english.people.com.cn. December 25, 2007.

313. Interview with Ernesto Fernández Taboda, November 7, 2007.

314. "China's Home-Grown Auto Brands Eager to Shed Low-Grade Image, Penetrate Overseas Markets (2)." *People's Daily Online*. Beijing, China. http://english.people.com.cn. July 16, 2007.

315. "Compañía china confirmó emprendimiento automotor en Uruguay." *Espectador*. Montevideo, Uruguay. http://www.espectador.com. July 17, 2007. See also "Latinoamérica es objectivo de autos chinos." *Nacion*. San José, Costa Rica. http://www.nacion.com. July 16, 2007.

316. Under the provisions of Mercosur, for example, Uruguay is able to export up to 2,000 autos to Brazil tariff-free. It is expected that Chery will leverage this quota in exporting its cars to Brazil. Tavares, 2007.

317. "Anunciaron inversion para la Argentina." *La Nacion*. Buenos Aires, Argentina. July 11, 2008.

318. Interview with Ernesto Fernández Taboda, November 7, 2007.

319. The deal was reportedly 80 percent financed by China Development Bank and guaranteed by the Argentine government. Ibid.

320. "China's First Private Aircraft Maker to Export 150 Planes." *China.org.cn*. Beijing, China. http://china.org.cn/english/news/188228.htm. November 8, 2006.

321. In addition, the telecommunications division of the Chinese logistics firm Hutchison-Whampoa operates a small fixed-telephony infrastructure in the northern part of Buenos Aires province, although its scope and growth have been modest relative to the expansion of its port operations in Latin America.

322. Hulse, 2007, p. 17.

323. Interview with Ernesto Fernández Taboda, November 7, 2007.

324. Hulse, 2007, p.7.

325. Ibid.

326. Ibid.

327. Cesarin, 2008, p. 25.

328. "Riesgo de défecit con China." *La Nacion*. Buenos Aires, Argentina. http://www.lanacion.com.ar. December 29, 2006.

329. "Argentina quiere prevenir 'dumping' brasileño y chino en textiles." *Nacion*. San José, Costa Rica. http://www.nacion.com. November 20, 2006.

330. "Peirano promete controlar las importaciones de China." *La Nacion*. Buenos Aires, Argentina. http://www.lanacion.com. August 15, 2007.

331. "Argentina tendrá défecit con China." *Clarín*. Buenos Aires, Argentina. http://www.clarin.com. August 18, 2007.

332. Annabella Quiroga, "Con la mira en productos de China, aplican un freno a las importaciones." *Clarín*. Buenos Aires, Argentina. http://www.clarin.com. August 18, 2007.

333. "China promete negocios por casi US$20 mil millones en diez años."

334. See Dreyer, 2006b, p. 89.

335. In part, the nonrealization of the hoped-for investment projects has reflected issues on the Argentine side, such as bureaucratic requirements and delays, as much as on the Chinese side. Part of the problem has also been, as discussed, the Chinese expectation that some or all PRC-sponsored investment projects would go to Chinese companies—a condition that has been difficult to reconcile with the formal requirement of merit-based contract awards, under Argentine law.

336. In many cases, the failure of the project to come to fruition was not because the Chinese reneged on their promises but, rather, because the terms offered by the Chinese were regarded as unacceptable by the other party. In some cases, for example, the Argentine government was legally unable to accept Chinese loans tied to the use of Chinese companies and workers.

337. "Buenos Aires Container Terminal." *Hutchison Port Holdings.* Official website. http://www.hph.com/business/ports/america/bactssa.htm. Accessed September 9, 2007.

338. Despite the presence of Hutchison, the trend in recent years has been a decrease in the use of this port in favor of other upstream ports. Interview with Ernesto Fernández Taboda, November 7, 2007.

339. Bussey, 2005.

340. These routes are reportedly considered problematic because they involve many curves. Interview with Ernesto Fernández Taboda, November 7, 2007.

341. "Un holding chino, interesado en la red de subtes." *La Nacion.* Buenos Aires, Argentina. http://www.lanacion.com.ar. July 2, 2008.

342. See "Tratados bilaterales: Republica Popular de China."

343. "China Signs 16 Int'l Space Cooperation Agreements, Memorandums in Five Years."

344. Hulse, 2007, p. 20.

345. Ibid.

346. Although Argentina traditionally has collaborated with the United States through the National Aeronautics and Space Administration (NASA) on space projects, the PRC also reportedly played a role in the developing and fielding of Argentina's SAC-C surveillance satellite. "Argentina explora cooperación con China en material nuclear." *El Universal.* Caracas, Venezuela. http://www.eluniversal.com. October 23, 2004.

347. Hulse, 2007, p. 21.

348. "China, Argentina Cooperate in Satellite Distance Measuring." *People's Daily Online.* Beijing, China. http://english.people.com.cn. February 21, 2006.

349. "China in Latin America: Trade, Not Military Involvement," p. 5.

350. "Argentina explora cooperación con China en material nuclear."

351. "Representaciones de Bio Sidus en el mundo." *Bio Sidus.* Official website. http://www.sidus.com.ar/web/biosidusweb.nsf/?Open. Accessed January 1, 2008.

352. See "Tratados bilaterales: Republica Popular de China."

353. Interview with Ernesto Fernández Taboda, November 7, 2007.

354. Moreover, the gentleman occupying the post passed away in late 2007, and as of late 2008, had not been replaced.

355. Interview with Ernesto Fernández Taboda, November 7, 2007.

356. "Macri firmó acerdos tecnológicos en China." *La Nacion.* Buenos Aires, Argentina. http://www.lanacion.com.ar. July 5, 2008.

357. Conference discussion. Fundación Pensar. Buenos Aires, Argentina. November 9, 2007.

358. Interview with Ernesto Fernández Taboda, November 7, 2007.

359. Ibid.

360. Ibid.

361. "Bancos de fomento de China y de Argentina firman convenio de cooperación." *El Comercio*. Quito, Ecuador. http://www.elcomercio.com. August 29, 2007.

362. "Impacto en la Argentina: Chinos compran 20% de Standard Bank." *Clarín*. Buenos Aires, Argentina. http://www.clarin.com. October 26, 2007.

363. Although limited by Andean geography, the presence of Chinese businesspeople and tourists is also on the rise. In October 2006, Argentina was put on the list of official Chinese tourist destinations, opening the door for a greatly expanded flow of tourists to the region. "Five New Tourism Destinations for Chinese Citizens." *People's Daily Online*. Beijing, China. http://english.people.com.cn. October 18, 2006.

364. "Confucius Institute to Be Opened in Argentina." *People's Daily Online*. Beijing, China. http://english.peopledaily.com.cn. May 22, 2008.

365. Based on a personal survey of conference attendees at the Congreso Latinoamericano y Caribeño de Ciencias Sociales, FLACSO Ecuador. Quito, Ecuador. October 29–31, 2007.

366. Ibid.

367. "Confucius Institute to Be Opened in Argentina." *ChinaView*. Beijing, China. http://www.chinaview.cn. May 22, 2008.

368. Based on a survey of participants at the Fifth Latin American System Dynamics Congress. Instituto Tecnológico de Buenos Aires. Buenos Aires, Argentina. November 9, 2007.

369. Ibid.

370. "China to Promote Strategic Partnership with Argentina." *People's Daily Online*. Beijing, China. http://english.people.com.cn. November 27, 2006. See also "Chinese, Argentine Vice Presidents Hold Talks."

371. "China to Boost Trade Cooperation with Argentina: Official." *People's Daily Online*. Beijing, China. http://english.people.com.cn. September 21, 2006.

372. "Chinese, Argentine Vice Presidents Hold Talks."

373. "Chinese, Argentine FMs Hold Talks in Beijing." *People's Daily Online*. Beijing, China. http://english.people.com.cn. November 27, 2006.

374. "Negocia la Argentina comprar helicópteros militares a China." *La Nacion*. Buenos Aires, Argentina. http://www.lanacion.com.ar. May 17, 2007. See also "Pacto militar con China." *Clarín*. Buenos Aires, Argentina. http://www.clarin.com. August 22, 2007. See also "Chinese Senior Legislator Meets Argentine Defense Minister." *People's Daily Online*. Beijing, China. http://english.people.com.cn. August 23, 2007.

375. Despite the close military relationship between Venezuela and China, for example, after an evaluation of comparative benefits, Venezuela decided to buy their major military weapon platforms, such as helicopters and fighter aircraft, from the Russians rather than from the Chinese.

376. Guido Bratslavsky, "Licitación de radares: Ya hay trece empresas interesadas." *Clarín*. Buenos Aires, Argentina. http://www.clarin.com. January 29, 2007. See also "Postergan la fecha para la licitación de radares." *Clarín*. Buenos Aires, Argentina. http://www.clarin.com. February 7, 2007.

377. *El Mercurio*. Santiago, Chile. http://diario.elmercurio.com. December 24, 2006.

378. "Argentina, China Pledge to Strengthen Bilateral Ties." *People's Daily Online*. Beijing, China. http://english.people.com.cn. October 28, 2005.

379. "Astori apuesta por comercio con China e India." *Espectador*. Montevideo, Uruguay. http://www.espectador.com. December 20, 2007.

380. "Mercosur trabado por las estrategias de sus socios." *El País*. Montevideo, Uruguay. http://www.elpais.com.uy. December 20, 2007.

381. In the continent of South America, only Paraguay continues to recognize the Republic of China as the legitimate government of the mainland.

382. "Intercambio comercial del país, por año, según región y país selecciona-do (miles $US): Período 1994; Al último dato disponible." *Republica Oriental de Uruguay. Instituto Nacional de Estadistica*. http://www.ine.gub.uy/economia/externo.htm. Accessed December 29, 2007.

383. Ibid.

384. "Poblacion: Uruguay en Cifras 2007." *Instituto Nacional de Estadistica*. http://www.ine.gub.uy/biblioteca/uruguayencifras2008/02%20poblaci%F3n.pdf. Accessed February 12, 2009, p. 13.

385. "¿Cómo vive la comunidad asiática en Uruguay?" *Espectador*. Montevideo, Uruguay. http://www.espectador.com. November 7, 2007.

386. Ibid.

387. Ibid.

388. Ibid.

389. "Bilateral Relations." *Ministry of Foreign Affairs of the People's Republic of China*. Official website. http://www.fmprc.gov.cn/eng/wjb/zzjg/ldmzs/gjlb/3533/default.htm. September 26, 2003.

390. "Ventas de lanas, carnes, y pieles aumentan 15,8 por ciento en Uruguay." *El Comercio*. Quito, Ecuador. http://www.elcomercio.com. September 5, 2007.

391. "Valor de las exportaciones, por año, según tipo de producto (en miles de dólares y porcentaje): Período 1990, al último dato disponible." *Republica Oriental de Uruguay. Instituto Nacional de Estadistica*. Official website. http://www.ine.gub.uy/economia/externo.htm. Accessed December 29, 2007.

392. As an example of developments in this area, in August 2005, a group of Chinese investors came to Montevideo to inspect Uruguayan Holland cattle. "China revisará ganado en los próximos días." *El País*. Montevideo, Uruguay. http://www.elpais.com.uy. August 11, 2005.

393. In an October 2007 speech, Uruguayan economics minister Danilo Astori suggested that the dilemma for Uruguay in entering markets such as China was that the products in which Uruguay is most competitive are those that are most protected. "Proteccionismo limita ingreso local en megamercados." *El País*. Montevideo, Uruguay. http://www.elpais.com.uy. October 20, 2007.

394. "Valor de las exportaciones, por año, según tipo de producto (en miles de dólares y porcentaje): Período 1990, al último dato disponible." "Valor de las exportaciones, por año, según tipo de producto (en miles de dólares y porcentaje): Período 1990, al último dato disponible." *Republica Oriental de Uruguay. Instituto Nacional de Estadistica*. Official website. http://www.ine.gub.uy/economia/externo.htm. Accessed December 29, 2007.

395. "Exportación de vino, por año, según paises (en litros): Período 1994, al último dato disponible." *Republica Oriental de Uruguay, Instituto Nacional de Estadistica*. Official website. http://www.ine.gub.uy/economia/externo.htm. Accessed December 29, 2007.

396. "Botnia manda celulosa a China." *Espectador*. Montevideo, Uruguay. http://www.espectador.com. December 19, 2007.

397. With an annual per capita income of $6,000 in 2006, Uruguay was the second-wealthiest country in South America, bested only by Chile. "Gross Domestic Product Per Capita, Current Prices (U.S. dollars)."

398. "Total Import and Export Value by Country (Region) (2007/01–12)."

399. "Bilateral Relations." *Ministry of Foreign Affairs of the People's Republic*

of China. Official website. http://www.fmprc.gov.cn/eng/wjb/zzjg/ldmzs/gjlb/3533/default.htm. September 26, 2003.

400. "Escáner del Puerto de Montevideo volverá a China." *Espectador.* Montevideo, Uruguay. http://www.espectador.com. December 6, 2007. See also "El Puerto tendrá escáner el año que viene." *Espectador.* Montevideo, Uruguay. http://www.espectador.com. December 6, 2007.

401. "Uruguay importa tecnología para seguridad pública y combate al narcotráfico." *Nacion.* San José, Costa Rica. http://www.nacion.com. July 9, 2008.

402. See, for example, "Banda de contrabandistas operaba en zonas francas." *El País.* Montevideo, Uruguay. http://www.elpais.com.uy. December 7, 2007. See also "Detectan contrabando en dirección de Aduanas." *Espectador.* Montevideo, Uruguay. http://www.espectador.com. December 13, 2007; and "Aduaneros investigados por maniobras en zonas francas." *Espectador.* Montevideo, Uruguay. http://www.espectador.com. December 13, 2007.

403. "Contact Us."

404. "ZTE's Global Sales Offices." *ZTE Corporation.* Official website. http://wwwen.zte.com.cn/main/about/Global%20Sales%20Offices/Representative%20offices/UVW/index.shtml?catalogId=13341. Accessed December 29, 2007.

405. Liu, 2006.

406. Huawei made Uruguay its test market for the introduction of its "3G" UMTS technology in Latin America. "Latin America's First UMTS Network Is Constructed by Huawei." *Huawei.* Press release. Montevideo, Uruguay. http://www.huawei.com/news/-view.do?id=1765&cid=42. September 4, 2006.

407. "Piden limitar ingreso para zapatos de China." *El País.* Montevideo, Uruguay. http://www.elpais.com.uy. August 31, 2007.

408. "Compañía china confirmó emprendimiento automotor en Uruguay." See also "Latinoamérica es objectivo de autos chinos."

409. Reflecting this combination of a manufacturing base, cheap labor, and access to Mercosur markets, by 2003 the PRC had established six small joint manufacturing ventures in Uruguay, with a modest investment of $1.83 million. "Bilateral Relations." *Ministry of Foreign Affairs of the People's Republic of China.* Official website. http://www.fmprc.gov.cn/eng/wjb/zzjg/ldmzs/gjlb/3533/default.htm. September 26, 2003.

410. "Misiones en China." *Ministerio de Relaciones Exteriores, Republica Oriental del Uruguay.* Official website. http://www.mrree.gub.uy/mrree/Embajadas_y_Consulados/-Misiones/Scripts_Misiones/por_pais.idc. Accessed December 29, 2007.

411. "Tratados y convenios internacionales." *Ministerio de Relaciones Exteriores.* Republica Oriental del Uruguay. http://www.mrree.gub.uy/Tratados/MenuInicial/busqueda/-Pais/PaisConsul.asp. Accessed December 29, 2007.

412. "Uruguay y China avanzan en sus relaciones." *El País.* Montevideo, Uruguay. http://www.elpais.com.uy. September 14, 2005.

413. "Tercer foro de comercio exterior organizado por Royal & SunAlliance Seguros." *Espectador.* Montevideo, Uruguay. http://www.espectador.com. October 24, 2007.

414. "En 2008 Lolita abrirá en Europa y África." *El País.* Montevideo, Uruguay. http://www.elpais.com.uy. December 30, 2007.

415. "¿Cómo vive la comunidad asiática en Uruguay?"

416. "Uruguay Becomes Tourism Destination for Chinese Citizens." *China View.* http://www.chinaview.cn. September 5, 2006.

417. Based on a personal survey of conference attendees at the Congreso

Latinoamericano y Caribeño de Ciencias Sociales, FLACSO Ecuador. Quito, Ecuador. October 29–31, 2007.

418. "Interview: China, Uruguay Committed to World Peace, Development; Uruguayan Parliament Speaker." *People's Daily Online*. Beijing, China. http://english.people.com.cn. January 19, 2007. See also "China, Uruguay to Upgrade Parliamentary Cooperation." *China View*. http://www.chinaview.cn. January 8, 2007.

419. Based on a personal survey of conference attendees at the Congreso Latinoamericano y Caribeño de Ciencias Sociales, FLACSO Ecuador. Quito, Ecuador. October 29–31, 2007.

420. "Mercosur trabado por las estrategias de sus socios."

421. The trip included the signing of a number of agreements, including approval of Uruguay by the PRC as an official tourist destination, and the establishment of a Confucius Institute for the promotion of the Chinese language and culture in Uruguay. "Interview: China, Uruguay Committed to World Peace, Development; Uruguayan Parliament Speaker." See also "China, Uruguay to Upgrade Parliamentary Cooperation."

422. "Bilateral Relations." *Ministry of Foreign Affairs of the People's Republic of China*. Official website. http://www.fmprc.gov.cn/eng/wjb/zzjg/ldmzs/gjlb/3533/default.htm. September 26, 2003.

423. "Chinese, Uruguayan Air Forces to Enhance Echanges, Cooperation." *People's Daily Online*. Beijing, China. http://english.people.com.cn. September 22, 2004.

424. "Uruguayan President Meets Head of Chinese Military Delegation." *People's Daily Online*. Beijing, China. http://english.people.com.cn. November 1, 2005.

425. "China, Uruguay Agree to Strengthen Military Exchanges." *China.org.cn*. http://www.china.org.cn. September 6, 2006. Visits to Uruguay by Chinese military officials have also included Chinese chief of staff Fu Quanyou (1998), president of the PRC National Defense University Xin Shizhong (1999), and Zhou Ziyu, deputy director of the PRC General Political Department (2000).

426. See, for example, "Chinese Merchandise Fair Held in Chile." *People's Daily Online*. Beijing, China. http://english.people.com.cn. November 15, 2005.

427. "Paraguay Proposes Free Trade with China." *People's Daily Online*. Beijing, China. http://english.people.com.cn. January 25, 2005.

428. The issue was not raised during the Mercosur summit in April 2005, and has not appeared in the public spotlight since that time. "No definen negociación con China continental." *ABC Digital*. Asunción, Paraguay. http://www.abc.com.py. April 16, 2005.

429. "Chinese Top Legislador Meets Paraguayan Delegation." *People's Daily Online*. Beijing, China. http://english.people.com.cn. July 31, 2001.

430. "Efemérides Paraguayas." *ABC Digital*. Asunción, Paraguay. http://www.abc.com.py/efemerides/efemerides.php?fec=2006-04-02. April 2, 2006.

431. "China, Central America Create Organization to Promote Ties." *People's Daily Online*. Beijing, China. http://english.people.com.cn. March 24, 2007.

432. Hanratty and Meditz, 1988.

433. "Taiwán promueve con 250 millones dólares inversiones en Paraguay." *Nacion*. San José, Costa Rica. http://www.nacion.com. May 6, 2006.

434. See, for example, "Policía decomisa 14 televisores en peaje de Ypacaraí." *ABC Digital*. Asunción, Paraguay. http://www.abc.com.py. December 13, 2007.

435. "Taiwán promueve con 250 millones dólares inversiones en Paraguay."

436. Ibid.

437. "Vice presidenta de Taiwán visitará América Latina." *Nacion*. San José,

Costa Rica. http://www.nacion.com. June 28, 2007. See also "Loss of Ally Prompts Taiwan to Take 'Extreme Precautions.'" *CNN.com.* http://www.cnn.com. June 7, 2007.

438. "Posible relación con China continental." *ABC Digital.* Asunción, Paraguay. http://www.abc.com.py. April 23, 2008.

439. "China acepta tregua de Taiwán, que tiene de aliado a Paraguay." *Ultima Hora.* Asunción, Paraguay. http://www.ultimahora.com. October 16, 2008.

440. "Total Import and Export Value by Country (Region) (2007/01–12)."

441. Ibid.

442. Ibid.

443. "Denuncian a Copaco ante Contraloría por inminente adjudicación a Ericsson." *ABC Digital.* Asunción, Paraguay. http://www.abc.com.py. November 23, 2007.

444. "Chinos quieren invertir en el país." *ABC Digital.* Asunción, Paraguay. http://www.abc.com.py. December 14, 2008.

445. "Taiwán promueve con 250 millones dólares inversiones en Paraguay."

446. "Ventas externas superan US$15 millones." *ABC Digital.* Asunción, Paraguay. http://www.abc.com.py. December 28, 2007.

447. "Primer auto chino en el país." *ABC Digital.* Asunción, Paraguay. http://www.abc.com.py. June 13, 2006.

448. "Ensambladora de motos produce 3.700 unidades en tres meses de operación." *ABC Digital.* Asunción, Paraguay. http://www.abc.com.py. April 10, 2005.

449. "Desean instalar ensambladora de vehículos con capital de China." *ABC Digital.* Asunción, Paraguay. http://www.abc.com.py. May 12, 2008.

450. "Uruguay y Perú distribuyen computadoras." *ABC Digital.* Asunción, Paraguay. http://www.abc.com.py. December 17, 2007.

451. "Toda la jornada del Jueves 7 de junio de 2007." *ABC Digital.* Asunción, Paraguay. http://www.abc.com.py. June 7, 2007.

452. "Posible relación con China Continental." *ABC Digital.* Asunción, Paraguay. http://www.abc.com.py. April 23, 2008.

453. Prior to the Lugo presidency, there had also been a series of low-level contacts between Paraguay and the PRC, including a March 2005 trip by a Paraguayan "friendship delegation" to Beijing, where they were received by senior Chinese official Cheng Siwei.

5
The Andes:
Fishmeal, Oil, and
Tenuous Alliances

———————■———————

ALTHOUGH COMMERCE BETWEEN THE PRC AND THE SOUTHERN
Cone nations is greater in value than China's trade with the Andean nations,
it is in the Andes that China is most clearly involved in the strategic and
ideological issues of Latin America.

The countries of the Andes are each attempting to deal with their long-
standing political, social, and economic maladies in very distinct ways.
Colombia and Peru are generally pursuing paths that rely on free-trade and
Western market mechanisms to generate wealth and overcome socioeconomic problems. Venezuela, Bolivia, and Ecuador, with varying degrees of
effectiveness, are following a socialist-populist course in which the state
seeks to capture revenues from primary-product industries and other strategic sectors, then direct those resources toward economic and social development programs. The distinct individual relationships that China has pursued with each of the Andean countries reflect the distinct political
situations prevailing in each, and the choices that each has made with
respect to ideological orientation and economic policy.

■ Venezuela

Due to the high-profile leadership style of Venezuela's leader, Hugo
Chávez, and his ability to capture the attention of the US press, Venezuela's
relationship with China is relatively well-known in the United States.
Venezuela is also the most recent of the four countries in the continent upon
which China has bestowed the title "strategic partner."[1] Venezuela's bilateral trade volume with China is significantly smaller than that of the PRC and

its other strategic partners,[2] highlighting that China's decision to bestow this title on Venezuela reflects its hopes about the future, as much as its present importance.

As China looks to the future, a key part of its interest in Venezuela, in superficial terms at least, is petroleum.[3] If the tarlike deposits found throughout Venezuela's Orinoco belt are certified as oil in the quantities anticipated, the nation will be credited with a total of 315 billion barrels of oil reserves. Although much of this oil is difficult to extract and requires special processes to refine, the quantity puts Venezuela ahead of Saudi Arabia as the nation with the world's largest oil reserves.[4]

Beyond possible oil trade, the rhetoric and policies pursued by the Chávez regime in Venezuela have generated new opportunities for the PRC to distinguish itself from Western countries and multinational companies as a partner. From satellites, computers, and telecommunications technology[5] to truck factories and trains, the Chinese have stepped in to build up the Venezuelan commercial infrastructure as Western and Venezuelan companies have been driven out. Reflecting such interests, Chinese investment in Venezuela in 2006 totaled $1.6 billion—greater than any other nation in Latin America with the exception of Ecuador—with an estimated investment of $2 billion in 2007.[6]

However, despite the opportunities for China represented by Venezuelan oil and other projects, the lack of a stable juridical and contractual framework in Venezuela, legal disputes that could disrupt supply—such as the $12 billion Venezuelan asset seizure in the ExxonMobil case—and the potential for Chávez's policies to destabilize the country and the region all signify risks for the PRC. Political chaos in Venezuela, or in the region more broadly, not only could hurt Chinese companies and undermine China's trade objectives in the region, but also could damage China's more important relationship with one of its primary export customers, the United States.

Historical Context

Venezuela and the PRC established diplomatic relations in June 1974; Venezuela was at the tail end of the first group of Latin American countries to do so. Despite diplomatic recognition, however, until Hugo Chávez assumed the presidency in 1999, Venezuela was generally aligned with the United States and was relatively restrained in its dealings with China.

Reflecting Venezuela's earlier conservative, pro-US political alignment, the first visit by a Venezuelan president (Luis Herrera Campins) to China did not occur until 1981, more than seven years after Venezuela extended diplomatic recognition to the PRC. The first visit of a Chinese premier to Venezuela came in November 1985, with the next Chinese visit at this level not occurring for another eleven years, with the trip by Premier Li Peng at the invitation of President Caldera. Thus, when Hugo Chávez became president in 1999, although the two countries had had diplomatic relations for more than twenty-five years, there had been only three presidential-level visits between them.

The ideological orientation of Hugo Chávez, and his interest in using the PRC as a counterweight to the United States in the region, have brought about a significant expansion of the Sino-Venezuelan relationship in all domains. Chávez made his first visit to China in October 1999, just months after assuming the presidency, and proceeded to visit the PRC three more times through the end of 2006. Reciprocally, Chinese president Jiang Zemin made a state visit to Venezuela in May 2001. Since that time, however, the closest that China has come to a state visit to Venezuela was the trip by Chinese vice president Zeng Quinghong in January 2005, in conjunction with the China-Caribbean Economic and Trade Summit.[7]

The Chinese Community in Venezuela

The Chinese community in Venezuela is one of the largest in Latin America, with approximately 130,000 people of Chinese descent living in the country.[8]

According to China's ambassador to Venezuela, Zhang Tuo, approximately 30–40 percent of Venezuelans of Chinese origin are found in the greater Caracas metropolitan area, with Maracaibo and Valencia each accounting for another 10 percent;[9] virtually all of this community came from the Guangzhou area. With respect to Caracas, a small "Chinatown" is located in its El Bosque district.[10]

As in other parts of Latin America, the Chinese community in Venezuela is known for its restaurants and small shops;[11] there are also doctors, lawyers, and government functionaries of Chinese descent.[12]

Although relations between Chinese Venezuelans and other groups in the ethnically diverse Venezuelan society have been relatively good, Venezuelans surveyed for this book often stated that the Chinese community maintains a degree of separation from the rest of society. An outbreak of violence against Chinese shopkeepers in Maracay and Valencia in November 2004[13] illustrates that some ethnic tensions do exist.[14]

The Heavy Investment Fund

One of the most important vehicles enabling Chinese projects in Venezuela is the Heavy Investment Fund, established with $6 billion in March 2007,[15] and expanded with the addition of an additional $6 billion in 2008.[16] Although not readily apparent in the way that the press represents it, the fund is potentially a powerful tool for enabling major projects in Venezuela and channeling the work on those projects to Chinese companies. The importance of the fund is, in part, a product of the capital crisis generated in Venezuela by the policies of the Chávez government, which combines significant social spending with an environment hostile to foreign investment. Although a number of Chinese companies are interested in doing business in Venezuela, and although the political will exists in Caracas to contract with them, the Venezuelan government does not have the resources to realize even a fraction of the projects to which it publicly commits. As a reflection of the uncertainties inherent in such an environment, Chinese companies have a strong preference for being paid by a Chinese entity in yuan, rather than by the Venezuelan government in its increasingly questionable currency. The Heavy Investment Fund remedies all of these problems, enabling projects to be committed to Chinese companies, paid for by Chinese institutions in yuan, but with the Venezuelan government ultimately paying the bill.

The Heavy Investment Fund is a pool of revolving credit created in November 2007, capitalized through $2 billion from the Venezuelan government and $4 billion in revolving credit from China Development Bank.[17] By mutual agreement, China administers the fund, although Venezuela is its guarantor, ultimately responsible for repaying the loans. Projects supported by the fund are decided by a committee in which the votes are proportional to the contributions of each country. Reflecting the ratio of capital contributed, China has forty votes to Venezuela's twenty, virtually guaranteeing that any work done under the fund in Venezuela will be channeled to a Chinese company, if one is in the competition. Moreover, China Development Bank physically provides the funds to the company doing the work, thus creating the system by which Chinese companies are paid by a Chinese bank in yuan, but with Venezuela responsible for the debt. For Chinese companies doing the work, this arrangement is particularly attractive, circumventing concerns over the reliability of the Venezuelan government as a source of funds, and of the Venezuelan currency, the bolivar. As of late 2008, $750 million from the fund had been earmarked toward $5.4 billion in railroad infrastructure improvements,[18] with an increasing number of projects seeking to be included in the fund, from transportation projects to petroleum to telecommunications.

China's Interest in Venezuelan Petroleum

A natural complementarity exists between China's significant and growing energy needs and Venezuela's position as a major petroleum supplier seeking to diversify its customer base to avoid dependence on sales to the United States.[19]

Venezuela is currently in the process of certifying and developing the heavy petroleum deposits concentrated in its Orinoco region as oil. In 2006,

Venezuela was recognized as having only 79 billion barrels of reserves.[20] By late 2008, through the ongoing process of certification of the new deposits (previously not considered to be recoverable as oil), this figure had surpassed 152 billion barrels.[21] If previous industry recovery rates are used, Venezuela may untimately be certified as having 315 billion barrels, putting the country ahead of Saudi Arabia as the country with the largest reserves in the world.[22] The sheer volume of these reserves when the heavy, high-sulfur oil of the Orinoco region is included makes the country of interest to China as a long-term supplier—particularly as sources of lighter crude oil throughout the world decline because of expanding demand not only from China, but also from the United States, the European Union, Japan, and elsewhere.

China's interest in Venezuelan oil is further heightened by obstacles that it has run up against in its pursuit of the heavy petroleum in the Alberta province of Canada. The oil believed to exist in this region would give Canada the world's third-largest petroleum reserves behind Venezuela and Saudi Arabia. The key Canadian developer, Enbridge, however, has focused on developing infrastructure to transport Canadian oil to the US market, leading to delays in building the $3.8 billion pipeline that would carry oil from Alberta to the Pacific for export to the PRC. Reflecting Chinese frustration with progress on the pipeline, in July 2007, CNPC announced that it was reducing its presence in Canada and would correspondingly increase its focus on Venezuela.[23]

China's interest in Venezuelan petroleum is not new. China's presence began in the early 1990s with the opening of the Venezuelan oil sector to outside players, which included the award of two marginal oil fields to CNPC in the third round of bidding: the Intercampo block in the Lake Maracaibo area of the northwest, and Caracol in the state of Anzoátegui in the southeast. CNPC was subsequently granted a number of other fields, including fifteen mature fields in Zumano,[24] as well as the Junin-4 and Carabobo blocks in the Orinoco belt[25] and the Poza field in the Gulf of Paria.[26]

In securing concessions for the potentially substantial oil fields of Orinoco,[27] the Chinese have made progress by holding on while others have abandoned the country. When Venezuela forced companies operating in Orinoco to renegotiate their contracts and give up their majority shares in May 2007,[28] for example, the Chinese were among those who agreed to the new terms.[29] Others choosing to stay included Iran's Petropars, India's Oil and Natural Gas Corporation (ONGC)–Videsh, and Russia's Lukoil.[30] Further, the decision by the Western multinationals ExxonMobil and ConocoPhillips to cease their activities in Orinoco, rather than agree to the new terms, positioned Chinese petrochemical companies such as Sinopec to take over the blocks being abandoned.[31]

The PRC's objective is to secure new and reliable oil supplies to accommodate China's needs, while Venezuela's is to diversify its list of clients away from the United States.[32] In 2004, Venezuela sold virtually no petroleum products to China; by May 2008, Venezuela was exporting an average of 80,000 barrels of crude oil per day to the PRC, plus an additional 220,000 barrels per day of fuel oil and other products.[33] By 2012, the Venezuelan national oil company, Petroleos de Venezuela, Sociedad Anonima (PdVSA), anticipates exporting 800,000 to 1,000,000 barrels of oil to the PRC.[34] If achieved, these export targets will represent 15 to 20 percent of total Chinese petroleum imports,[35] making Venezuela a strategically important supplier for China.[36]

In addition to exploration and development by Chinese companies in Venezuela, PdVSA bought Chinese drilling rigs,[37] to supplement those that the Chávez regime expropriated, beginning in May 2007, from foreign oil companies operating in the country.[38] The first thirteen rigs are to be imported from China, with the other fourteen specified in the initial contract to be partially produced in Venezuela.[39] Within the framework of the agreement, PdVSA sent a number of engineers and experts to the PRC during 2007 and 2008 to receive training on the operation of the rigs and to map out a plan for transitioning production to Venezuela.[40]

Although China and Venezuela are pursuing a number of cooperative initiatives in the oil sector, Venezuela's ambitious efforts to increase dramatically its oil exports to China are overshadowed by a growing disjunction between what is being promised, what is being done, and what is technically feasible. Although not admitted by either the Chinese or the Venezuelans, a dynamic is currently playing out whereby the Chinese are moving forward on projects that are based on supply guarantees that Venezuela will not be able to realize. This situation will ultimately force Venezuela to decide whether to break its current supply commitment to its professed adversary, the United States, to avoid breaking its commitment to its strategic partner, the PRC. Even by mid-2008, a falloff in oil supplies to the United States could be seen—from 1.28 million down to 1.13 million barrels per day over the first four months of the year—as Venezuela boosted its exports to the PRC.[41]

A number of technical issues also cast doubt on whether Venezuela will be able to produce the oil promised to the PRC. Although part of this increase is expected to come from an expansion of production from 40,000 to 100,000 barrels per day in the 15 mature fields that CNPC operates in Zumano,[42] doing so will require the injection of gas into the fields through pipelines not yet built or by other technologies not yet planned. Similarly, although noteworthy new production is anticipated to come from areas of the Orinoco belt,[43] such as the Chinese-operated Junin-4 block,[44] significant challenges remain with respect to transportation and storage that will make it difficult for these areas to meet production goals by 2012.[45]

Unresolved questions also exist with respect to upgrading and refining the planned new oil. Although Venezuelan oil being extracted from mature fields is of a grade that can be refined in a number of facilities, much of that to be extracted from the Orinoco fields requires a number of additional operations to upgrade it to the point where it can be refined by traditional processes. One option is to upgrade it close to the point of extraction; an alternative is to mix it with a solvent so it can be moved to a different location for upgrading. In pursuing the first option, Venezuela has considered the construction of a 400,000-barrel-per-day facility near the town of Cabruta,[46] as well as the reopening of smaller facilities in Barinas or Caripito. Such options are generally considered impractical, however, because of the remoteness of the area in general and its propensity to flood, and because PdVSA lacks the capital to pay for such a project.

An alternative to upgrading facilities in Orinoco is to construct simpler mixing facilities there, transport the mixed product to new upgrading facilities that would be constructed on the northern coast, and, from there, ship the product to facilities in China or other parts of the world for further refinement.[47] Although this option is generally regarded as the most likely, it still implies significant investment in new mixing and upgrading facilities, as well as the availability of surplus capacity in existing petroleum pipelines to move the solvent and product.

These questions involving production and refinement are complemented by challenges in transporting the oil from Venezuela to China, where it would be further refined and ultimately consumed. Despite the fact that Venezuela is acquiring new oil tankers[48]—and China and Venezuela have signed an ambitious accord for a new tanker fleet[49]—as with other projects, it is not clear that PdVSA will be able to finance this expansion unless it, too, is financed through indirect loans from China.[50]

One of the agreements signed during the March 2007 visit to Venezuela by Chinese Politburo member Li Changchun was for the construction of three new refineries in the PRC to process up to 800,000 barrels per day of Venezuelan crude oil.[51] The refineries, theoretically, would be operated through a partnership controlled 60 percent by the Chinese and 40 percent by PdVSA.[52] In May 2008, the two nations signed an accord further affirming their intention to explore the construction of at least one of these facilities, a 400,000-barrel-per-day refinery in China's Guangdong province.[53] As of November 2008, some evidence suggested that the PRC was moving forward with work on the refineries, but that participation by PdVSA was uncertain, since the organization did not have the capital to participate.[54]

In addition to the refineries in China, another option for refining the heavy oil coming out of Orinoco is a refinery being constructed near the Brazilian city of Pernambuco.[55] Originally, the Brazilian partner in the project, Petrobras, expected that PdVSA would finance 50 percent of the venture, aimed at refining heavy oil extracted from that part of Orinoco in which Petrobras was operating. However, the inability of PdVSA to help finance the project, in combination with the discovery of significant new oil deposits in Brazil itself in 2007, will probably lead Petrobras to use Pernambuco to refine Brazil's own oil, rather than shipping oil from Orinoco large distances to Pernambuco to be refined.

Compounding these logistical challenges are contractual challenges arising from the new legal and regulatory framework imposed in May 2007 on all oil companies operating in Orinoco. Under the new system, all oil extracted by Chinese companies in Orinoco must be sold to PdVSA, which, at its discretion, may resell it to customers such as the refineries in China. By contrast, oil extracted from non-Orinoco areas, such as the CNPC operations in Intercampo or Zulia, can be exported directly to China for refining, generating greater confidence in the supply, and potentially greater profits. In the short term, thus, the Chinese have strong incentives to focus their resources on the operation of the mature wells, rather than on developing the greater potential of the petroleum in Orinoco.

Although virtually all of these challenges can be addressed with sufficient time and money, PdVSA is not making such investments, and perhaps cannot without significant new infusions of Chinese capital, which would likely be coupled with a significant loss of Venezuelan control over many of these projects. One senior industry expert has estimated that Venezuela will need $250 billion in investment in the petroleum sector from 2008 to 2018, or $25 billion per year, to realize its production targets; yet, programmed investment for 2008 was a mere $15.6 billion.

Finally, PdVSA's ability to supply oil to China will also be impacted by its ability to resolve outstanding legal challenges, such as the battle by ExxonMobil to seize $12 billion in PdVSA's assets, due to a dispute over compensation of the oil company for the nationalization of its assets in 2007. Fighting such legal battles will continue to divert the attention of PdVSA executives from implementing a viable plan to produce promised oil; further, the escalation of this dispute will potentially change the context of the dilemma. A cutoff in supply to the United States, depending on the capability of Chinese and other refineries to process Venezuelan heavy crude at the time that it occurred, either would force a catastrophic drop in revenues that would bring down the Chávez regime or would resolve the supply dilemma, freeing up oil to be refined in the PRC, or both.

Aside from context-changing events such as those flowing out of PdVSA's legal disputes, if the organization cannot meet its commitments to supply oil to China based on new production,[56] its manner of resolving the dilemma may well depend on who is in power in Caracas. If Chávez or one of his allies controls the government, it is likely that Venezuela would prefer to break its contracts to supply refineries on the US Gulf Coast in order to keep its commitment to the PRC, Venezuela's strategic partner. However, if a more market-oriented, less anti-US government is in power when the dilemma arises, the logic of existing contracts and relative costs will lead Venezuela to break its commitments to China in order to honor its existing relationships with US refineries.

China's Interest in the Venezuelan Mining Sector

While Venezuela's economy is dominated by petroleum, the mining sector also plays an important role in the nation's economy, with metals exports accounting for 19 percent of the nation's exports in 2006.[57] The PRC purchases modest quantities of Venezuelan iron,[58] and Chinese companies are present in the sector. In December 2005, for example, the Chinese mining companies Jin Yan and Shandong Gold Mining began operations in the Venezuelan gold mine Sosa Méndez in the state of Bolívar, including a modest initial investment of $13 million.[59] Separately, the Chinese steel producer China Metallurgical Group has signed memorandums of understanding concerning an iron mine, with the potential construction of a plant, in the state of Bolívar, to process the ore into pellets for export.[60] It is also possible that some portion of future Chinese investment in the sector will be channeled through the Heavy Investment Fund. Although no specific mining projects have been chosen for the fund, Gustavo Hernandez, vice minister of Investment Promotion for Basic Industry and Mining (MIBAM), estimates that approximately 8 percent of the fund could go to the mining sector.[61]

China's Interest in Other Venezuelan Products

As we have seen with other countries of the region, a handful of Venezuelan companies are seeking to position themselves in the Chinese market, using national and brand recognition to sell high-end products to the growing Chinese middle class. The Venezuelan gourmet-coffee maker Arabia, for instance, is seeking to join others, such as Starbucks and Café Britt, in the growing Chinese market. Similarly, in 2008, the internationally known Venezuelan rum manufacturer Santa Teresa, which has previously exported to the Japanese market, was evaluating possibilities for exporting to China. Exports of Venezuelan cacao to China have also been mentioned, given the international reputation of Venezuelan chocolate, although currently, the quantities of cacao produced in the country are limited and virtually all cacao exports are absorbed by France. In keeping with Venezuela's comparative strength in the petroleum industry, perhaps the nation's best prospect for export involves a related sector, petrochemicals. According to experts interviewed for this book, the Venezuelan petrochemicals company Glassven has set up a modest production operation in the PRC.

Venezuela as a Market for Chinese Goods and Services

Because of both the political orientation of the Chávez regime and the collapse of domestic production, Venezuela is a growing market for Chinese exports. The concentration of the Venezuelan economy on petroleum and related industries creates a need to import a broad range of products, with very little competition from domestic producers. Venezuelan oil revenue also makes the country the second wealthiest in South America, with funds to buy such goods (at least in some sectors).[62]

Demand exists in Venezuela for both low-end Chinese merchandise and more expensive goods. Venezuela has a sizable poor population for whom the cheapness of such Chinese products as textiles and footwear is particularly important. Venezuela also has a large and growing informal sector, into which such goods are often introduced as contraband,[63] generally coming into Panama, then shipped to Colombia, and smuggled across the border into Venezuela.[64]

In addition to low-end products, a range of more sophisticated Chinese products are available, including consumer appliances from the Chinese company Haier.[65] Goods of this type are generally brought into the country by large retailers. However, Venezuela's difficulty in obtaining access to foreign currency for transactions (if the goods are not on the prioritized list of imports) in general limits its ability to import products..

At the top end of the retail sector, Venezuela is becoming a market for more sophisticated Chinese goods, from consumer electronics and computers to motorcycles, cars, and trucks. The Chinese car brands Chery, Geeley, and Great Wall are currently available in Venezuela, principally through the distributor Cinescar, although they have not yet experienced a significant takeoff in sales. Chinese motorcycles are widely available throughout the country—although sold under non-Chinese brand names, such as "Jaguar."

Chinese companies are beginning to explore setting up manufacturing facilities in Venezuela, taking advantage of relatively generous tax treatment and infrastructure subsidies from the Venezuelan government. In October 2007, for example, the consortium Civetchi announced that it would begin importing Chinese Dongfeng busses, with a plan to build by 2009, in the Venezuelan state of Carabobo, a factory that would produce Dongfeng busses for the Venezuelan, Colombian, and Ecuadorian markets.[66]

In the personal-computer market, the Chinese brand Lenovo is widely sold, leveraging the sales and distribution infrastructure of International Business Machines (IBM), from whom Lenovo's personal-computer division was purchased in 2005. In December 2006, the Venezuelan government announced another venture—although not on the same scale as Lenovo's—in which the Chinese firm Lang Chao would assemble computers in Venezuela from Chinese components, in a facility in the industrial free-trade zone of Paraguaná, in the state of Falcon.[67] The Venezuelan government planned to purchase the initial output of the plant,[68] providing a guaranteed market that complements subsidies involved in the facility and operation itself,[69] although Lang Chao also indicated plans to sell the computers in the commercial market.[70]

In the domain of heavy equipment, the PRC has sold to Venezuela railroad boxcars and twelve diesel locomotives, which were delivered in December 2006.[71] The transaction, which represented the first sale by the PRC of such equipment in South America, followed anther sale of a dozen locomotives to Cuba in 2005,[72] helping China to advance its train industry and position itself for sales to larger markets, such as Brazil and Argentina.

In addition to sales of goods, Chinese telecommunication companies such as Huawei and ZTE have actively worked to develop a position in the Venezuelan market. As of 2006, Venezuela had signed contracts with Chinese companies for an estimated $140 million in deals in this sector, with a potential for more than $300 million.[73]

Huawei entered the Venezuelan telecom market in July 1999[74] and established its first branch office in the country in 2001. By 2007, Huawei had 3 offices in the country, 97 service centers, and approximately 210 employees.[75] The company provides services to a range of clients, including private enterprises like Telcel, Digitel, and Movistar-Telfonica, as well as such state firms as Compañía Anónima Nacional Teléfonos de Venezuela (CANTV) and Compañía General de Minería de Venezuela (CVG).[76] Beyond providing network services and components, in June 2007, Huawei entered a joint venture with the telecommunications branch of the state firm CVG to manufacture cellular telephones in a new facility under construction in Ciudad Zamora.[77] The plant is expected to manufacture a million units in its first year of operation,[78] with plans to sell the output throughout Venezuela and South America. In addition, in 2004, Huawei won an important contract to build a fiber-optic network in Caracas,[79] and by 2008 was partnered with Ericsson in the construction of a new national cellular telephone infrastructure for CANTV, based on GSM technology. Unfortunately for Huawei, however, the nationalization of its client CANTV has diverted the latter organization's resources away from capital projects in order to fulfill its social mission.[80]

In addition to Huawei, the Chinese firm ZTE has established a strong presence in Venezuela.[81] The company has a variety of government and private-sector clients, including PdVSA, CVG, and the electric company Compañía Anónima De Administración y Fomento Eléctrico (CADAFE). Among its other projects, it has been awarded a contract to build a backup data center for the Venezuelan national tax administration, Servicio Nacional Integrado de Administración Tributaria (SENIAT), and, in 2006, was awarded a concession for a 7,000-kilometer extension of the Venezuelan fiber-optic network to poor areas in the south of the country.[82]

Beyond their activities in providing infrastructure to the Venezuelan telecom sector, both Huawei and ZTE have plans in place to build a production facility with the government to produce cell phones in Los Valles del Tuiy. These phones will be for sale within the Venezuela market, Central America, and the Caribbean, with the first ones expected out in 2009 or 2010.[83]

Infrastructure Projects

By contrast with other countries of the region, Venezuela has focused surprisingly little effort on infrastructure projects that would connect it to ports on the Pacific Ocean. Although for years Venezuela has contemplated the construction of an oil pipeline from Maracaibo across Colombia to Tribugal, most of the nation's current plans to export its oil to China involve use of its Atlantic ports. Beyond oil, Venezuela has little to export to Asia, and those businesses that import products from Asia have little weight in determining the nation's few infrastructure investments. Furthermore, Venezuela's poor relations with Colombia, in combination with risks from Colombian guerillas and from organized crime in crossing overland, help to suppress enthusiasm for new infrastructure projects involving Colombia.

Perhaps the most significant Venezuelan infrastructure project concerning China is an ambitious plan to modernize and extend the nation's railroad system. A Chinese company and an Italian company currently are working to modernize and extend this infrastructure in Venezuela's northwest. An even more ambitious follow-up project would extend this rail network from the coast to the interior of the country in support of petroleum operations. In addition to the projects mentioned above, the Venezuelan government signed an accord with the Chinese State Commission for Reform and Development for $10 billion of work involving the construction or improvement of 1,500 kilometers of rail lines.[84]

Technology Cooperation

In addition to supporting Venezuela in petroleum and other primary-product sectors, the PRC has been a significant goods and service provider to Venezuela in a number of technology sectors.[85] In November 2005, for example, Venezuela announced that China would provide the country with its own telecommunications satellite. The Zhongxing-22A satellite, called "Simon Bolívar," launched in November 2008 from the Cosmodrome in the Chinese city of Xian, includes Chinese-provided hardware, launch services, and two ground stations in Venezuela,[86] including a command-and-control facility at La Carlotta Airport.[87] To support the project, military technical students from the Venezuelan armed forces university, Universidad Nacional Experimental Politécnica (Unefa), were sent to the PRC for training as part of the agreement,[88] with the consequence that Venezuela may have more personnel in China on official business than any other Latin American country.[89]

Government and Business Infrastructures

Venezuela's governmental infrastructure for doing business with the PRC is much more sophisticated than the corresponding infrastructure in the private sector, although the capabilities of the government also present serious shortcomings.

Because of their strategic-partner relationship, China and Venezuela have a permanent binational High-Level Mixed Commission, which has met annually since 2001 to address bilateral issues, alternating meeting locations between the two countries. The November 2007 meeting took place in Caracas and was attended by 130 Chinese functionaries.[90] The commission includes 6 subcommittees, specializing in various topics and integrating various bureaucracies, including the ministries of planning, petroleum, and finance on the Venezuelan side. Despite the work of the commission, and despite the 213 agreements signed between China and Venezuela during 30 years of bilateral relations,[91] the two nations have surprisingly few agreements to facilitate private-sector trade, such as accords on investment protection, phytosanitation, or the resolution of disputes.

The Venezuelan government's infrastructure in China is one of the largest among its Latin American peers, although much more focused on state-to-state projects than on the promotion of private-sector interactions. Venezuela has, for example, both an embassy in Beijing and a representative office in Shanghai, which opened in March 2007.[92]

Interestingly, the Chinese diplomatic presence in Venezuela differs significantly from Venezuela's diplomatic presence in China in the active promotion by the Chinese of their commercial interests. Both the previous and current Chinese ambassadors have been extremely active in providing a voice not only for Chinese state-owned companies, but also for Chinese commercial entities doing business in Venezuela, helping them present their positions to the Venezuelan government and facilitating resolutions of their issues.[93]

For the promotion of trade with China, the Venezuelan counterpart of such organizations as ProChile and Fundación Exportar is the Banco Comercio Exterior de Venezuela (BANCOEX), which provides lines of credit for commercial transactions, works with Venezuelan companies to help them export, and leads commercial groups to important events (e.g., the China–Latin America Business Summit in Santiago in November 2007) as well as to trade fairs (e.g., the one held in Xiamen in September 2007). Because of the relative absence of Venezuelan companies attentive to the

Chinese market, however, the principal focus of BANCOEX has been to put Chinese companies interested in doing business in Venezuela in touch with the right people, rather than vice versa.[94]

Although some private-sector initiatives are beginning to emerge, they appear primarily oriented to fostering more sales of Chinese goods in Venezuela, rather than the sale of Venezuelan goods in China. In June 2008, to give one instance, seventy Chinese companies held a Chinese industrial products fair in Caracas, promoting Chinese wares from industrial equipment and agricultural machinery, to cars and car parts, to construction materials, to appliances.[95]

In addition to state-to-state initiatives in sectors such as petroleum, mining, technology cooperation, and infrastructure projects, the China-Venezuela relationship features a plethora of social projects. The Chinese state company City Group, for example, has been working to construct 20,000 low-cost housing units in Venezuela. In the agricultural sector, although China has not shown significant interest in importing Venezuelan agricultural goods, the Chinese international projects company of Zhonggong and the Venezuelan Foundation for the Development of Agriculture, Fishing, and Forestry (FONDAFA) have agreed to donate Chinese agricultural goods to Venezuela. Separately, the Shenzen-based Sino-Venezuelan Agricultural Investment Company has signed a contract with CVG for the construction of a "model farm." Plans are also under way for the creation of an agricultural academy to improve the planting and processing of rice.

With respect to the financial sector, China and Venezuela have almost no banking infrastructure to support transactions, other than the activities of China Development Bank and the Heavy Investment Fund. As of November 2008, there were no Venezuelan banks with a presence in China. Although Banco Industrial de Venezuela had previously explored opening a representative office in China, the financial difficulties of the bank have at least temporarily derailed such plans. Reciprocally, beyond China Development Bank's small representative office in Caracas, there is no Chinese banking presence in Venezuela.

Intellectual Infrastructure

Although most activity in the China-Venezuela relationship is at the government-to-government level, the nation's universities have modest offerings in China studies and the Mandarin language. The Universidad Central de Venezuela, for example, has a modest Mandarin program to train Venezuelan government officials, and the Venezuelan government sponsors a modest exchange program with China, giving ten scholarships for Venezuelans to study in the PRC. Nonetheless, other important Venezuelan universities, such as Universidad Católica Andrés Bello, Universidad Simon Bolívar, and Universidad del Zulia, either do not have degree programs that feature China or Chinese-language studies or provide nondegree Chinese-language courses only through an affiliated institute.

Political and Military Relations

Venezuela, as noted earlier, is one of four nations in Latin America that China designates as a strategic partner.[96] While the Chávez regime has been vocal in its support for the PRC, it is not always clear if the Chinese are as enthusiastic about their relationship with Venezuela.[97] China's ambassador to Venezuela, Zhang Tuo, emphasizes that China's decision to recognize Venezuela as a strategic partner reflected, in part, the nation's economic and political potential, including its influence in the region.[98] Although China has avoided taking a position with respect to many of Venezuela's statements and actions in the international arena, as a strategic partner, it has supported Venezuela on a number of issues, including backing Venezuela's candidacy for a position on the UN Security Council.[99]

In addition to the strategic partnership and diplomatic alignment between the two countries, the level of political interaction between China and Venezuela is significant. As of the end of 2008, Venezuelan president Hugo Chávez had visited China five times during his presidency, including a trip in September 2008 that included an agreement for China to expand the Heavy Investment Fund from $6 billion to $12 billion.[100] Reciprocally, Venezuela has been a stop for various Chinese leaders and functionaries, including a visit by Politburo member Li Changchun in April 2007[101] and a trip by Chinese vice president Zheng Quinghong in January 2005.[102]

A substantial number of agreements have been negotiated between Venezuela and China, establishing mechanisms that deepen their political and cultural cooperation. In April 2006, for example, the two countries signed an accord on the exchange and training of television and radio broadcasters.[103] In December 2006, they agreed on a cultural cooperation pact, with interchanges of experts, artists, specialists, and various other groups.[104]

In the military realm, Chinese-Venezuelan cooperation has been strong but constrained. On one hand, the Chinese have neither established a permanent military presence in the country nor sold the Venezuelans significant quantities of lethal hardware, as the Russians have. On the other hand, reflecting the desire by the Chávez government to free itself from dependence on US and other Western military hardware, the Venezuelans have bought a range of Chinese military goods, including eighteen Chinese K-8 training aircraft that can be fitted with air-to-ground or air-to-air munitions, to be delivered in the first half of 2009.[105] China also sold ten mobile air defense radar to Venezuela from 2004 through 2008, which were subsequently deployed along Venezuela's northern coast.[106] Chávez has claimed, moreover, that the Simon Bolívar satellite constructed by China for Venezuela will provide communications security for the Venezuelan armed forces,[107] and even will be part of an "integrated ground- and space-based air defense system"[108]—though such claims are dubious, given the technology involved.

In addition to these items, the Chinese have sold Venezuela logistics aircraft, military uniforms, and other nonlethal military supplies. Venezuela also explored the possibility of purchasing FC-1/J-10 fighter aircraft from China in 2005, but ended up pursuing a procurement of twenty-four Russian Sukhoi-30 fighter aircraft instead.[109] The Venezuelan choice of Russia for major weapons purchases like helicopters, fighter aircraft, and machine guns reflects the superior reputation enjoyed by the Russians in the quality and performance of such equipment. However, it also opens the door to purchases of Chinese equipment over the long term, insofar as many Chinese munitions are based closely on, or are exact copies of, Russian equipment, and, for many categories of armaments, Russian equipment can be supported by Chinese munitions and components.

Venezuela has also expanded its officer exchange and training programs with the Chinese. One Venezuelan expert interviewed in January 2008 estimated that the Chinese had approximately thirty officers on long-term assignment at the Caracas military base Fuerte Tiuna, with a similar number of senior Venezuelan military officers receiving command- and general staff–level training in China. The use of China for significant military training dates back to April 2002, when the Chávez government was ousted by the Venezuelan military and briefly replaced with the civilian government of Pedro Carmona. When Chávez returned to power, he eliminated perceived threats, expelling US military trainers, who Chávez believed had supported the actions against him. The US trainers, including special-operations personnel, were replaced by trainers from the PRC,[110] providing the Chinese a valuable opportunity to learn US tactics, techniques and procedures, and the content of US training programs from the Venezuelan soldiers who had recently worked closely with US trainers.

■ Ecuador

Ecuador's relationship with the PRC is characterized by cycles of rapid advance interrupted by strategic pauses. In 2005, a consortium of Chinese oil companies purchased the Ecuadorian assets of the Canadian firm EnCana, catapulting the PRC's fixed investment in the country to $1.8 billion, thus making Ecuador the largest recipient of Chinese capital in Latin

America.[111] During the same period, Ecuador's imports from China increased by 32 percent and its exports to the PRC jumped by 62 percent.[112] The PRC appeared ready to play a role in a number of strategically important projects in the country, from a new $6 billion refinery in the province of Manabí, to participation in the development of a major new oil field, to construction of a multimodal transit corridor from the port of Manta to Brazil's Atlantic coast. Then, in 2007, progress seemed to halt, as the country focused on reviewing not only its constitutional framework but also its relationship with oil companies and other foreign entities, in a manner that appeared to make Chinese investors as nervous as their Western counterparts.[113] Suddenly, Venezuela was being discussed in the press as the principal investor in the Manabí refinery,[114] and the opening of the environmentally sensitive Yasuni national parklands for oil exploration was put on hold. The end of 2007 brought indications that the Sino-Ecuadorian relationship was again moving forward: Ecuador's president, Rafael Correa Delgado, made a major trip to China and Ecuador promised to remove the minor US military presence from the Manta airport and transform the airport into a major international airfield supporting regular flights to China. Like Ecuador's political process, for better or worse, the nation's relationship with the PRC is wide open with possibilities whose prospects of realization evolve on a daily basis, along with the political landscape of the country.

As is true for Western investors, a key concern for the Chinese in expanding their position in Ecuador is the stability of the latter's legal and juridical framework. In 2007, for example, Ecuador began reviewing all of its twenty-two investment pacts and treaties with foreign countries, including those with the PRC.[115] Such uncertainties were magnified by the Constituent Assembly process, which rewrote the nation's constitution during 2007–2008. Reflecting concerns over institutional unpredictability, in an interview for this book, the Chinese ambassador to Ecuador, Cai Runguo, emphasized the importance of the legal framework for the Chinese, and the hope of his government that both the review of the Chinese-Ecuadorian investment framework and the Constituent Assembly process would be resolved quickly so that the PRC could proceed to develop its commercial relationship with Ecuador.[116] At the time that this book went to press, Ecuador was preparing for April 2009 elections to choose its first government under the new constitution.

Historical Context

The modern history of Ecuador's relationship with the PRC is replete with both good intentions and false starts. Although Ecuador did not officially establish diplomatic relations with the PRC until 1980, interest by the

Ecuadorian government in doing so was publicly manifested as early as 1968–1972, when it abstained from a series of votes in the United Nations seeking to block a seat on that body for the PRC.[117] During the period 1971–1975, China and Ecuador deepened their commercial and diplomatic ties, including the signing of a bilateral accord establishing commercial offices in each other's countries. In 1976, however, the Ecuadorian government of General Guillermo Rodriguez Lara was ousted in a military coup and replaced by a regime less friendly to the PRC. The return to civilian rule in 1979, with the election of Jaime Roldós Aguilera, allowed Ecuador and China to continue developing commercial and political ties, culminating in the establishment of diplomatic relations in January 1980.[118]

From the establishment of diplomatic relations to the present, Ecuador and the PRC have generally maintained a positive relationship, although one that was relatively limited in scope until recently. The first visit by one head of state to the other was the trip by Ecuadorian president Oswaldo Hurtado to China in May 1984. Following the Hurtado trip, however, the next presidential-level visit did not occur for another ten years, when President Sixto Duran traveled to the PRC in March 1994. Subsequently, President Jamil Mahuad went to China in August 1999 and President Gustavo Noboa, in March 2002.[119] Not once has a Chinese head of state traveled to Ecuador, however.

The Chinese Community in Ecuador

Approximately 50,000 people of Chinese origin live in Ecuador.[120] Although the Chinese community in Ecuador is not as large as that of Brazil or Peru, it nonetheless has significant social and economic weight in the country.[121]

The largest concentration of ethnic Chinese in Ecuador is found in Guayaquil, the nation's principal port city and commercial hub. Another significant Chinese community is found in Quevedo, which was historically a center of agriculture, attracting Chinese immigrants seeking employment in that sector. Another important Chinese population is found in Machala, a center of Ecuador's fishing industry in the south of the country.

Chinese Ecuadorian communities play an important role in the nation's economy. The Chinese-Ecuadorian conglomerate Grupo Wong, for example, is one of the major players in the banana industry,[122] the nation's most significant traditional product. Similarly, the Chinese-Ecuadorian company Sol del Oriente is a chief producer of noodles, exporting its product throughout Latin America. In addition to Chinese Ecuadorians owning these large companies, the Chinese communities in Guayas and Los Rios are a significant part of Ecuador's agriculture sector, while those in Machala participate in the nation's shrimp and fishing industry. In addition, Chinese Ecuadorians are well-known nationwide for their small shops and for their restaurants (known as *chifas*), representing a blend of Chinese cuisine and local spices.

As with Chinese immigrants in other parts of Latin America, the Chinese in Ecuador began to arrive in the nineteenth century, driven by political chaos and a lack of economic opportunity in their home country. The initial destination of Chinese immigrants to the region during this period was Peru; by 1880, Chinese immigrants from Lima began arriving in the Ecuadorian province of Guayas.[123] Like Chinese immigrants in other Latin American nations, many Chinese immigrants in Ecuador initially worked in the country's agricultural sector, while others set up restaurants and other small businesses.

The assimilation of the Chinese into Ecuadorian society was facilitated by a series of relatively effective, well-disciplined social organizations, like the China Beneficence, which helped to establish these immigrants in jobs in agriculture, restaurants, and the retail sector, and provided them with various forms of social support. The China Beneficence later gave rise to the China-Ecuador Society and, eventually, to the Ecuador-China Chamber of Commerce, still important today in connecting Chinese Ecuadorians, businesspeople from the PRC interested in Ecuador, and Ecuadorians interested in doing business with China.[124]

From the beginning, the Chinese community made a determined effort to integrate into the broader Ecuadorian society, maintaining a low profile socially and politically. Many changed their surnames and even avoided public conversation in their native tongues to avoid calling attention to their Chinese ancestry. Over the long run, such behavior had two important consequences. First, the combination of the discretion adopted by the community and the comparative tolerance of Ecuadorian society contributed to a relative absence of ethnic tensions, in contrast to the experience of Chinese communities in other parts of Latin America, such as Mexico. Second, because immigrants avoided using Mandarin in public and did not teach it to their children, a large percentage of subsequent generations of Chinese Ecuadorians lost the ability to read or write the language.[125] As a consequence, the most established and successful members of the Chinese Ecuadorian community today are limited in the linguistic and cultural ties that would help them promote the support industries for the nation's growing Sino-Ecuadorian commerce.

Although Chinese Ecuadorians have lived in relative harmony with the rest of society, the standing of ethnic Chinese in the country was tarnished somewhat during the administration of Lucio Gutierrez by a scandal involving the improper granting of visas to thousands of Chinese. The investigation, which ultimately involved charges against the Ecuadorian director of immigration, Renato de Campo, revealed that the authorities had taken bribes in exchange for the granting of some 4,000 visas.[126]

In addition to the negative publicity, the visa scandal highlighted an immigration dynamic that has tested the established Chinese community in Ecuador in recent years. The established population of Chinese Ecuadorians arrived many years ago, primarily from the Chinese province of Guangzhou.[127] While newly arriving Chinese immigrants, predominantly from the province of Fushien, are generally poorer and less literate, they bring valuable skills, including the ability to speak and, in some cases, write Chinese. The flow of Chinese immigrants into Ecuador increased significantly after the Ecuadoran government eliminated the requirement that Chinese apply for visas in order to enter the country in June 2008.[128] Although many of the newly arriving Chinese are only traveling through Ecuador en route to the United States, a significant number of Chinese do stay in the country, at least temporarily. One of the challenges of the established Chinese Ecuadorian community and groups such as the China-Ecuador Society is how to integrate these populations into a coherent community.[129]

China's Interest in Ecuadorian Petroleum

Although Ecuadorian oil reserves are not as large as those of Venezuela, they are nonetheless significant. Moreover, the combination of low domestic oil consumption, Pacific coast ports, and an existing Pacific-oriented oil pipeline infrastructure makes the export of Ecuadorian oil to the PRC a viable proposition.

As noted previously, it is the Chinese venture in Ecuador's petroleum sector that accounts for the vast majority of the reported $1.8 billion in PRC investments in the country. The figure is particularly striking given the relative lack of PRC investment in other sectors of the Ecuadorian economy, signifying that, almost solely through oil investments, Ecuador has become one of the leading recipients of Chinese capital in Latin America.

The deal that accounts for the lion's share of Chinese activity in the Ecuadorian petroleum sector was the $1.42 billion purchase, finalized in 2005, of the Ecuadorian holdings of the Canadian firm EnCana.[130] For more than a decade prior to the EnCana purchase, Chinese petroleum companies were involved in five of the country's oil fields.[131] The purchase of the Ecuadorian EnCana assets by a Chinese consortium gave the Chinese not only a number of important new oil fields, but also the 450,000-barrel-per-day Oleoducto Crudo Pesado (OCP) pipeline—the newest and most reliable of Ecuador's two major pipeline systems.[132] Chinese corporations now account for more than a quarter of all planned spending in the petroleum sector, including programmed spending by Ecuador's national oil company.[133]

While the EnCana acquisition is, by far, the largest Chinese investment initiative in Ecuador, Chinese companies have also been active as service providers elsewhere in the oil sector. In one instance, when the US firm Occidental Petroleum (Oxy) was forced to leave the country in February 2005 due to a dispute with the Ecuadorian government,[134] Chinese firms stepped in, signing contracts with the Ecuadorian national petroleum company, Petroecuador, to operate and conduct exploration in several fields that had previously belonged to Oxy.[135] In addition, Petroecuador contracted out operations of the Atacapi Parahuachu field to the Chinese state-owned firm Changquing Petroleum Exploration Bureau.[136] In June 2007, Petroecuador further signed a five-year strategic agreement with CNPC to collaborate on a broad range of activities, including exploration and development, transportation, storage, and even management and training.[137]

Beyond ongoing work in the sector, a number of future projects contemplated by the Ecuadorian government have the potential to expand China's presence in the oil sector significantly. The Ecuadorian government is currently considering opening up the Ishpingo Tambococha Tiputini (ITT) oil block for exploration and development. The development of ITT has been under consideration since the mid-1990s, but is a matter of significant controversy since the area to be developed is located in Yasuni National Park, an environmentally sensitive and protected area, where development would encroach on the lives of relatively isolated communities of indigenous peoples.[138] The reserve is believed to contain as much as one billion barrels of oil,[139] and possibly twice that,[140] putting it on a par with Ecuador's most productive oil fields in the northeast of the country.[141] In July 2007, Petroecuador signed a memorandum of agreement with a consortium consisting of China's Sinopec, Petrobras of Brazil, and Enap of Chile to develop a plan for exploring and developing ITT.[142] A final decision on opening ITT, however, was postponed multiple times to see if the international community will compensate Ecuador for not exploiting the reserve.[143] As of late 2008, a decision to open the reserve had not yet been made. If the Ecuadorian government eventually chooses to open ITT,[144] a substantial amount of the $5 billion required to develop the fields could come from Sinopec or other Chinese companies.[145]

As a complement to ITT, Chinese companies may also play a major role in the El Aroma refinery project initiated in July 2008 as a joint venture between Petroecuador and the Venezuelan national oil company, PdVSA. The refinery, which will have the capacity to process up to 300,000 barrels of heavy crude oil per day, will require an estimated $6.6 billion in funding, which the government has indicated will be raised from external sources,[146] such as the Chinese. Beyond El Aroma, the Ecuadoran minister of petroleum and mining, Galo Chiriboga, has indicated that the Chinese companies CNPC and Sinopec have expressed interest in projects to expand and modernize two other refineries currently in the country, Shushufindi and La Libertad.[147]

While the combination of Chinese participation in ITT, El Aroma, and other refinery projects would represent an enormous expansion in the already substantial Chinese presence in Ecuador, it is possible that ultimately neither will take place. In 2008, the Ecuadoran government sought to increase state control over the operations of major oil companies and tax the "extraordinary" earnings of these companies at rates up to 99 percent. The affected companies included CNPC and Petrochina, which had just invested $1.42 billion in the country two years earlier to acquire the assets of EnCana and form a new entity, Andes Petroleum, as well as to acquire the operations of another, smaller Chinese company, Petroriental.

China's future in the Ecuadorian petroleum sector is impacted not only by these projects but also by its present experience in Ecuador, including difficulties that the Chinese have experienced with local populations and with the Ecuadorian government.

Like other oil companies operating in remote areas, Chinese companies operating in the northeastern part of Ecuador have repeatedly come into conflict with local populations. The area is populated by a volatile combination of indigenous peoples, narcotraffickers, guerillas, and others displaced by the war in Colombia.[148] In November 2006, indigenous activists in the department of Tarapoa seized control of an oil field belonging to CNPC, taking thirty workers hostage and causing production to fall from 42,000 to 14,000 barrels per day.[149] In July 2007, in the department of Orellana, operations of the Chinese oil company Petroriental were paralyzed for more than a week when protests degenerated into violent confrontations with the authorities.[150] The violence, which caused over $1 million in damage and lost production,[151] left thirty-one people injured, and included peasants throwing dynamite at soldiers,[152] as well as sabotage to the firm's pipeline in the vicinity of the town of Dayuma.[153] In November, yet another outbreak of violence forced the government to declare a state of emergency in the area.

Chinese entities in the petroleum sector have also been affected by legal and administrative actions by the Ecuadorian government. As with other petroleum operations in the country, the EnCana properties purchased by the Chinese consortium Andes Petroleum were subject to a significant increase in taxes and royalty payments in 2006.[154] In 2008, the Ecuadorian government further sought to have all of the petroleum companies operating in its territory, including Andes, renegotiate their contracts, moving from ownership to service agreements.[155] In August 2008, Andes and Repsol YPF became the first two oil companies in the country to accept a new contract, with Andes Petroleum agreeing to a provisional one-year service contract, but leaving its relationship with the government over the long term uncertain.[156]

China's Interest in the Ecuadorian Mining Sector

Ecuador also has significant, although undeveloped, potential as an exporter of minerals and metals to the PRC.[157] One analyst, with an eye to the Chinese market, noted that Ecuador's reserves of copper could be as important as its petroleum reserves.[158] The country's minerals and metal deposits principally lie in the south—among others, in provinces El Oro and Zamora Chinchipe. In addition, the Condor mountain range, which forms the eastern border between the province of Zamora Chinchipe and Peru, has potential reserves of uranium that China might have an interest in if it begins to look to Latin America to supply materials to its expanding nuclear power industry.[159]

The owners of the territory in which Ecuador's mineral wealth potentially exists have been relatively slow to exploit it. In part, this reflects concessionary terms for landowners, which, while they are highly favorable, do not create incentives to mine the land. In an attempt to correct the underdevelopment of this sector, legislators incorporated a number of reforms of the mining law into the new Ecuadorian constitution approved in 2008 to give the state more power to award and regulate mining concessions. As of December 2008, the new law was being considered by the Congresillo, Ecuador's transitional legislature, with approval likely.[160]

In the event that traditional mining interests are forced out or are discouraged from investing under the new laws, PRC firms such as China Minmetals could be brought in to develop Ecuador's mineral wealth.

China's Interest in Other Ecuadorian Goods

Although Ecuador lacks a diversified export sector, the nation produces a number of primary products other than petroleum, metals, and minerals that are of potential interest to the PRC, including bananas, coffee, lumber products, seafood, cacao, and scrap metal. By the end of 2008, however, the Ecuadorian government was beginning to openly express frustration with its inability to sell products to China beyond petroleum.[161]

Ecuador clearly hopes to increase exports of bananas and other traditional products as it expands its commercial relationship with the PRC. Bananas are Ecuador's second-largest export product after petroleum,[162] and China was a key focus when the Global Banana Congress met in Guayaquil in April 2007.[163] At that congress, the vice minister of the Ministry of Agriculture promised to work with the Ministry of Foreign Relations to promote banana exports to China.[164] Ecuador's banana industry includes not only politically powerful conglomerates such as the Noboa Group, but also such organizations as the Cansing Group, and the Wong Group, founded by one of the pillars of the Chinese Ecuadorian community, the late Segundo Wong.

Despite its interest in exporting bananas to China, Ecuador arguably does not have a comparative advantage in doing so, as suggested by its limited success thus far. Bananas are a relatively labor-intensive crop; in such an industry, Ecuador cannot compete well on a cost basis against bananas grown in China or the Philippines, where labor is cheaper and transportation costs are lower.[165] Ecuadorian banana exporters are further prejudiced by the entry into the market of new suppliers in the Philippines, who are close to the Chinese market, with lower transport costs than Ecuadorian producers.[166]

Ecuador's fishing industry is a candidate for exports to the PRC of such goods as high-quality tuna and shellfish. Moreover, Chinese Ecuadorians play a role in this sector, including purchasing the products of local merchants and creating a wholesale market that supports the export sector. The Chinese have also provided technical assistance, helping to solve the white-spot blight that had caused significant damage to the Ecuadorian shrimp industry.[167] Nonetheless, to date, the majority of Ecuador's fishing industry products have been sold to the United States rather than to the PRC. In part, this is because China has its own commercial fishing industry, turning out the same types of products as Ecuador does. For example, although shrimp is the star product of Ecuador's fishing industry,[168] China is the world's largest shrimp-producing country, accounting for almost 40 percent of global production.[169] Progress in the Chinese market is also hampered by a combination of existing fishing treaties and commercial arrangements, and by the use of the dollar as the Ecuadorian currency—all of which previously made Ecuadorian products relatively noncompetitive for export to China, in comparison with those of neighboring Peru and Chile.

By contrast to bananas and fish, Ecuador has had some success in niche industries in which the Ecuadorian origin of the product gives it a special appeal or a reputation for quality. Aromatic cacao from Ecuador, for example, is considered among the best in the world. Cacao, used in chocolate, is found principally in Balao and is exported to China and other destinations as a premium product.

Although labor-intensive Ecuadorian agricultural businesses like the banana industry currently are not cost competitive in the PRC, Ecuador has considered following the lead of Argentina and Brazil to grow and export soy products, in which the use of large quantities of land and agricultural machinery play a larger role in production. Although as of 2007, Ecuador was a net importer of corn, the government presently is attempting to expand corn production in response to increasing international prices for corn because of its role in the expanding biofuels market.[170] The Chinese have also expressed an interest in growing other crops in Ecuador as alternative fuels. In one project under consideration in 2007, for example, a Chinese-backed firm, Bejar Trade Company, had a plan to plant African palm trees in Ecuador, extracting the palm oil and converting it into biodiesel fuel.[171]

As with other countries in the region, Ecuador's success in exporting agricultural products to the PRC has been limited by a lack of phytosanitary agreements between the two countries. Currently, phytosanitary regulations effectively block Ecuador from exporting milk products, meat, and a variety of similar products to the PRC.[172] As of November 2008, the Ecuadorian government was in discussions with the PRC to establish a basic agreement on phytosanitary standards and categories, in order to expand the sale of Ecuadorian goods on the Chinese market.[173]

Finally, Ecuador's lumber industry exports to China and has the potential to expand those exports. As with aromatic cacao, a special Ecuadorian wood, teca, is valued for its high quality and unique properties; the volume exported is relatively limited, however, because much of the wood is located in protected areas of the Amazon region.[174] With respect to wood available for export, the Chinese have historically come to Ecuador with their own equipment to cut and extract the timber, contributing relatively little value-added to the local economy.[175]

Ecuador as a Market for Chinese Goods

Although the size of the Ecuadorian economy has limited the potential of the nation as a market for Chinese goods, Ecuador has nonetheless emerged as an important purchaser of a broad range of Chinese products. China sells Ecuador not only a significant quantity, but also a broad variety, of goods, exporting some 2,600 different products to the country, according to data from the Ministry of Foreign Relations.[176] Although as recently as 2000, nine other countries sold more goods to Ecuador than did the PRC, by 2006, according to records from Ecuador's central bank, China was the nation's fourth-largest source of imports.[177]

In recent years, the importation of goods by 50,000 Chinese Ecuadorians in the country has been eclipsed by the rapidly expanding sale of Chinese consumer goods to the broader society.[178] The PRC increasingly sells low-end goods (textiles, footwear, toys) to Ecuador. Although the quality of local goods is generally regarded to be higher than that of Chinese wares, the latter are significantly cheaper, making them enormously attractive to the poorer segments of Ecuadorian society.

The entry of Chinese goods into Ecuador also involves an enormous contraband market. According to one account, although China reported selling some $3 billion in goods to Ecuador, Ecuadorian customs only reported receiving $900 million in goods, suggesting that the vast majority of Chinese goods entering Ecuador pass into the informal economy, without being subject to customs duties.[179]

China is an important supplier of consumer products and electronic goods to Ecuador, as it is to many Latin American countries. According to one report, some 81.5 percent of all portable computers entering Ecuador in 2006 came from China, although many were manufactured there by Western companies such as Hewlett-Packard and Dell.[180] In some cases, Chinese consumer products are imported by local manufacturers, who put their own names on the products and certify them for entry into the Ecuadorian market. One example of this is Grupo Terno, which specializes in importing Chinese household appliances, motorcycles, and other goods and selling them in the Ecuadorian market.[181]

Although Ecuador imports toys, textiles, footwear, and other low-end products from the PRC, China also supplies it with an increasing quantity of higher value–added products as well. The Chinese automobile brand QMC is well established in Ecuador,[182] for example, and was featured in the annual auto show in Guayaquil. The show also highlighted a number of new Chinese car brands entering the Ecuadorian market, including Chery, Hefei, Zxalito, Saic, Wuling, and Byd Changhe.[183] China has also sold busses in Ecuador, including thirty-six bought by the transportation company Libertad Peninsular, reported in October 2007.[184]

Unlike the state of affairs in Argentina and Brazil, Chinese contraband and displacement of local producers have created relatively little political backlash in Ecuador. One analyst suggests that this is due, in part, to the relative lack of political organization of small producers and associated laborers in the country.[185]

Infrastructure Products

Ecuador, with its Pacific ports of Manta and Guayaquil, is emerging as a strategic gateway for Chinese access to Brazil and other Latin American markets. Two landmark events in China's commercial relationship with Ecuador were the awarding of the concession to operate and develop the port of Manta to a consortium led by the Chinese firm Hutchison Port Holdings, and a commitment to transform the Manta airport into an international hub linking China to Latin America. With respect to the port of Manta, Hutchison has committed to invest $423 million to enlarge its capabilities, including constructing more offloading cranes at the site, expanding the commercial fishing pier, and dredging the channel to permit operations by larger commercial vessels.[186] Regarding the airport, the Ecuadorian government has agreed to focus the facility on international flights to Asia when the US concession to operate a military facility there ends in 2009.[187] The plans, publicly highlighted by President Correa during his November 2007 visit to China and presented in detail in the 2007–2010 national development plan, include attracting Chinese airlines to establish a presence in

Manta, making direct flights between the airport and China, and possibly granting a Chinese firm the right to operate the airport.[188]

The schemes for the port and the airport are both significant because they have the potential to transform the pattern of commerce in Ecuador, and in Latin America as a whole. Hutchison's development of the port should be understood in the context of the increasing Chinese commerce with Ecuador[189]—a context that includes the construction of a new refinery in Manabí and the possibility that petroleum output from newly opened ITT oil fields would be sent to Manta for refining and subsequent export.[190]

The development of Manta also has a political dimension, insofar as Guayaquil is the seat of Ecuador's traditional commercial elite, which views the current Ecuadorian government of Rafael Correa with suspicion.[191] Over the long term, the development of Manta as a new logistics hub for Asian commerce could help to give rise to a new commercial elite in Ecuador.

Perhaps the most ambitious dimension of the transformation of Manta is the potential role that it would then play as the Pacific anchor of a new interoceanic corridor linking it to the Brazilian city of Belém, on the Atlantic coast.[192] The project, if it goes forward, would create a new link between Pacific ports and Brazilian markets, competing not only with the Panama Canal, but also with other ventures currently in the works, such as interoceanic highways from Arica and Iquique in Chile and from the Peruvian ports of Ilo and Paita.

The significance of the Manta-Manaus-Belém corridor for Ecuador is largely a function of the enormous volume of commerce between China and Brazil. Currently, Brazil not only is one of Latin America's largest purchasers of Chinese goods, but also is responsible for almost 36 percent of Latin America's exports to China.[193] Although a number of interoceanic highway projects are in the works, Brazilian exports to the PRC are currently transported overland to Atlantic ports, from where they are shipped by sea either in a westerly direction through the Panama Canal or in an easterly direction around the Horn of Africa. Virtually all current routes connecting Brazil to the PRC involve transit times of forty or more days.

With the Manta-Manaus-Belém corridor, products would be shipped by river through the Brazilian Amazon, then via smaller rivers to a transfer station in Ecuador,[194] and, from there, overland via a newly improved highway or rail corridor to Manta, where the products would be reloaded on ships in Manta's newly expanded, high-volume port. In a similar fashion, Chinese goods bound for Brazilian markets could enter the port of Manta, then be sent by highway or rail to a river transfer station, and loaded onto barges for shipment to Manaus or all the way to Belém.[195]

To the extent that the Manta-Manaus-Belém corridor would be used instead of current routes, or instead of the alternative interoceanic highways currently in the works, the volume of commerce going through Ecuador would expand by an order of magnitude, with the possibility that an enormous new logistics and service industry would grow up around the currently modest port of Manta. The demand for China-oriented service providers under such a scenario would draw not only on the modest number of Ecuadorian university graduates with such training, but also could leverage nearby Chinese Ecuadorian communities in Guayaquil and Quevido.

Although Latin America has a history of infrastructure projects that are planned but never realized, the Manta-Manaus-Belém corridor has the advantage of a commitment from the leaders of Brazil and Ecuador. During their first summit meeting in April 2006, Ecuador's then–newly elected president Rafael Correa and President Lula of Brazil specifically agreed to proceed with the project.[196] Moreover, the Manta-Manaus-Belém axis has received repeated attention from the Ecuadorian government in its dealings with China, including statements by President Correa while visiting China,[197] and has been incorporated into the 2007–2010 national development plan.[198]

Other Projects Expanding
China's Strategic Presence in Ecuador

Chinese companies are increasingly participating in other sectors of the Ecuadorian economy beyond petroleum and agriculture. In April 2006, for example, investors representing ten Chinese companies expressed interest in a series of hydroelectric developments in the country; this interest included a potential $500 million investment in the 600-megawatt Sopladora-Cardenillo generator,[199] although the job was subsequently awarded to another consortium.[200] Chinese investors were also among a group of bidders for the Toachi-Piliton hydroelectric project in the department of Pichincha,[201] although, again, the $458 million project was ultimately awarded to another firm, Hydrotoapi.[202]

In addition to commercial projects, the PRC carries out a variety of aid and social development projects in Ecuador, as well as programs that support the technical capabilities of the Ecuadorian government. Such undertakings, coordinated through the Ecuadorian Institute for International Cooperation (INECI), include the construction of schools and medical facilities, and a limited number of training programs for Ecuadorian government officials in areas like network administration.[203] During his visit to Ecuador in March 2007, for example, Chinese Politburo member Li Changchun signed accords that included the construction of a hospital in the city of Poyo, the rehabilitation of a hospital in Quito, and the provision of medical supplies.[204] While the scale of such aid is relatively limited, the funds play a valuable role in building goodwill toward China in Ecuadorian society and generating tangible results for the government of Rafael Correa.

Government and Business Infrastructures

Ecuador has largely unrealized potential to develop government and business infrastructures to support commerce with Asia. The Ministry of Foreign Relations represents Ecuador in China through its embassy in Beijing, whose capabilities are complemented by those of the Corporation for the Promotion of Exports (CORPEI),[205] though the resources available to help Ecuadorian businesses promote exports and build commercial relationships in China remain limited.

In the private sector, Ecuador has a modest but growing capacity for doing business with the PRC. This facility is spearheaded by the relatively effective Ecuador-China Chamber of Commerce, which provides leadership and organization for a range of China-oriented activities, from leading delegations to trade fairs in China, to coordinating between business and state delegations during official visits (such as President Correa's trip to China in November 2007).[206] The chamber is also active in building the administrative infrastructure to facilitate commercial interactions with the PRC. In November 2005, for example, the organization signed an agreement with its Chinese counterpart, CCPIT, creating a standard framework in which resolution of disputes arising out of commercial agreements between Chinese and Ecuadorian companies may be referred to a quasi-private Ecuadorian body tied to the Chamber of Commerce, the Center of Arbitration and Mediation.[207]

Despite the activities of the Ecuador-China Chamber of Commerce, the principal commercial infrastructure possessing a familiarity with Chinese culture, language, and business practices remains within the Chinese Ecuadorian community itself. While Chinese Ecuadorian businesses such as Grupo Wong, Sol de Oriente, and the myriad of *chifas* and Chinese-owned shops make important contributions to the Ecuadorian economy, the ties that these businesses have to the PRC itself are few to none.

Finally, another important but largely underdeveloped area for Sino-Ecuadorian commerce is the banking sector. Although China and Ecuador have very few banking connections, in 2006, investors from the Chinese Sampo Group consortium indicated interest in investing in the Ecuadorian finance sector and, potentially, in other sectors.[208]

Intellectual Infrastructure

Despite a relatively strong and well-organized Chinese Ecuadorian community, the country's intellectual infrastructure to support ties with China is relatively underdeveloped.

The Chinese Ecuadorian community, including such organizations as the Ecuador-China Chamber of Commerce and the China-Ecuador Society, contributes to a greater understanding of China and Chinese culture within the country.[209] However, relatively few programs in Ecuador's universities or other institutes focus on Chinese language or culture. As an example, Ecuador's FLACSO affiliate still does not have a Chinese-language program.[210] Similarly, Escuela Superior Politécnica del Litoral (ESPOL), in Guayaquil, one of Ecuador's leading technical universities, has a single Mandarin program in its Center for Foreign Language Studies, which, as of the summer of 2007, had a total enrollment of six students.[211] As of late 2008, however, ESPOL was in the process of establishing a new China studies program. Arguably, the leading program for Mandarin language and China studies in Ecuador is the private Universidad de San Francisco. In 2006, the university created a Department of Oriental Studies, with a master's degree in Chinese culture beginning in the fall semester of 2007.[212] Beyond these universities, a handful of specialized institutions also provide Chinese-language training. In Guayaquil, for example, Colegio Ecuatoriano-Chino, a well-known private secondary school, offers curricula on Chinese culture and language, with coordination with and support from the Chinese Ecuadorian community.[213] The country is also slowly expanding its pool of people with Chinese cultural and linguistic knowledge through coordination with the Chinese government. Through INECI and the Ecuadorian Institute for Educational Credit and Scholarships, the Chinese government has provided a number of scholarships to Ecuadorians to study Mandarin and other skills in the PRC.[214]

Political and Military Relations

Although political and military relations between Ecuador and China have historically been limited, the orientation of Ecuador's president Rafael Correa has facilitated the expansion of ties with the PRC in all domains, as an alternative to Ecuador's traditional bonds with the United States. President Correa made a high-profile state visit to Beijing in November 2007, signing fourteen bilateral accords and proposing to make Ecuador China's point of entry to Latin America.[215] The visit followed a lower-level but important trip to Ecuador by Chinese Politburo member Li Changchun in March 2007.[216] Notably, however, Ecuador was not one of the countries on the agenda of Chinese president Hu Jintao when he traveled to Latin America in November 2008 in conjunction with the APEC Leader's Summit forum in Lima, Peru.

In the military realm, ties between Ecuador and China have, until recently, been fairly circumscribed. In March 2006, Minister of Defense Oswaldo Jarrin traveled to Beijing to meet with his Chinese counterpart, Cao Gangchuan.[217] Previously, in December 2004, the chairman of the Joint Chiefs of Staff of the Ecuadorian armed forces had traveled to Beijing to meet with Liang Guanglie, chief of staff of the PLA.[218]

The Ecuadorian military has also begun to exchange officers with their

Chinese complements; this exchange includes participation in various professional military education programs. In the material realm, in 2006, China provided two transport aircraft to the Ecuadorian military,[219] in addition to selling it nonlethal goods such as military uniforms.[220]

■ Bolivia

The prospect of a significant expansion of Bolivia's political and commercial relationships with China was highlighted by Evo Morales's visit to China as president-elect in January 2006, and continued with the December 2007 visit to China by Bolivian foreign minister David Choquehuanca.[221] Although the Morales administration has given Bolivia's relationship with China a new flavor of ideological alliance, Bolivian interest in Chinese investment has also been a theme for prior administrations, including those of Gonzalo Sanchez de Lozada, Carlos Mesa Gisbert, and Eduardo Rodriguez Veltze. Most of the PRC investment in Bolivia has been in primary-product sectors, although Chinese companies have made advances in other sectors, such as telecommunications.[222]

Although Chinese companies, including Shengli Oil, Huanji, and the logistics firm Shandong Luneng, expressed an interest in investing in Bolivia during the administrations of Carlos Mesa and Eduardo Rodriguez, uncertainty over the political stability and the legal framework of the country has prevented a number of projects from going forward.[223] Bolivia received a mere $488 million in foreign investment in 2005; of this, only $46,000 was from the PRC.[224] Sources of concern include the management of the petroleum sector's nationalization and the management of the awarding of the El Mutún iron concession. These worries were further compounded by uncertainty during the political instability associated with Bolivia's writing of a new constitution, and later, seeking ratification of the new document, including initiatives by the resource-rich departments of the Media Luna to secure greater independence and the possibility that they could secede from the country.

While China's economic, political, and military relationships with Bolivia have expanded significantly during the regime of Bolivian president Evo Morales, it is important to point out that the Chinese have been very cautious in taking the relationship forward. Although, as noted previously, the PRC welcomes opportunities to strengthen sources of resistance to US hegemony in the region, it is also aware that this policy could backfire if managed poorly. Bolivia is in a period of political unrest—with a turbulent Constituent Assembly and regional demands for autonomy—that could give rise to civil war, leaving the PRC tied to a radicalized and discredited regime.[225]

Historical Context

The PRC has not traditionally had a close relationship with governments in La Paz. From 1964 until 1985, Bolivia was ruled by a series of conservative military governments that, by contrast to their counterparts in Argentina and Chile, chose not to recognize the revolutionary communist regime in China. In 1985, Bolivia underwent a process that produced democratic elections and returned the country to civilian rule. On July 9, 1985, just days before elections were held, the military leadership of the country signed a communiqué establishing diplomatic relations with the PRC.

The first executive-level visit between the two nations occurred in May 1992, seven years after the establishment of diplomatic relations, when Bolivian president Jaime Paz Zamora traveled to the PRC for a state visit, which included a meeting with Chinese president Yang Shangkun. Five years later, in March 1997, Bolivian president Gonzalo Sanchez de Lozada also visited China, meeting with Chinese president Jiang Zemin.

Despite a diplomatic history in which Bolivia was one of the last countries on the continent to recognize the PRC, the orientation of Evo Morales's government has been impacted positively by the history of the Chinese revolution. Morales, a leftist activist who grew up in a world in which the PRC was a revisionist power broadcasting revolutionary messages in Quechua to the Andean highlands, has expressed a sense of affinity with Chinese revolutionary leaders such as Mao Zedong.[226] This relationship has continued in recent years as well, with modest yet symbolically important aid and technical assistance to rural areas of the country.[227]

The Chinese Community in Bolivia

The Chinese community in Bolivia is very small, with an estimated 12,000 people of some Chinese ancestry living in the country.[228] Zhang Tuo, Chinese ambassador to Venezuela and a former Chinese senior diplomat in Bolivia, estimates that the greatest concentration of ethnic Chinese in the country is found in Santa Cruz, with approximately 1,500 people of Chinese origin; followed by La Paz, with no more than 100 ethnic Chinese; and, after it, other major cities, each with no more than 10 or 20 Chinese Bolivian citizens.[229] The use of Bolivia by Chinese human-smuggling networks (highlighted by the recent high-profile case of the group Red Dragon)[230] may have expanded this community somewhat, yet the total numbers remain small.

China's Interest in Bolivian Petroleum

Chinese companies have shown some interest in the Bolivian hydrocarbons sector, although the politically charged nature of the gas export issue, in combination with significant changes in the sector, cast doubts as to whether Bolivia is in a position to supply gas reliably to the PRC in the foreseeable future.

During the administrations of Bolivian presidents Carlos Mesa (October 2003–June 2005) and Eduardo Rodriguez Veltze (June 2005–January 2006), Chinese petrochemical companies, including Shengli Oil and Huanji, expressed an interest in a number of natural gas–related projects in Bolivia. In March 2004, Shengli, an affiliate of Sinopec, announced plans to form a partnership with the then–partially privatized Bolivian petroleum organization Yacimientos Petrolíferos Fiscales Bolivianos (YPFB) to explore jointly for petroleum in the north of the country.[231] Later the same year, Shengli announced that it was considering an investment in the Bolivian hydrocarbons sector that could total $1.5 billion over ten years.[232] In October 2004, as a follow-up, fourteen executives from Shengli traveled to Bolivia for an extended stay to identify and evaluate possible oil projects, bringing with them a preliminary investment of $15 million as a demonstration of commitment.[233] As an illustration of the uncertainty that has come to prevail in the sector, however, there was apparently some confusion as to whether the representatives of Shengli who made investment commitments in late 2004 were actually part of the Shengli Oil affiliated with Sinopec.[234]

In addition to Shengli's interest in a possible project, in 2005, the Chinese firm Huanji proposed a $600 million investment project to construct a plant in Bolivia that would liquefy natural gas[235]—a capability that Bolivia does not currently have, but that would be critical for the transport of gas to overseas destinations.

Despite the initiatives by Shengli and Huanji, overt indications of China's interest in the sector virtually disappeared with the assumption of the presidency by Evo Morales and the nationalization of the hydrocarbons sector, publicly initiated in May 2006. As Luisa Palacios argues, this was due to Bolivia's political instability, "which has postponed investments in the country not only by the Chinese, but also by other international oil companies."[236] In addition to casting doubts on the legal framework within which Chinese investors in Bolivia would be operating, the nationalization was implemented badly, with significant delays and demands for the resignation of the leadership of both the national petroleum company[237] and the hydrocarbons minister.[238] Indeed, the final series of renegotiated contracts had to be resubmitted to the Bolivian Congress multiple times after errors came to light.[239] To many players in the sector, such events made it apparent that the Bolivian government and the state hydrocarbons firm, YPFB, did not yet have the capacity to enter into sustainable, detailed contracts or otherwise manage the oil sector in a manner that gave confidence to investors.

Such uncertainty may have given companies such as Shengli and Huanji pause in pressing ahead with projects, even though corporate representatives of the PRC have conducted business in other politically volatile states.

China's interest in the sector has been further undercut by mixed signals from Bolivia with respect to whether it will make its gas available for export at all. The 2003 plan by the Bolivian government of Gonzalo Sanchez de Lozada to send Bolivian gas to a refinery to be built in Arica, Chile, proved politically unacceptable and led to violent protests that ultimately brought down the government.[240] Sanchez de Lozada was succeeded in office by his vice president, Carlos Mesa, who won popular support for a vaguely worded referendum to use Bolivian gas as a diplomatic weapon to force Chile to negotiate a Bolivian access to the sea; however, Mesa was forced to resign before such a policy could be pursued in earnest. The man who replaced him—after two others in line for succession turned down the job—Supreme Court head Eduardo Rodriguez Veltze, claimed that he lacked the political authority to address the gas export issue, and avoided taking action on it. Although the current Morales government has nationalized the gas industry, and although options exist for the export of Bolivian gas via Peru[241] as well as Chile,[242] doubts exist as to whether Bolivia will be able to meet its expanding domestic gas demand and existing export commitments, let alone increase gas exports to other parties. Domestic demand for Bolivian gas will increase as the processing facility at the new Bolivian mineral field at El Mutún comes online. Moreover, as noted above, preliminary indications suggest that Bolivia may not be able to meet its commitments to Brazil and Argentina for expanded exports of its gas.[243]

Despite the nervousness of Chinese investors in the Bolivian hydrocarbons industry, by the end of 2008 the political situation in Bolivia had begun to stabilize, and Chinese companies were cautiously expanding their activities in the country. In June 2008, for example, the Chinese company Eastern Petrogas signed an agreement to do a study of reserves in the country.[244] In November 2008, the Bolivian national petroleum company, YPFB, took an even bigger step, indicating that it would enter into a strategic alliance with China's National Petroleum Company in the first part of 2009.[245]

In addition to such direct ties, Venezuela's partnership with Bolivia in the petroleum sector may help to bring the Chinese into the country on a contract basis, paid for by Venezuelan resources. Venezuela has committed to assist Bolivia with the construction of a $600 million liquid natural gas (LNG) separation plant on Bolivia's border with Argentina, as well as a $480 million petrochemical plant to make plastics, medicines, and fertilizers. In both cases, Venezuela arguably lacks the human resources to do the project, and, if either goes forward, industry experts have suggested that experienced workers could be brought in from the PRC to provide assistance.

Bolivia is also benefiting indirectly from Chinese equipment, through the former's alliance with Venezuela. In July 2008, for example, the Venezuelan government provided one of the drilling rigs that it had obtained from China to the Bolivian national oil company, YPFB, for use in the vicinity of Santa Cruz.[246]

China's Interest in Bolivian Mining

In the short term, the PRC is arguably more interested in Bolivian minerals than in the country's gas and oil. The focus of much recent activity in the mineral sector has been the development of the iron deposits of El Mutún. El Mutún, in the Bolivian department of Santa Cruz, is believed to contain the largest deposits of iron in South America—making Brazilian-based firms such as CVRD nervous because of the potential of the Bolivian field to overshadow their own deposits.[247]

The PRC first expressed an interest in El Mutún in 1997, although it took the Bolivian government almost ten years to conduct a public auction and award a contract for the development of the area. On the Chinese side, the firm Shandong Luneng participated in initial selection rounds as one of the prequalified bidders.[248] At the same time, and with an eye to the logistics of exploiting El Mutún, Shandong Luneng was talking with the Peruvian government concerning a proposed $10 billion investment to expand and modernize the Peruvian port of Tacna[249] and to construct highway and rail links from Tacna through La Paz to El Mutún.[250] Had Shandong Luneng been awarded the El Mutún concession, the proposed investment in Peru would have enabled the PRC to achieve a secure supply chain: extracting iron from El Mutún, transporting it via rail to Tacna, and processing it there for export to China.[251]

The concession to exploit 50 percent of El Mutún was eventually made to China's competitor, the Indian firm Jindal, which promised to invest some $2.5 billion over eight years in the development of the field.[252] If the loss to Jindal soured China's enthusiasm for participation in the Bolivian mining industry, the difficulties that Jindal later experienced in dealing with the government must also have given pause to the PRC and other countries interested in Bolivia's mining sector. Post-award negotiations between the Bolivian government and Jindal quickly became bogged down over details that had been left ambiguous, such as the specific territory that was to be developed by Jindal and the price at which Bolivian gas was to be supplied to the operation for different processes.[253] Moreover, during the dispute with Jindal, Bolivian government officials made continual references to other firms interested in the concession—insinuating that the deal could be reversed. To add insult to injury, in the middle of the dispute with Jindal, the Bolivian government publicly indicated that the other half of El Mutún would be developed through a new partnership with the Venezuelan government[254] (this commitment was later retracted).[255] As of 2008, Bolivia and China were still exploring the possibility of granting the remaining half of El Mutún to a Chinese firm.[256]

China's interest in the Bolivian mining sector extends to other sites as well. In February 2006, a private Chinese company, Mines Company, indicated its intention to invest in Bolivia to develop the Socavones mines in Huanuni, the Chorolque mine in Oruro, and TelaMayu mine in Potosí.[257] In July 2006, the PRC further expressed interest in the San José mine in Oruro, offering to the Bolivian state mining organization Coimbol to do a free feasibility study on the possibility of resuming operations at the mine to extract lead, silver, antimony, and tin.[258]

In addition to Chinese interest in specific mines in Bolivia, the PRC is a purchaser of the output of the Bolivian mining sector, and therefore has a stake in the country's political situation and the functioning of its mines. As an example, the majority of the output of the Huanuni mine—which was the site of significant labor unrest in October 2006—is destined for the PRC.[259]

China's Interest in Other Bolivian Goods

Aside from mining industry products and hydrocarbons, the Bolivian goods that account for the majority of the nation's exports to the PRC in recent years are wood, leather, and scrap metal.[260] A 2005 study by the Bolivian Institute of Foreign Trade concluded that, in addition to the other two sectors, Bolivia's growing commerce with China was likely to continue to favor these three industries.[261] Other Bolivian products with export potential in the near term include soy[262] and sunflower products,[263] as well as Bolivian beef, noted for its distinct flavor—although export markets and associated infrastructures have not yet been developed for these items.

Inspired by the potential to export a range of products to the PRC, in 2004, representatives from the Bolivian and Chinese governments held preliminary meetings to explore the possibility of a free-trade agreement.[264] Little progress has occurred on this front, however,[265] due to the current process of political change in Bolivia. Moreover, Bolivian exports to the PRC in general remain relatively stagnant compared to the increases by other countries in the region. As of 2006, the PRC remained in fifteenth place among Bolivia's export partners.[266]

Bolivia as a Market for Chinese Goods

According to statistics from the World Bank, Bolivia's per capita annual income in 2006 was $1,100, making it the poorest country in South America.[267] Although the nation's poverty limits its potential as a market for Chinese goods, the relatively large informal market in Bolivia and its appetite for inexpensive goods have nonetheless created important opportunities for Chinese vendors on the low end of the product spectrum.

The PRC presence in Bolivia has been particularly strong with respect to Chinese contraband goods in the extensive Bolivian informal sector, where controls against pirated goods are virtually nonexistent. Sources interviewed for this book indicated that the free-trade zones in Corumbá, Brazil, and Iquique, Chile, are significant sources for the entry of Chinese goods into Bolivia. Although it is difficult to estimate the quantity of Chinese contraband goods in the country, the seeming omnipresence of these goods on the streets of cities like Santa Cruz contrasts dramatically with official trade statistics, which indicate that six other countries send more goods to Bolivia than does the PRC.[268]

Bolivia, like other Latin American countries, is an increasingly important market for Chinese cars and motorcycles. Chinese motorcycles have been featured in Expocruz—Santa Cruz's annual international trade fair—as well as other venues. Chinese motorcycles are sold with a line of spare parts compatible with more expensive, established brands such as Yamaha and Suzuki, but at a cost less than half that of the Japanese competition.[269] Chinese consumer electronics brands, such as Haier, are similarly commonplace in the retail sector in the larger cities.[270]

In the telecommunications sector, as well, Chinese companies are competing aggressively to expand their position in Bolivia. The firm Huawei, with an office in La Paz,[271] is an important supplier of antennas, high-frequency (HF) equipment, and related services. It was also the winner of an important contract, whose value is estimated at $25–40 million, for the Next-Generation Network (NGN) wireless network modernization project in Santa Cruz. In addition, Huawei is expected to be one of the strongest competitors to build Bolivia's proposed new Wymax network. The Chinese firm ZTE Telecom also has a significant presence in the country as a supplier of ADCL routers to Cooperativa de Telecomunicaciones Santa Cruz (COTAS).[272]

Infrastructure Projects

Over the long term, the ability to realize the potential of Sino-Bolivian commerce will depend heavily on Bolivia's ability to complete its portion of infrastructure projects that will provide the country with more economical access to Pacific ports. As noted previously, a number of railway projects and highway improvements are under way, or in the planning stages, that would connect Bolivia with Pacific ports, such as Tacna or Ilo in Peru, or Arica and Iquique in Chile. The bi-oceanic highway, which received a presidential-level commitment in December 2007,[273] would connect Bolivia to Santos, Brazil, on the Atlantic coast, and to the ports of Arica and Iquique on the Pacific. According to the president of Bolivia's highway administration, the new route would carry some 70 percent of Bolivian exports.[274] Other contemplated infrastructure projects could also play important roles in enabling Chinese commerce with Bolivia. The southern route of the intercoastal highway connecting Peru and Brazil, for example, skirts the Bolivian border in the vicinity of Lake Titicaca, with the potential to link up to the Bolivian highway system at that point, if Bolivia can fund its part of the route. Other connections, such as the previously mentioned highway and rail corridor that would connect the iron fields of El Mutún to the Peruvian port of Tacna, also have the potential to energize Bolivian commerce with China.

Although Bolivia's lack of access to the sea has been considered a commercial impediment, its position on the continent of South America is also a potential asset. Once the Andes Mountains are crossed, for example, the Bolivian city of Santa Cruz occupies a central location, with relatively flat terrain connecting the city to important ports in both Brazil and Argentina. Given this location, and the ability of the country to overcome its endemic political instability, the city that already has the best-developed commercial infrastructure in the country could develop into a new transportation and distribution hub for the emerging Asian trade.

Although the Chinese stand to be more beneficiaries than investors with respect to Bolivia's transportation infrastructure, Chinese technicians may play a role in a number of important projects in Bolivia's power infrastructure. As one indication of this, in August 2007, the Venezuelan and Bolivian governments signed an agreement for the construction of a gas-fired thermoelectric plant in the Chapare region of Bolivia.[275] In the 2008 Bolivian national investment plan, the project was budgeted to receive $800 million in investment.[276] According to persons knowledgeable in the industry, one possibility for the project is that Venezuela would bring in Chinese technicians and workers to support the project, in order to compensate for weaknesses in Venezuelan resources and technical capabilities.

Government and Business Infrastructures

Although considerable interest exists on both the Chinese and Bolivian sides to expand commercial relations, the infrastructures necessary at all levels are still relatively lacking.

At the government level, sources interviewed off the record for this book in 2007 indicated, for example, that the Bolivian embassy in Beijing has neither the manpower nor the organization to help Bolivian firms to make connections, set up operations, or conduct transactions in China. Similarly, Bolivia lags behind other Latin American governments in establishing representative offices in important Chinese commercial centers, such as Shanghai.

Although Bolivia, like other Latin American countries, has an official trade promotion organization, Centro de Promoción Bolivia (CEPROBOL), the organization reportedly has focused on promoting exports to other countries of Latin America, the United States, and the European Union, rather than to Asia. On its Web site, none of the contacts listed on the entity's "International Organizations" page are Asian or have significant ties to Asia.[277] Similarly, although CEPROBOL provides country profiles for six export destinations, none of them are Asian.[278] In its calendar, the organization listed an event in Beijing that had occurred the previous month, but listed no upcoming events in Asia.[279]

Bolivia has very little private-sector infrastructure, either, for expanding commerce with the PRC. Although the logical private-sector organization to support the development of such ties is the Bolivian Institute of Foreign Commerce (IBCE), the organization currently does not devote significant resources to Asia.[280] Similarly, at the time that this was written, the Camara de Industria, Comercio, Servicios y Turismo de Santa Cruz (CAINCO), the chamber of commerce of Santa Cruz, Bolivia's most prosperous city, had begun to develop contacts in China—sending an exploratory delegation to the fall 2007 Canton trade fair[281] and including Chinese businesses in local events, like its September 2008 business roundtable[282]—although such activities remained limited.

For Bolivia, part of the problem is a lack of individual companies with capability or experience in doing business with China. In an informal survey of the economically prosperous eastern region of the country, only one organization could be found performing this function: a combination import-export firm and chamber of commerce called CHIMBOL. However, a small but promising number of Chinese companies are establishing contacts in Bolivia. In the 2007 version of the Expocruz trade fair, the most significant internationally oriented commercial event in the country, sixteen Chinese entities were registered to promote their products,[283] and the number continues to expand.[284]

Effectively, by November 2008 no financial infrastructure was in place to facilitate Bolivian businesses in China or Chinese businesses in Bolivia. There were, for example, no Bolivian banks with representative offices or similar capabilities in China. Indeed, the only bank in the east of the country with international reach, Banco Santa Cruz, lost this reach when its former parent bank, Banco Santander, sold it to a local firm, Banco Mercantil.[285]

Intellectual Infrastructure

One of the principal limitations on the growth of relationships at the business and popular levels continues to be the lack of familiarity in Bolivia with the Chinese language and culture. In general, there are very few business-oriented programs in Bolivian universities focused on China. Although Universidad Privado de Santa Cruz offers a master's degree in international business, it does not yet offer extensive, practical courses or materials on doing business with China.

A similar situation exists in the domain of language training. In late 2007, for example, Universidad Gabriel René Moreno in Santa Cruz, one of the most prestigious public universities in the country, was conducting preliminary discussions with China for setting up a Confucius Institute,[286] although by the beginning of 2009 nothing had come of the initiative.

At the same time, despite a limited offering in the domain of Chinese language or China studies, Bolivia is host to a number of organizations oriented toward promoting commercial and cultural ties with China, such as the Bolivian Association for Friendship with China, of La Paz, and the Association of China-Bolivia Friendship, in Santa Cruz.[287]

Political and Military Relations

While Bolivian-Chinese commercial relations have been comparatively limited, relations between the two countries in the political and military spheres are making important advances.

In the political realm, relations have been bolstered by the ideological affinity that Bolivia's leader, Evo Morales, feels toward China as a historically revisionist power and champion of the rights of third-world interests.[288] The two countries took an important step to strengthen these relations in December 2007, when Bolivian foreign minister David Choquehuanca traveled to the PRC for a visit that included a Bolivian proposal to form an "alliance" with China,[289] and that culminated in the signing of an agreement for expanded technical and economic cooperation between the two countries.[290]

The PRC has also worked to bolster its benevolent image through various types of assistance. Much of this, ironically, has taken the form of gifts of vehicles and associated equipment. In February 2005, the PRC donated 120 Lifan motorcycles to the Bolivian police;[291] in January 2006, it gave $4 million for the construction of a new building for the Ministry of Housing.[292] In November 2006, the PRC provided $2.6 million in goods (including computers and ambulances) and credits for the supply of technical cooperation and materials.[293] In October 2006, the PRC made a larger contribution to Bolivia, including 200 tractors to support agricultural development,[294] and, in the same month, made a commitment to donate various pieces of heavy equipment for the construction of a new highway between La Paz and Cochabamba.[295] In December 2007, China presented Bolivian police forces with a modest gift that included 30 bicycles, 20 televisions, and 2 motorcycles.[296]

In the military domain, the Sino-Bolivian relationship has expanded notably in recent years. In 1995–1996, the PRC first established a modest officer exchange between Escuela de Altos Estudios Nacionales and its counterpart in China. The initial relationship included a number of exchange programs varying in duration from six months to two years. Between 1987 and 1996, as well, China donated some 10,000 Chinese-made AK-47 assault rifles to the Bolivian military.[297]

Overall, however, the military-to-military relationship between the two countries remained relatively limited, by comparison to the US-Bolivia military relationship, until the election of Evo Morales in January 2006, which represented a landmark change in the ideological orientation of the country. The increasing isolation of the Bolivian military leadership and the new ideological orientation of the Morales government were reinforced by a purge of the country's military leadership over a politically controversial transfer of obsolete Chinese anti-aircraft munitions to the United States.[298]

The replacement of most of the senior Bolivian military leadership, whose career experience and training had generally given them a favorable orientation toward the United States, set the stage for a progressive ideological reorientation of the military, accompanied by a steady deepening of its relationship with the PRC. In August 2006, Bolivian defense minister Walker San Miguel traveled to the PRC to meet with his Chinese counterpart, Cao Gangchuan.[299] Four months later, the PRC announced a modest but symbolically important gift of military equipment, including twenty-five–person assault craft, infantry and artillery munitions, night vision goggles, and Kevlar helmets.[300] In March 2007, Bolivia publicized a more significant project: the leasing of two MA-60 military cargo and passenger aircraft from the PRC, as part of a larger deal that included the acquisition of other transport aircraft from Venezuela.[301] The Chinese MA-60 aircraft were paid for by a $38.3 million loan from the PRC[302] and delivered in February 2008. In April 2007, the joint commander of the Bolivian armed forces, Wilfredo Vargas, traveled to China, meeting with Cao Gangchuan, China's defense minister, and committing to still broader military exchanges between the two countries.[303] In August of the same year, China donated forty-three transport vehicles to the Bolivian military—thirty-four trucks and five busses from the company First Automobile Works (FAW), three Toyota Land Cruiser SUVs, and a tow truck.[304]

■ Peru

Although Peru is not recognized as a strategic partner by the PRC, and although Mexico, Brazil, Chile, and Argentina surpass Peru in terms of volume of bilateral trade with China,[305] Peru possesses a combination of attributes that position it to play a key role in China's future relationship with Latin America. Peru, like Bolivia and Brazil, has a mining sector of interest to the PRC. Like Venezuela, Bolivia, Colombia, and Ecuador, it has both natural gas and oil in which Chinese firms have shown an interest. Like Chile, Peru has a well-developed fishing industry, which already supplies a significant quantity of the PRC's imports from this sector, as well as a growing export-oriented agricultural industry. Like Ecuador, Colombia, and Chile, Peru's location and established Pacific ports give it a strategic geographic position vis-à-vis current and potential overland routes connecting it to the much larger markets and primary-product sources of Brazil.

Although the Peruvian presidential elections of 2006 raised the possibility that the nation would elect a populist government along the lines of Venezuela, Ecuador, and Bolivia, the triumph of Alan Garcia reaffirmed the market orientation of the country. His election laid the groundwork for Peru to develop a commercially oriented relationship with the PRC similiar to that pursued by Chile, rather than the more ideologically charged, state-centered relationships that Venezuela, Ecuador, and Bolivia have with China.

In 2007, China surpassed the United States to become Peru's largest commercial partner.[306] By contrast to the situation in other Andean nations, such as Ecuador and Colombia, this expanding relationship has generated a continuing trade surplus for Peru with respect to China. In 2006, to take one statistic, China exported $1.01 billion in goods to Peru, while importing $2.91 billion in goods,[307] contributing to the sense that Peru's expanding business relationship with the PRC is beneficial for Peru.[308]

The positive and expanding relationship between the two countries was highlighted during the APEC summit, in Lima in November 2008. The summit included the signing of a free-trade agreement between China and Peru, the second such agreement to be signed by the two countries.[309]

Historical Context

Peru established diplomatic relations with the PRC in November 1971, making it the second nation in South America to do so, following recognition of China by the Chilean government of Salvador Allende in December 1970.

Although Peru, like other Latin American nations, had relatively limited trade ties with the PRC through the end of the 1990s, the nation was a leader among the states of South America with respect to its diplomatic interactions with China during this period. Peruvian president Alberto Fujimori made the PRC an important focus of his foreign policy, visiting China four times between 1991 and 1995.[310] The first visit by a Chinese leader to Peru, however, did not occur for almost twenty-four years after diplomatic recognition, with the groundbreaking trip by Chinese premier Li Peng to Peru in 1995.[311] APEC, of which Peru is one of two Latin American members, also has been an important platform for interactions involving the Chinese leadership. In November 1998 and September 1999, for example, President Fujimori met with Chinese president Jiang Zemin in successive APEC forums. APEC similarly served as the basis for meetings between President Jiang and the new Peruvian president, Alejandro Toledo, in October 2001 and October 2002.

The Chinese Community in Peru

Peru has the second-largest Chinese community in Latin America, behind Brazil, as well as a substantial number of citizens of Japanese and other Asian ancestry. Although estimates of the size of the Chinese community in Peru vary widely, one report approximates that up to 4.2 million Peruvians, or 15 percent of the population, have some Chinese lineage.[312]

The first significant group of Chinese in Peru was brought to the region in the nineteenth century to work in its sugar plantations, as well as in the guano industry and other agricultural areas.[313] Indeed, many of the earliest Chinese immigrants arriving in other countries of the region, such as Ecuador and Chile, had first come to Peru.

The first Chinese immigrants to Peru were recorded in 1849. By 1874, the flow from China to Peru was sufficient to give rise to a treaty of "commerce, friendship, and navigation" between the two countries.[314] The 1912 nationalist revolution in China led to another major wave of Chinese immigration to Peru, with a third wave following the communist revolution of 1949.

As occurred in other Latin American countries, the Chinese community in Peru was subject to anti-immigrant sentiment and periodic anti-immigrant policies, including a 1909 campaign that led to the expulsion of more than 1,000 ethnic Chinese from the country.[315] Other unfortunate events of this period included the tearing down of the Lobatón house, a well-known Chinese landmark in Lima, as well as the "clearing out" of the Otaysa zone, another symbol of the Chinese presence in the city.[316]

Despite a troubled history, the Chinese community in Peru has achieved great commercial success and prosperity.[317] Today, most Chinese Peruvians continue to be concentrated in the capital city, Lima, although there is also a sizable Chinese population in the northeast jungle region, near the city of Iquitos.[318] One sign of the Chinese presence in many cities is the *chifa;* these restaurants are well-known throughout the country, with some 4,500 in the capital city alone, representing a blend of Chinese and local influences.[319]

China's Interest in Peruvian Petroleum

Peru produces modest amounts of oil and natural gas, which are of direct and indirect interest to the Chinese. The nation's oil production is concentrated in the Amazon basin in the northeast of the country; oil was also discovered in the northwest, off the coast, in June 2005.[320] The Amazon basin of northeastern Peru includes two of the largest and most productive oil fields, Block 1A-B and Block 8, which together account for 65 percent of the country's current petroleum output;[321] both are owned by the Argentine firm PlusPetrol Norte. The firm China National Offshore Drilling Corporation (CNODC) has a 45 percent stake in PlusPetrol Norte, giving China another significant stake in Peru's oil-production operations. In addition, CNPC signed contracts to develop oil fields in the Amazon jungle region in 2005,[322] in addition to the mature Talara oil fields that its subsidiary Sapet operates near Talara, on the northwest coast of Peru.[323]

Although Peruvian petroleum production has generally been in a state of protracted decline,[324] important new discoveries were made in 2006 and 2007 in areas operated by the Chinese; included among these discoveries, Sapet announced, was petroleum in areas of the Amazon.[325]

Peru is also becoming a net exporter of natural gas through the development of major new fields known as Camisea, in the jungle region in eastern Peru.[326] Both the Chinese company Sapet and PlusPetrol Norte, which is 45 percent owned by CNPC, have been awarded licenses to explore in the south, where Camisea gas has been found.[327] Nonetheless, Peru's gas reserves are modest compared to those of Venezuela, Bolivia, and Ecuador;[328] additionally, to date, Peruvian gas from Camisea has been destined for export to Mexico.[329]

China's Interest in Peruvian Mining

Peru's mining industry is not only the source of significant exports to the PRC, but also one of the areas in which China is most actively engaged in acquiring Latin American assets. The abundant mineral wealth possessed by Peru, and the availability of Pacific coast ports to export those minerals, are natural complements to China's need for metals and minerals as factor inputs in manufactured goods, as well as for building new plants and producing new equipment in China.

The flagship operation of the Chinese presence in Peru's mining sector is the Shougang Hierro Peru, which owns and operates a key mine in the department of Ica. The mine is Peru's largest producer of iron,[330] with 70 percent of the mine's product exported, principally to China and other Asian destinations.[331]

In addition to symbolizing China's interest in Peru's metals and minerals, Shougang demonstrates the potential of the Chinese presence in Latin America to generate controversy and social unrest. Since purchasing Hierro Peru in 1993, Shougang has been mired in a series of disputes with both the Peruvian government and the miners. The Peruvian government has complained that Shougang has repeatedly violated environmental laws[332] and failed to fulfill promised investment commitments in the mine and in the surrounding community.[333] The mineworkers, for their part, have staged an average of one to two strikes per year,[334] including four over the course of 2006.[335] During one strike, in August 2006, an outbreak of violence between 600 striking workers and authorities left 10 injured and 3 workers detained by police.[336]

Despite the difficulties experienced by Shougang, Chinese companies are aggressively expanding their presence in the Peruvian mining sector. In September 2007, a mission from the PRC traveled to Peru to meet with personnel from the Peruvian Ministry of Energy and Mines, indicating that the PRC wanted to move beyond the problems of Shougang and that many Chinese companies were interested in investing in the sector.[337] Within months of the meeting, specific deals began to emerge. In April 2007, the Chinese Zijin Mining Group purchased a controlling stake in the English mining company Monterrico Metals, which operates the Rio Blanco copper mine in Piura; Zijin also made a $44 million offer for the nearby copper mine in Michiquillay, believed to contain the fourth-largest copper deposit in Peru.[338] The Chinese parent company, Shoudu Iron and Steel Group, indicated intentions to increase imports of iron ore from Peru from 7 million tons to 20 million tons over the course of the next three years.[339] Under terms of the contract granting Zijin control of Michiquillay, the Chinese firm could invest as much as $700 million.[340] In July 2007, the Aluminum Corporation of China (Chinalco) purchased the Peruvian holdings of the Canadian mining company Peru Copper for $792 million. The project included an initial position in the Toromocho mine, which could become one of the biggest copper mines in the country, with a production of 300,000 tons of copper per year.[341] In May 2008, Chinalco was awarded a $2.15 billion concession contract to operate the Toromocho mine, under-written by China Development Bank,[342] with a contract with the Peruvian government for the operation. In December 2007, China Minmetals and Jiangxi Copper Corporation purchased the Canadian firm Northern Peru Copper for $446 million. The purchase included the firm's operation in Cajamarca, where it was mining copper, gold, silver, and molybdenum.[343] The transactions also highlight how copper exports from Peru to China are becoming relatively more important, even though early PRC involvement in the sector concentrated in iron. Indeed, almost 70 percent of Peruvian mining exports to China in 2007 were copper, according to Peru's National Society of Mining, Petroleum, and Energy (SNMPE).[344]

China's Interest in Peruvian Agriculture

China is a major purchaser of Peruvian fishmeal and has a growing interest in the fishing sector, as well as in other forms of Peruvian agriculture.

Peru has an extensive commercial fishing industry, oriented toward the production of fishmeal, which is used as poultry feed. Indeed, fishmeal is Peru's second most important export, behind copper, though output may vary greatly in any given year as a result of the El Niño weather phenomenon.[345] Peru, together with Chile, supplies 80 percent of all PRC imports of fishmeal.[346] The industry, which has been consolidated considerably in recent years, is also a target of interest for Chinese investors.[347] In June 2006, China Fishery Group purchased Peru's Alexandria Fishing Company for $100 million.[348] Throughout 2006 and 2007, the group continued buying Peruvian assets, including fishing fleets, fishmeal, and canning plants. Purchases by China Fishery Group also include the December 2006 acquisition of Pesquería Isla Blanca, including its fleet of eighteen fishing vessels,[349] the June 2007 acquisition of Peruvian fishmeal producers Pesquería Maru and Pesquería El Pilar,[350] and the acquisition of a fishmeal-processing plant in Chimbote in October of the same year.[351] The strategy, according to public statements by China Fishery Group, is to increase its capabilities for acquiring fish from its own fleet and local sellers, and then to transform the fish rapidly and efficiently into products for export to the PRC.[352]

In addition to the fishmeal industry, other areas of the Peruvian agriculture sector could be sources of significant exports to the PRC in the future, including coffee, asparagus, paprika, and mangoes.[353] In October 2007, an analysis by the Peruvian Association of Exporters (ADEX) for the event Semana de Comercio Exterior 2007, identified 359 agricultural products—representing current export sales of $979 million—whose potential for export to the Chinese market has been largely unrealized.[354] In addition, the Chinese have shown interest in Peruvian wood products.[355]

Peruvian agricultural technology is also of potential interest to the PRC. Peru, like China, has limited terrain suitable for agriculture, and limited supplies of fresh water where such terrain does exist. Despite these limitations, it has achieved remarkable success in expanding agricultural production through a combination of extensive irrigation and genetically engineered crops. As a reflection of such achievements, a Chinese delegation traveled to Ica, in the south of Peru, in 2006 to learn more about Peru's application of advanced agricultural techniques.[356]

Peru as a Market for Chinese Goods

Like other middle-income Latin American countries, Peru is of interest to the PRC as a market for its goods, from textiles, footwear, and toys to cars, appliances, and computers. Although Peru's per capita income of $3,584 in 2007 was lower than that of most of the Southern Cone nations (with the exception of Venezuela), it surpassed those of its peers in the Andes.[357] Moreover, upper-class suburbs of Lima, like San Isidro and Miraflores, as well as smaller urban areas, such as the El Golf suburb of Trujillo, are centers of prosperity that offer important markets for Chinese products. In

2007, according to the PRC Ministry of Commerce, the PRC sold $1.68 billion in products to Peru, representing an expansion of 66 percent over the prior year.[358]

As in other parts of the region, major Peruvian cities, like Lima, have been used as a test market for the introduction of Chinese cars. The products of Chinese automakers Great Wall, Hefei, Geeley,[359] and FAW debuted in the Peruvian market in November 2006, after having been introduced previously in Colombia and Venezuela.[360] In July 2008, the Chinese automakers SAIC and Wuling, along with the US manufacturer General Motors, announced a joint venture to sell cars in Peru.[361] However, the marketing of Chinese automobiles in Peru has not been without public scandal, based in part on the cars' reputation for poor quality. In September 2007, the Peruvian Interior Ministry backed out of a purchase of 698 Chinese autos (brands Geeley and Huanghai) that were to be used as patrol cars.[362] The Chinese had won a competitive bid with the Interior Ministry based on price, but the Peruvian government was forced to delay awarding the contract when the quality of the cars and their suitability for use as police cruisers were publicly questioned.[363]

Peruvian Infrastructure Projects

Over the long term, Peru's strategic value to the PRC goes beyond its role as a market for Chinese goods and beyond the products from its petroleum, mining, agriculture, and fishing sectors: Peru is located in the middle of the Pacific coast of Latin America. Although the Andes mountains have historically been an obstacle to the flow of goods across the continent (and then on to Asia), many of the routes that connect Brazil, Bolivia, and Argentina to Pacific coast ports go through Peru.

Peru's strategic geographic position and its expanding business with the PRC are reflected in the rapidly growing volume of trade going through the port of Callao, near Lima, which currently handles 80 percent of cargo entering or leaving the country. Up to $1.5 billion in new investment may be put into the improvement of Callao to accommodate this escalating traffic. As Peru's president, Alan Garcia, proclaimed, "The Callo port is going to be the biggest, most profitable port on the Pacific Coast. It is going to be a platform for investment and trade."[364]

The geographic significance of Peru is also highlighted by the interoceanic highway project, which Garcia called "the most important public work that is currently being realized in South America."[365] Contracts had been awarded and construction had begun on road segments by November 2008, with an expected completion date between 2009 and 2011.[366] The project includes two parallel routes across the Andes: the northern route, initiated in May 2006 and expected to require $220 million in total investment, begins at the Peruvian port of Paita and goes through Piura to the city of Yurimagua (on the eastern side of the Andes), finally linking up to the Amazon River near Iquitos.[367] The southern route, for which construction was begun in October 2007,[368] starts at the Peruvian port of Ilo,[369] ascends the mountains to Puno, on the western edge of Lake Titicaca, then goes north to Puerto Maldonado (avoiding Bolivian territory),[370] before reaching Brazil at Iñapari.[371]

In addition to these two routes, the infrastructure connecting other Peruvian ports to other parts of the continent has received attention. As an example, in 2006, the Chinese firm Shandong Luneng publicly discussed investing $2 billion to construct a megaport complex in the southern port of Tacna,[372] ultimately linking that city via an improved road and rail route to both Lima, Peru, and La Paz, Bolivia.[373] The project, which was the subject of special legislation passed by the Peruvian Congress authorizing the development of the port,[374] reflected interest by the company in exporting and processing output from the Bolivian iron fields of El Mutún. As with the previously mentioned highway routes, the improved infrastructure from Tacna to El Mutún ultimately could have made it easier to transport Chinese goods to Bolivian and Brazilian markets, as well as served as an export route for a variety of Bolivian and Brazilian products, from iron to soybeans.[375] However, when the concession to operate El Mutún was ultimately awarded to the Indian firm Jindal rather than to Shandong Luneng, interest in developing Tacna and the highway and rail links connecting it to the iron fields evaporated.

Government and Business Infrastructures

Although Peru is not as advanced as Chile in its development of business and regulatory infrastructures to support expanding trade with China, it has been making rapid progress in doing so.

At the governmental level, Peru has a relatively well-developed infrastructure to support commerce with China. The Peruvian Ministry of Foreign Relations has offices in Shanghai and Hong Kong, in addition to its office in Beijing. As a complement, the Peruvian government also promotes exports to the PRC through activities of organizations such as the Commission to Promote Exports and Tourism (PromPeru)[376] and the Peruvian investment-promotion agency ProInversión. In October 2006, for example, ProInversión, in coordination with its Chinese counterpart, CCPIT, established a Peru-China business committee.[377] In addition, ProInversión, cosponsored—with CCPIT and the Peru-China Chamber of Commerce—two China-Peru investment summits, the first in December 2007[378] and the second in October 2008.[379] Overall, experts surveyed for this book suggested that Peru ranks among the top five Latin American governments in terms of the effectiveness of its trade-promotion activities in China.

Peru is seeking to strengthen and expand its growing commodity trade with the PRC by negotiating a China-Peru free-trade agreement similar to that signed between Chile and the PRC in October 2005. The hope is that such a treaty will not only enable Peru to expand its own commerce with the PRC, but also allow it to leverage both its geographic position on the Pacific coast of South America and its substantial Chinese ethnic community, so that it may serve as a gateway between Asia and Latin America.

Like Chile, Peru's development of trade ties with the PRC is assisted by its membership in the Asia-Pacific Economic Cooperation forum, which provides a vehicle for high-level economic and governmental interchanges. The November 2006 APEC summit in Hanoi, Vietnam, for example, afforded the opportunity for a meeting between the Peruvian foreign minister, José Antonio García Belaúnde, and his Chinese colleague, Li Zhaoxing, over increasing economic cooperation and commercial coordination between the two countries.[380] As noted previously, Peru was host to the fifteenth APEC meeting, held in November 2008, in Lima.

In addition to its membership in APEC, Peru currently is seeking to strengthen its trade infrastructure, including a bilateral free-trade accord with the PRC that it signed during the November 2008 APEC summit in Lima, complementing similar agreements that it had previously signed with the United States and with Singapore[381] with plans to negotiate new agreements with South Korea and Japan.[382]

In the private sector, Peru has a reasonably well-developed infrastructure for trading with the PRC, including the Peru-China Chamber of Commerce (CAPECHI).[383] Among its other activities, CAPECHI has led delegations of Peruvian businesspeople to the Canton trade fair and other events, and serves as a clearinghouse for Peruvian businesses with respect to other China-related commercial events and opportunities.[384]

Another important dimension of the infrastructure to support growing ties between Peru and China has been the establishment of banking relationships between the two countries, although those relationships are just beginning to develop. In August 2007, Grupo Interbank became the first Peruvian financial institution to open an office in China, with the hope of providing services to Peruvian companies looking to do business in the country.[385] In November 2008, China Development Bank and Peru's Banco de la Nacion de Perú (BNP) signed a strategic partnership, enabling them to cooperate in matters such as lending to Peruvian local government organizations and microfinance.[386]

Intellectual Infrastructure

The development of a business infrastructure to support commerce between Peru and China is supported by educational institutions with strong and growing offerings in Chinese-language programs and business courses focused on China. One example is Universidad de Lima, one of Peru's two most prestigious universities, in which the business school has created a number of new course offerings in recent years involving commerce with Asia, as well as expanded its Mandarin offerings through the foreign languages department. Universidad de Lima has also created the new Center for Asia-Pacific Studies, to support and capitalize on the selection of Lima to host the 2008 APEC summit.[387] Lima's other leading university, La Pontificia Universidad Católica, also teaches Mandarin, but has no China-oriented programs in its law or economics department.[388]

Peru made a significant step forward in Chinese-language and China studies in December 2007, with the establishment of the country's first Confucius Institute. This occurred through an agreement between the Chinese government and three Peruvian universities: Pontificia Universidad Católica del Perú, Universidad de Piura, and Universidad Católica de Santa María de Arequipa.[389]

In addition to these programs, the intellectual infrastructure of Peru vis-à-vis China benefits from the substantial Chinese community in the country, and this infrastructure will likely improve in coming years because of the expanding interactions with the PRC—including a boost from China's designation of Peru as an official tourist destination,[390] paving the way for a significant increase in visits by Chinese travelers.[391]

Political and Military Relations

Sino-Peruvian political and military relations have been rapidly expanding, even while Peru has sought to maintain its close relationship with the United States.

In the political realm, Peru and the PRC have had regular interactions, including interchanges between officials at the highest levels of government. In January 2005, Chinese vice president Zeng Quinghong visited Peru as part of a five-nation tour of Latin America and the Caribbean. Three months later, then–Peruvian president Alejandro Toledo made a state visit to the PRC, seeking in part to promote commerce between the two nations and Chinese investment in Peru.[392] Following this trip, there were no official presidential-level contacts until September 2006, when Alan Garcia, the newly elected Peruvian president, met with then–PRC vice foreign minister Yang Jiechi in Lima to discuss the expansion of bilateral ties.[393] In April 2007, Chinese Politburo member Li Changchun visited Peru while on a five-nation trip to Latin America; he met with President Garcia[394] as well as with Mercedes Cabanillas, head of the Peruvian legislature.[395] President Garcia made a point of meeting with his Chinese counterpart, Hu Jintao, during the 2007 APEC summit in Sydney, Australia.[396] In March 2008,

Garcia made a state visit to China, in which he strongly affirmed Peru's support for two key political issues of importance to the PRC: nonrecognition of Taiwan and support for China's political control over Tibet.[397] The latter was particularly important, insofar as Garcia's trip to China coincided with unrest in Tibet.[398] Garcia also met with President Hu when the Chinese president came to Lima in November 2008 for the APEC summit.[399]

China's relationship with Peru also includes activities designed to generate goodwill, such as the former's donation of $100,000 in July 2008 to help Peru remove mines from the Condor mountain range forming its border with Ecuador.[400]

In the military realm, China's relationship with Peru has received consistent high-level support and attention. In November 2007, for example, Peruvian defense minister Allan Wagner traveled to the PRC, where he met with his Chinese counterpart, Cao Gangchuan, proclaiming that China was Peru's most important ally in the Asia-Pacific region.[401] The Wagner visit also included the signing of several important military agreements, including the sale by China of some $800,000 in military equipment to Peru, and Peru's granting the PRC access to its military bidding and acquisition system—making it easier for the PRC to supply military goods to Peru in the future.[402]

The Wagner visit was notable for both the positive tone used by the Peruvian defense minister and the achievements of the visit. Nonetheless, visits between Peruvian and Chinese military leaders have been a relatively regular occurrence in recent years. In September 2006, for example, Liang Guanglie, chief of staff of the People's Liberation Army, met in China with Felipe Conde, commanding general of the Peruvian air force, committing to a continued strengthening of exchanges between the two militaries.[403] Earlier, in July 2005, then–Peruvian defense minister Roberto Chiabra met in Beijing with Cao Gangchuan.[404] Before that, in August 2003, Victor Bustamante, chairman of the Joint Chiefs of Staff of the Peruvian armed forces, had met with his PLA counterpart, Liang Guanglie, in Beijing.[405]

▒ Colombia

China's relationship with Colombia has been relatively limited compared to its relationships with Colombia's Andean neighbors. In part, this is because Colombia historically has not been a major exporter of the primary products China seeks. In addition, a long-standing combination of war and criminality has impeded the development of Colombia's Pacific coast infrastructure (and associated commerce with Asia). Moreover, Colombia's close strategic relationship with the United States has hindered, to some extent, its development of a strong relationship with the PRC.

Colombia is currently in a state of transition. The nation is simultaneously moving past a legacy of decades of civil war and violence, reviving its petroleum and export-oriented agricultural sectors, and building new relationships with Asia. From the perspective of the PRC, Colombia is a potential source of minerals, petroleum, and agricultural products, as well as a middle-income nation that offers a market for Chinese goods. Moreover, Colombian Pacific coast ports potentially serve as points of entry for Chinese commerce with the Andean region.

While the political differences between Colombia and its Andean neighbors have derailed some projects of interest to China, such as a long-discussed pipeline for carrying Venezuelan petroleum across Colombia to the Pacific, the pro-US stance of Colombia has not prevented its government from actively seeking Chinese trade and investment.

Historical Context

Colombia was one of the last nations in South America to establish relations with the PRC, granting diplomatic recognition to China in February 1980. The first executive-level visit occurred five years later, when the Chinese premier paid a visit to Colombian president Belisario Betancur. In addition, Colombian president Virgilio Barco, who ruled the country from 1986 to 1990, played an important but indirect role in the growth of Chinese-Colombian ties by focusing on the importance of Colombia's insertion into the economy of the Pacific.[406]

Despite Barco's focus, however, the next major state visit did not occur until October 1996, during a period of difficult Colombia-US relations, when President Ernesto Samper traveled to the PRC to meet with President Jiang Zemin.[407] Three years later, in May 1999, President Andres Pastrana also met in China with Jiang Zemin, signing agreements on economic and technological cooperation, cultural and educational cooperation, and environmental protection cooperation. Following the Pastrana visit, however, little activity took place at the presidential level until April 2005, when President Alvaro Uribe visited the PRC.[408]

The Chinese Community in Colombia

The Chinese community in Colombia is one of the smallest in Latin America. Although some Chinese Colombians can be found in various parts of the country, the largest group is found near the city of Barranquilla, with another community of notable size located in Cali, just inland from Colombia's major Pacific port, Buenaventura. Although violence directed against the Chinese in Colombia has been overshadowed by civil war and rampant criminality, which have dominated parts of Colombia during much of the last half century, Colombia's ethnic Chinese have been marginalized, nonetheless—socially, economically, and politically. Indeed, as in some other parts of Latin America, calling a person *chino* (Chinese) in Colombia is generally regarded as giving an insult—one implying, however wrongly, that the person is deceitful, devious, untrustworthy, and unintelligent.[409]

Colombia currently is experiencing a small, new wave of Chinese immigrants into Cali, Bogotá, and other urban areas, brought in largely through illegal, human-trafficking networks. Stories of groups of Chinese detained by police or other authorities appear periodically in Colombian papers; in October 2007, for example, 23 Chinese were detained in an immigration operation in Cauca, adding to 160 detained in Bogota five months earlier.[410]

By contrast to Chinese communities in other Latin American countries, the Chinese Colombian community is not organized sufficiently to play a leading role in the expansion of Sino-Colombian commerce. As of late 2008, for example, there was no established China-Colombia chamber of commerce or similar organization at the national level, nor other strong Chinese-Colombian social institutions, such as those found in many other countries of the region.

China's Interest in Colombian Petroleum

In his April 2005 visit to China, President Alvaro Uribe invited the PRC and its companies to expand their investment in the largely untapped Colombian oil sector.[411] Chinese companies have responded favorably, and a series of partnerships and projects in the sector have emerged.

Many believe that substantial oil deposits will someday be found in the country. While Colombia's currently known oil reserves, concentrated in the Bahia de Santa Marta basin on the country's Caribbean coast,[412] are modest and declining,[413] much of the country has never been explored for oil.[414] The land that extends along the Andean ridge from the north of Ecuador through Colombia and into Venezuela is believed by some to be geologically favorable for oil deposits.[415] Significant amounts of petroleum have been found in both the Ecuadorian and the Venezuelan segments of the same geography, suggesting that the Colombian segment of this strip of land could also contain quantities of oil worth exploiting.[416] Unfortunately, attempts to date to explore portions of the area's potential reserves, such as Los Llanos, have not produced the hoped-for results.[417]

Although, thus far, Chinese oil exploration in Colombia has been limited, the PRC is cautiously moving forward through a number of initiatives. The most significant commercial venture by the PRC in the Colombian oil sector was the September 2006 acquisition of a stake in the Colombian firm Omimex, through a joint venture between the Chinese national oil company, CNPC, and the Videsh subsidiary of an Indian company, ONGC.[418] The deal, valued at $850 million,[419] gives each partner a 50 percent stake in the firm, which controls the majority of Colombian petroleum assets not under the control of the state firm, Ecopetrol.[420] As Luisa Palacios has noted, the first-of-its-kind cooperation between CNPC and ONGC-Videsh was also significant symbolically, given the increasing competition between Chinese and Indian firms globally because of expanding demand by both countries for energy and raw materials.[421]

In addition to the Omimex acquisition, Chinese companies are competing as both principals and associates in bids for exploration and development in thirteen new exploration blocks that Colombia opened up along its Caribbean coast and offshore.[422]

While the PRC is interested in the possibility of importing petroleum produced in Colombia, the Colombian petroleum industry also plays an important role in helping the PRC to extract petroleum from the much larger reserves found in neighboring Venezuela. For example, natural gas in the eastern parts of Colombia is imported by Venezuela for injection into the mature Venezuelan oil fields in the Lake Maracaibo region in order to maintain production. A pipeline was completed in October 2007 to carry gas from the Colombian gas fields of Punta Ballenas to the Lake Maracaibo region of Venezuela for this purpose.[423] The injection of Colombian gas into Venezuelan oil fields thus helps Chinese companies maintain pressure in those fields so the oil can be extracted and shipped to China.

In addition to the Colombia-Venezuela gas pipeline, Colombia may serve as the route for a liquid petroleum pipeline that would transport Venezuelan oil to a Pacific port, such as Tribugal, with the possibility that a refinery would be constructed on Colombian territory to process the product.[424] During his visit to China in April 2005, Colombian president Uribe explicitly invited the Chinese to consider investing in the project,[425] although the project was still on hold as of late 2008.

China's Interest in Colombian Mining

Although Colombia traditionally has been associated with agricultural exports like coffee, fruit, and bananas, the nation's current exports to the PRC are dominated by metals. Indeed, the number one Colombian export to China in 2006 was nickel, accounting for 47.5 percent of the nation's total exports to the PRC that year.[426] Virtually all of this nickel production comes from the Cerro Matoso mine in the province of Córdoba, operated by BHP Billiton.[427]

Colombia's coal resources are also of potential interest to the PRC, although China is itself a significant coal producer. Indeed, during President Uribe's visit to China in April 2005, coal was one of the explicit areas in which the Colombian leader invited the Chinese to invest.[428] Colombia's coalfields, located in the northeast of the country in the province of Guajira, include El Cerrejón, the largest open-pit coal mine in the world.[429] Cerrejón is owned, in part, by the same mining firm—BHP Billiton—that exports nickel from Cerro Matoso to China, although the output of El Cerrejón currently is destined for other customers.

In addition to nickel and coal, Colombia has modest amounts of uranium and other metals and minerals of potential interest to the PRC. A number of companies are currently conducting exploratory operations for uranium in Colombia in the provinces of Santander and Norte de Santander, including Energentia Resources,[430] Mega Uranium,[431] and Blue Sky Uranium Corporation.[432] If significant quantities of uranium are found in this area, it would introduce a number of new considerations into Colombia's relationship with both the United States and the PRC, since the area involved is host to significant activity by paramilitaries, guerillas, and various criminal gangs.[433]

China's Interest in Colombian Agriculture

Colombia's traditional exports, such as coffee, livestock products, fruits, and flowers, have not yet played a significant role in exports to China. In 2006, for example, Colombia exported a modest $1.4 million in coffee to the PRC, accounting for just 0.32 percent of the nation's total exports to China. Colombia also reported a modest $9.6 million in exports of leather to the PRC during this period, representing just over 2 percent of total Colombian exports to that country. Similarly, although Colombia is a significant producer of flowers, beef, bananas, and exotic fruits, none of these items appear on the list of Colombia's top twenty-five exports to the PRC.[434]

Colombian agricultural exports to the PRC have been limited by a combination of strict Chinese phytosanitary requirements and competition with other suppliers of these goods in Asia. As is true for Ecuadorian bananas, Colombian bananas have not been price competitive in Chinese markets when competing with local Chinese producers and Filipino suppliers. Similarly, the PRC appears to be purchasing the majority of its coffee from Vietnam,[435] although it is also developing ties with other Latin American suppliers, for instance Costa Rica.

The Colombian government is working to put an infrastructure in place to increase sales to the PRC. During the April 2005 visit of President Uribe to China, the governments signed a series of phytosanitary agreements that would facilitate the entry of Colombian agriculture products into the country.[436] Later in the same year, the Colombian trade-promotion organization Proexport opened an office in Beijing,[437] and sought to identify key Colombian products with good prospects for making headway into the

Chinese market. Among the products identified were exotic fruits, fruit pulp, and flowers.

Although, to date, Colombia has sold relatively little coffee to China, this also may change with the significant expansion expected in Chinese demand in the coming years. According to a report in the official newspaper *Shanghai Daily*, Chinese coffee consumption was expected to increase by 40 percent in 2007 alone.[438] Colombia's best prospects, however, may be indirect sales of green coffee to coffee-retailer chains such as Starbucks. Although the Colombian National Association of Coffee Growers has been pursuing a plan since 2006 to establish Colombian-style coffeehouses in China,[439] initial efforts to spearhead exports through the brand Juan Valdez had mixed results. In addition, Colombia is competing for the expanding Chinese coffee market, not only with Chinese producers and closer countries, such as India, but also with other Latin American coffee producers like Costa Rica, Venezuela, Ecuador, Guatemala, and Brazil.

Beyond coffee, Colombia has significant potential as an exporter of fruits and vegetables. In addition, Colombian beef has a reputation for high quality, although such imports are made extremely difficult by PRC phytosanitary restrictions.

Infrastructure Projects

Due in part to a half century of civil war, Colombia is a country that has not focused a great deal of attention on its commerce with the rest of the world. To the extent that Colombia has had commercial aspirations beyond the Andean region, they have been principally aimed at the United States, and to a lesser extent, at the European Union. In external trade, Colombia has had a historical orientation toward the Atlantic, reflected in the relatively modern infrastructure of its Atlantic coast ports, from Urubá to Cartagena to Santa Marta, and the relative neglect of its Pacific coast port infrastructure.

Colombia's major Pacific port, Buenaventura, is characterized by aging equipment and limited capacity. Companies that have used it for commerce with China note a variety of problems, including significant delays, which, on some occasions, have forced shipments to be diverted through the Panama Canal to Atlantic coast ports to circumvent congestion in Buenaventura.[440] Experts interviewed for this book have also suggested that the port of Buenaventura is effectively controlled by major narcotrafficking organizations.

Responding to the growing interest in commerce with the PRC and other Asian partners, the Colombian government is making major improvements in the port of Buenaventura, including the installation of multiple new loading cranes, the expansion of the docks, and the dredging of the port's access channel, to permit access for larger, deep-draft commercial vessels.[441] The project is part of a national plan put together by the Colombian National Council for Economic and Social Policy (CONPES), which contemplates an investment in the port of $560 million in private funds and $450 million in public funds over the coming years.[442]

Beyond the port itself, entrance to Buenaventura is also limited by the aging highway that connects it to the nearby city of Cali. Landslides closed the highway for two weeks in 2006, blocking container traffic into and out of the port, and resulting in a pile-up of freight that left the port congested for months.[443] Although the Colombian government has plans to turn the road from Cali to Buenaventura into a highway,[444] the zone in which the road and the port are located has a strong presence of both paramilitary and guerilla groups, and is one of the parts of Colombia most beset by kidnappings, guerrillas, and criminal activities.[445]

In addition to improving Buenaventura, the government has given consideration to transforming the very small port of Cupica, in Antioquia, into a major commercial operation, and building the associated infrastructure to give Colombia a second major Pacific coast port.

Colombia as a Market for Chinese Goods

Although Colombia ranks second to the bottom of South American countries in per capita income,[446] the islands of prosperity that characterize its major urban areas make the country an attractive market for Chinese goods. In 2007, according to the Chinese Ministry of Commerce, Colombia purchased $2.26 billion in goods from the PRC—up 51 percent from the prior year—generating a $1.16 billion single-year trade deficit with China.[447]

At the low end of the value-added chain, Chinese sales to Colombia have included toys, textiles, and footwear. Such goods, however, do not show up in significant quantities in official Colombian trade data. Textiles, for example, do not even appear on the list of the top twenty-five Colombian imports from China. Footwear imports occupy only three categories in the middle of this list, accounting for approximately 3.5 percent of all Colombian imports from the PRC in 2006.[448] Nonetheless, such competition is acutely felt by Colombian manufacturers and has led the Colombian government to take steps to block Chinese imports in some cases. In February 2006, for instance, the government imposed a 95 percent tariff against certain categories of Chinese textiles to protect Colombian textile producers from the rapid expansion of Chinese textiles into the Colombian market following the 2006 expiration of quotas established under the Multi-Fiber Agreement.[449] In addition, the Colombian government has taken steps to crack down on contraband goods, including limiting the number of ports through which goods can enter Colombia, since a substantial amount of Chinese contraband goods is believed to come into Colombia from Panama.[450]

In addition to being a market for Chinese light manufactured goods, Colombia buys more sophisticated products from the PRC, such as cars and motorcycles. Chinese cars first became available for sale in Colombia in 2005, and quickly expanded their market share due to their very low prices.[451] As of July 2007, numerous Chinese car brands had a presence in Colombia, including Great Wall Motors,[452] Fotón,[453] Hafei,[454] First Auto Works (FAW), Geeley, Dongfeng, Shanghai Automobile Industrial Corporation (SAIC), and Chery.[455] As in other Latin American countries, these brands are principally sold through partnerships with Colombian dealer networks, for example Cinescar de Colombia, which, since March 2007, has represented four Chinese auto brands in the country.[456] Similarly, the brand Hafei is distributed in Colombia by the local firm Harbin Motor Colombia.[457] Indeed, reflecting the emerging importance of the Chinese auto industry in Colombia, one of the first meetings of Colombian president Alvaro Uribe upon visiting China in April 2005 was with the directors of an auto company, FAW.[458]

Like automobile makers, Chinese motorcycle manufacturers, including Jialing and Jincheng,[459] have made significant advances in Colombia. One dealer with a presence throughout Colombia, AKT Motors, sells Chinese motorcycles as its principal product line.[460] In the Colombian city of Barranquilla, a joint venture between a Colombian and a Chinese firm reportedly is in the works that would produce another motorcycle, using Chinese components, to be sold in Colombia and throughout Latin America.[461] Although the introduction of a significant number of new Chinese auto brands and motorcycles did not occur until 2007, in 2006, Colombia imported some $87 million in Chinese motorcycles, putting these imports behind only "telephone equipment" in terms of sales volume.[462]

Beyond cars and motorcycles, Colombia also buys appliances and consumer electronics goods from China. Indeed, in 2006, according to the Colombian Ministry of Commerce, Industry, and Tourism, twelve of the top twenty-five categories of items imported into Colombia from China were technology goods. Together, these top dozen accounted for almost 20 percent of all Colombian imports from China.[463]

Finally, the PRC is a significant seller of telecommunications services and associated goods to Colombia; Huawei, for example, is the largest Chinese commercial operation in Colombia, with offices in Bogotá and Medellín.[464] Huawei has constructed numerous GSM networks in the country, including work for a broad range of local clients, including Móvil, EDATEL, ETP, and EMTELSA. Similarly, with respect to UMTS, Huawei is one of the few companies that supplies both of the key players in the market, Movistar and Colombia Móvil. For 2005, Huawei registered $80 billion in sales in Colombia as a whole.[465] In addition to Huawei, the ZTE corporation has a strong presence in Colombia; it first established itself in the country in 2004, serving the Buenaventura market, then expanded in 2005 when it won an $11 million project to construct a multiservice network in Cali.[466]

Colombia as an Assembly Platform

As with Mexico, Colombia's relatively well-developed manufacturing sector, in combination with the potential for its goods to have tariff-free access to the US market, makes the nation an attractive manufacturing partner for the PRC. Although it is further from the United States than is the north of Mexico, where many maquiladora facilities are located, the distance between Colombia and the United States is not significant compared to the distance from China to the United States; and, like Mexico, Colombia has a relatively sophisticated, well-educated labor force.

Currently, under the provisions of the Andean Trade Preferences Drug Enforcement Act (ATPDEA) certain categories of goods manufactured in Colombia can enter the United States tariff-free. In 2006 when Colombia was in the process of negotiating a free-trade agreement with the United States (rejected by the US Congress in 2008), the Colombian consulting firm Araújo, Ibarra, and Associates carried out a study (in conjunction with the Colombian trade-promotion organization Proexport and the Chinese trade-promotion organization CCPIT) identifying some 500 products that potentially could be manufactured in Colombia with Chinese factor inputs and sold in the United States tariff-free.[467] Although the global recession that began in 2008 has temporarily decreased the opportunities for selling to the US market, the logic of producing products in Colombia for export to the United States remains valid over the long term.

Government and Business Infrastructures

As Colombia emerges from the prolonged period of civil war and violence that has besieged the country, it is awakening to the potential presented by its commercial relations with Asia. The trip by President Alvaro Uribe to Beijing in April 2005 was a demonstration that the Colombian government recognizes the importance of Asia and is actively pursuing an expanded commercial interchange. In November 2008, Colombian president Alvaro Uribe met with Chinese president Hu Jintao while both leaders were in Lima, Peru, for the APEC summit. At the meeting, the two leaders signed an agreement providing reciprocal protection for Chinese investments in Colombia and Colombian investments in China.[468]

Colombia's current bid to join APEC, if successful, will strengthen that nation's institutional economic ties with China and other Asian governments. Although Colombia is not yet a member of APEC, the nation hosted the Pacific Basin Forum for the Latin American members of APEC in Cali, in January 2007.[469] Moreover, Peru and Chile, which are both members of APEC, have expressed their support for Colombia's bid to join.[470] The APEC members voted during their September 2007 meeting in Sidney, Australia, to postpone the acceptance of new members into the forum until 2010;[471] it is likely that Colombia's bid will be looked upon favorably at that time.

In addition to its attempt to join APEC, the Colombian government is expanding its institutional capabilities for doing business with the PRC. The government has taken the initial steps to enable its embassy in Beijing to provide information to Colombian companies who wish to develop business relationships in China. Additionally, the Colombian foreign ministry works in coordination with Colombia's small business–oriented trade-promotion organization, Proexport, to support Colombian exporters to China, having a Proexport representative in the Colombian embassy in Beijing.

Despite such capabilities, the staff and resources of the Colombian government in China remain small in relation to the work required to help Colombian businesses establish themselves in the PRC. Moreover, unlike the ministries of some other Latin American countries, as of late 2008, the Colombian Ministry of Foreign Affairs did not yet have offices in other parts of China to facilitate business beyond the capital.

Regardless of growing interest in the private sector and support from the government, Colombia remains somewhat behind other Latin American countries (e.g., Chile and Peru) in private-sector infrastructure for doing business with China. Although Colombia has a number of respectable consulting firms, including Araújo, Ibarra, y Asociados and China Business (CHB), to help its firms build ties with the PRC, Colombia does not yet have a truly coordinated, national-level Chinese-Colombian chamber of commerce.[472] On the positive side, Colombian firms are increasingly sending personnel to China to fact-find and to establish business ties, such as the trip by representatives from the Asociación Colombiano de Pequeños Industriales (ACOPI) in 2006. Various Colombian companies also participate in trade fairs and other commercial events in China, like the famous biannual event in Canton,[473] although as of late 2008, government organizations were not playing a major role in such activities.

In terms of financial and legal infrastructures, although a number of preliminary accords were signed between the Colombian government and the PRC during President Uribe's 2005 trip to China,[474] much work remains to be done. Colombian banks have almost no presence in China, with the result that Colombian companies wishing to do business in the PRC must use outside international financial institutions, such as Citigroup. Moreover, as is the case with most other Latin American countries, effective mechanisms (e.g., financial derivatives or standard arbitration bodies) do not yet exist for mitigating risk for Colombian companies doing business in the PRC.

Intellectual Infrastructure

Colombia's intellectual infrastructure to support commerce with the PRC is relatively limited. While some major universities, such as Universidad Nacional and Universidad de Los Andes in Bogotá, offer Mandarin programs,[475] many other important universities do not—for instance, Universidad Autónoma de Colombia, Universidad del Valle in Cali, Universidad de Caldas, Universidad de Manizales, and Universidad de Cauca.[476]

Projects are under way across a broad range of Colombian universities to meet the perceived need for expanded Chinese-language and China studies programs. In 2005, Universidad EAFIT, one of the nation's most prestigious private universities, established its Center for Asia-Pacific Studies, in parallel with a new offering of Chinese-language instruction and new courses about Asian business and culture.[477] In May 2007, EAFIT and Universidad de Antioquia entered an agreement with the Chinese government to establish the first Confucius Institute in Colombia. This institute will allow both universities to offer a certified Chinese-language program, with visiting faculty from China.[478] Corresponding with the effort at Universidad EAFIT, in 2004, Universidad Sergio Arboleda in Bogotá established its own Center of Asia-Pacific Studies.[479] Similarly, in 2005, Corporación Unificada Nacional initiated a new Chinese-language program and Asian-oriented business courses.

Political and Military Relations

Colombia's political and military relationships with the PRC have grown in a cautious fashion, in parallel with Colombia's continuation of its close relationship with the United States.[480] As Juan Gabriel Tokatlian argues, "China's rapprochement with Colombia has been cautious, indicating that Beijing understands the significance of Bogotá for Washington today."[481] Similarly, Colombia's leadership has also endeavored to avoid the impression that there is any conflict between Colombia's special relationship with the United States and its pursuit of closer relations with the PRC.

The landmark event in Colombia's relationship with China was arguably the visit to the PRC by President Alvaro Uribe in 2005. The trip included a broad range of agreements and activities, with the signing of five accords to deepen cooperation across a spectrum of matters, from telecommunications to cinema to production technology. The presidential delegation itself included not only 25 government representatives, but also 140 businesspeople and 44 university officials.[482] As noted previously, the two leaders also met at the November 2008 APEC summit, where they signed an important investment-protection agreement.

In addition to high-level diplomacy, the PRC has undertaken various initiatives aimed at building goodwill with the Colombian government and its people. In November 2006, for example, China donated $1.46 million in goods to Colombia, including medical and agricultural equipment, as well as various items for Colombia's schools, such as computers, desks, and supplies.[483] The Chinese government also confers approximately twenty scholarships each year for Colombians to study in the PRC.[484] A different fund provides scholarships for Chinese students to study in Colombia at a variety of different universities; twenty of these students arrived in October 2007.[485]

In the military realm, although contacts between China and Colombia have been relatively low-key, they have been persistent and meaningful, including officer exchanges. In June 2006, Cao Gangchuan, the Chinese minister of defense, met with his Colombian complement, Juan Manuel Santos, in Beijing and signed an accord to expand military-to-military exchanges and deepen Chinese-Colombian defense cooperation.[486]

Colombia is also one of a number of Latin American countries that have obtained military goods from the PRC. For a number of years, China has supplied specialized cold-weather gear to Colombian high-mountain battalions, although the Colombian Ministry of Defense has generally not publicized such transactions.[487] In December 2007, the purchase of 50,000 bulletproof vests by the Colombian army became a matter of open scandal when a public complaint was launched by the Chinese Arms Ministry over alleged unfairness in the bidding process.[488]

■ Notes

1. The others are Mexico, Brazil, and Argentina.
2. "Imports by Major Categories (2007/01–12)." *Ministry of Commerce of the People's Republic of China.* http://english.mofcom.gov.cn/aarticle/statistic/ie/200802/20080205372493.html. February 4, 2008.
3. Further evidence for this "future orientation" is suggested by the agreements signed between the two nations in June 2007 in the energy and transportation sectors, with a potential value of $11 billion if the activities are realized as planned. "Petrolera Sinopec negocia extracciones en la faja." *El Universal.* Caracas, Venezuela. http://www.eluniversal.com. June 29, 2007. See also "Petrolera China negocia contratos en Venezuela." *Diario Financiero.* Santiago, Chile. http://www.df.cl. June 29, 2007.
4. As of 2006, Saudi Arabia claimed 260 billion barrels of proven reserves. "Venezuela Looks to Tar Deposits to Supply Surging Global Energy Needs." *Latin Petroleum Magazine.* http://www.latinpetroleum.com. May 30, 2006.
5. Eduardo Camel Anderson, "Tecnología china apoyará las telecomunica-

ciones locales." *El Universal*. Caracas, Venezuela. http://www.eluniversal.com. February 20, 2007.

6. "China estima que inversión en el país llegará a $2.000 millones." *El Universal*. Caracas, Venezuela. http://www.eluniversal.com. March 30, 2007.

7. "Alto funcionario chino visitará México, Venezuela, Surinam, Perú, y Samoa." *El Universal*. Caracas, Venezuela. http://www.eluniversal.com. March 12, 2007. See also "Senior Chinese Party Official Wraps Up Mexico Visit." *People's Daily Online*. Beijing, China. http://english.people.com.cn. March 26, 2007.

8. Yolanda Ojeda Reyes, "Ciudanos chinos reciben protección." *El Universal*. Caracas, Venezuela. http://www.eluniversal.com. November 11, 2004.

9. Interview with Zhang Tuo, ambassador of the People's Republic of China to the Republic of Venezuela. Caracas, Venezuela. January 15, 2008.

10. Ojeda Reyes, 2004. El Bosque is only a few square blocks in size, but includes a Chinese social center and has a thriving market, particularly on Sunday afternoons.

11. In this capacity, the Chinese community in Venezuela is also believed to play an important role in the importation of Chinese consumer goods for the Venezuelan market.

12. Interview with Zhang Tuo, ambassador of the People's Republic of China to the Republic of Venezuela. Caracas, Venezuela. January 15, 2008.

13. The violence was associated with the national strike of 2002 and political protests of 2004. Some Chinese shops, located in poor neighborhoods, closed their doors in sympathy with the protests. In some cases, the shops were looted by mobs in the neighborhoods, both because the pro-Chávez mobs were angry that the shopkeepers were aligning themselves with the opposition and because the people in the neighborhoods were poor and needed the food and other goods that the shops sold.

14. Ojeda Reyes, 2004.

15. The revolving fund, which theoretically is to be replenished on a three-year cycle, would include $2 billion in Venezuelan capital, plus up to $4 billion in Chinese credits and loans through China Development Bank. "China dio visto bueno a fondo con Venezuela." *El Universal*. Caracas, Venezuela. http://www.eluniversal. com. April 30, 2007.

16. "Aporte al fondo pesado con China surge del fonden." *El Universal*. Caracas, Venezuela. http://www.eluniversal.com. March 1, 2008.

17. Interview with Zhang Tuo, ambassador of the People's Republic of China to the Republic of Venezuela. Caracas, Venezuela. January 15, 2008.

18. "Chávez dice que es 'más que suficiente' el petróleo a entre 80 y 90 dólares." *El Universal*. Caracas, Venezuela. http://www.eluniversal.com. October 18, 2008.

19. At the same time, the relationship is underlined by an ongoing uncertainty that Venezuela will be able to deliver on the promised oil sales.

20. "China Wins Heavy Oil Area in Venezuela." *Alexander's Gas and Oil Connections* 11(21). November 9, 2006.

21. "Venezuela aumenta sus reservas certificadas de petróleo a más de 152 mil millones de barriles." *El Nacional*. Caracas, Venezuela. http://www.el-nacional.com. October 29, 2008.

22. Similarly, certification of heavy petroleum products as oil in the Canadian province of Alberta would give Canada the second- or third-largest oil reserves in the world.

23. "CNPC cambia centro de petróleo de Canadá a Venezuela." *El Universal*. Caracas, Venezuela. http://www.eluniversal.com. July 14, 2007.

24. "Venezuela Maps Out Plan for Chinese Oil Investment." *Reuters.* http://www.reuters.com. March 28, 2007.

25. "China Wins Heavy Oil Area in Venezuela."

26. In January 2007, PdVSA and China National Petroleum Corporation entered an agreement to explore and produce oil in the Posa field, in the Gulf of Paria. The oil block is expected to produce 400,000 barrels of oil per day by 2011. "Venezuela Creates Joint Oil Venture with China." *Reuters.* http://www.reuters.com. January 29, 2007.

27. The Chinese presence in the Junin field of Orinoco alone gives China control of 35 billion of the 236 billion barrels of new Venezuelan heavy oil expected to be certified in the area. "China Wins Heavy Oil Area in Venezuela."

28. "Chávez nacionaliza la gigantesca faja petrolífera del Orinoco." *Nacion.* San José, Costa Rica. http://www.nacion.com. May 1, 2007.

29. Under the terms of the new partnership agreements that China and other foreign entities operating in the Orinoco belt signed with Venezuela, the Chinese companies conducting the exploration and development activities will have a 40 percent stake in the entity, while PdVSA will have the other 60 percent, giving them control of the operations. Alejandra M. Hernández F., "Venezuela aumentará suministros de crudo a China." *El Universal.* Caracas, Venezuela. http://www.eluniversal.com. March 24, 2007. See also "Venezuela y China concretan acuerdos para impulsar integración estratégica." *El Universal.* Caracas, Venezuela. http://www.eluniversal.com. March 26, 2007. Nonetheless, beyond the technicalities of the new partnership, the Chinese generally will be exporting oil that they themselves are extracting from new production blocks. See "Petrolera Sinopec negocia extracciones en la faja."

30. See "OVL Likely to Form Joint Venture with Venezuelan Co." *Hindu Business Line.* http://www.thehindubusinessline.com. January 9, 2007. Petropars is currently operating in the Ayacucho region of Venezuela. "Venezuela e Irán inician exploración petrolera conjunta." *Nacion.* San José, Costa Rica. http://www.nacion.com. September 19, 2006.

31. "Petrolera China negocia contratos en Venezuela."

32. Venezuela has also shipped limited quantities of oil to India and other Asian customers. In December 2005, for example, PdVSA reportedly exported 3.4 million barrels of crude and fuel oil to Singapore. "Venezuela Reports on Oil Exports to China and Singapore." *Alexander's Gas and Oil Connections* 11(2). January 26, 2006. Venezuela has also been working actively to promote the use of its petroleum and gas throughout Latin America, through a number of proposed refinery projects, pipelines and other infrastructure projects, and promotional terms. Such promotions include the supply of Venezuelan oil to Caribbean states through PetroCaribe, and the supply of oil on preferential terms to member countries of the Alternativa Bolivariana (ALBA). See "Petroleo y bono para el ALBA." *El Universal.* Caracas, Venezuela. http://www.eluniversal.com. April 30, 2007.

33. "Venezuela Puts $12 Bn Cost on New China Oil Deal." *Reuters News.* http://uofaweb.ualberta.ca/chinainstitute. May 13, 2008.

34. "Venezuela y China crean fondo estratégico y firman 5 acuerdos." *El Universal.* Caracas, Venezuela. http://www.eluniversal.com. March 27, 2007.

35. "Hugo Chávez viajará a China." *El Economista.* Mexico City, Mexico. http://eleconomista.com.mx/. August 15, 2006.

36. Reflecting this importance, CNPC and China Petroleum and Chemical Corporation (CPCC) alone have invested an estimated $5 billion in exploration and development activities in Venezuela in recent years, and plan to invest much more.

"Embajador asegura que Venezuela vende a China 200 mil barriles de petróleo." *El Universal*. Caracas, Venezuela. http://www.eluniversal.com. March 29, 2007.

37. As of October 2007, Venezuela had purchased some thirteen drilling rigs from China, with plans to purchase more. "PdVSA aumentará el número de taladros." *El Universal*. Caracas, Venezuela. http://www.eluniversal.com. October 21, 2007.

38. "Gobierno reafirma que nacionalizará taladros de exploración petrolera." *El Universal*. Caracas, Venezuela. http://www.eluniversal.com. May 14, 2007.

39. "Venezuela Receives Drilling Rigs from China." *Latin America News Digest*. http://www.uofaweb.ualberta.ca. June 11, 2008. Under the deal, valued at $434 million, a capability is to be developed to produce eight drilling rigs per year in Venezuela. "PdVSA, CNPC to Produce 8 Rigs Annually." *Business News Americas*. http://www.uofaweb.ualberta.ca. June 23, 2008. See also Marianna Párraga, "China absorbe los barriles que Venezuela le quita a EEUU." *El Universal*. Caracas, Venezuela. http://www.eluniversal.com. October 22, 2007.

40. Industry experts interviewed for this book have suggested, however, that it is likely that the motor, which is the core of the drill, will continue to be produced in China as a component, while final-assembly operations will take place in Venezuela, fulfilling the letter of the agreement.

41. Rachel Jones, "Venezuela Sends Less Oil to US, More to China." *Associated Press*. http://www.uofaweb.ualberta.ca. June 30, 2008.

42. "Venezuela Maps Out Plan for Chinese Oil Investment."

43. According to the deal, for example, 200,000 barrels per day would come from the CNPC-controlled Junin-4 block in the Orinoco strip, and 400,000 barrels per day would come from the Carabobo block there. Ibid.

44. PdVSA projects, for example, that, within two to three years, the Junin-4 block of the Orinoco belt, where CNPC is now certifying reserves for the Venezuelan government, will go from currently producing no oil to producing 600,000 barrels of oil per day. See also "Venezuela y China crean fondo estratégico y firman 5 acuerdos."

45. For example, for the heavy oil from Orinoco to be shipped to China or to other parts of Venezuela, it will require the construction of a pipeline over very difficult terrain in the Orinoco delta to reach the Gulf of Paria. Before the oil can be moved, it must be mixed with a solvent, such as naphtha, which will have to be brought into Orinoco through another pipeline, or by truck or rail via an infrastructure that is currently nonexistent. The development of Orinoco also will require an estimated 1,200 new wells, in addition to the 900 that currently exist there, and a massive quantity of oil industry personnel. While none of these obstacles is insurmountable, the quantity of investment required could exceed $30 billion. Moreover, the fact that none of the supporting infrastructure is yet in the works suggests that it will be virtually impossible for PdVSA to meet its targets for increasing oil production.

46. The 2005 PdVSA strategic plan included reference to a new refining facility to be built in Orinoco, although subsequent studies cast doubt on the project, causing it to be put on hold.

47. According to industry experts, this approach would involve moving solvent via pipeline from the coast to the mixing facilities, where it would be combined with the tar sludge and shipped back to the coastal facilities via the same pipeline infrastructure (assuming that the existing pipeline infrastructure is constructed as a circuit) to be upgraded from 8 API to 22 API at the new coastal facility.

48. In addition to the twenty-one tankers in its current fleet, Venezuela has ordered two tankers from an Argentine shipyard. "China construirá 18 embarca-

ciones para PDV marina." *El Universal.* Caracas, Venezuela. http://www. eluniversal.com. May 11, 2006. PdVSA has also added four tankers to the ten that it currently has on order from Brazilian shipyards. "PdVSA to Buy Oil Tankers from China." *Alexander's Gas and Oil Connections* 11(11). June 8, 2006.

49. PdVSA has ordered eighteen new tankers for $1.3 billion through a joint venture with China State Shipbuilding Corporation (CSSC) and China Shipbuilding Industry Corporation (CSIC), and plans to acquire a total of forty-two new tankers through this arrangement by 2012, implying a total investment in tankers of approximately $2.8 billion. "Venezuela y China construirán buques petroleros." *El Universal.* Caracas, Venezuela. http://www.eluniversal.com. May 10, 2006. See also "China to Build 18 Oil Ships for Venezuela." *El Universal.* Caracas, Venezuela. http://www.eluniversal.com. September 4, 2006.

50. When Chinese Politburo member Li Changchun visited Venezuela in April 2007, he signed a number of protocols with the Venezuelans, including an agreement by which Venezuela and China would jointly operate the new fleet through a 50–50 ownership arrangement, to supply Venezuelan oil to China. "Venezuela y China concretan acuerdos para impulsar integración estratégica." Oil industry experts suggest, however, that PdVSA probably does not have the money to participate directly in such a project; and if it does participate, it would probably do so through the Heavy Investment Fund, implying the that shipbuilding work would probably go to a Chinese company, such as CSSC, financed principally by China Development Bank, with PdVSA ultimately paying back the loan from China through oil

51. "Venezuela y China crean fondo estratégico y firman 5 acuerdos."

52. Ibid.

53. Peter Haldis, "China, Venezuela Sign Refinery Agreement." *Hart's Global Refining and Fuels Report.* http://www.uofaweb.ualberta.ca. May 21, 2008.

54. Oil industry experts interviewed off the record indicated that the projects in China had broken ground.

55. PdVSA announced in November 2006 that it was entering into a partnership with Petrobras to build a new $2.5 billion refinery in the Brazilian city of Pernambuco to be called "Pedro Leon." See "Donado terreno para refinería de Pernambuco." *El Universal.* Caracas, Venezuela. http://www.eluniversal.com. August 17, 2006.

56. PdVSA's failure to meet its supply commitment to the PRC would not be without precedent. Indeed, just weeks before the announcement of the accord for the construction of the three new refineries, PdVSA stated that it was backing out of a commitment made in 2004 to supply China with 1.8 million tons per year of the heavy petroleum product ormulsion. "$1.500 millones en envíos a China." *El Universal.* Caracas, Venezuela. http://www.eluniversal.com. August 24, 2005. See also "Áreas estratégicas." *El Universal.* Caracas, Venezuela. http://www. eluniversal.com. August 23, 2005. See also "China sólo se quedará con dos tercerios de la ormulsión del segundo módulo." *El Universal.* Caracas, Venezuela. http:// www.eluniversal.com. April 11, 2006. With the increase in the price of oil, PdVSA decided that it was more profitable to blend the heavy petroleum product used with ormulsion with a lighter grade of crude, and sell the resulting product as oil, rather than dedicate the substance to the production of ormulsion, which commands a much lower price. Unfortunately for the Chinese, however, the petroleum company PetroChina had built two 600-megawatt generators in Zhanjiang province specifically designed to consume ormulsion. See Jubany and Poon, 2006, p. 30. Petrochina initially sought damages from PdVSA, since it was forced to suspend operations at the plant while retooling it to use a different fuel. "Cierra sus puertas en China plan-

ta que usaba ormulsión." *El Universal*. Caracas, Venezuela. http://www.
eluniversal.com. August 31, 2007. See also "China usará carbón para reemplazar
orimulsión." *El Universal*. Caracas, Venezuela. http://www.eluniversal.com. April
11, 2007.

57. Following the mineral products sector (which includes petroleum) and the
metals sector, Venezuela's next-largest export sector is chemical products, also
largely tied to the petroleum industry, representing 6.7 percent of the nation's
exports, followed by transportation equipment, with 3.6 percent of exports by value.
"Valor de las exportaciones efectuadas por Venezuela, según sector económico,
Enero–Diciembre, 2006–2007." *Instituto Nacional de Estadística. Republica
Bolivarana de Venezuela*. http://www.ine.gov.ve/comercio/comercioindice.asp.
Accessed August 5, 2008.

58. "China estima que inversión en el país llegará a $2.000 millones."

59. "Minera china empezará a trabajar en el estado Bolívar este año." *El
Universal*. Caracas, Venezuela. http://www.eluniversal.com. March 31, 2006.

60. "Venezuela y china crean fondo estratégico y firman 5 acuerdos." As of
January 2008, however, no action had been taken to begin work on the pelletizing
facility.

61. "Proyectos del Mibam recibirán financiamiento de fondo Venezuela-
China." *El Universal*. Caracas, Venezuela. http://www.eluniversal.com. October 25,
2006.

62. "Gross Domestic Product per Capita, Current Prices (U.S. dollars)."
International Monetary Fund. World Economic Outloook Database. http://www.imf.
org/external/pubs/ft/weo/2007/01/data/index.aspx. April 2007.

63. Although contraband goods are a serious problem, one expert interviewed
for this book notes that the problem has been mitigated somewhat by the implementation of regulations in 2003 requiring all products entering the country to specify
for whom and by whom they had been produced.

64. The relatively high levels of corruption in the country increase the proba-
bility that such contraband goods will be able successfully to enter the country and
be sold without legal penalty.

65. The subject of an investment by Haier to create an appliance factory in
Venezuela was raised by the Mixed Commission in November 2007. Interview with
Zhang Tuo, ambassador of the People's Republic of China to the Republic of
Venezuela. Caracas, Venezuela. January 15, 2008. Nonetheless, the Venezuelan mar-
ket remains dominated by the Mexican manufacturer Mabe.

66. "Producirán camiones chinos en Venezuela." *El Universal*. Caracas,
Venezuela. http://www.eluniversal.com. October 29, 2007.

67. Joseph Poliszuk, "Gobierno lanza 'computadoras bolivarianas' desde Bs
870.175." *El Universal*. Caracas, Venezuela. http://www.eluniversal.com. December
19, 2006.

68. Daniel Ricardo Hernández, "La computadora bolivariana está lista." *El
Universal*. Caracas, Venezuela. http://www.eluniversal.com. January 26, 2007.

69. None of the Venezuelan subject-matter experts interviewed for this book,
however, were aware of any specific plans to use the computers in government facilities. Some suggested that the government plans to donate the computers to public
"infocenters" in poor areas of the country.

70. Interview with Zhang Tuo, ambassador of the People's Republic of China
to the Republic of Venezuela. Caracas, Venezuela. January 15, 2008.

71. "China Sells High Power Diesel Locomotives to Venezuela." *People's
Daily Online*. Beijing, China. http://english.people.com.cn. December 19, 2006.

72. Ibid.

73. Anderson, "Tecnología China apoyará las telecomunicaciones locales."

74. "Venezuela CANTV Selected Huawei Technologies to Upgrade Its Optical Fiber National Backbone Network." *Huawei.* Official website. http://www.huawei.com/news.view.do?id=198&cid=42. Accessed January 10, 2008.

75. "Venezuela." *Huawei.* Official website. http://www.huawei.com/es/catalog.do?id=343. Accessed January 10, 2008.

76. See "Venezuela CANTV Selected Huawei Technologies to Upgrade Its Optical Fiber National Backbone Network." See also "Venezuela." *Huawei.* Official website. http://www.huawei.com/es/catalog.do?id=343. Accessed January 10, 2008.

77. The facility, producing telephones with the new GSM technology, is anticipated to begin production in 2008. See "Huawei and CVG Telecom to Produce GMS Handsets in Venezuela." *Telecomworldwire.* June 1, 2007. See also "CVG Telecom colocará mañana piedra fundacional de fábrica de celulares." *El Universal.* Caracas, Venezuela. http://www.eluniversal.com. November 13, 2006.

78. "Venezuela y China inician fábrica de teléfonos celulares."

79. The project was put on hold, however, following the nationalization of CANTV and the initiation of efforts to integrate existing fiber-optic networks.

80. Industry experts interviewed for this book have suggested that the GSM network could be a candidate for inclusion in the Heavy Investment Fund in the future, to help free the project from the increasing capital constraints of CANTV.

81. Beyond Huawei and ZTE, the telecommunications firm Alcatel Shanghai Bell has also been active in Venezuela, serving both government and private-sector clients.

82. "Complementarán el desarrollo de fibra óptica con la CANTV." *El Universal.* Caracas, Venezuela. http://www.eluniversal.com. February 2, 2007. See also "CVG Telecom suscribirá 6 contratos con empresas Chinas." *El Universal.* Caracas, Venezuela. http://www.eluniversal.com. October 16, 2006. The near-term benefits of the investment are not yet clear, however, since the fiber-optic lines are being installed to such relatively remote rural areas as the Amacuro Delta, Amazonas, Monagas, Anzoátegui, Sucre, and Táchira, which do not yet have a significant user base. "Complementarán el desarrollo de fibra óptica con la CANTV."

83. "Venezuela tendrá fábricas de celulares entre 2009 y 2010, según ministra." *Nacion.* San José, Costa Rica. http://www.nacion.com. July 31, 2008.

84. The contemplated extension of the national rail system would include segments from San Cristóbal to Barinas, from Barinas to Tinaco, and from Tinaco to Anaco. According to Venezuelan president Chávez, a significant portion of the funding would come from the Chinese, and the Chinese would build a factory in Venezuela to assemble rails and train cars. "Chávez afirma que triplicará venta de petróleo a China." *La Razón.* La Paz, Bolivia. http://www.la-razon.com. August 25, 2006. It also appears likely that the Heavy Investment Fund would be a major contributor to such a project, with the work ultimately channeled to a Chinese firm.

85. Although some products have appeared to involve technology transfer to Venezuela, the long-term benefits to Venezuela are often superficial, and the country is paying well, in hard currency, for the services that the PRC is providing.

86. Roberto Guisti, "En 2008 tendremos un satélite chino." *El Universal.* Caracas, Venezuela. http://www.eluniversal.com. April 1, 2007. See also Anderson, 2007.

87. According to Venezuelan officials interviewed off the record for this book, in 2008 China and Venezuela were building a Center of Technology Innovation, in La Carlota Airport in the center of Caracas. Projects planned for the center include

not only work with mobile communication technologies, but also the monitoring of signals from the Simon Bolívar satellite as well as the monitoring and control of the nation's newly integrated fiber-optic network.

88. "Egresados de la Unefa cursarán estudios de satélites en China." *El Universal.* Caracas, Venezuela. http://www.eluniversal.com. February 25, 2006.

89. China and Venezuela have also discussed the construction of a second, smaller satellite for climatic study, and a follow-on to the Simon Bolívar satellite when its useful life expires within fifteen years. "UIT apoya proyecto satelital de Venezuela." *El Universal.* Caracas, Venezuela. http://www.eluniversal.com. October 26, 2007.

90. Interview with Zhang Tuo, ambassador of the People's Republic of China to the Republic of Venezuela. Caracas, Venezuela. January 15, 2008.

91. When Venezuelan president Hugo Chávez came to power in 1999, there were only thirty-seven agreements in effect between Venezuela and China.

92. As a reflection of the emphasis on government projects, Venezuela has only one commercial attaché, working out of the embassy in Beijing.

93. Although all ambassadors have some commercial role, Venezuelan experts interviewed for this book indicate that the level of engagement by Chinese ambassadors in Venezuela stands out in sharp contrast to the activities of other diplomats in Caracas.

94. Although experts note that the organization was never particularly well resourced, its effectiveness was undercut when its president was removed on corruption charges in late 2007.

95. "China organiza feria industrial en Caracas." *El Universal.* Caracas, Venezuela. June 17, 2008.

96. "Senior Chinese Party Official Meets with Venezuelan President." *People's Daily Online.* Caracas, Venezuela. http://english.peopledaily.com.cn/. March 27, 2007.

97. Although there is no public standard for why China chooses to bestow the title "strategic partner" on certain nations and not others, Venezuela stands out among China's strategic partners Mexico, Brazil, and Argentina in that the level of Chinese-Venezuelan trade is notably lower than that between China and its other Latin American "strategic partners." See, for example, "Total Import and Export Value by Country (Region) (2007/01–12)." *Ministry of Commerce.* People's Republic of China. http://english.mofcom.gov.cn.aarticle/statistic/ie/200802/20080205371690.html. February 4, 2008. Moreover, China's other three strategic partners have relatively modern, diversified economies, and have historically exercised roles of leadership in the region. The strategic partnership between Venezuela and China, by contrast, appears to concentrate much more on the oil reserves that Venezuela possesses, as well as on the strong expressions of political alliance made by the Chávez government, and the substantial number of shared investment projects between the two countries. Indeed, some have suggested that the Chinese did not initially wish to grant the status of strategic partner to Venezuela, and did so only at the insistence of Chávez. Domínguez, 2006. See also "China in Latin America: Trade, Not Military Involvement." *Latin America–Asia Review.* July 2006, p. 5.

98. Interview with Zhang Tuo, ambassador of the People's Republic of China to the Republic of Venezuela. Caracas, Venezuela. January 15, 2008.

99. "China apoyará a Venezuela en la ONU." *El País.* Bogotá, Colombia. http://www.elpais.com. February 2, 2007.

100. "Aporte al fondo pesado con China surge del fonden." *El Universal.* Caracas, Venezuela. http://www.eluniversal.com. March 1, 2008.

101. During the March 2007 visit by Chinese Politburo member Li

Changchun, the leader held meetings with a variety of members of the Venezuelan ruling party, the Movimiento del Quinto Republica (MVR), including the president of the National Assembly, Cilia Flores. "China y Venezuela revisan ejecución de acuerdo bilateral." *El Universal.* Caracas, Venezuela. http://www.eluniversal.com. March 27, 2007. See also "Senior Chinese Party Official Meets with Venezuelan President." Previously, in January 2007, legislators from the two nations had announced plans to form a "friendship group" to increase coordination between their legislative bodies. "Constituirán grupo de amistad China-Venezuela." *El Universal.* Caracas, Venezuela. http://www.eluniversal.com. January 12, 2007. See also "Senior Chinese, Venezuelan Leaders Meet to Strengthen Bilateral Ties." *People's Daily Online.* Beijing, China. http://english.people.com.cn. January 12, 2007.

102. "Senior Chinese Party Official Meets with Venezuelan President."

103. "Venezuela, China Sign Agreement on Broadcaster Training, Production, Exchange." *China View.* Beijing, China. http://www.chinaview.cn. April 19, 2006.

104. "Venezuela y China firman intercambio cultural." *El Universal.* Caracas, Venezuela. http://www.eluniversal.com. December 5, 2006.

105. "Venezuela comprará 18 aviones de China para entrenar a sus pilotos." *ABC Digital.* Asunción, Paraguay. http://www.abc.com.py. November 2, 2008. See also María Daniela Espinoza, "Aviones chinos de entrenamiento tienen capacidad de combate." *El Universal.* Caracas, Venezuela. http://www.eluniversal.com. May 14, 2008.

106. Although Venezuela indicated that the purpose of the radar was to combat narcotrafficking, their military role was highlighted by the fact that they were put under the control of the Venezuelan air force, whereas three other radars acquired from Italy during the same time period were placed under the control of the Venezuelan civil aviation organization. "Venezuela instala radares para combatir narcotráfico." *El Universal.* Caracas, Venezuela. http://www.eluniversal.com. December 15, 2006.

107. "Satélite blindará comunicaciones de la FAN." *El Universal.* Caracas, Venezuela. http://www.eluniversal.com/index.shtml. August 27, 2008.

108. Arostegui, 2007.

109. Russia has been Venezuela's principal supplier of arms, with an estimated $3 billion in Venezuelan purchases from Russia, including 53 helicopters, 24 Sukhoi-30 aircraft, and 100,000 Kalashnikov rifles during 2006 and 2007; the government also has plans to purchase 5 diesel-electric submarines and an air-defense system. "Presidente dice que submarinos rusos son para 'defender la revolución.'" *El Universal.* Caracas, Venezuela. http://www.eluniversal.com. June 29, 2007.

110. Jubany and Poon, 2006.

111. Virtually all of this investment is, however, in the petroleum sector, and is accounted for by the purchase by the Chinese consortium Andes Petroleum of the Ecuadorian assets of the Canadian firm EnCana. "China apoya inclusion de Ecuador a APEC." *El Comercio.* Quito, Ecuador. http://www.elcomercio.com.ec. March 28, 2007.

112. "Total Import and Export Value by Country (Region) (2006/01–12)."

113. See Palacios, 2008, p. 172. See also, interview with Cai Rungo, ambassador for the People's Republic of China to Ecuador. Quito, Ecuador. July 9, 2007.

114. "Ecuador y Venezuela firmarán acta de conformación de nueva refinería en Manabí." *El Universo.* Guayaquil, Ecuador. http://www.eluniverso.com. February 1, 2008.

115. "El Ecuador renegociará todos los tratados de inversions." *El Comercio.* Quito, Ecuador. http://www.elcomercio.com. May 31, 2007.

116. Interview with Cai Rungo, ambassador for the People's Republic of China to Ecuador. Quito, Ecuador. July 9, 2007.

117. In 1971, both the president and foreign minister of Ecuador declared on various occasions the desire to establish diplomatic and commercial relations with China. Liu Yuquin, 2006, p. 16.

118. "Bilateral Relations." *Ministry of Foreign Affairs of the People's Republic of China.* Official website. http://www.fmprc.gov.cn/eng/wjb/zzjg/ldmzs/gjlb/3493/default.htm. September 2003.

119. In addition to these trips, there have been various ministerial-level exchanges between the two countries and the signing of commercial accords. Ibid.

120. Interview with Harry Sun Soria Laman, Ecuador-China Chamber of Commerce. Guayaquil, Ecuador. July 13, 2007.

121. Ibid.

122. Grupo Wong's product is known in Ecuador under the brand "Rey van Pac." Ibid.

123. Hago, 2005, p. 64.

124. Interview with Harry Sun Soria Laman, Ecuador-China Chamber of Commerce. Guayaquil, Ecuador. July 13, 2007.

125. Ibid.

126. "Fiscal acusó por emission de visas falsas a favor de ciudadanos extranjeros." *Boletines Enero 2006: Fiscalia de Ecuador.* Official website. www.fiscalia.gov.ec/Boletines/Docs/2006/ENERO.pdf. January 27, 2006.

127. Indeed, the status and economic importance of the established Chinese community in Guayaquil are reflected in a project that is currently in the works, to create a major new "Chinatown" urban district, south of the Guayaquil international airport, to serve as a center for business and culture for the Chinese community of the city.

128. "Ecuador no pedirá visas a turistas." *El Universo.* Guayaquil, Ecuador. http://www.eluniverso.com. June 12, 2008.

129. Interview with Harry Sun Soria Laman, Ecuador-China Chamber of Commerce. Guayaquil, Ecuador. July 13, 2007.

130. "China CNPC preocupada e interesada por Ecuador." *El Universal.* Caracas, Venezuela. http://www.eluniversal.com. June 1, 2006. See also Mercedes Alvaro, "Ecuador's President Seeks Stronger Ties with China." *Dow Jones Emerging Markets Report.* http://www.uofaweb.ualberta.ca/chinainstitute/. March 29, 2007.

131. "China CNPC preocupada e interesada por Ecuador."

132. The other major Ecuadorian pipeline is Sistema del Oleoducto Transecuatoriano (SOTE), which is owned by the Ecuadorian national oil company Ecopetrol, and is older and prone to breakdowns. Jubany and Poon, 2006.

133. Interview with Alberto Panche, Ministry of Energy and Mines. Quito, Ecuador. July 9, 2007.

134. "El bloque 15 decendió al ritmo de Petroecuador en producción." *El Comercio.* Quito, Ecuador. http://www.elcomercio.com. October 25, 2006. "Correa niega cambio de posición en el caso Occidental." *El Comercio.* Quito, Ecuador. http://www.elcomercio.com. June 23, 2007.

135. These include Block 15, Eden-Yuturi, and Limoncocha. See "El bloque 15 decendió al ritmo de Petroecuador en producción." Sinopec subsequently ran into some difficulties with Petroecuador over declining production in these fields, due to delays in bringing exploration rigs to the area because of commitments for the rigs elsewhere.

136. Alvaro, 2007.

137. "Petroleras de Ecuador y China firman alianza." *El Comercio*. Quito, Ecuador. http://www.elcomercio.com. June 5, 2007.

138. Because of the environmental sensitivity of the land to be developed, the government is asking the international community to provide Ecuador with $350 million not to develop the land. "La alternativa para explotar el ITT avanza." *El Comercio*. Quito, Ecuador. http://www.elcomercio.com. July 9, 2007.

139. "Ecuador extiende plazo para no explotar petróleo en reserva natural." *El Universal*. Caracas, Venezuela. http://www.eluniversal.com. January 11, 2008. See also Pablo Ortiz García, "Una locura cuerda." *El Comercio*. Quito, Ecuador. http://www.elcomercio.com. June 29, 2007. See also "Petrobras planea explotar 230 milliones de barriles de crudo en Ecuador." *El Comercio*. Quito, Ecuador. http://www.elcomercio.com. May 16, 2007. See also Alvaro, 2007.

140. "PdVSA estudia asociaciones con Ecuador en yacimientos de ITT." *El Universal*. Caracas, Venezuela. http://www.el-universal.com. April 17, 2007.

141. Interview with Alberto Panche, Ministry of Energy and Mines. Quito, Ecuador. July 9, 2007.

142. "La alternativa para explotar el ITT avanza."

143. "ITT: Utopía camina hacia la realidad." Boletín: Dirección de Comunicación Social, Ministerio de Energia y Minas, Republica del Ecuador. No. 182. www.menergia.gov.ec. July 3, 2007.

144. Although the regime of Rafael Correa looks favorably upon Chinese investors, he is also sensitive to the indigenous and environmentalist constituencies that do not want ITT to be opened. The degree to which the Chinese presence expands in exploration and development in the Ecuadorian petroleum sector is thus partly a function of whether ITT is opened up by the Correa regime or by a future regime that may be less oriented toward Chinese investors.

145. "Empresas de once países están interesadas en explotar el ITT." *El Comercio*. Quito, Ecuador. http://www.elcomercio.com. March 13, 2007. See also Mercedes Alvaro, "Chinese State-Owned Oil Co Agrees to Raise Output in Ecuador." *Dow Jones International News*. http://www.uofaweb.ualberta.ca/chinainstitute. February 13, 2007.

146. "Correa y Chávez en pacto petrolero." *El Universo*. Guayaquil, Ecuador. http://www.eluniverso.com. July 15, 2008.

147. "Ecuador: China deberá comprar algo más que petróleo." *El Universo*. Guayaquil, Ecuador. http://www.eluniverso.com. November 25, 2007.

148. For a discussion of how the war in Colombia has impacted neighboring Ecuadorian provinces, see Zambrano, 2006.

149. "Petrolera china dice que incidentes en Amazonia no afectarán sus intereses en Latinoamérica." *El Comercio*. Quito, Ecuador. http://www.elcomercio.com. November 14, 2006. See also Juliette Kerr, "Protests Against Chinese Company's Oil Operations End in Ecuador." *Global Insight Daily Analysis*. http://www.uofaweb.ualberta.ca/chinainstitute/. November 13, 2006. Despite the violence and the disruption of its operations, however, the Chinese reaction was remarkably low-key, indicating that such actions were a traditional manner by which the people in Ecuador expressed their political views. "Petrolera China desestima que protesta en Tarapoa haya afectado sus intereses."

150. "Protestas contra Petroriental dejan 31 heridas en ocho días." *El Comercio*. Quito, Ecuador. http://www.elcomercio.com. July 4, 2007.

151. "Petroriental perdió cerca de un millón de dólares por protesta." *El Comercio*. Quito, Ecuador. http://www.elcomercio.com. July 7, 2007.

152. "Campesinos armados de Ecuador buscan paralizar actividad de Petrolera China." *El Universal.* Caracas, Venezuela. http://www.eluniversal.com. July 23, 2007.

153. "Petroriental denuncia atentado en oleoducto en China." *El Universal.* Caracas, Venezuela. http://www.eluniversal.com. July 21, 2007.

154. "Borja anunció cambios en el reglamento de hidrocarburos." *El Universo.* Guayaquil, Ecuador. http://www.eluniverso.com. July 6, 2006.

155. "Min. de Minas y Petróleos espera concluir renegociación de contratos petroleros antes de fecha fijada por Correa." *El Comercio.* Quito, Ecuador. http://www.elcomercio.com. February 8, 2008. Andes Petroleum was also impacted by the dispute between Occidental Petroleum and the Ecuadorian government, which raised the prospect that Andes might have to forfeit certain assets previously purchased from Oxy. Ultimately, however, the matter was resolved in an amiable manner. "China CNPC preocupada e interesada por Ecuador."

156. "La Andes Petroleum y Repsol logran un acuerdo." *El Universo.* Guayaquil, Ecuador. http://www.eluniverso.com. August 9, 2008.

157. In part, the development of Ecuador's mining industry has been relatively limited because the thick foliage covering potentially mineral-rich land makes identification of mineral veins more costly than in terrain without such foliage, such as in the coastal regions and mountains of Peru.

158. Benjamín Rosales, "Ecuador minero." *El Comercio.* Quito, Ecuador. http://www.elcomercio.com. April 19, 2007.

159. Prior to the war between Ecuador and Peru in 1995, the area encompassed by the mountain range was all Ecuadorian territory. The 1998 treaty between Ecuador and Peru that delimited the border established that the eastern side of the mountain range was Peruvian territory, giving Peru mineral exploration rights in the area as well. Interview with Gustavo Solórzano, Escuela Superior Politécnica del Litoral (ESPOL). Guayaquil, Ecuador. July 12, 2007. Curiously, in July 2008, the Chinese government made a $100,000 donation to the Peruvian government to help it to clear mines from this territory, left over from the war, an action that could also facilitate exploration of the region for uranium and other mineral wealth. "China donó US$100.000 a Perú para retirar minas de frontera con Ecuador." *Diario Financiero.* Santiago, Chile. http://www.df.cl. July 24, 2008.

160. "Ley minera pasó primer debate en 'Congresillo.'" *El Universo.* Guayaquil, Ecuador. http://www.eluniverso.com. December 19, 2008.

161. "Ecuador espera con China un trato comercial equitativo." *El Universo.* Guayaquil, Ecuador. http://www.eluniverso.com. October 31, 2008.

162. "Ecuador busca ampliar exportaciones bananeras a China." *El Universo.* Guayaquil, Ecuador. http://www.eluniverso.com. April 4, 2007.

163. "Ecuador busca más mercados bananeros." *El Comercio.* Guayaquil, Ecuador. http://www.elcomercio.com. April 26, 2007.

164. "Ecuador busca ampliar exportaciones bananeras a China."

165. "Ecuador vende menos banano a EE.UU y a la UE." *El Comercio.* Quito, Ecuador. http://www.elcomercio.com. June 11, 2007.

166. "Bananeros buscan exportar más a China." *El Universo.* Guayaquil, Ecuador. http://www.eluniverso.com. June 19, 2006.

167. Interview with Harry Sun Soria Laman, Ecuador-China Chamber of Commerce. Guayaquil, Ecuador. July 13, 2007. See also Interview with Gustavo Solórzano, Escuela Politécnica de Litoral (ESPOL). Guayaquil, Ecuador. July 12, 2007.

168. According to industry data, Ecuador is the leading producer of shrimp in

Latin America. "El camarón con valor agregado permitirá competir con Asia." *El Comercio*. Quito, Ecuador. http://www.elcomercio.com. October 18, 2007.

169. Ibid.

170. Similarly, Ecuador has also planted some 50,000 hectares of sugarcane and 50,000 hectares of African palm, focused on the use of these products for the production of ethanol and biodiesel fuel. "Ecuador busca aumentar produccion de maiz." *El Comercio*. Quito, Ecuador. http://www.elcomercio.com. October 16, 2007.

171. See also Interview with Gustavo Solórzano, Escuela Politécnica de Litoral (ESPOL). Guayaquil, Ecuador. July 12, 2007.

172. "Ecuador-China relaciones comerciales." Unpublished background paper. *Ministerio de Relaciones Exteriores*. July 10, 2007.

173. Ecuadorian government involvement in the negotiations included the head of export promotion and investment of agricultural health. Interview with Fernando Guzman, Ministry of Foreign Relations. Quito, Ecuador. July 10, 2007.

174. Interview with Cai Rungo, ambassador for the People's Republic of China to Ecuador. Quito, Ecuador. July 9, 2007.

175. In one case, after repeated visits, the Chinese company set up a small operation in Ecuador to facilitate the extraction and processing of lumber. Interview with Marlene de Auson, director, International Business Division, Ecuador-China Chamber of Commerce. Guayaquil, Ecuador. July 12, 2007.

176. "Ecuador-China relaciones comerciales."

177. "China es el principal proveedor de motos, jugetes y calzado." *El Comercio*. Quito, Ecuador. http://www.elcomercio.com. August 28, 2007.

178. A traditional source of demand for Chinese goods in the Ecuadorian market has been Ecuador's Chinese community. In particular, elements of this community that established themselves in the restaurant and retail sector often import products and other specialty goods from China for use in their businesses. See Soria, 2007.

179. See also Interview with Gustavo Solórzano, Escuela Politécnica de Litoral (ESPOL). Guayaquil, Ecuador. July 12, 2007.

180. "Las computadoras portátiles ganan más espacio en el mercado nacional." *El Comercio*. Quito, Ecuador. http://www.elcomercio.com. September 11, 2007.

181. See also Interview with Gustavo Solórzano, Escuela Politécnica de Litoral (ESPOL). Guayaquil, Ecuador. July 12, 2007.

182. Ibid.

183. The last brand is offered for sale in Ecuador through the distributor Cinascar. See "Con una feria se intenta mejorar la venta de autos para este año." *El Comercio*. Quito, Ecuador. October 28, 2007, p. 14.

184. "En la terminal de Guayaquil operán nuevos buses." *El Comercio*. Guayaquil, Ecuador. http://www.elcomercio.com. October 29, 2007.

185. See also Interview with Gustavo Solórzano, Escuela Politécnica de Litoral (ESPOL). Guayaquil, Ecuador. July 12, 2007.

186. Of this investment, $15 million had already been spent by Hutchison within the first seven months of the operation of the port, for, among other things, the installation of the first movable crane and the conclusion of bathymetric studies, necessary for the dredging operations. See "USD15 millones se invirtieron en el puerto de Manta en 7 meses." *El Comercio*. Quito, Ecuador. http://www.elcomercio.com. October 19, 2007. The port of Manta currently supports vessels with a draft of thirteen meters. The improvements contemplated by Hutchison include deepening the channel to support entry by ships with a draft of eighteen meters, thus enabling the port to support operations by larger commercial vessels,

such as those transiting the Pacific to and from Asia. "Eje Manta-Manaos, alternativa al Canal de Panamá para desarrollo de Amazonía." *El Comercio*. Quito, Ecuador. http://www.elcomercio.com. May 6, 2007.

187. "Aeropuerto de Manta se habilitará para vuelos con Asia." *El Universo*. Guayaquil, Ecuador. http://www.eluniverso.com. November 22, 2007.

188. "Correa le propone a China que Manta sea su ruta de comercio." *El Universo*. Guayaquil, Ecuador. http://www.eluniverso.com. November 23, 2007.

189. In representing the award of the Manta port concession to the Ecuadorian press, the Chinese delegation emphasized their vision for developing the port, and Ecuador in general, as a major point of entry for Chinese commerce with South America. See "TIDE toma las riendas del puerto." *El Comercio*. Quito, Ecuador. http://www.el-comercio.com. February 2, 2007.

190. Without the Manabí refinery, Ecuadorian oil would be sent to Esmereldas for refining, or simply shipped out through the port of Esmereldas or Guayaquil for refining abroad. In addition, the decision of the Ecuadorian government to move forward with the refinery in Manabí in July 2007 also represented a defeat for elements within Ecuador that had wanted to construct a refinery further to the south, in Monteverde, closer to Guayaquil. See also Interview with Gustavo Solórzano, Escuela Politécnica de Litoral (ESPOL). Guayaquil, Ecuador. July 12, 2007.

191. Indeed, in discussing the award of the Manta concession, representatives from Hutchison noted that they had previously negotiated with authorities in Guayaquil for locating the expanded port facilities there, but those with whom they had spoken had not shared their vision. "TIDE toma las riendas del puerto."

192. "Eje Manta-Manaos, alternativa al Canal de Panamá para desarrollo de Amazonía."

193. "Total Import and Export Value by Country (Region) (2007/01–12)."

194. Some analysts have concerns about the navigability, during the dry season, of the rivers in the middle section of the corridor.

195. "Eje bioceanico multimodal Pacifico-Atlantico Ecuador-Brasil Manta-Manaus-Belém." Unpublished briefing. Manta Port Authority. Manta, Ecuador. May 2007.

196. Zambrano, 2007.

197. See "Correa hace más ofertas a China." *El Universo*. Guayaquil, Ecuador. http://www.eluniverso.com. November 22, 2007.

198. "Correa le propone a China que Manta sea su ruta de comercio." The Chinese have also reportedly expressed an interest in helping to fund the project, although the official Chinese position is that they would like to see Ecuador and Brazil proceed with the project, then formally ask China for funding at a later point in time when it is more mature. Interview with Cai Rungo, ambassador for the People's Republic of China to Ecuador. Quito, Ecuador. July 9, 2007.

199. "Empresas chinas interesada en generación hidroeléctrica en Ecuador." *Nacion*. San José, Costa Rica. http://www.nacion.com. April 12, 2006.

200. In December 2007, the project was awarded to a consortium of Conelec and Hidropaute. See "El Presidente asiste en Cuenca a la suscripción del contrato para construcción de proyecto hidroeléctrico Sopladora." *Gobierno Nacional de la Republica de Ecuador*. http://www.presidencia.gov.ec/noticias.asp?noid=9036. December 28, 2007.

201. See also Interview with Gustavo Solórzano, Escuela Politécnica de Litoral (ESPOL). Guayaquil, Ecuador. July 12, 2007.

202. "Proyecto hidroeléctrico Toachi Pilatón empezará a construirse en el 2008." *El Universo*. Guayaquil, Ecuador. http://www.eluniverso.com. October 11,

2007. See also Ramiro Gonzalez J., "Hydro Power Project Toachi Pilatón." Government of the Province of Pichincha. Presentation. www.pichincha.gov.ec/ download/pilatoac/presingl.pdf. Accessed December 28, 2007.

203. Interview with Fernando Guzman, Ministry of Foreign Relations. Quito, Ecuador. July 10, 2007. See also "Perfil de los cooperantes: Republica Popular de China." *Instituto Ecuatoriano de Cooperacion Internacional (INECI)*. http://www. mmrree.gov.ec/ineci/perfiles/china.asp. Accessed December 28, 2007.

204. Interview with Fernando Guzman, Ministry of Foreign Relations. Quito, Ecuador. July 10, 2007.

205. In 2000, the Ecuadorian Ministry of Foreign Relations established a coordination agreement with CORPEI through which the latter can leverage the diplomatic resources of the ministry to promote Ecuadorian goods in China and provide information to Ecuadorian companies looking to do business there. The agreement, which was renewed in 2006, also contains provisions for the designation of a single person within the foreign ministry to coordinate activities with CORPEI. Reflecting the new spirit of integration, the Ecuadorian vice minister of foreign commerce and integration, Antonio Ruales, is also a member of CORPEI. Interview with Fernando Guzman, Ministry of Foreign Relations. Quito, Ecuador. July 10, 2007. See also Hilton Heredia G., "Privados andinos logran respaldo en EEUU para ampliar el Atpdea." *El Deber*. Santa Cruz, Bolivia. http://www.eldeber.com.bo. May 17, 2007.

206. In November 2007, in coordination with the official trip by President Rafael Correa to China, the Ecuador-China Chamber of Commerce sent its tenth annual delegation of businesspeople to the PRC. Interview with Harry Sun Soria Laman, Ecuador-China Chamber of Commerce. Guayaquil, Ecuador. July 13, 2007. Furthermore, in 2007, the former president of the Ecuador-China Chamber of Commerce, Washington Hago, was named as Ecuador's ambassador to China.

207. Hago, 2005, p. 64.

208. "Petróleo y sector financiero Ecuador en mira de empresas chinas." *Nacion*. San José, Costa Rica. http://www.nacion.com. April 5, 2006.

209. Similarly, although Ecuador was declared by China to be an official tourist destination, the number of Chinese tourists who have thus far traveled to the country has been limited, due to the lack both of formal accords eliminating requirements such as visas for entry and of a Chinese-speaking tourist infrastructure. Interview with Marlene de Auson, director, International Business Division, Ecuador-China Chamber of Commerce. Guayaquil, Ecuador. July 12, 2007.

210. Indeed, within the Latin American FLACSO system, only the Argentina affiliate offers Chinese-language courses. Based on a personal survey of conference attendees at the Congreso Latinoamericano y Caribeño de Ciencias Sociales, FLACSO Ecuador. Quito, Ecuador. October 29–31, 2007.

211. See also Interview with Gustavo Solórzano, Escuela Politécnica de Litoral (ESPOL). Guayaquil, Ecuador. July 12, 2007.

212. Interview with Dr. Adrian Bonilla, Facultad Latinoamericano de Ciencias Sociales. Quito, Ecuador. July 10, 2007.

213. Interview with Harry Sun Soria Laman, Ecuador-China Chamber of Commerce. Guayaquil, Ecuador. July 13, 2007.

214. "Perfil de los Cooperantes: Republica Popular de China."

215. "Correa hace más ofertas a China." See also "Ecuador acerca su diplomacia a la gigante China." *El Universo*. Guayaquil, Ecuador. http://www. eluniverso.com. November 21, 2007. See also "China e Ecuador firman acuerdos de cooperación bilateral." *El Universo*. Guayaquil, Ecuador. http://www.eluniverso. com. November 20, 2007.

216. "Senior Chinese Party Official Meets with Ecuadorian President." *Xinhua.* http://www.uofaweb.ualberta.ca/chinainstitute. March 29, 2007. See also "China apoya inclusion de Ecuador a APEC."

217. "Chinese Defense Minister Hold Talks with Ecuadorian Counterpart." *People's Daily Online.* Beijing, China. http://english.people.com.cn. March 22, 2006.

218. "China, Ecuador Vow to Further Military Ties." *People's Daily Online.* Beijing, China. http://english.people.com.cn. December 2, 2004.

219. Interview with Guido Zambrano, Ministry of Transportation and Public Works. Quito, Ecuador. July 8, 2007.

220. Interview with Cai Rungo, ambassador for the People's Republic of China to Ecuador. Quito, Ecuador. July 9, 2007.

221. "El canciller Choquehuanca firma un convenio de cooperación en China." *La Razón.* La Paz, Bolivia. http://www.la-razon.com. December 20, 2007.

222. A 2005 study by the Bolivian Institute for Foreign Commerce emphasized the complementary nature of the Bolivian and Chinese economies, with Bolivia mainly being a primary-product exporter, and China being a significant importer of such products. The study "El Dragón Disperta" argues that the growth of the Chinese economy definitely favors Bolivian exports, particularly in sectors such as mining and forestry. Herberto Quispe, "Comercio exterior con China." *El Diario.* La Paz, Bolivia. http://eldiario.net/noticias. April 5, 2005.

223. See, for example, Juan L. Cariaga, "Planes económicas sin inversion." *La Razón.* La Paz, Bolivia. http://www.la-razon.com. June 24, 2007.

224. "Bolivia: Inversión extranjera directa por año según país de origen (p), 1996–2005." *Instituto Nacional de Estadística: Bolivia.* http://www.ine.gov.bo. Accessed December 26, 2007.

225. Although such uncertainty makes the Chinese caution understandable, it does not fully explain why the Chinese have shown relatively more caution in their dealings with Bolivia than in their relationship with Ecuador, which has a similar history of political instability.

226. In January 2006, shortly alter being elected president of Bolivia, but prior to assuming office, Morales traveled to China, where he met with Hu Jintao and other Chinese leaders. In his meeting with Hu, Morales called China an "ideological ally" and expressed his hopes for closer cooperation between the two nations, including his hopes that China would participate in Bolivia's gas industry. Joe McDonald, "Bolivian Leader Labels China 'Ideological Ally.'" *Washington Times.* Washington, DC. http://www.washingtontimes.com. January 10, 2006.

227. The PRC Ministry of Foreign Affairs claims seven sets of projects between the establishment of diplomatic relations in 1985 and 2003, including well drilling, the construction of a cultural center and a small hydropower station, and three technical cooperation projects, including rice and vegetable cultivation. "Bilateral Relations." *Ministry of Foreign Affairs of the People's Republic of China.* Official website. http://www.fmprc.gov.cn/eng/wjb/zzjg/ldmzs/gjlb/3468/default.htm. September 26, 2003.

228. Population Division of the Department of Economic and Social Affairs of the United Nations Secretariat, 2004.

229. Interview with Zhang Tuo, ambassador of the People's Republic of China to the Republic of Venezuela. Caracas, Venezuela. January 15, 2008.

230. "Con trabajo en equipo se destapó el caso de las visas." *La Razón.* La Paz, Bolivia. http://www.la-razon.com. December 13, 2006.

231. "Empresa China se alía con YPFB e invertirá $US 1.500 millones." *Los Tiempos.* Cochabamba, Bolivia. http://www.lostiempos.com September 3, 2004.

232. "Gobierno rechaza inversión de Shengli." *El Diario*. La Paz, Bolivia. http://eldiario.net. August 24, 2005. See also "EEUU preocupado por influencia económica y política de China." *El Diario*. La Paz, Bolivia. http://eldiario.net. April 11, 2005.

233. "Shengli Oil decidió apostar por Bolivia con gas natural." *Los Tiempos*. Cochabamba, Bolivia. http://www.lostiempos.com October 21, 2004.

234. "Petrolera China niega vínculo con la Shengli." *Correo del Sur*. Sucre, Bolivia. http://correodelsur.net. August 23, 2005.

235. "Grandes empresas chinas invertirán en Bolivia." *Portal Minero*. http://www.portalminero.com. January 10, 2006.

236. Palacios, 2008, p. 180.

237. "Ortiz se fue de YPFB y denuncia manoseo." *El Nuevo Día*. La Paz, Bolivia. http://www.el-nuevodia.com. February 27, 2007. See also "Renuncia presidente de YPFB." *Prensa.com*. Panama City, Panama. http://mensual.prensa.com/mensual/contenido/2007/01/28/hoy/negocios/873568.html. January 28, 2007. See also "El presidente de YPFB renuncia por falta de apoyo a su gestión." *El Economista*. http://www.eleconomista.es. December 26, 2006.

238. "Evo rechaza la renuncia de Ministro de Hidrocarburos." *Los Tiempos*. Cochabamba, Bolvia. http://www.lostiempos.com. February 12, 2007.

239. Ibid.

240. From a Bolivian perspective, the solution was politically objectionable on multiple counts. Not only did the plan export Bolivian gas, rather than use it to support the energy needs of the country, but also it exported the gas via the Chilean port of Arica—across territory that had once belonged to Bolivia. The need to export the gas via Chile was a reminder that Chile had taken the territory from Bolivia in the 1879 War of the Pacific, leaving the country without access to the sea. To add insult to injury, the plan involved refining the gas in Arica before exporting it, conducting one of the most significant value-added steps on Chilean territory that had once belonged to Bolivia.

241. Bolivia could, for example, export its gas from the Margarita gas fields to China and other Pacific destinations via the Peruvian port of Ilo. Although the distance involved is somewhat longer than that involved for the principal alternative of export via the Chilean port of Ariqua, Ilo is part of a diplomatic agreement negotiated between the Peruvian government of Alberto Fujimori and the Bolivian government of Jaime Paz Zamora, which lays the groundwork for partial Bolivian sovereignty over the use of the route. Nonetheless, it is unlikely that a project to develop the infrastructure to export Bolivian gas via Ilo will go forward until the Chilean route and the possibility of a new Bolivian corridor to the sea have been definitively resolved.

242. Upon assuming power, Morales expressed a desire, on various occasions, to talk to his Chilean counterpart regarding Bolivian access to the sea. "Morales espera hablar del mar." *Los Tiempos*. Cochabamba, Bolivia. http://www.lostiempos.com. March 9, 2006.

243. "Bolivia, la potencia gasífera, pasa aprietos para abastecer." *La Razón*. La Paz, Bolivia. http://www.la-razon.com. December 14, 2007.

244. "La inversion petrolera en el país es de las más bajas." *La Razón*. La Paz, Bolivia. http://www.la-razon.com. July 6, 2008.

245. "Aún tardará la solución a los combustibles." *La Razón*. La Paz, Bolivia. http://www.la-razon.com. November 5, 2008.

246. "PdVSA despachó taladro chino con destino a Bolivia." *El Universal*. Caracas, Venezuela. http://www.el-universal.com. July 10, 2008.

247. "Acusan a brazileña EBX de violar normas ambientales de Bolivia."

Nacion. San José, Costa Rica. http://www.nacion.com. April 14, 2006. El Mutún is believed to be the sixth-largest mineral field of its type in the world. "A la espera de Jindal." *La Razón.* La Paz, Bolivia. http://www.la-razon.com. November 20, 2006.

248. "Grandes empresas Chinas invertirán en Bolivia."

249. Talks were sufficiently advanced with respect to the Tacna portion of the deal that the Peruvian Congress approved a law authorizing the construction of the megaport at Tacna and the highway and rail infrastructure to connect Tacna to El Mutún. "Congress Passes Bill to Build Tacna Megaport: Bolivia, Peru." *Business News Americas.* http://www.bnamericas.com. February 27, 2006.

250. Reportedly, the talks included not only the creation of a Tacna-Mutún railway, but also the creation of a free-trade zone in the port of Tacna itself. Interview with Dr. José Antonio de Chazal, executive director of Universidad Virtual. Santa Cruz, Bolivia. August 15, 2007.

251. "Un dragón en la puerta." See also "Alan García frenta a Bolivia." *La Razón.* La Paz, Bolivia. www.la-razon.com. August 9, 2006.

252. "Los papeles de la Jindal." *La Razón.* La Paz, Bolivia. http://www.la-razon.com. June 1, 2007. See also "El gobierno pone plazo a los de Jindal." *El Nuevo Día.* http://www.el-neuvodia.com. May 22, 2007.

253. "Confusión sobre el Mutún." *La Razón.* La Paz, Bolivia. http://www.la-razon.com; and "Congress Passes Bill to Build Tacna Megaport: Bolivia, Peru."

254. "Bolivianos critican acuerdo entre Morales y Chávez." La Paz, Bolivia. *El Nuevo Herald.* Miami, Florida. September 11, 2007. p. A1.

255. Shortly after the announcement that the remaining half of El Mutún would be developed in collaboration with Venezuela, a group of Chinese investors traveled to Bolivia to discuss Chinese participation in that half, leading the Bolivian government apparently to retract its initial commitment to Venezuela and announce that there was "room for all of the countries that want to invest in Bolivia and explore the reserves" of El Mutún. "Bolivia gestiona con China explotar fabuloso yacimiento de hierro." *El Universal.* Caracas, Venezuela. http://www.eluniversal.com. September 27, 2007.

256. "Bolivia Talking with China for El Mutún Development." *Economic Times.* http://economictimes.indiatimes.com. January 7, 2008.

257. "China quiere invertir en las minas potosinas." *El Potosí.* Potosí, Bolivia. http://www.elpotosi.net. February 12, 2006.

258. "La minería en el Plan de Desarrollo." *La Razón.* La Paz, Bolivia. http://www.la-razon.com. July 12, 2006.

259. "Los mineros pedieron $US 250 mil durante el conflicto." *La Razón.* La Paz, Bolivia. http://www.la-razon.com. October 7, 2006.

260. "El comercio exterior con China." *El Diario.* La Paz, Bolivia. http://eldiario.net. April 25, 2005.

261. Heriberto Quispe, "Comercio exterior con China." *El Diario.* La Paz, Bolivia. http://eldiario.net. April 5, 2005.

262. According to one source, Bolivia was one of several nations in South America that substantially increased the amount of land dedicated to soy production in 2005, due in part to Chinese demand. See "American Farmers Afraid of Losing Soybean Market in China." *People's Daily Online.* Beijing, China. http://english.people.com.cn. August 30, 2006.

263. "Bolivia: Exportaciones según producto." *Instituto Nacional de Estadística: Bolivia.* http://www.ine.gov.bo. Accessed December 26, 2007.

264. "Bolivia y China abren posibilidad de un TLC." *Portal Minero.* http://www.portalminero.com. February 23, 2005.

265. It is likely that interest within Bolivia to expand exports to China will receive an added push in 2009 if, as expected, Bolivia's preferential access to markets in the United States is cut off with the expiration of the Andean Trade Preferences Drug Enforcement Act (ATPDEA). The program was created to reward and compensate nations of the Andean region for their cooperation with the United States in drug enforcement activities. As is also the case with Ecuador, the tariff levied on Bolivian goods entering US markets will increase from 0 percent to 17 percent, significantly hurting the competitive position of Bolivian products exported to the United States and creating incentives to seek new markets—such as China—for those exports. ATPDEA originally was scheduled to expire in June 2007, but was extended by the US Congress. Milton Heredia G. "Privados andinos logran respaldo en EEUU para ampliar el ATPDEA." *El Deber.* Santa Cruz, Bolivia. http://www. eldeber.com.bo. May 17, 2007.

266. "Bolivia—Estadísticas Económicas: Sector Exportaciones (2006)." *Instituto Nacional de Estadística: Bolivia.* http://www.ine.gov.bo. Accessed December 26, 2007.

267. Bolivia Data Profile. *World Bank Group.* http://devdata.worldbank.org/external/CPProfile.asp?SelectedCountry=BOL&CCODE=BOL&CNAME=Bolivia&PTYPE=CP. Accessed September 22, 2007.

268. "Bolivia—Estadísticas Económicas: Sector Importaciones (2006)."

269. Interview with David Suarez Nuñez del Prado. Chamber of Commerce, Industry, Commerce, and Tourism of Santa Cruz (CAINCO). Santa Cruz, Bolivia. August 15, 2007.

270. "Las tiendas lanzan sus ofertas y descuentos especiales por Navidad." *El Deber.* Santa Cruz, Bolivia. http://www.eldeber.com.bo. December 2, 2007.

271. "Contact Us." *Huawei.* Official website. http://www.huawei.com/about/officeList.do#Chile. Accessed December 30, 2007.

272. "ZTE to Provide High-End Router Switch Products to Bolivia's COTAS." *Global Executive Forum.* http://www.globalexecutiveforum.net/China.htm. June 11, 2007.

273. "Brazil Gets Port on Pacific Coast and China Becomes Much Closer." *Brazzil Magazine.* São Paulo, Brazil. http://www.brazzilmag.com. December 17, 2007.

274. Ibid.

275. David Moreno and Gonzalo López. "Chávez impulsa Petroandina y oferta invertir en petroquímica." *El Deber.* Santa Cruz, Bolivia. http://www.eldeber. com.bo. August 10, 2007.

276. Marco Chuquimia. "Vice: Hay nuevo modelo económico." *El Deber.* Santa Cruz, Bolivia. http://www.eldeber.com.bo. June 9, 2008.

277. "Organismos Internacionales." *Centro de Promoción Bolivia (CEPROBOL).* Official website. La Paz, Bolivia. http://www.ceprobol.gov.bo/enlacesint.aspx. Accessed December 26, 2007.

278. "Perfil País." *Centro de Promoción Bolivia (CEPROBOL).* La Paz, Bolivia. http://www.ceprobol.gov.bo/ppais.aspx. Accessed December 26, 2007.

279. "Calendario de Eventos." *Centro de Promoción Bolivia (CEPROBOL).* Official website. La Paz, Bolivia. http://www.ceprobol.gov.bo/ecalendario1.aspx. Accessed December 26, 2007.

280. Each of the editions of the organization's bulletin, *Exportemos,* for example, contains a profile of a specific foreign market for its exporters. None of the twelve bulletins maintained on the organization's website, however, contained information about an Asian market. Similarly, none of the summaries of the organization's trade magazine, *Comercio Exterior,* from 2003 through 2007, contained a reference to China. See *Instituto Boliviano de Comercio Exterior.* Official website. http://www.ibce.org.bo. Accessed December 26, 2007.

281. Interview with David Suarez Nuñez del Prado. Chamber of Commerce, Industry, Commerce, and Tourism of Santa Cruz (CAINCO). Santa Cruz, Bolivia. August 15, 2007.

282. "Empresarios de China confirman presencia en rueda de negocios." *El Deber*. Santa Cruz, Bolivia. http://www.eldeber.com.bo. September 1, 2008.

283. Interview with David Suarez Nuñez del Prado. Chamber of Commerce, Industry, Commerce, and Tourism of Santa Cruz (CAINCO). Santa Cruz, Bolivia. August 15, 2007.

284. "Vuelve a brillar la feria de Santa Cruz." *La Razón*. La Paz, Bolivia. http://www.la-razon.com. September 29, 2006. See also "La Expocruz cerró con más de 460.000 visitas." *La Razón*. http://www.la-razon.com. La Paz, Bolivia. October 1, 2007.

285. See "Historia del Banco." *Banco Mercantíl Santa Cruz*. Official website. https://www.bmsc.com.bo/Institucional/bncHistoria.aspx. Accessed December 26, 2007.

286. Interview with Jenny Ampuero Justiniano, director of the National and International Relations Program, Universidad Autónoma Gabriel René Moreno. Santa Cruz, Bolivia. August 17, 2007.

287. "Hay dos Asociaciones de Amistad Bolivia-China." *La Razón*. La Paz, Bolivia. http://www.la-razon.com. March 21, 2007.

288. See, for example, Joe Macdonald, "Bolivian Leader Names China Ideological Ally." *Washington Times*. Washington, DC. http://www.washington-times.com. January 10, 2006.

289. "Ministro Choquehuanca pide a Primer Ministro chino 'alianza' Bolivia-China." *Journadanet*. La Paz, Bolivia. http://www.journadanet.com. December 22, 2007.

290. "El canceller Choquehuanca firma un convenio de cooperación en China." *La Razón*. La Paz, Bolivia. http://www.la-razon.com. December 20, 2007. See also "Convenio de cooperación técnica en Pekín." *Journadanet*. La Paz, Bolivia. http://www.journadanet.com. December 20, 2007.

291. "China dona 120 motos a la policía boliviana." *Los Tiempos*. Cochabamba, Bolivia. http://www.lostiempos.com. February 10, 2005.

292. "China da 4 millones de dólares a Bolivia." *Correo del Sur*. Sucre, Bolivia. http://correodelsur.net. January 21, 2006.

293. "China ortorga una ayuda de 2,6 millones de dólares a Bolivia." *Los Tiempos*. Cochabamba, Bolivia. http://www.lostiempos.com. November 21, 2006.

294. "El Gobierno ya entregó 346 tractores para el agro." *La Razón*. http://www.la-razon.com. October 24, 2006.

295. "Empiezan las obras para la nueva ruta a Cochabamba." *La Razón*. La Paz, Bolivia. http://www.la-razon.com. October 13, 2006.

296. "China, EEUU e Irán apoyan a la policía con vehículos." *La Razón*. La Paz, Bolivia. http://www.la-razon.com. December 12, 2007.

297. The sale came to light during a political dispute in 2008, in which the Bolivian government sought to demonstrate that the armaments had not been supplied by Venezuela. See "Bolivia aclara que 10.000 fusiles fueron donados por China y no por Venezuela." *El Universal*. Caracas, Venezuela. June 26, 2008. See also "Dos ex autoridades dudan de la llegada de los AK-47." *La Razón*. La Paz, Bolivia. http://www.la-razon.com. June 28, 2008.

298. "Gobierno descarta malestar entre militares por nuevo Alto Mando." *Los Tiempos*. Cochabamba, Bolivia. http://www.lostiempos.com. January 26, 2006.

299. "China ortorga una ayuda de 2,6 millones de dólares a Bolivia." *Los Tiempos*. Cochabamba, Bolivia. http://www.lostiempos.com. November 21, 2006.

300. "China donó equipos a las fuerzas armadas." *Los Tiempos*. Cochabamba, Bolivia. http://www.lostiempos.com. December 16, 2006.

301. "El gobierno decide potenciar la fuerza aérea." *La Razón*. La Paz, Bolivia.

http://www.la-razon.com. February 19, 2007. See also "La FAB se fortalece con un avión de carga." *La Razón*. La Paz, Bolivia. http://www.la-razon.com. August 2, 2007. See also "Chávez donará dos aeronaves a Bolivia." *El Universal*. Caracas, Venezuela. http://www.eluniversal.com. February 20, 2007.

302. "In 2007, Bolivia sextuplicó su deuda." *El Deber*. Santa Cruz, Bolivia. http://www.eldeber.com.bo. January 31, 2008.

303. "China, Bolivia Vow to Enhance Military Exchanges." *People's Daily Online*. Beijing, China. http://english.people.cn. April 29, 2007.

304. "China regaló 43 vehículos a las fuerzas armadas." *El Deber*. Santa Cruz, Bolivia. http://www.eldeber.com.bo. September 11, 2007. See also "El gobierno elogia la ayuda de China 'sin condiciones.'" *La Razón*. La Paz, Bolivia. http://www.la-razon.com/versiones/20070911_006026/nota_256_478432.htm. September 11, 2007.

305. "Total Import and Export Value by Country (Region) (2007/01–12)."

306. "Vicecanciller destaca potencial en intercambios comerciales con China." *El Comercio*. Lima, Peru. http://www.elcomercio.com.pe/ediciononline. July 3, 2007. See also "Exportaciones peruanas crecieron en 2006 un 35.6%." *El Comercio*. Lima, Peru. http://www.elcomercio.com.pe/ediciononline. January 23, 2007.

307. "China y Perú iniciarán conversaciones hacia TLC en los próximos días." *Los Tiempos*. Cochabamba, Bolivia. http://www.lostiempos.com. March 19, 2007.

308. "El Perú destacó durante una semana en la televisión china." *El Comercio*. Lima, Peru. http://www.elcomercio.com.pe/ediciononline. August 6, 2006.

309. "Tras TLC con China, Perú negocia con Corea y Japón." *El Universo*. Guayaquil, Ecuador. http://www.eluniverso.com. November 18, 2008.

310. "Bilateral Relations." *Ministry of Foreign Affairs of the People's Republic of China*. Official website. http://www.fmprc.gov.cn/eng/wjb/zzjg/ldmzs/gjlb/3513/default.htm. September 26, 2003.

311. Ibid.

312. "Los nuevos herederos del dragón." *Asociación Peruano-Chino*. http://www.apochi.-com. October 29, 2005.

313. Quesada, 2006.

314. "Republic Popular de China." *Ministerio de Relaciones Exteriores del Perú*. Official website. http://www.rree.gob.pe/portal/Pbilateral.nsf/PaisTipo/54D756B7EB6CC86B0-5256C60005BF189?OpenDocument. Accessed December 20, 2007.

315. "El barrio chino: Lo asiático en Lima." *El Commercio*. Lima, Peru. http://www.elcomercio.com/ediciononline. May 15, 2007.

316. Ibid.

317. Ibid.

318. "Crece influencia china en America Latina." *BBC Mundo*. http://news.bbc.co.uk/hi/spanish/misc/newsid_7039000/7039671.stm. October 15, 2007.

319. "Perú y sus 'chifas.'" *El Mercurio*. Santiago, Chile. http://diario.elmercurio.com. May 16, 2007.

320. "Peru." Country Analysis Brief. Energy Information Administration. http://www.eia.doe.gov. Updated June 2008.

321. Ibid.

322. Palacios, 2008, p. 180.

323. "CNPC Says Oil Discovered in Peru's Northern Jungle: Ministry." *Platts Commodity News*. http://www.uofaweb.ualberta.ca/chinainstitute. March 29, 2007.

324. "Peru." Country Analysis Brief, 2008.

325. "Filial de transnacional china descubre petróleo en la selva norte." *Portal Minero*. www.portalminero.com. 30 March, 2007. See also "CNPC Says Oil Discovered in Peru's Northern Jungle: Ministry."

326. Arriagada, 2006, p. 11.

327. "Statistics." *Perú Petro, S.A.* Official website. http://mirror.perupetro. com.pe/estadisticas01e.asp#link7. Accessed December 21, 2007.

328. Peru has 8.7 trillion cubic feet of proven gas reserves, for example, compared to 151 trillion cubic feet of reserves in Venezuela. "Peru." Country Analysis Brief, 2008. See also *Venezuela: Country Analysis Briefs.* Energy Information Administration. http://www.eia.doe.gov. September 2006.

329. "Peru." Country Analysis Brief, 2008.

330. "Peru—Mining: Iron Ore Mining." *MBendi.* http://www.mbendi.com.za. January 3, 2007.

331. *China Shougang Internacional Trade and Engineering Corporation.* Official website. http://www.zs.com.cn/en/abroad/peru.htm. Accessed March 1, 2006.

332. Chauvin, 2006.

333. Hildegard Willer, "Del sueño americano que se esfumó en un barco chino." *Ideele.* No. 130. http://www.idl.org.pe/idlrev/revistas/130/pag54.htm. August 2000.

334. Ibid.

335. Chauvin, 2006.

336. "Diez heridos y tres trabajadores detenidos de minera Shougang deja enfrentamiento con la policía." *CPN Radio.* http://www.cpnradio.com.pe. August 12, 2006.

337. "Empresas chinas están interesadas en invertir en sector minero de Perú." *Portal Minero.* http://www.portalminero.com/noti/noticias_ver.php?codigo=3504. September 12, 2007.

338. "Mineras Zijin de China y CVRD de Brazil figuran entre interesados por proyecto minero Michiquillay en Perú." *Portal Minero.* http://www.portalminero. com. April 30, 2007.

339. "China and Peru Cozy Up over Energy and Mineral Resources." *Interfax.* Downloaded from http://www.uofaweb.ualberta.ca. March 27, 2008.

340. "China planea inversión minera en Perú." *El Mercurio.* Santiago, Chile. http://diario.elmercurio.com. November 16, 2006.

341. "Asiática Chinalco adquire Peru Copper por US$792 milliones." *Portal Minero.* http:///www.portalminero.com/noti/noticias_ver.php?codigo=3314. July 12, 2007.

342. "Chinalco adquiere concesiones para explotación de proyecto cuprífero en Perú." *Diario Financiero.* Santiago, Chile. http://www.df.cl. May 5, 2008.

343. "China Minmetals concertaría operación para adquirir mineria Northern Peru Copper de Canadá." *Portal Minero.* http://www.portalminero.com. December 7, 2007.

344. "El 68.99% de las exportaciones mineras peruanas a China corresponden al cobre." *Portal Minero.* http:www.portalminero.com. July 15, 2008.

345. "Peru Fishing." *Nation's Encyclopedia.* http://www.nationsencyclopedia. com/Americas/Peru-FISHING.html. Accessed December 21, 2007.

346. "Cepal: América Latina debe aprovechar potencial de China e India." *El Economista.* http://www.eleconomista.es/economia/noticias/69851/09/06/Cepal-America-Latina-debe-aprovechar-potencial-de-China-e-India.html. September 14, 2006.

347. "Pesqueras peruanas en la mira de inversionistas asiáticos." *Diario Gestión.* Lima, Peru. http://www.gestion.com.pe. June 25, 2006.

348. "China Pacific Andes compró Alexandra por US$100 millones." *Diario Gestión.* Lima, Perú. http://www.gestion.com.pe. June 15, 2006.

349. "Pacific Andes' Singapore-Listed Subsidiary China Fishery Strengthens Fishing Fleet in Peru to 18 Licensed Vessels with Latest Acquisition." *China Fishery Group Ltd.* Press release. http://www.chinafisherygroup.com/newsroom_press.htm. December 27, 2006.

350. "China Fishery Furthers Strategic Roadmap with New Acquisitions in Peru." *China Fishery Group Ltd.* Press release. http://www.chinafisherygroup.com/newsroom_press.htm. June 4, 2007.

351. "China Fishery Acquires New Plant in Peru's Largest Fishing Port." *China Fishery Group Ltd.* Press release. http://www.chinafisherygroup.com/newsroom_press.htm. October 10, 2007. See also Ho Choon Seng, "China Fishery Group Limited: Raising the Stakes in Fishmeal Processing; CIMB." *World Press.* http://sgmarkettalk.wordpress.com/2007/10/16/china-fishery-group-limited-raising-the-stakes-in-fishmealprocessing-cimb. October 17, 2007.

352. "China Fishery Acquires New Plant in Peru's Largest Fishing Port." See also Ho Choon Seng, 2007.

353. Lozada, 2007.

354. Ibid.

355. "China y Perú estiman que la firma de su TLC se producirá en 2008." *Bilaterals.* http://www.bilaterals.org/. May 22, 2007.

356. "Empresarios chinos llegan a Ica para entablar nuevos negocios." *El Comercio.* Lima, Peru. http://www.elcomercio.com.pe/ediciononline. January 10, 2006.

357. "Gross Domestic Product per Capita, Current Prices (U.S. Dollars)."

358. This level of consumption of Chinese products puts Peru in the middle of its peers in the Andean region: ahead of Bolivia and Ecuador, yet behind Venezuela and Colombia. "Total Import and Export Value by Country (Region) (2007/01–12)."

359. "En el Perú, ya se venden autos de la marca Geely." *El Comercio.* Lima, Peru. August 1, 2007. Sec. A, p. 2.

360. "Four Chinese Leading Auto Brands Debut in Peru." *People's Daily Online.* Beijing, China. http://english.people.com.cn. November 9, 2006.

361. "Empresa mixta de General Motors en China comienza a exportar camionetas a Perú." *El Comercio.* Lima, Peru. http://www.elcomercio.com.pe/ediciononline/HTML/2008-07-18/-empresa-mixta-General-Motors-China-comienza-exportar-camionetas-Peru.html. July 18, 2008.

362. Álvaro Gastañduí Ramírez and Luis García Panta, "Policía probará los patrulleros chinos antes de firmar contrato con provedor." *El Comercio.* Lima, Peru. August 1, 2007. Sec. A, p. 2.

363. "Ministerio declara desierta la compra de patrulleros chinos." *El Comercio.* Lima, Peru. August 24, 2007. Sec. A. p. 11.

364. Chauvin, 2006, p. 32.

365. "García dice que la Carretera Interoceánica es la obra más importante de la región." *Terra.* http://actualidad.terra.es. Madrid, Spain. July 13, 2007.

366. "¿Qué nos traerá la Interoceánica?" *Los Andes.* Puno, Peru. http://www.losandes.com.pe. December 13, 2007.

367. "Por fin: Interoceánica Norte en marcha." *Carretera Interoceánico.* http://www.car-reterainteroceanica.com/modules/news/article.php?storyid=4. May 6, 2006.

368. "Se inicia construcción de carretera Interoceánica Sur." *Radio Programas del Perú.* http://www.rpp.com.pe. October 31, 2007.

369. "Ministra de Transportes, se comprometio licitar tramo 5 de la interoceánica." *Pachamama Radio.* Puno, Peru. http://www.pachamamaradio.org.pe.

May 22, 2007. The port of Ilo has also been mentioned as a possible route for the export of Bolivian natural gas, whether to Asia or other destinations. Hannah Hennessey, "Bolivia Signs Big Gas Deal." *BBC News*. http://news.bbc.co.uk/1/hi/world/americas/3535644.stm. August 4, 2004.

370. "Inauguran nuevo tramo de la carretera interoceánica en Perú." *El Universal*. Caracas, Venezuela. http://www.eluniversal.com. July 2, 2007.

371. "García dice que la carretera interoceánica es la obra más importante de la región."

372. China also reportedly was interested in establishing a free-trade zone in the port. "Una millonaria inversión busca unir La Paz con Tacna." *La Razón*. La Paz, Bolivia. http://www.la-razon.com. August 29, 2006.

373. "Un megapuerto en Tacna." *La Razón*. La Paz, Bolivia. http://www.la-razoncom. September 3, 2006. See also "Congress Passes Bill to Build Tacna Megaport: Bolivia, Peru."

374. Ibid.

375. Brazilian soybeans and other agricultural goods bound for Asia are currently shipped long distances over poor roads and rail lines to ports on the Atlantic coast of Brazil. See "Un megapuerto en Tacna." See also "Congress Passes Bill to Build Tacna Megaport: Bolivia, Peru."

376. See *PromPeru*. Official website. http://export.promperu.gob.pe. Accessed December 22, 2007.

377. "Se estableció el Comité Empresarial Perú-China ProInversión y Consejo Chino de Promoción del Comercio Internacional (CCPIT) lo presiden." *ProInversion* 2(18). http://www.proinversion.gob.pe/RepositorioAPS/0/0/JER/NEWSLETTER/octubre/Nota4.htm. October 2006.

378. "Peruvian PM Attends the China-Peru Investment Summit." *China Council for the Promotion of International Trade (CCPIT)*. Official website. http://english.ccpit.org/Contents/Channel_410/2007/1212/79931/content_79931.htm. Accessed December 12, 2007.

379. "Las inversiones chinas en Perú podrían acumular US $1.000 mlls. en el 2009." *El Comercio*. Lima, Peru. http://www.elcomercio.com.pe/ediciononline. August 29, 2008.

380. "Perú y China buscaran vías para aumentar cooperación económica." *Nacion*. San José, Costa Rica. http://www.nacion.com. November 20, 2006.

381. Victor Juárez, "El TLC de Perú entra en etapa de definición." *El Comercio*. Quito, Ecuador. http://www.elcomercio.com. September 11, 2007.

382. "Tras TLC con China, Perú negocia con Corea y Japón."

383. *Camara de Comercio Peruano-Chino (CAPECHI)*. Official website. http://www.capechi.org.pe/. Accessed December 22, 2007.

384. "Actividades." *Camara de Comercio Peruano-Chino (CAPECHI)*. Official website. http://www.capechi.org.pe/ca_actividades.htm. Accessed December 22, 2007.

385. "El Grupo Interbank abre una oficina de representación en China." *El Comercio*. Lima, Peru. http://www.elcomercio.com.pe/ediciononline. August 7, 2007.

386. Victor Raul Trujillo de Zela, "Convenio Banco de Desarrollo de China-Banco de la Nación." *La Razón Online*. Lima, Peru. http://www.larazon.com.pe. November 27, 2008.

387. "A un paso de Perú 2008." *Universidad de Lima*. Official website. http://www.ulima.edu.pe/webulima.nsf/Noticias/BEDFC70A51F9AF77052571C7004658D6?OpenDocument. Accessed December 22, 2007.

388. Based on a personal survey of conference attendees at the Congreso Latinoamericano y Caribeño de Ciencias Sociales, FLACSO Ecuador. Quito, Ecuador. October 29–31, 2007.

389. "Universidades peruanas firman convenio en China para ser sedes del 'Instituto Confucio.'" Press release No. 274-07. *Ministerio de Relationes Exteriores del Perú*. Official website. http://www.rree.gob.pe/portal/boletinInf.nsf/mrealdia/ B6EA69F5EE7-0EBFB052573B700034ABF?OpenDocument. December 19, 2007.

390. "El Perú destacó durante una semana en la televisión china."

391. As early as 2005, iconic Peruvian tourist sites such as Machu Picchu were already offering tours in Chinese. Alvaro Vargas Llosa, "Llosa: China Dangerous for Latin America?" *NewsMax*. http://www.newsmax.com. October 14, 2005.

392. "Peruvian President Invites Further Investment from China." *People's Daily Online*. Beijing, China. http://english.people.com.cn. June 3, 2007.

393. "Peruvian President Meets Top Chinese Diplomat on Cooperative Ties." *People's Daily Online*. Beijing, China. http://english.people.com.cn. September 19, 2006. Following this visit, in January 2007, Mauricio Mulder Bedoya, general secretary of Peru's ruling Aprista Party, visited China to facilitate cooperation on energy, trade, and economic issues; his visit included a meeting with his legislative counterparts in the Communist Party of China. "China Appreciates Peru Support on Issues of Taiwan, Tibet, Human Rights." *People's Daily Online*. Beijing, China. http:// english.people.com.cn. January 26, 2007.

394. "Senior Chinese Party Official Emphasizes Friendship with Peru." *People's Daily Online*. Beijing, China. http://english.people.com.cn. April 1, 2007.

395. "Senior Chinese Party Official Meets with Peruvian Congress Leader." *People's Daily Online*. Beijing, China. http://english.people.com.cn. March 30, 2007.

396. "China, Peru Launch FTA Talks." *People's Daily Online*. Beijing, China. http://english.people.com.cn. September 7, 2007.

397. "García advierte boicot contra China y defiende su unidad." *El Comercio*. Lima, Peru. http://www.elcomercio.com.pe. March 28, 2008.

398. "El presidente Alan García llegará a China en el peor momento político de ese país en años." *El Comercio*. Lima, Peru. http://www.elcomercio.com.pe. March 28, 2008.

399. Reynaldo Muñoz. "Presidente de China inicia visita oficial a Perú antes de Cumbre APEC." *La Prensa Grafica*. San Salvador, El Salvador. http://www. laprensagrafica.com. November 19, 2008.

400. "China donó US$100.000 a Perú para retirar minas de frontera con Ecuador."

401. "Wagner dice que China es el aliado más importante del Perú en el Asia-Pacífico." *El Comercio*. Lima, Peru. http://www.elcomercio.com.pe/ediciononline. November 9, 2007. The visit was originally set for September, but was postponed due to a deadly earthquake in the south of Peru. "El Ministro de Defensa suspende viaje a China a causa del terremoto." *El Comercio*. Lima, Peru. http://www. elcomercio.com.pe/ediciononline. August 18, 2007.

402. "Perú y China firman un convenio de cooperación por 800 mil dólares." *El Comercio*. Lima, Peru. http://www.elcomercio.com.pe/ediciononline. November 11, 2007.

403. "China, Peru Pledge to Beef Up Military Ties." *People's Daily Online*. Beijing, China. http://english.peopledaily.com.cn. September 2, 2006.

404. "Chinese, Peruvian Defense Ministers Vow to Consolidate Military

Cooperation." *People's Daily Online*. Beijing, China. http://english.people.com.cn/. July 12, 2005.

405. "Chief of PLA General Staff Meets Peruvian, Laotian Guests." *People's Daily Online*. http://english.peopledaily.com.cn. August 28, 2003.

406. "Uribe visita Pekín." *BBC Mundo.com*. http://news.bbc.co.uk/hi/spanish/latin_america/newsid_4417000/4417505.stm. April 6, 2005.

407. "Bilateral Political Relations." *Ministry of Foreign Affairs of the People's Republic of China*. Official website. http://www.fmprc.gov.cn/eng/wjb/zzjg/ldmzs/gjlb/3483/de-fault.htm. September 26, 2003.

408. "Chinese, Colombian Presidents Hold Talks." *People's Daily Online*. Beijing, China. http://english.peopledaily.com.cn. April 7, 2005.

409. Correspondence with Maria Velez de Berliner, president of Latin Intelligence Corporation. McLean, Virginia. February 8, 2008.

410. "Autoridades retuvieron ayer a otros 30 chinos." *El País*. Cali, Colombia. http://www.elpais.com.co. October 16, 2007. Similarly, in May 2004, the newspaper *Vangurdia Liberal* reported the presence of some 500 recently arrived, illegal Chinese immigrants in Bucaramanga, brought in by an organization called "Head of the Serpent." "Denuncian tráfico illegal de inmigrantes asiáticos." *Vanguardia Liberal*. Bucaramanga, Colombia. http://www.vanguardia.com. May 9, 2004. Indeed, the flow of illegal Chinese immigrants into Colombia has exceeded the resources of the Colombian government to purchase plane tickets to return them to China. In most cases, these immigrants remain in the informal economy, working in restaurants and other parts of the service industry.

411. "Colombia President Welcomes China to Invest in Oil." *People's Daily Online*. http://search.people.com.cn. Beijing, China. April 8, 2005.

412. Correspondence with Maria Velez de Berliner, president of Latin Intelligence Corporation. McLean, Virginia. February 8, 2008.

413. According to 2006 data, Colombian oil production is declining rapidly; if major new reserves are not found, the country could become a net oil importer as early as 2010. See Arriagada, 2006, p. 9.

414. "Uribe busca inversiones chinas." *EFE*. http://www.esmas.com/noticierostelevisa/internacionales/437262.html. April 6, 2005.

415. Similarly, the Orinoco River basin, in which some of Venezuela's most significant heavy oil deposits have been found, also extends into Colombia.

416. The oil-rich Orinoco region of Venezuela, for example, is adjacent to the department of Arauca, in Colombia, where some oil has been found. Bill Weinberg, "Colombia vs. Venezuela: Big Oil Turns Up Heat in Border Region." *Pacific News Service*. http://news.pacificnews.org/news/view_article.html?article_id=141c7d84bf2dc0a00a9af42fa9253d40. April 22, 2005.

417. Correspondence with Maria Velez de Berliner, president of Latin Intelligence Corporation. McLean, Virginia. February 8, 2008.

418. "ONGC and SINOPEC's Joint Acquisition of Producing Colombian Oil Assets." *ONGC Videsh*. Official website. http://www.ongcvidesh.com. September 21, 2006.

419. ONGC Videsh and Sinopec each paid $425 million for the acquisition. "ONGC-Sinopec Acquires Columbian Oil Firm." *The Hindu Business Line*. New Delhi, India. http://www.thehindubusinessline.com/2006/09/22/stories/2006092202200200.htm. September 21, 2006.

420. China Leaving Imprint on Latin American Energy." *Alexander's Oil and Gas Connection* 12(9). May 12, 2007.

421. Palacios, 2008, p. 180. The Omimex deal represents the first time China

and India collaborated on a major acquisition in Latin America, and suggests a possible strategy in which the two emerging Asian giants would work together to acquire Latin American assets at the lowest possible price, rather than permit an asset-bidding war that would largely benefit Latin America.

422. In addition to direct Chinese participation, China is indirectly represented in the bidding through CNPC ownership of a 45 percent stake in the Argentina-based firm PlusPetrol Norte. "Asian, US Oil Companies Eyeing Colombia." http://www.uofaweb.ualberta.ca/chinainstitute. May 29, 2007.

423. "Colombia, Venezuela Inaugurate Binational Gas Pipeline." *People's Daily Online*. Beijing, China. http://english.people.com.cn/90001/90777/6282188. html. October 13, 2007. See also "Venezuela, Colombia, Start Building Gas Pipeline." *CNN*. http://money.cnn.com/2006/07/08/news/venezgas_reut/index.htm. July 8, 2006.

424. Simon Romero, "Ideological Opposites, Colombia and Venezuela, Begin to Attract." *International Herald Tribune*. London, England. http://www.iht.com/articles/2007/10/18-/asia/latin.php. October 18, 2007. See also Arriagada, 2006, p. 10.

425. "Doctorado Honoris causa cierra la visita del Presidente Uribe a China." *Caracol Radio*. http://www.caracol.com.co/noticias/166103.asp?id=166103. April 8, 2005.

426. Beyond nickel, scrap metal accounts for another 46.1 percent of Colombian exports to the PRC. "Relaciones Bilaterales de Comercio Colombia–Republica Popular China." *Ministerio de Comercio, Industria y Turismo.* http://www.mincomercio.gov.co. Accessed August 11, 2007.

427. Interview with Pablo Echavarría, former Colombian ambassador to the People's Republic of China. Medellín, Colombia. August 11, 2007.

428. "Firman China y Colombia 5 documentos de cooperación." *Xinhuanet.* http://www.spanish.xinhuanet.com/spanish/2005-04/07/content_100364.htm. July 4, 2005.

429. *Cerrejón.* Official website. http://www.cerrejoncoal.com/secciones/CER-WEB/ENG-HOME/seccion_HTML.html. Accessed August 11, 2007.

430. "Energentia Announces Positive Results at Zapatoca." *Energenta Resources, Inc.* Press release. http://micro.newswire.ca/release.cgi?rkey=1511086233&view=10470-0&-Start=0. November 8, 2007.

431. "Mega Acquires Uranium Exploration Properties in Columbia." *Mega Uranium Corp.* Press release. http://www.megauranium.com/main/?newsRoom&18. November 3, 2006.

432. "Blue Sky Uranium Enters Letter of Agreement for Projects in Colombia." *Blue Sky Uranium Corp.* Press release. http://www.blueskyuranium.com/s/NewsReleases.asp?-ReportID=177023. March 14, 2007.

433. Correspondence with Maria Velez de Berliner, president of Latin Intelligence Corporation. McLean, Virginia. February 8, 2008.

434. "Relaciones Bilaterales de Comercio Colombia–Republica і ᴏрᴀᴦᴀᴦ China."

435. Interview with Pablo Echavarría, former Colombian ambassador to the People's Republic of China. Medellín, Colombia. August 11, 2007.

436. "Se avanzará en un tratado de protección recíproca de inversiones." *Observatorio del Asia Pacífico.* Universidad Sergio Arboleda. http://www.usergioarboleda.edu.co/asia/negocios_viaje_uribe.htm. April 4, 2005.

437. "Oficina Comercial Beijing." *Proexport Colombia.* Official website. http://www.pro-export.gov.co/vbecontent/newsDetail.asp?id=1115. Accessed December 19, 2007.

438. "Demanda de café en China podría crecer 40%." *Nacion.* San José, Costa Rica. http://www.nacion.com. February 8, 2007.

439. Reportedly, the organization established an initial facility in Shuhai, near Maccao, but later sold the operation. Interview with Pablo Echavarría, former Colombian ambassador to the People's Republic of China. Medellín, Colombia. August 11, 2007.

440. Ibid.

441. "El puerto de Buenaventura acelera su modernización." *El País.* Cali, Colombia. http://www.elpais.com.co. October 11, 2007.

442. Ibid.

443. "Buenaventura, Colombia Port Congestion." *BDP Internacional.* http://www.bdpint.com/news/BuenaventuraColombiaportCongestion.asp. August 23, 2006.

444. "Comunicado sobre Buenaventura." Unpublished fact sheet. *Ministerio de Transporte.* August 10, 2007.

445. See, for example, Jeremy McDermott, "Colombia's New Urban Drugs War." *BBC News.* http://news.bbc.co.uk/1/hi/programmes/from_our_own_correspondent/695-1683.stm. August 18, 2007.

446. Colombia's per capita income in 2006 was estimated to be $2,888, putting it behind every country in South America with the exception of Bolivia. "Gross Domestic Product per Capita, Current Prices (U.S. Dollars)."

447. "Total Import and Export Value by Country (Region) (2007/01–12)." Indeed, according to the Colombian Ministry of Commerce, Industry, and Tourism, the volume of goods sold by China to Colombia leapt from $355.8 million in 2000 to $2.219 billion in 2006, causing Colombia's trade deficit with the PRC to jump from $326.4 million to $1.767 billion in that period. "Relaciones bilaterales de comercio Colombia–Republica Popular China."

448. "Relaciones bilaterales de comercio Colombia–Republica Popular China."

449. "Gobierno impuso salvaguardia temporal a las importaciones de ropa interior china." *El Tiempo.* Bogota, Colombia. http://www.eltiempo.com. February 10, 2006.

450. "Analizan impacto de China en la region." *El Universal.* Caracas, Venezuela. http://www.eluniversal.com. October 22, 2007.

451. "La llegada de automóviles chinos consolida la industria automotriz oriental en Colombia." *El Tiempo.* Bogota, Colombia. http://www.eltiempo.com. January 18, 2006.

452. "Se crecen los chinos." *El País.* Cali, Colombia. http://www.elpais.com.co. July 29, 2007.

453. "Fotón, los chinos ahoras son pesados." *El País.* Cali, Colombia. http://www.elpais.com.co. March 17, 2007.

454. "Notas del sector." *El País.* Cali, Colombia. http://www.elpais.com.co. July 29, 2007.

455. "La llegada de automóviles chinos consolida la industria automotriz oriental en Colombia." *El Tiempo.* Bogota, Colombia. http://www.eltiempo.com. January 18, 2006.

456. "Cinascar, empresa ideal que le apuesta al Valle." *El País.* Cali, Colombia. http://www.elpais.com.co. April 14, 2007.

457. It is marketed by the firm as as an inexpensive taxi, with a new model costing approximately $14,000 USD. "Notas del Sector." *El País.* Cali, Colombia. http://www.elpais.com.co. July 29, 2007.

458. Presumably, the visit was made with the expectation of attracting FAW to

set up a production facility, or otherwise invest in Colombia. See "Uribe busca inversions chinas." *Esmas.* http://www.esmas.com/usa/index.html. April 6, 2005.

459. Henry Delgado Henao, "Motocicletas, las aliadas del bolsillo." *El País.* Cali, Colombia. http://www.elpais.com.co. August 20, 2007.

460. *AKT Motors.* Official website. http://www.aktmotos.com/VBeContent/NewsDetail.asp?ID=7&IDCompany=125. Accessed August 11, 2007.

461. Interview with Pablo Echavarría, former Colombian ambassador to the People's Republic of China. Medellín, Colombia. August 11, 2007.

462. This calculation is based on the combination of two categories of motorcycle imports in the trade data: "Motorcycles of displacement equal or less than 185 cm^3" and "Motorcycles (including mopeds and bicycles with piston motors)." "Relaciones bilaterales de comercio Colombia–Republica Popular China."

463. Ibid.

464. Zhao Xuemei, 2007.

465. Written correspondence with Pablo Echavarría Toro, former Colombian ambassador to the People's Republic of China. November 18, 2008.

466. "Colombia se conecta a la inversión china." *Topcomm.* http://www.topcomm.biz/ShowContent.asp?ContentId=31830&ChannelId=1. October 25, 2005.

467. Jorge Ramirez Ocampo, "Las empresas nacen, crecen, se reproducen, envejecen, envejecen . . . y mueren: 500 productos nuevos de exportación a Estados Unidos." *Araújo Ibarra & Asociados, S.A.* Presentation. Bogotá, Colombia. http://www.colombiadigital.net. June 12, 2006.

468. "Colombia y China acuerdan protección a inversiones." *La Prensa.* Managua, Nicaragua. http://www.laprensa.com.ni. November 22, 2008.

469. "En Cali, foro ministerial de los países del Pacífico." *El País.* Cali, Colombia. http://www.elpais.com.co. January 23, 2007. See also "Cali quere ser el puente de Colombia con Asia." *El País.* Cali, Colombia. January 30, 2007. p. 1.

470. "En Cali, foro ministerial de los países del Pacífico."

471. "Los líderes cierran hasta 2010 las puertas de APEC a nuevos miembros." *El Comercio.* Quito, Ecuador. http://www.elcomercio.com. September 9, 2007.

472. Interview with Pablo Echavarría, former Colombian ambassador to the People's Republic of China. Medellín, Colombia. August 11, 2007.

473. Although the quality of such trips varies widely, at least one company, Araujo Ibarra & Asociados, offers a trip that includes training and a directed experience in China, to help Colombian businesspeople build Chinese business ties in the most effective manner possible.

474. "Información general sobre la República Popular China." *Ministerio de Relaciones Exteriores: Gobierno de Colombia.* Official website. http://www.minrelext.gov.co/Web-ContentManager/webapp/display.jsp?sid=9902&pid=7243. August 28, 2006.

475. Universidad Industrial de Santander also has a modest offering of Mandarin courses, which it was in the process of expanding in 2007.

476. Based on a personal survey of conference attendees at the Congreso Latinoamericano y Caribeño de Ciencias Sociales, FLACSO Ecuador. Quito, Ecuador. October 29–31, 2007.

477. As such programs expand, Asia-themed conferences and other events are becoming increasingly common in Colombia. One such example was the Asia-Pacific Week event put on by Universidad EAFIT in Medellín in August 2007. Cooperative efforts are being fueled by the Chinese side as well.

478. Interview with Pablo Echavarría, former Colombian ambassador to the People's Republic of China. Medellín, Colombia. August 11, 2007.

479. Interview with Juvenal Infante, director, Centro de Estudios del Asia-Pacífico, Universidad Sergio Arboleda. Medellín, Colombia. August 10, 2007.

480. Colombia is one of the United States' strongest allies in Latin America, and the one in which the United States has invested the most. Colombia has followed political and economic policies closely aligned with the United States; the relationship includes close collaboration between the two nations' military and police institutions, and the joint signing of a free-trade agreement (FTA) in 2006. In return, Colombia has received significant US military, counternarcotics, economic, and institution-building support, largely through Plan Colombia. A report by the US Congressional Research Service noted that US aid to Colombia from 2000 through 2005, including foreign military and Department of Defense funding, totaled $4.5 billion. Veillette, 2005.

481. Tokatlian, 2008, p. 71.

482. "Uribe visita Pekín." *BBC Mundo*. http://news.bbc.co.uk/hi/spanish/latin_america/newsid_4417000/4417505.stm. April 6, 2005.

483. "Donación millionaria de China a Colombia." *El País*. Cali, Colombia. http://www.elpais.com.co. July 29, 2007.

484. Interview with Pablo Echavarría, former Colombian ambassador to the People's Republic of China. Medellín, Colombia. August 11, 2007.

485. "Estudiantes chinos viajan a Colombia." *El País*. Cali, Colombia. http//www.elpais.com.co. October 20, 2007.

486. "Los Ministerios de Defensa de China y Colombia ampliarán cooperación." *Radio Caracol*. http://www.caracol.com.co/nota.asp?id=299857. June 19, 2006.

487. The PRC has been exploring military sales to Colombia for some time. In January 2005, for example, the head of the Chinese People's Liberation Army, Cao Gangchuan, raised the issue during a meeting with the commander-in-chief of the Colombian armed forces, General Carlos Ospina, although doing so in a manner that demonstrated considerable sensitivity to the special relationship between the Colombian armed forces and those of the United States.

488. "Casa de Nariño indaga queja de China sobre chalecos antibalas." *El Tiempo*. Bogotá, Colombia. http://www.eltiempo.com. December 18, 2007. See also "Licitación para compra de 50 mil chalecos antibalas fue aplazada por el gobierno." *El Tiempo*. Bogotá, Colombia. http://www.eltiempo.com. December 18, 2007.

6

Mexico, Central America, and the Caribbean: Strategic Position and the Taiwan Card

———————————————————■———————————————————

FROM PANAMA TO THE NORTH, CHINA'S RELATIONSHIP WITH THE countries of the subregion is dominated by two factors: their strategic geographic position vis-à-vis the United States, and the issue of Taiwan.

The strategic position of the nations of this region has both a commercial and a military component. From a commercial perspective, the proximity of this area to the US market is a powerful competitive advantage in terms of logistics costs and service responsiveness. These advantages are increased by the fact that goods produced in Mexico and Central America enter the US market with few or no tariffs, creating potent incentives for the PRC to locate final-assembly operations in these countries as part of supply chains serving US and Latin American markets. From a military perspective, the proximity of the region to the United States gives rise to the possibility that Chinese facilities there could be used in time of conflict to collect intelligence data or as a launching point for operations against the United States.

With respect to Taiwan, it is significant that approximately half of the nations in the world that continue to recognize the government of the Republic of China (ROC) as the legitimate government of China are concentrated in this region. The critical role of the Taiwan issue in the domestic politics of the PRC leads the latter to pay particular attention to other nations' positions on this topic, although as of early 2009, an informal "truce" was in place between China and Taiwan not to seek to change countries recognizing Taiwan to recognize the PRC, or vice versa. In relative terms, the matter takes on greater importance for the PRC in Central America and the Caribbean because these states generally do not have significant quantities of the primary products that the PRC is interested in buying; nor, with the exception of Mexico, do the economies of this subregion offer significant markets for Chinese manufactured goods. At the same time, the very smallness of these nations makes them more easily influenced by relatively small aid packages and other forms of reward or pressure.

▪ Mexico

Mexico is one of four nations in Latin America recognized by China as a "strategic partner," with the others being Brazil, Venezuela, and Argentina. China's conferral of this status on Mexico is relatively recent, having taken place in 2003.[1] Although there are no clear criteria by which the PRC defines who is a "strategic partner," China appears to have awarded this honor to Mexico because of the latter's importance as a trading partner and because of the leadership role that it has historically played in the region, particularly among the states of Central America.[2]

Although the economic relationship between China and Mexico has reached its current proportions only during the last several years, the political alignment between the two countries is long-standing. Mexico has historically provided important support to the PRC in international bodies such as the United Nations, and has facilitated participation by the PRC in Latin American institutions, including helping China to attain observer status in the Organization of American States (OAS), and supporting China's bid for membership in the Inter-American Development Bank (IADB).[3]

Despite a history of political congruence between the two nations, their relationship in the economic realm has been tense because that trade has increasingly favored the PRC as it has grown. In general terms, Mexico's trade relationship with China has expanded dramatically since the early 1970s. When Mexico established diplomatic relations with the PRC in 1972, bilateral trade between the two was $13 million per year.[4] By 2005, China had become Mexico's second-largest trading partner in terms of bilateral trade,[5] and by 2007, this trade had reached $15 billion per year.[6]

Perhaps the most troublesome aspect of the expansion of Sino-Mexican trade, from the Mexican perspective, is that the PRC has consistently had a significant balance-of-trade surplus with Mexico. According to the PRC Ministry of Commerce, for example, in 2007, Mexico had $3.3 billion in exports to the PRC, versus $11.7 billion in imports from the PRC.[7] Because Mexico consumes, rather than exports, the vast majority of its primary products, the country has benefited relatively little from the significant growth of Chinese consumption of these goods in recent years. At the same time, studies show that sales of Mexican labor-intensive manufactured goods (e.g., textiles and footwear) have gone head to head with sales of PRC exports in these categories—both in Mexico itself and in the nation's traditional export markets, such as the United States—and have been losing ground in this competition.[8]

Despite such rivalry, Mexico's economic relationship with the PRC has begun to evolve from competition to partnership. In part, the evolution is rooted in Mexico's competitive advantages, which include a combination of technological knowledge in high value–added manufacturing sectors, such as autos; physical proximity to the United States; and tariff-free access to the US market, for a subset of goods, under the provisions of the North American Free Trade Agreement (NAFTA). Increasingly, the Chinese have sought to work with their Mexican counterparts to form integrated global production chains: producing basic components in the PRC, while performing final assembly in Mexico for shipment of finished goods to markets in the United States and Latin America.[9]

Concurrent with the expansion of the Chinese presence in Mexico, a wide range of Mexican companies have sought to do business in China. The Mexican government has attempted to promote its nation's exports to China, with mixed results. Nonetheless, Mexico has enjoyed some success in expanding exports in the consumer goods sector, where such major corporate entities as FEMSA, Grupo Modelo, and Bimbo have built distribution networks and realized significant sales in the PRC by leveraging the growth of the Chinese middle class, with its emergent taste for Western consumer goods.

Historical Context

China and Mexico have a long history, although the level of commerce between the two has been relatively modest until recent years. Some claim that the first contacts between them date back to the fifth century when, according to some accounts, Chinese monks arrived in Mexico.[10] Similarly, Mexico was arguably one of the first nations in the Americas to establish trade relations with China, in the sixteenth century, selling China cotton, cocoa, and cassava and purchasing Chinese embroidery, textiles, flatware, and silk.[11] In contemporary history, Mexico was one of the first nations in Latin America to extend diplomatic recognition to China and has supported the PRC politically in a range of international bodies since that time.[12]

In 2003, as noted earlier, China recognized the economic and political importance of its bilateral relationship with Mexico, conferring upon it the status of strategic partner. The level of attention given by the PRC to Mexico has generally been consistent with this status, including a state visit by Chinese president Hu Jintao just two months before his landmark trip to the region in November 2004 in conjunction with the APEC summit.[13]

The Chinese Community in Mexico

As with some Chinese communities in other parts of Latin America, the number of ethnic Chinese in Mexico is relatively small. Although figures are often dated and vary widely according to the bases used in the estimates, one report estimates that there are 31,000 people who speak various dialects of the Chinese language in the country.[14]

The first Chinese arrived in Mexico to work on the railroads and other projects at the turn of the twentieth century.[15] Although the Chinese led a relatively low-profile existence, separate from other Mexican communities, they were caught up in the wave of anti-Asian sentiment that accompanied the social unrest in the country in the first part of the twentieth century.[16] Difficulties persisted after the revolution as well. In the Mexican state of Sonora, for example, marriages between Chinese and Mexicans were outlawed in 1931, and official discrimination forced many Chinese Mexicans to leave the region.[17]

Currently, Chinese Mexicans live not only in Mexico City, but also in towns along the US border, such as Mexicali,[18] and throughout the northern part of the country. The cultural festival[19] put on each year by the Chinese community of Tampico, on the eastern coast, highlights the existence of Chinese Mexicans even in relatively small cities of the country.

China's Interest in Mexican Petroleum

By contrast to some other Latin American countries, Mexico's commercial dealings with China in the petroleum sector have been very limited. Although Mexico is a substantial producer of petroleum, its oil fields are generally mature, and its reserves are declining.[20] The output of Mexico's largest oil-production complex, Cantarell, for example, fell 20 percent between January 2006 and January 2007, fueling concern over the future of Mexico as an oil-producing nation.[21] Compounding such problems, Mexico's ability to explore for new petroleum and increase production in existing fields is limited by inefficiencies in the Mexican national oil company, Petróleos Mexicanos (PEMEX), as well as constitutionally rooted prohibitions on investment by foreign interests in the Mexican oil sector.[22]

Mexico's worsening position as a petroleum supplier limits its ability to enter into new deals, including those with the Chinese. In April 2007, Mexico caused considerable ire, during a summit meeting between Plan Puebla Panama member countries, when it announced that it was unable to provide 230,000 barrels a day for a new refinery project in Central America, and would have to reduce its commitment to just 80,000 barrels per day—making the $8 billion project significantly less financially viable for China National Petroleum Corporation (CNPC), the principal investor.[23]

Compounding problems of declining supply, obligations to give priority to domestic markets, plus contractual commitments to supply the United States, limit Mexico's flexibility to enter into new deals with the PRC.[24] Without the ability to increase production, any oil Mexico sold to China would have to be diverted from an existing customer, located closer to Mexico; so it is neither politically viable nor economically beneficial for Mexico to increase oil supplies significantly to the PRC at the present time.

Attempts by the Calderón government to push through reforms for PEMEX in 2008 were stopped by the political opposition through actions that included large-scale protests and the occupation of the Mexican Senate to block debate on the reform legislation. Defeat of the reforms cast doubt on Mexico's ability either to give Chinese companies an equity stake in the country's oil production or to have excess petroleum to export to China in the foreseeable future. Although Chinese oil company China National Offshore Development Corporation (CNODC) is reportedly looking for partners to conduct deepwater exploration in the Gulf of Mexico, its activities will probably be limited to the non-Mexican portion of those waters, because the Mexican national oil company, PEMEX, cannot enter into equity partnerships with foreign firms, nor does it have the capital or technical expertise to perform deepwater exploration at the present time.[25]

China's Interest in Mexican Agriculture

Agriculture is one area in which Mexico could expand its exports to the PRC. Countries resembling Mexico in economic structure, such as Brazil and Argentina, have had significant successes in selling land-intensive agricultural commodities (such as soy) to China, while Chile and Peru have had similar successes with fishmeal.

Although Mexico has not sought to increase production of agricultural products most imported by China, it has worked with China to expand the quantity of those goods that it currently exports to the PRC. Through a series of Sino-Mexican binational commissions, for example, Mexico's Office of the Secretary of Agriculture, Livestock, Rural Development, Fishing, and Food (SAGARPA) has sought to eliminate barriers to Mexican agricultural products entering Chinese markets.[26] In July 2008, for example, the governments of Mexico and China reached a high-level agreement to permit the import of Mexican pork into China.[27]

Mexico as a Market for Chinese Goods

As with other middle-income countries in Latin America, Mexico is attractive to the PRC as a market for a broad range of Chinese goods. In 2007, according to the PRC Ministry of Commerce, China sold $11.71 billion in goods to Mexico, representing a 32.7 percent increase over the prior year. During the same period, Mexican exports to the PRC expanded by a more modest 25.1 percent (to $3.26 billion), generating a net trade deficit with China of $8.45 billion.[28] In addition, Chinese imports to Mexico were expected to expand after December 2007, when Mexico ended a six-year-long period of compensatory quotas against goods from the PRC in compliance with its 2001 agreement with China, in which it dropped its objections to the PRC's entry into the WTO.[29]

China's penetration of the Mexican market in low-end manufactured goods like textiles and footwear has received a great deal of attention in the press, both inside of Mexico and beyond. According to a market survey in the town of Zapotlanejo, seven out of ten articles of clothing sold in the town were from Asia.[30] A symbolic illustration of the extent of this penetration is that the iconic figures of the Virgin of Guadalupe that are sold to tourists in the Zócalo, Mexico City's central square, are made in China.[31]

China is also making rapid headway in the sale of more sophisticated products to the Mexican market, such as motorcycles, computers, appliances, and cars. In 2007, it was expected that a total of thirty thousand Chinese cars would be sold in the Mexican market.[32] One of the projects with the greatest potential to throw open the Mexican market to Chinese cars is the partnership announced in November 2007 between the Mexican appliance and electronics conglomerate Grupo Electra and the Chinese automaker First Automobile Works (FAW) to sell Chinese cars through Elektra's retail outlets.[33] The partnership promises to be particularly effective for the Chinese because Elektra already has a consumer credit infrastructure integrated with its retail outlets through its affiliate Banco Azteca.[34] Much of Elektra's previous retail success came from getting poor clients to buy the company's products through high-interest consumer loans. In the same fashion, the company may now be positioned to sell inexpensive Chinese cars on credit to Mexicans previously considered too poor to purchase a car. Moreover, the Elektra retail infrastructure, including its affiliation with Banco Azteca or other local partners, spans Latin America, so that the Elektra model for selling Chinese autos, if successful, could be copied rapidly throughout the region, doing an end-run around traditional auto distributor networks.

China companies have become increasingly important providers of components and services in the telecommunications sector, paticularly the principal Chinese companies, Huawei and ZTE. In addition to the previously mentioned ZTE deal to provide a wireless telecommunications network in Mexico City, the Chinese telecom giant Huawei announced in November 2006 that it was investing $20 million in Mexico to establish a new center of operations and training there.[35] Following the July 2008 visit by Mexican president Felipe Calderón to Beijing, Huawei announced that it was expanding this center, adding a new software research-and-development facility.[36]

Manufacturing: From Competition to Complementarity

Historically, the trading relationship between Mexico and China has been characterized more by competition than by complementarity, with a net balance-of-payments position heavily favoring the PRC.[37] A review of the literature on China's economic relationship with Latin America reveals that virtually every study that compares Mexican and Chinese export structures or the competitiveness of LAC exports in the world singles out Mexico as a country in which competition with China overshadows trade complementarity, because of the similarities in the export structures of the two countries.[38] Mexico, like China, has a significant manufacturing sector, and has leveraged the price competitiveness of its labor relative to that of the United States to sell goods with a high labor component to the US market. For Mexico, thus, the globalization of trade, including milestone events such as the acceptance of China into the WTO in 2001,[39] has meant greater competition from the PRC in Mexico's traditional export markets (e.g., the United States), as well as significant penetration by Chinese manufactured goods into Mexico's domestic markets. Indeed, because of the structural similarities between the Mexican and Chinese economies, a 2006 World Bank study identified Mexico as the country in Latin America most adversely affected by the expansion of trade with the PRC and other Asian countries.[40]

The signing of NAFTA by the United States and Mexico in 1994 allowed products manufactured in Mexico, and meeting certain criteria, to enter the United States virtually tariff-free. NAFTA thus created incentives for US manufacturers to move their production operations to Mexico, where labor was substantially cheaper than in the United States. The result was the dramatic expansion of the maquiladora sector in the north of the country, in which factories (largely owned and operated by foreign corporations) use inexpensive Mexican labor to manufacture products for the US market.[41] Consequently, until being displaced by China in 2003, Mexico was the largest supplier of goods to the United States.[42]

Since the price differential between Mexican and US labor made it attractive for firms to move certain types of manufacturing operations with high labor content to Mexico, the same logic also created an incentive for manufacturers to move such operations to the PRC, where labor was even cheaper.[43] Between October 2000 and December 2002, Mexicans lost 270,000 manufacturing jobs.[44] According to the Mexican National Textile Industry Chamber of Commerce (CANAINTEX), between 2003 and 2006, 250,000 jobs were lost in the textile sector alone.[45] Indeed, one study estimates that 40 percent of all the losses in the maquiladora sector during this period were due to companies moving their operations to Asia.[46]

A key watershed event in the competition with China was the expiration of the Multi-Fiber Agreement (MFA) in January 2006,[47] which demonstrated dramatically that China-based manufacturers could easily outcompete their Mexico-based counterparts in an open competition based on price. Within seven months of lifting the MFA, which had established quotas on textile imports into the US market, Mexico saw its share of the textile market fall from 10 to 3 percent, while the PRC share of the US market jumped from 25 to 56 percent.[48]

The damage felt by Mexican companies from competition with China has been a key factor in the push by Mexican industry, and the local politicians representing it, to secure protection from the government against Chinese goods.[49] Calls for protection frequently appear in the Mexican press, such as the appeal from the governor of the state of Jalisco to reconsider lowering trade duties on cell phones, to avoid the displacement of production from his state to the PRC.[50]

The lack of significant Mexican primary-product exports to China, and the competition that has characterized the relationship between these two countries in manufactures, are reflected, likewise, in the relatively limited presence of Chinese companies in Mexico. Mexico City mayor Marcelo Ebrard noted in October 2006, for example, that although there were, at that time, 251 Chinese businesses in Mexico, none of China's major national companies, such as CNPC or China Minmetals, had a presence there.[51]

Despite such difficulties, there are reasons for optimism for Mexico in its commercial relationship with China. The competition in manufactures is slowly evolving into partnerships involving integrated, global production chains, with a portion of production operations located in Mexico. This trend is an emerging, constantly shifting compromise between the imperatives to produce in China and the imperatives to produce in Mexico.

A number of factors argue for performing some final-assembly operations in Mexico. The fact that certain categories of goods produced in Mexico can enter the United States tariff-free under NAFTA is an incentive to perform work on those goods, in Mexico, to the minimum extent necessary to meet domestic-content requirements for entering the US market. The maquiladora sector is oriented to perform precisely this type of assembly operation.[52] Although labor costs in Mexico are generally higher than those in China, the ability of Mexican goods to avoid taxes when entering the US market represents an important offset. Relatively inexpensive but bulky goods fall into this category, where tariff avoidance complements costs savings in shipping finished goods to the United States from Mexico, rather than from China.[53] The value of performing final assembly in Mexico is even greater for those goods in which demand is volatile or delivery is time-sensitive, thus the long transit time from the PRC to the United States is a significant liability. In addition, production in Mexico may also present certain strategic benefits for the growth of the Chinese company, including opportunities to acquire new technologies and improve production processes through partnerships with Mexican firms.[54]

Chinese have been pursuing numerous initiatives to position them-selves in the maquiladora sector to leverage such benefits, although the global financial crisis of 2008 put many of these initiatives on hold. To detail a few of the initiatives in the automotive sector, in September 2007, the Chinese automaker Zhongxing announced plans to invest $400 million to construct a plant in Tijuana to assemble cars—largely for export to the United States—beating its rivals, such as Hefei, into the market.[55] The proj-ect, later reported to be on hold,[56] would have been the first instance of a Chinese company's conducting final auto-assembly operations in Mexico for cars designed for the US market.[57] Amid the uncertainty over the Zhongxing deal, in November 2007, the Chinese automaker FAW announced plans to invest $150 million to build an auto plant in the Mexican state of Michoacán as part of its partnership with the Mexican dis-tributorship and financing infrastructure of Grupo Elektra (see section above).[58] The factory, to open in 2010, will, as currently envisioned, have a capacity to produce 100,000 cars per year and employ an estimated 2,000 workers.

In addition to FAW's plans in Mexico, in July 2008, following a state visit to China by President Felipe Calderón, China's largest auto manufac-turer, Geeley, announced plans to invest $130 million to build an auto-assembly plant in the Mexican state of León, with an annual production capacity of 50,000 vehicles. Geeley declared its intention to invest $269 million over the long run to create a capacity to manufacture 120,000 cars per year in Mexico.[59]

A number of other initiatives have also been explored. In April 2007, Chinese investors from the province of Ningbo visited the Mexican city of Aguascalientes to explore the possibility of establishing an automotive-oriented industrial park in the area, noting that the prospective project had the support of the Chinese government.[60] In the Mexican state of Hidalgo, according to the Mexican Foreign Ministry, the Chinese firm Giant Engine Company has invested $50 million to acquire another auto-assembly plant.[61] Prior to the recession of 2008, which put many contemplated manu-facturing projects on hold, total plans for Chinese auto production in Mexico were estimated to be 1.6 million cars per year by 2012.[62]

The emerging global-supply-chain partnership with the PRC has not been limited to the automotive industry. In the state of Northern Baja California, which borders the United States, as of late 2007, 12 Chinese companies had factories employing 765 workers and representing a modest but nontrivial $1.5 million in Chinese investment over the preceding five years.[63] In 2007, the Chinese firm Golden Dragon announced plans to invest $100 million in the construction of a plant to produce copper tubes in the state of Coahuila.[64] Following the July 2008 state visit to China by the Mexican president, the Chinese computer manufacturer Lenovo announced plans to build a new assembly plant and operations center in Monterrey, with a capacity of 5 million computers per year.[65] Finally, in the port sector, which represents another crucial component of the global supply chain, the logistics company Hutchison Port Holdings has advanced funds to establish operations in a number of key Mexican ports, including the deepwater port Lazaro Cardenas in the state of Michoacán and the port of Ensenada in Baja California; Hutchison is also investing in a container-handling operation at the port of Manzanillo. On the Atlantic coast, Hutchison has a presence in the port of Veracruz.[66] President Calderón, during his visit to China, actively encouraged Chinese companies to take advantage of the opportunities offered by Mexico's plans to expand its national infrastructure, to invest further in the nation's port sector.[67]

Although direct investment in the PRC amounted to a meager $66 million between 1999 and 2007, potential projects discussed during Calderón's 2008 China trip totaled $900 million.[68]

While the emerging collaborative relationship between Mexico and China is a positive trend for their economic relationship, a number of complications and pitfalls also exist. First, much of their plans' success depends on the continuing growth of the US market, to which such exports are principally aimed. According to one estimate, for example, 85 percent of Mexican exports are destined for the United States.[69] As noted previously, the global recession of 2008 temporarily cast doubt on many of the projects in the maquiladora sector oriented toward the US market. Moreover, trade disputes threaten to derail cooperation. In April 2007, for example, the Mexican government added itself to a complaint filed by the United States against China in the WTO over inadequate Chinese protection of intellectual property.[70] In September of the same year, the WTO began an investigation, backed by Mexico and the United States, of unfair Chinese subsidies of its exports, prompting an outcry on the Chinese side.[71] Thus, the health of the US market and the ability of the two governments to resolve associated disputes satisfactorily will have a significant bearing on Mexico's and China's ability to move successfully from competition to complementarity.

Mexican Corporate Initiatives to Enter the Chinese Market

Although the story of the Mexico-China relationship is dominated by the lack of major primary-product exports and by competition and complementarity in manufacturing, a handful of important Mexican companies are establishing themselves in the Chinese market and, in the process, providing a number of lessons and insights for others across Latin America. These companies, including such entities as Grupo FEMSA, Grupo Modelo, Grupo Maseca, Vitro y Domos, Gruma, Bimbo, and Televisa, are large managers of internationally recognized brands. They are selling their brands to an expanding and increasingly affluent Chinese middle class that is developing a taste for a broad variety of foreign goods. The experience of these companies in the Chinese market serves as a useful reference for many Latin American producers, although it is not necessarily a model that all companies have the resources, expertise, or competitive strength to pursue successfully.

One common element of the strategy of these companies has been targeting the expanding Chinese middle class as a market. FEMSA, for example, started out in the Chinese market in 1992 with a very modest presence in Hong Kong, marketing internationally recognized brands of Mexican beer to Western businesspeople and tourists,[72] and in its expansion has leveraged growing Chinese interest in Western beer and the increasing group of Chinese consumers who can afford such products.

A second common strategic element of this group has been working with local Chinese partners to build sales and distribution networks in China. FEMSA, for example, has worked with local partners to develop supplier networks in China's southern coastal provinces before seeking to extend its presence into the center of the country. Grupo Modelo employed a similar strategy, forming a strategic partnership with Anheuser Busch, which already had a presence in the region.[73] In many cases, the strategy has also involved purchasing or building production facilities in China. To take two examples, Gruma invested $100 million to build a tortilla factory near Shanghai,[74] while Bimbo purchased a Spanish firm with a presence in the Beijing and Tianjin markets to advance its distribution network.[75]

A third common strategic element has been leveraging a product's Mexican identity to appeal to Chinese consumers' growing interest in foreign goods. In January 2007, to give one example, the Mexican restaurant chain El Fogoncito opened its first restaurant in Beijing, with plans to open as many as thirty more locations in China over the following three years, targeting an expanding market in China for authentic Mexican cuisine.[76] Reportedly, four other Mexican restaurant chains also have plans to enter China.[77] In the telecommunications sector, capitalizing on a different dimension of Mexican identity, the communications company Televisa announced in May 2007 that it was exploring the establishment of a Chinese-language television channel in the PRC,[78] featuring Latino content, including a version of the successful Mexican telenovela *Betty la fea* in Mandarin.[79]

For the Mexican companies analyzed, a frequent complication and expense arising out of sales of premium goods to the Chinese middle class has been the resources required to protect patents and "brand authenticity." Companies such as FEMSA have had to invest significant time and money in protecting the position of their product against copycat brands.[80] An important dimension of such battles has been the establishment of improved frameworks for legal protection at the governmental level. In one instance of this, in April 2007, Mexico and China signed a agreement providing protection for origin-based branding, paving the way for the broader marketing of goods such as Mexican tequila.[81]

Government and Business Infrastructure

Despite criticism of the effectiveness of the Mexican government's trade-promotion policies,[82] the attention the government has given to the issue is evident at both the senior and working levels. When President Calderón visited the PRC in July 2008, for example, he highlighted issues of commerce and investment, signing a number of high-level agreements (including one permitting the import of Mexican pork into China),[83] meeting with the heads of computer manufacturer Lenovo and steelmaker Baosteel, promoting Mexico's participation in the upcoming 2010 Shanghai trade expo, advertising Mexican investments in China by entities such as Grupo Maseca, and inviting Chinese investment in Mexico in areas such as port infrastructure.[84] As another example, in August 2007 Mexican secretary of the economy Eduardo Solo led a trade delegation to Beijing, including some fifty businesspeople and trade representatives.[85] The trip was the first major initiative toward China by the new government of Felipe Calderón, and reflected, in some sense, a continuity of the interest in China demonstrated by the February 2006 China trip by Luis Derbez, the foreign minister under the previous government of Vicente Fox.[86]

At the national level, the Mexican government has been working with the PRC to build administrative and legal infrastructures to facilitate trade between the two countries. In 2005, for example, following China's recognition of Mexico as a strategic partner, the two nations established a Mexico-China Permanent Binational Commission. As a parallel to the permanent bodies that the PRC has established with its other strategic partners, the commission holds annual meetings, working through subcommittees to identify and address issues across a range of areas from trade to technological cooperation.[87] It was this group, for example, that arrived at a high-level accord in July 2008, allowing Mexican pork exports into China.[88]

In addition to the work of this permanent body, the Mexican government is negotiating a number of agreements with the PRC to facilitate trade, including an accord for the reciprocal protection of investments, which was addressed at the fifteenth Mexico-China Plenary Reunion, in March 2007,[89] as well as various agreements on phytosanitary protocols for individual products, such as those for the export of Mexican "Persian lemons" and the import into Mexico of Chinese oranges.[90] Although the number of products that could benefit from pacts remains enormous, between 2004 and 2007 the two nations put fifteen new agreements in effect, bringing the total number of agreements that exist between them to twenty-one.[91]

Mexican trade-promotion organizations are involved in a number of partnerships with the private sector to promote commerce with the PRC, from organizing trade delegations and official visits to supplying information and promoting Mexican products. These organizations include ProMexico and El Consejo Mexicano de Comercio Exterior.[92] Their support also includes various conferences and events sponsored by government organizations, but oriented toward promoting contacts in the private sector. In August 2007, for instance, the Mexican Committee of Foreign Trade, in coordination with its Chinese counterpart, CCPIT, held its sixteenth China-Mexico Entrepreneur Conference in China.[93]

Despite the considerable effort of the Mexican government to promote trade with the PRC, much remains to be done. One senior leader in the Mexican Foreign Commerce Bank (BANCOMEXT) has noted, for example, that spending by the Mexican government on the promotion of Mexican products abroad is relatively limited compared to that of other countries, such as Spain.[94] Others argue that the government has not effectively identified or leveraged Mexico's competitive advantages or targeted the types of products that China wishes to purchase. One executive of a major Mexican corporation indicated that the Mexican consulate in Beijing could do much more to maintain information and facilitate contacts to help companies with the mundane tasks of establishing supplier relationships and wading through the myriad bureaucratic requirements involved in doing business in China. Such criticisms, however, can also be applied to many other nations of the region in their dealings with the PRC.

One strength of Mexico's infrastructure for dealing with the PRC is that initiatives can be found at all levels of government. One of the first acts of Marcelo Ebrard, upon becoming mayor-elect of Mexico City, for example, was to travel to China to promote ties with businesses represented within his constituency.[95] The trip included a meeting with the mayor of Beijing, Wang Qi Shan, and the signing of an agreement with the company Sinosure to launch infrastructure projects and investments.[96] The new mayor was able to show a payoff in April 2007, when he signed a deal with the Chinese telecommunications firm ZTE Telecom to supply a system of 4,000 surveillance cameras and a network to provide free wireless Internet service to residents of the entire Mexican capital region.[97]

Mexico's regional governments have also been active in their promotion of trade with China. Representatives from the capital region participated in the presidential-level delegation that went to China in July 2008 and, at the end of this trip, announced that Mexico City would be receiving some $200 million in Chinese investments in the months to follow.[98] In April 2007, the governor of the state of Guanajuato announced a trip to the PRC and Singapore to attract investment and technology, with the objective of promoting the emergence of the region as a logistics hub serving the North American market.[99]

Mexican businesspeople and universities are likewise very active in terms of conferences and visits to China to make contacts and expand commercial connections. Numerous delegations have made commercially oriented trips, such as that by a group of Mexican businesspeople from Zacatecas in April 2007.[100] Consultancies have sprung up as well, dedicated to providing support services to companies interested in entering the Chinese market or in importing goods from the PRC.[101]

Finally, as with other Latin American countries, the Mexican banking sector is slowly building ties to the PRC to facilitate commerce. For instance, BANCOMEXT has opened up a series of offices in the PRC to support Mexican corporations doing business there[102] and has sponsored a series of trade fairs, primarily designed to help small and medium-sized enterprises market their goods to China.[103]

Intellectual Infrastructure

Despite its persistent trade deficit with China, Mexico's intellectual infrastructure is among the best developed in Latin America in supporting commerce with the PRC. Universidad Nacional Autónoma de México arguably was the first Latin American university to create a center dedicated to China studies.[104] In addition, the country has some thirty universities and centers with programs for teaching Mandarin. In an unprecedented move, in September 2006, Bulmaro Fuentes, national executive director of Mexico's technical institutes, signed a decree that all of the country's technical institutes begin teaching the language as soon as possible.[105] Mexico was also the first country in Latin America to establish a Confucius Institute, doing so in 2006;[106] it continues to lead Latin America in the number of such institutes, with plans under way to establish new ones in Universidad de Nuevo León, Universidad Nacional Autónoma de México, Universidad de Yucatán, and Universidad de Chihuahua.

Some of the strongest intellectual infrastructures for doing business with China, not surprisingly, are found in the northern part of Mexico, where the maquiladora sector dominates. Prestigious private schools, such as Instituto Tecnológico de Mexico (ITESM), are expanding their Mandarin-language programs and the portion of their business curriculum focused on doing business in Asia. ITESM, for example, has representative offices in three Chinese cities—Beijing, Shanghai, and Guangzhou—as well as ties to ten Chinese universities. In 2004, 200 of its students spent time in the PRC.[107] Other universities have been involved as well. As one example, in August 2007, Universidad Anónima de Baja California conducted an economic, cultural, and business forum in Tijuana, with investors from the PRC in attendance, interested in investing in Mexico.[108]

At the popular level, knowledge of the PRC and interest in developing business ties there are likely to grow with the expansion of contacts between the two countries. In 2004, the Chinese government recognized Mexico as an official tourist destination, facilitating the flow of Chinese businesspeople and tourists to Mexico.[109] Mexico also increasingly is connected to China by transportation links, including a direct Aeroméxico flight between the Mexican city Tijuana and the Chinese commercial center Shanghai, inaugurated in May 2008.[110]

Political and Military Relationships

Mexico's political and military relationships with China continue along positive but cautious paths. For China, Mexico has played a valuable role as a diplomatic ally, not only supporting a range of PRC positions on the world stage, but also helping the PRC in its bid to secure a place in Latin American institutions such as the Organization of American States (OAS) and the Inter-American Development Bank (IADB). Mexico's diplomatic position of nonrecognition of Taiwan has been particularly useful for the PRC as it has sought to convince other states of Central America and the Caribbean to adopt a similar position. Likewise, Mexico has been willing to use its influence in Central America on behalf of the PRC in exchange for its support in international forums. In 2005, when Mexico wanted PRC support for its bid to become a permanent member of the United Nations Security Council, it convened a group of Central American states for a meeting with a PRC dignitary to discuss the recognition issue.

For Mexico, which sees itself as an important actor in the international community, China is one of other key players with whom Mexico should have a relationship. In addition, from the Mexican perspective, its relationship with the PRC has been a useful vehicle to demonstrate its political independence from its neighbor to the north, the United States.[111] The importance that Mexico places on China was highlighted in July 2008 by President Felipe Calderón's state visit to the PRC and his meetings with Chinese president Hu Jintao and other government officials.[112]

As a reflection of its importance to China, Mexico is regularly included in visits by senior Chinese diplomats and political figures to the region. Although Mexico was not a stop on President Hu Jintao's landmark five-nation visit to Latin America in November 2004, Chinese vice president Zheng Quinghong included the country in his trip to attend the China-Caribbean Trade and Economic Cooperation forum two months later. Following this trip, in September 2005, President Hu visited Mexico to hold talks with President Vicente Fox, a trip that included the signing of six bilateral agreements to reinforce diplomatic relationships.[113] Subsequently, in March 2007, Chinese Politburo member Li Changchun also visited Mexico during his own five-nation trip to Latin America.[114]

In the military realm, Mexico's interactions with China have been limited, serving primarily as an extension of the diplomatic relationship between
the nations and a vehicle for Mexico to provide an international experience
for its officer corps. Significant milestones in this relationship include an
April 2004 meeting in Mexico between General Xu Caihou and the Mexican
secretaries of defense and the navy,[115] as well as participation by Mexican
military observers in a group of fifty servicemen attending an amphibious
landing exercise in China's Guangdong province in September 2004.

■ Costa Rica

Costa Rica is an outlier with respect to the relations between China and the
countries of Central America. It was the first country in the region in the
post–Cold War period to diplomatically recognize China, and the only
country other than Cuba to be visited by Chinese president Hu Jintao when
he traveled to the region in November 2008 in conjunction with the APEC
summit in Lima, Peru.

Even before switching diplomatic recognition from Taiwan to China in
June 2007, Costa Rica had a significant commercial relationship and a balance-of-payments surplus with the PRC. For Costa Rica, the PRC has growing weight as an export market, although, to date, these exports have been
computer chips made by Costa Rica's Intel plant and sold to computer manufacturers such as Lenovo, Hewlett-Packard (HP), and Dell, whose assembly plants are located in China.[116] In 2006, China was Costa Rica's number
two export market after the United States,[117] accounting for 13.2 percent of
the nation's export sales.[118] In 2007, the volume of bilateral trade between
Costa Rica and China was over $2.87 billion,[119] with an increase of 33 per-
cent over the previous year.[120] Costa Rica's diplomatic recognition of the
PRC moved these nations beyond exports into a new, strategic partnership,
with the expectation on the Costa Rican side that the relationship would
bring the country preferential access to Chinese investment and markets.[121]
Symbolic of its expectation, Costa Rica named as its new ambassador to
China Antonio Burgués, who had previously been the economics minister
and president of the Chamber of Exporters of Costa Rica (CADEXO).[122]

Although Costa Rica also has a variety of other information technology
industries and a burgeoning biomedical sector, Intel is at the heart of the
information technology character of Costa Rica's modern economy. It is this
modern, technology-oriented sector of the Costa Rican economy that has
allowed Costa Rica to stand out among the nations of Central America as the
one with a positive trade balance with China, and the only one in which
change in that balance has been moving in a positive direction.[123] Beyond
technology, Costa Rica is seeking to position itself both as a key tourist des-

tination for the Chinese and as an exporter to niche markets serving the growing Chinese middle class, including high-end goods like luxury coffee.

Costa Rica is also emerging as a major hub for Central American commerce with the PRC, providing a relatively large portion of the region's business contacts and leadership of many of the region's trade delegations to China. Costa Rica's June 2007 decision to recognize the PRC is likely to further broaden the nation's access to Chinese markets and to help consolidate its role as the Central American gateway to China.[124]

Historical Context

Prior to June 2007, Costa Rica maintained diplomatic ties with the Republic of China, not with the People's Republic of China. Although its diplomatic posture limited economic, political, and social contacts between the two countries, Costa Rica nonetheless exported a significant quantity of computer chips to the PRC. This export relationship, which allowed Costa Rica to enjoy strong exports and a balance-of-payments surplus with the PRC, was, however, a result of the decision by the chip manufacturer Intel to locate a production facility in Costa Rica in 1999. When the Chinese computer company Lenovo purchased the personal computer division of IBM in May 2005, it inherited this production relationship and chose to continue it.[125]

Shifting Diplomatic Recognition from Taiwan to the PRC

Costa Rica's recognition of the People's Republic of China in June 2007 was a bold action driven by the personal convictions of the nation's two-time president, Oscar Arias. During his candidacy, Arias had indicated that he would review the nation's foreign relations comprehensively, although it was not obvious at the time that this implied diplomatic recognition of the PRC.

Despite the surprise generated both domestically and internationally by Costa Rica's recognition of China, the action was consistent with the pragmatism and international orientation of President Arias and with his goal of expanding Costa Rica's engagement with the international community.[126] Despite Costa Rica's long-standing and positive relationship with Taiwan, which involved ties to communities throughout the country, and despite its differences with the PRC regarding democracy and human rights in the PRC,[127] Costa Rica saw the move as necessary to ensure that it had a relationship with the country that was emerging as the driver of global economic growth.[128] Indeed, without coordination, multiple people interviewed for this book linked the decision to other pragmatic moves by which Costa Rica was seeking to broaden its engagement with the rest of the world, including the relocation of the Costa Rican embassy in Israel from Jerusalem to Tel Aviv as part of Costa Rica's rapprochement with the international Arab community.[129]

Because of the sensitivity of what was being contemplated both for Taiwan and in the domestic political arena, negotiations were conducted in great secrecy. Serious negotiations began in earnest in 2006, with President Arias sending his young foreign minister, Bruno Stagno, to China to conduct preliminary talks.[130] The talks reportedly were conducted with such secrecy that the only people other than President Arias who were aware of the contemplated change were the president's brother, Estaño, and the housing minister, who had participated in the talks.[131]

Many of the nation's own ministers and political figures were taken by surprise, learning about the decision by hearing the announcement on television. At the time of the announcement, preparations were under way for a much-needed $60 million upgrade to the highway from Naranjo to San José, which included a planned $15 million donation from the Taiwanese government; the Costa Rican government arranged to cover this from other funds.[132] Similarly, at the time of the pronouncement, the Ministry of Public Security had just received $2 million in equipment from the Taiwanese government and was expecting to take delivery of an additional $3 million in goods. Moreover, because the Taiwanese embassy had been working directly with Costa Rican municipalities, a significant but unknown quantity of local projects were left to uncertain fates.[133] The use of funds from the Taiwanese government would continue to generate questions in Costa Rican politics long after the issue of recognition was closed.[134]

Once the formal proclamation of Costa Rica's recognition of the PRC was made, both nations moved forward rapidly with the concrete tasks required to build diplomatic and commercial relations. A PRC embassy in Costa Rica was opened in August 2007.[135] The new ambassador, Wang Xiaoyuan, fluent in Spanish and with previous experience as Chinese ambassador to Uruguay, moved quickly to establish ties with a range of business and social groups across the country, from Costa Rica's Chinese community[136] to business groups such as CADEXO and the Costa Rican Chamber of Commerce.[137] Marco Vinicio Ruiz, intimately involved in the process as Costa Rica's minister of foreign trade, noted that the features of the new relationship that most impressed him were the directness and pragmatism with which the Chinese worked with their new Costa Rican counterparts to put the infrastructure in place to expand both diplomatic and commercial relations.[138]

Although the new relationship with the PRC tended to focus more on loans and technical cooperation than on monetary donations,[139] it nonetheless involved a significant amount of new assistance. One of the key activities by the Costa Rican Ministry of Foreign Affairs in preparation for the October 2007 Arias trip to China was coordination with other ministries to identify areas in which assistance had been lost from Taiwan, or in which assistance was otherwise needed.[140] Overall, an estimated $220 million in potential donations and projects were promised or discussed during the period preceding Costa Rican recognition of the PRC, and while setting an agenda for the October 2007 trip to China.[141] Major Chinese contributions to Costa Rica that have materialized since the change in recognition include $73 million for a new 40,000-person national stadium,[142] and purchases by the PRC of an undisclosed portion of a $300 million Costa Rican government bond issue.[143] New assistance from the PRC also included a $21 million contribution to a national emergency fund, in October 2007, in response to damage from flooding in the province of Guanacaste.[144]

The Chinese Community in Costa Rica

Relative to its size, Costa Rica has a rather significant Chinese community. According to Wang Xiaoyaun, China's ambassador to Costa Rica, there are 60,000 people of Chinese origin in the country.[145] Chinese immigrants began arriving in Costa Rica in the nineteenth century, fleeing political chaos and economic hardship. Many were contracted (with varying degrees of awareness as to what they were getting themselves into) to work on the nation's railroad system. A small but steady stream of Chinese migrants has continued to arrive in Costa Rica since that time, including those smuggled into the country by human-trafficking organizations, seeking to make their way to the United States.

Chinese Costa Ricans today are principally employed in the retail sector,[146] working in small grocery stores, known as *pulperías,* and in small restaurants. Indeed, Chinese restaurants were historically one of the first options for dining out in Costa Rica, before the tradition became widespread and led to the growth of other types of restaurants.[147] As in Ecuador, Costa Rica's Chinese community has been able to coexist in a relatively harmonious fashion with the rest of the society, with modest levels of intermarriage[148] and without a history of significant anti-Chinese violence,[149] such as that found in northern Mexico.

Largely reflecting the locations of the railroad work engaged in by the first Chinese immigrants, Costa Rica's Chinese community today is concentrated in the east coast port of Limón, the west coast port of Puntarena, the province of Guanacaste,[150] and the capital, San José.[151] Although the section of San José (including the Paseo de los Estudiantes) where the majority of Chinese shops are concentrated is only a few blocks in size, in January 2008, the municipality of San José proposed the creation of a formal Chinatown in the area.[152]

China's Interest in Costa Rican Agriculture

Costa Rica's recognition of the PRC in June 2008 opened the door for officials and businesspeople from both countries to build new commercial relationships.[153] While the rapid pace of expansion is arguably driven by a Chinese desire to demonstrate to other countries the tangible benefits that arise from recognition, the patterns of commerce between the two countries are also shaped by the logic of what China wants to buy and what Costa Rica has to sell.

In general, Costa Rica is not seeking to become an exporter of bulk agricultural commodities to China. Regarding such traditional crops as coffee, bananas, and pineapple, it recognizes that it neither has the surplus labor force nor the land to increase its agricultural exports sufficiently to serve the Chinese market.[154] Moreover, Costa Rica is a relatively high-wage country compared to its Central American neighbors and to regions of Asia. Costa Rica's strategy, thus, has been to focus on relatively high value–added niches, such as luxury coffees, that combine its competitive advantages in quality and international brand recognition with the growing demand of a Chinese middle class interested in Western consumer goods.[155]

Costa Rica hopes to sell more of its green coffee both directly in the premium sector of the Chinese market and through retail chains with a presence in China, such as Starbucks (which purchases an impressive 20 percent of Costa Rica's coffee crop).[156] The Costa Rican coffee retailer Café Britt has had a presence in China since 2004, selling not only coffee but also its line of gourmet chocolates and other goods,[157] as well as using Chinese facilities to produce artisan products, like decorated coffee mugs, to sell in its shops worldwide.[158]

Costa Rica is also pursuing a niche market for its bananas. Indeed, bananas were the only item for which a specific phytosanitary accord was signed during the October 2007 visit of Oscar Arias to China.[159] The nation's bananas are regarded as high-quality but too expensive to compete in the Chinese market on the basis of cost alone.[160] Unlike the case with coffee, some believe that room exists for a meaningful expansion of Costa Rican banana production to supply the new Chinese market.[161] The prospect for expanding banana sales to China is particularly attractive for Costa Rica due to a trade dispute with the European Union in 2007–2008, which threatened access for its banana exports to the European market.[162]

Costa Rica has identified a range of other agricultural products with potential to be exported to China, including fruit juices, fish, vegetables, fruits, bread products, and shellfish,[163] although more detailed studies of where the opportunities and Costa Rica's competitive advantages lie have yet to be completed.[164] One of the most significant successes for Costa Rican agricultural exports was the signing of a $150 million contract by the firm Talmana to export Costa Rican shellfish to China.[165]

Costa Rica has been successful, as well, in supplying agricultural niche markets in China beyond foodstuffs. The Costa Rican company Coopeindia, for example, has been exporting the decorative plant *caña india* to Asia since 1984, with the PRC coming to represent 63 percent of its export sales by 2006.[166]

China's Interest in Costa Rican Petroleum and Refining

In addition to agriculture, Costa Rica's diplomatic recognition of the PRC has created new possibilities in the nation's modest-sized petroleum industry. During his visit to China, President Arias held discussions with China National Petroleum Corporation, leading to an agreement between the Costa Rican state petroleum company, Refinadora Costarricense de Petróleo (Recope), and CNPC, by which the latter would help Recope to increase its refining capability,[167] including possible construction of a new refinery, potentially in the Costa Rican Pacific port of Barranca.[168] The agreement also included possible exploration for petroleum by the Chinese in Costa Rican waters.[169] Although the refinery, and any new Costa Rican oil, could ostensibly be used to supply other nations of Central America, the participation of CNPC in the project, in conjunction with a refinery in Barranca that could use an offshore platform to load very large crude carriers, suggests that Costa Rica might supply petroleum to China and other Asian destinations.[170] During his visit to Costa Rica in November 2008, Chinese president Hu Jintao signed an accord advancing the project by creating a joint company to modernize the existing refinery, with a contemplated investment of up to $1.2 billion.[171]

China's Interest in Costa Rica's Information Technology Sector

The information technology (IT) sector has played a major role in establishing Costa Rica as the only nation in Central America with a positive balance of trade with the PRC.[172] As noted previously, Costa Rican IT exports to China are largely a function of computer chip production by Intel, and the government and business infrastructures that support it. According to the statistics from PROCOMER, 86.2 percent of Costa Rican exports to China in 2006 were integrated circuits and related products.[173] Intel was in place in Costa Rica as a supplier of chips to the personal-computer division of IBM when that division was bought by the Chinese in May 2005,[174] and simply continued supplying chips to the parent computer manufacturer, even when the owner of the manufacturer became Lenovo. While it is not known whether China is interested in expanding its technology purchases from Costa Rica to other companies and sectors, Costa Rican government officials interviewed for this book made it clear that this is the type of commerce with China that Costa Rica wishes to promote.[175]

China's Interest in Costa Rica as a Tourist Destination

In one of the accords signed during the October 2007 visit by Oscar Arias to China, the PRC recognized Costa Rica not only as an *authorized* tourist destination, but as a *recommended* destination for Chinese traveling abroad.[176] The combination of Costa Rica's favorable climate, ecological diversity, relatively low crime rate, and existing tourism industries makes tourism a logical vehicle by which Costa Rica can expand its commerce with China.[177] Chinese investors have recognized the potential of Costa Rica as a tourism destination as well, with the company Mandarin Oriental constructing a 130-room hotel on the booming Pacific northwest coast of Costa Rica, to be completed in 2009.[178]

Costa Rica as a Market for Chinese Goods

Aside from Panama, whose earnings are distorted by income in the Canal Zone, Costa Rica has the highest per capita income in Central America.[179] Although the overall size of the Costa Rican economy is small compared to those of some other nations, such as Brazil, its people's earnings make it a logical market for Chinese goods, including not only textiles, toys, and footwear, but also consumer electronics, appliances, motorcycles, cars, and other manufactured goods.[180]

Chinese consumer appliances are increasingly available in Costa Rica through such retail outlets as Casa Blanca and Importadora Monge.[181] Costa Rican retail companies, like CEMACO and Universal, also play an important role in importing Chinese products.[182] Similarly, in the automotive sector, Chinese cars (e.g., Great Wall, Geeley, and Golden Car) are available through the nation's network of existing dealerships.[183]

Finally, Costa Rica is also of interest to the PRC as a market for its telecommunication companies. As of October 2007, the Chinese firms Huawei and ZTE had offices and contracts in Costa Rica[184] and were exploring possibilities to expand their presence; Huawei had a potential interest, as well, in establishing a facility in one of the nation's free-trade zones to produce flat-panel displays and cellular telephones. In part, these plans by Huawei and ZTE are contingent upon the reform of the Costa Rican telecommunications sector, as required under the provisions of the Central American Free Trade Agreement (CAFTA), and as taken up in the general telecommunications law, which was passed by the Costa Rican parliament in February 2008. Under these laws, companies such as Huawei and ZTE are now able to offer services directly to the Costa Rican public, in contrast to the previous situation, in which they had to act as subs to the Instituto Costarricense de Electricidad (ICE), the national telecom monopoly.[185] Reinforcing the impact of telecommunications reform, during Arias's trip to China in 2007, the two nations signed an accord further committing Costa Rica to this course of action, permitting Huawei and ZTE to bid for cellular telephone or Internet infrastructure projects in the country.[186]

Costa Rica as an Assembly Platform

In combination with a potential free-trade agreement with China, CAFTA makes Costa Rica attractive to the PRC as a final-assembly hub for certain types of Chinese products, complementing the former's proximity to east coast and west coast markets, its educated labor force, its effective government and physical infrastructures, and other attributes.

With respect to tariffs, with the passage of a national referendum on October 7, 2007, Costa Rica officially cleared the way to finalize its participation in CAFTA.[187] As a complement, in 2007 the Costa Rican government initiated a study of a free-trade agreement between Costa Rica and China.[188] In July 2008, the Costa Rican working group assigned to study the issue recommended that the government proceed in seeking such an accord.[189] In November 2008, in conjunction with the visit to Costa Rica by Chinese president Hu Jintao, the two nations announced that they would formally begin negotiations on a free-trade agreement in the beginning of 2009. This type of agreement, in combination with Costa Rican participation in CAFTA, creates the possibility of a production chain through which components could be imported from China, assembled in Costa Rica, and sold as final products in the US market with low or no tariffs.[190]

In addition to tariff incentives—and by contrast to other nations of Central America—Costa Rica has a relatively sophisticated business infrastructure in high value–added sectors in which the Chinese are interested, such as information technology and biotechnology. It also has a relatively well-educated labor force, as well as good, technically oriented public and private universities providing a supply of trained technicians and managers.[191] Thus, particularly in the domain of technologically sophisticated products and complex manufacturing operations, Costa Rica is able to make a strong case to be the logical final-assembly location for Chinese companies who are seeking to enter the US market.[192]

On the other hand, although Costa Rican government representatives, such as the minister of commerce, welcome China's interest in locating manufacturing facilities in Costa Rica,[193] a significant expansion of traditional manufacturing is arguably not the thrust of Costa Rica's orientation toward China. Indeed, in an interview, Costa Rica's minister of labor, Francisco Morales, argued that Costa Rica's current focus is on the expansion of jobs in the service sector, such as those represented by Intel and Hewlett Packard.[194]

Government and Business Infrastructures

Given the size of Costa Rica and the brief time that diplomatic relations have been established between Costa Rica and China, the governmental and commercial infrastructures for doing business with China and the quantity of events that these infrastructures support are truly impressive. On the government side, this infrastructure includes the Ministry of Commerce (MIN-

COM) and its quasi-public trade-promotion companion organization, PRO-COMER.[195] The activities of MINCOM and PROCOMER in providing services and information for companies seeking to do business in China[196] are complemented by a number of public/private organizations, such as the Costa Rican Chamber of Exporters (CRECEX), and the now-separate initiative, China Ya, which organizes and leads Central American delegations traveling to China,[197] as well as others, such as the China–Costa Rica Chamber of Commerce and Industry.

Even before the establishment of diplomatic relations, Costa Rica was the bridge to China for much of Central America. In April 2006, PROCO-MER and its Chinese counterpart, CCPIT, signed an accord by which each organization would provide support to businesspeople from the other country.[198] That same month, CRECEX, in combination with PROCOMER and the Costa Rican business council CADEXO, led 110 Central American businesspeople to participate in the Canton trade fair, in addition to visiting Shanghai and other Chinese cities under "China Ya 2006."[199] In August 2007, for example, the Chinese trade-promotion organization CCPIT, in coordination with the Costa Rican government, organized an economic and social forum and trade fair in San José, Costa Rica, attracting 30 Chinese companies and 25,000 visitors, including delegations from Nicaragua, Panama, Mexico, the Dominican Republic, and the United States.[200] In September of the same year, PROCOMER led a group to the international commerce and investment trade fair in Xiamen, China,[201] including representatives from the Costa Rican investment promotion agency (CINDE).[202] A month later, during October 15–20, PROCOMER, in coordination with CRECEX, led a delegation of 25 companies to represent Costa Rica at the Canton trade fair.[203] Although the exhibit was a modest 36 square meters, Costa Rica was among only six Latin American countries represented at the fair.[204] The following week, in Beijing, PROCOMER held a major exhibition of Costa Rican products—with 30 Costa Rican companies and filling a 1,900-square-meter facility dedicated to the event at the China International Exhibition Center[205]—while at the same time opening its representative office in the city and playing host for the visit of President Oscar Arias.[206]

In addition to services provided by organizations such as PROCOMER,[207] associations of Costa Rican businesses, like CADEXO, participate in initiatives (e.g., China Ya) to expand Costa Rica's commercial interactions with China,[208] maintaining close contact with PROCOMER and MINCOM, and complementing their activities.[209]

Beyond such activities, Costa Rica is building the financial connections that will facilitate commerce between the two nations. In October 2007, for example, China Development Bank and Banco Nacional of Costa Rica signed a cooperative agreement that will facilitate the importation of Costa Rican goods, such as bananas, into China.[210] In the private sector, in 2007,

Hong Kong Bank of China (HSBC) bought out Banco Exterior (BANEX),[211] supplying at least a degree of potential reach into the Asian market through the parent company. In addition, Banco Cathay operates in Costa Rica, although this institution is primarily oriented toward Costa Rican residents of Chinese origin, rather than promoting international business ties.[212]

In addition to these initiatives, Costa Rica has a pending application to join the APEC forum when the possibility of accepting new members is revisited in 2010.[213] If Costa Rica's application is accepted, the nation will become the only one in Central America to enjoy this institutional relationship with China and the other economies of Asia.[214]

Intellectual Infrastructure

Costa Rica's intellectual infrastructure to support commerce with China consistently stands out among the nations of Central America and the Caribbean. Within the region, Costa Rica has the largest and most well-regarded universities with Asia-focused business programs. An example is Centro de Investigación de Mercados Sostenibles, attached to the business school of Costa Rica's most prestigious private university, the Instituto Centroamericano de Administracion de Empresas (INCAE). This center not only has China-oriented programs of study, but has actively participated in leading trips to China, in coordination with CRECEX and PROCOMER.[215]

INCAE and a number of other highly thought-of private universities and institutes have Mandarin offerings; additionally, the prestigious Humbolt School, a private high school in San José, has a Mandarin club.[216]

In the public domain, Universidad de Costa Rica has a Mandarin program, with instructors coming from China in February 2008 to expand the program, and with plans to establish a Confucius Institute.[217]

Political Relations

Prior to Costa Rica's 2007 decision to grant diplomatic recognition to the People's Republic of China, political relations between the two countries were almost nonexistent. Costa Rica's recognition of the PRC not only enabled the expansion of economic interactions between the two countries, but also enhanced cooperation in the political sphere.

Four months after Costa Rica recognized the PRC, President Arias traveled to China with a delegation of fifteen, including the Costa Rican minister of the presidency, Rodrigo Arias, and the minister of foreign relations, Bruno Stagno,[218] both of whom had played a key role in the process leading to recognition. As noted previously, the visit included the signing of eleven agreements across a broad range of topics, from Chinese investment in a new Costa Rican refinery, to the opening up of the Costa Rican telecommunications market to Chinese firms, to a range of symbolic projects, including the remodeling of Costa Rica's national sports stadium and assistance to flood-damaged areas. Beyond such tangible benefits, however, through recognition, Costa Rica forged an important new political alliance that supported President Arias's goal of expanding the nation's role in international politics; for example, China has indicated that it will look "very positively" on Costa Rica's bid for a nonpermanent seat on the United Nations Security Council in the future.[219] Similarly, in October 2007, Chinese president Hu Jintao committed China to back Costa Rica's application for membership in APEC, assuming that the moratorium on new membership is terminated in 2010.[220]

■ Panama

China's interest in Panama is dominated by the importance of the Panama Canal for trade between China and Atlantic coast ports. This commerce includes exports of soy and other primary products from Brazil and Argentina, as well as Chinese exports bound for those countries. The Panama Canal also supports the even greater Chinese bilateral trade with the East Coast of the United States, and is one of the key routes for Venezuela to export its petroleum to the PRC. Chinese businesses profit not only indirectly from the canal, but also directly, through operation by the Chinese logistics firm Hutchison of key Canal Zone facilities at Cristobal, Balboa, and Rodman Point. Chinese firms such as the China Ocean Shipping Company (COSCO) Pacific also play an important role in the ongoing efforts to expand and modernize the canal.

In addition to the canal, like other nations in Central America and the Caribbean, Panama is of political interest to the PRC because it continues to give diplomatic recognition to Taiwan. When Costa Rica chose to recognize the PRC in June 2007, Panama became the focus of widespread speculation that it could become the next nation to do so.

Commercial interactions between PRC producers and Panamanian consumers are overshadowed by transactions that relate directly or indirectly to the canal. In 2006, China accounted for a minuscule 1.43 percent of total Panamanian exports, with fifteen other countries purchasing more from Panama than did the PRC.[221] However, although Panama's net balance-of-payments position with the PRC is negative, such figures do not fully reflect the direct and indirect revenues generated by the Canal Zone because of the growing traffic to and from China.

Historical Context

Despite the lack of diplomatic relations between Panama and the PRC, China has long maintained low-level trade relations with the former because shipping companies use the Panama Canal to ship goods to and from China. The United States' return of sovereignty over the canal to Panama in 1999 became the occasion for an expansion of the Chinese commercial presence in the country. In 1996, Panama and the PRC established representative trade offices in each other's countries to facilitate commercial transactions, and, in 1999, on the eve of the turnover of the canal to Panama, the Chinese firm Hutchison Whampoa was awarded two consecutive twenty-five-year leases to operate major facilities there.

In the diplomatic arena, Panama and the PRC have generally avoided engaging each other, although tension over Panama's recognition of the ROC has occasionally come to the fore. In 1997, for instance, the PRC worked to prevent world leaders from attending an international forum in Panama on the future of the canal, due to sponsorship of the event by Taiwan.[222] Although no official high-level exchanges between Panama and the PRC have taken place in recent years, periodic informal meetings between decisionmakers do occur. These include the 2001 trip to China by Hector Aleman, chairman of the Foreign Affairs Committee of the Panamanian Congress, and his meeting with Li Peng, chairman of the Standing Committee of the National People's Congress.[223]

The Chinese Community in Panama

The contemporary Chinese community in Panama can trace its roots to the Chinese workers, known as "coolies," who came principally from the province of Canton.[224] The first group of Chinese arrived in the country in 1954 to work on the Panama Railroad,[225] and continued to be brought into the region to work on a range of projects associated with the Panama Canal. Due to a combination of tropical diseases and harsh working conditions, the mortality rate of Chinese laborers on these projects was so high that the Chinese government sought to put an end to contracting workers in China for projects in Panama. Chinese have continued to arrive in Panama as a result of various traumatic events in the PRC, such as the political crackdown in 1989 after the events of Tiananmen Square. Panama, moreover, is part of the transit zone for Chinese being smuggled overland into the United States by human-trafficking networks, contributing to a modest proportion of Panama's population.

The number of people of Chinese descent living in Panama today is at least 150,000, and up to a third of Panama's total population may have some Chinese ancestry.[226] Whatever criteria are used for the estimate, the Chinese community in Panama is one of the largest in Latin America. The presence of this ethnic group in the capital, Panama City, is marked by an aging commercial Chinatown, known locally as the *barrio chino*.[227] A substantial Chinese community also exists in Colón, where the government maintains a free-trade zone populated by numerous Chinese and Taiwanese businesses.[228]

Today the Chinese Panamanian community is a mix between the relatively established descendants of previous generations of immigrants and more recent arrivals from Taiwan, Hong Kong, and various provinces of mainland China. As with other Chinese communities in Latin America, the Chinese community in Panama is represented through various social organizations, principally the China Association (Asociación China).[229]

China's Interest in Panamanian Agriculture and Other Products

Panama has a modest export-oriented agricultural sector, but the PRC's interest in Panama is largely focused on two other areas: the canal (and services related to crossing it) and Panama's recognition of Taiwan. According to statistics from the PRC Ministry of Commerce, Panama exported a mere $7.9 million to the PRC in 2007—a quantity that is particularly small in comparison with other Latin American nations and with Panamanian purchases from China, the latter amounting to $5.58 billion during the same period.[230]

Panama's difficulty in exporting products to the PRC is similar to that faced by other Central American countries. It principally exports such goods as fish, fruits, and scrap metal, with smaller exports of coffee, wood, and various animal products.[231] As with comparable exports from other Latin American countries, Panamanian fruit exports are generally not competitive in the PRC. China has demonstrated an interest in purchasing fishing industry products and scrap metal from a variety of Latin American countries, and could expand its purchases of such items from Panama as well.

Panama as a Market for Chinese Goods

By contrast to other countries of Central America, Panama is—at least on paper—a significant market for Chinese goods. In 2007, China exported some $5.58 billion in goods to Panama, making the latter the third-best customer of the PRC in Latin America, behind only Brazil and Mexico.[232] Indeed, it is interesting to note that, during this period, Panama actually imported more goods from China than did Chile.[233]

In part, the high number of Panamanian imports from China reflects the relative affluence of the country vis-à-vis the rest of Central America. Indeed, in 2007, Panama had the highest overall per capita income in the region, slightly ahead of Costa Rica's.[234] In addition to low-end products such as textiles, toys, and footwear, Panama purchases more sophisticated goods from the PRC, such as motorcycles and cars. In July 2007, for example, the company Ameristar Sales and Leasing began to introduce Chinese busses into its service in Panama.[235]

Panama's high level of imports from China is also an artifact of the nature of commerce in the Canal Zone. Because the area is a major international logistics hub, the companies that operate there consume significant quantities of goods and services in support of canal traffic; many of the key operators have ties to China. Not only does the Chinese firm Hutchison operate vital Panamanian port facilities at Cristobal, Balboa, and Rodman Point, but also the PRC firm COSCO, the second-largest shipping company in the world[236] and the second-largest user of the canal,[237] has a number of facilities there.[238]

Perhaps the most important factor in explaining Panama's large volume of purchases of Chinese goods is that the nation is also a key point of access and distribution for Chinese goods entering Latin America in general. Various companies have facilities in the Canal Zone that receive and warehouse Chinese goods, subsequently shipping them to retailers or other distribution nodes in Latin America. In some cases, the goods are repackaged or modified in some small way, causing them to be registered as "Panamanian imports" from China, then subsequently as "Panamanian exports" to other Latin American countries. A number of such operations take place in the Colón free-trade zone (among others), which is host to a number of Chinese and Taiwanese companies.[239] There, the Chinese manufacturer Kitomi (as one example) assembles motorcycles for export throughout Latin America.[240]

Although much of the commerce that takes place in the Canal Zone is legitimate, the area is also believed to be an important point of access for Chinese contraband products entering Latin America.[241]

Infrastructure Projects

The Panama Canal currently plays an important role in the commerce between China and destinations on the Americas' Atlantic coast. In addition to its importance for the shipment of Chinese goods to markets on the East Coast of the United States, the Panama Canal is crucial in Chinese access to markets in Brazil, Argentina, and Uruguay, as well as in the shipment of vast quantities of iron and soy products from those nations to the PRC. The Panama Canal, as well, could be involved in Venezuelan plans to ship its petroleum to China, if these plans go forward.[242] Overall, an estimated 40 percent of all traffic going through the canal is tied to China in one way or another.[243]

Currently, the Chinese firm Hutchison-Whampoa operates facilities on both the Atlantic and Pacific sides of the Panama Canal. In addition, the Chinese firm COSCO Pacific is one of the leading partners in Panama's current massive project to increase the capacity of the canal, involving the construction of a new set of three-chamber locks on each end of the canal with the capacity to handle ships that are too large to use the existing canal locks.[244] The modernization and expansion of the canal, scheduled to run until 2014, is estimated to require $5.25 billion in investment.[245] As of late 2008, COSCO Pacific was also one of two bidders for the construction of a megaport on the Pacific side of the canal at Farfán, although as of late 2008, legal battles and the global recession had delayed the project.[246]

The PRC is also an interested party in a proposed project to increase the capacity of the trans-Panama pipeline and reverse its flow.[247] The principal proponent of the project is Hugo Chávez in Venezuela,[248] so that Venezuela would be able to ship oil from its Atlantic coast ports to Panama, then move it across the country to holding facilities on the west coast, where it could be loaded onto very large crude carriers (VLCCs) for shipment to the PRC and other Asian destinations. The pipeline, and a prospective new Panamanian refinery to process the unique heavy Venezuelan crude oil, were mentioned by Chávez when he traveled to Panama in June 2006 to sign an energy cooperation accord with the Panamanian government.[249]

Another important petroleum-sector infrastructure project that would complement the trans-Panama pipeline is the creation of a petroleum complex called the Centro Energético de las Américas (CELA). Such a complex would integrate the new pipeline with new processing, storage, and loading facilities on both the Pacific and Atlantic sides of the canal, providing a capacity to refine two million barrels of petroleum per day,[250] significantly increasing the importance of Panama as a key node in processing and transporting petroleum bound for China and other Asian destinations.

The Impact of Alternatives to the Canal

Currently, the Panama Canal plays a key role in China's commerce with the Americas, and the geography of the Americas implies that this role will be a permanent fixture of China's commercial relationship with the Americas. In the future, however, a number of proposed or ongoing projects may alleviate a portion of the growing demand currently being placed on the canal.

In the petroleum sector, the principal options that would reduce the amount of tanker traffic through the canal involve projects to build or upgrade pipelines. The trans-Panama pipeline, for example, could offer an important new alternative to the use of the canal for the shipment of Venezuelan, and perhaps Brazilian, petroleum to the PRC and other Asian destinations. Other alternatives include the somewhat more remote possibilities of an oil pipeline across Colombia from Maracaibo to Tribugal, as well as a pipeline across Nicaragua.

Beyond the petroleum sector, a number of transcontinental infrastructure projects represent other ways of moving goods to and from the Pacific without using the canal. These include the Manta-Manaus-Belém multimodal corridor, the Peru-Brazil interoceanic corridor, the improvement of the rail and highway infrastructure from Tacna to Santa Cruz, and the corridor connecting Santos to Arica and Iquique. Similarly, improvement of the mountain passes connecting Argentina and Chile would give Argentina better options for exporting its agricultural products via Chilean ports during the winter months. Each of these options, if realized, would divert some of the growing commercial demand on the Panama Canal and give rise to new centers of trade and commerce serving the region.

Government and Business Infrastructures

Handling the volume of Chinese goods that move through the Panama Canal Zone has given the Panamanian government and business community in the area significant experience in dealing with China and Asian companies. Because the Panamanian government has a well-developed infrastructure to administer the zone, it is relatively sophisticated in its dealings with the major Chinese companies that operate there, such as Hutchison-Whampoa, and COSCO, as well as the various smaller companies that have manufacturing and import-export operations in such areas as the Colón free-trade zone.

One expression of the ongoing ties between China and the local business community in Panama is the annual China Trade Exposition. The ninth China Trade Exposition, for example, held in Panama in 2006,[251] generated an estimated $12 million in business.[252] The tenth such exposition, hosted a year later, featured more than a hundred Chinese companies from Beijing, Tianjin, Shanghai, Chongqing, and nine Chinese provinces.[253] The eleventh exposition, held in Panama City in November 2008, enjoyed similar success.[254]

Additionally, support for commercial transactions is increasing in the financial sector. The only branch office that Bank of China has in Latin America, for example, is located in Panama City.[255]

Finally, like Colombia, Ecuador, Costa Rica, and other nations of Latin America, Panama has expressed an interest in becoming a member of the Asia-Pacific Economic Cooperation forum, if the moratorium on the entry of new members is lifted in 2010.[256] As with pending applications, Panama's membership in APEC could further strengthen the nation's institutional ties to the PRC and to Asia in general.

The Question of Panamanian
Diplomatic Recognition of the PRC

Although Panama does not have official diplomatic relations with the PRC, representatives from the two countries interact on a regular basis through a series of unofficial channels—for instance, the October 2007 trip to the PRC by a delegation (headed by Panamanian party leader Juan Carlos

Varela) to meet with its counterparts in the Chinese Communist Party.[257] The Panama Canal, making the nation a logistics hub for the region, has helped Panama to develop a significant commercial relationship with the PRC, even in the absence of diplomatic ties.[258] Chinese foreign minister Yang Jiechi implicitly made this point in a September 2007 meeting with his counterpart, Samuel Lewis Navarro, in which Yang reaffirmed interest by the PRC in expanding commerce between the two countries.[259]

Despite Panama's strong relations with the ROC, the question of granting diplomatic recognition to the PRC has been a persistent theme in Panamanian politics in recent years. During the 2004 presidential election, Guerrmo Endara Galimany, of Panama's Solidarity Party, openly advocated recognition of the PRC,[260] but was soundly beaten by Martin Torrijos. Nonetheless, the June 2007 recognition of the PRC by neighboring Costa Rica generated a reexamination of the issue within Panamanian editorial pages[261] and across the Panamanian political spectrum. Following Costa Rica's action, former Panamanian president Ernesto Perez, a member of the ruling Revolutionary Democratic Party (PRD), called upon the Panamanian government to follow suit. Despite such statements, however, in March 2008 Panamanian president Torrijos reaffirmed that Panama would continue to maintain diplomatic relations with Taiwan, even while pursuing commercial relations with China.[262] Nonetheless, although this is the position of the current administration, Panama has elections scheduled for May 2009, and the statements discussed in the previous paragraphs suggest that there are currents within both the ruling party and the opposition that advocate a change in position.[263]

■ Other Nations of Central America

With a number of exceptions, such as the the Panama Canal Zone and the information technology sector in Costa Rica, the states of Central America continue to be primary-product economies oriented toward the United States, including trade relationships that will deepen through implementation of the Central American Free Trade Agreement (CAFTA) and through the growing flow of remittances from Central Americans living in the United States.

Beyond the exceptions noted previously, Central America does not possess the governmental and commercial infrastructures that would allow it to take advantage of the opportunities represented by the PRC. The region generally does not export in great quantities the types of primary products that the PRC is seeking to import. Nor do the states of Central America have well-developed physical infrastructures or commercial mechanisms for collecting, inspecting, and packaging the production of its small farmers and exporting it to the PRC in large amounts on a sustained basis. With a few exceptions, the region also generally lacks large companies with an internationally recognized brand identity and with the resources, experience, and products to set up sales and distribution networks in the PRC; nor do the governments of Central America yet possess well-resourced trade-promotion organizations with representative offices beyond Beijing to facilitate major deals. Further, in general, the nations of Central America do not have a large number of Mandarin speakers to support business and government institutions that might otherwise realize commercial opportunities.

The countries of Central America are among those in the region most challenged by poverty, crime, and violence; failing systems of public education; and a range of other difficulties, limiting their potential as markets for Chinese products or as attractive sites for Chinese investors.

The informal truce that emerged in 2008 in the battle to change the diplomatic posture of countries recognizing Taiwan, and the prospect for a broader reconciliation between the two Chinas, could diminish even more the level of interest that Central America holds for China. From a Central American perspective, if the short-term truce between Taiwan and China were to break, the continuing likelihood of a reconciliation between the two Chinas over the long term could set in motion a scramble among countries of the region to switch recognition from Taiwan to the PRC while something remains to be gained by doing so.

China's Interest in Central American Products

Central America has largely unrealized potential as an exporter of agricultural and other products to the PRC. As a whole, the region has been slow in developing the commercial relationships that support export sales to China; traditionally, it has been dominated by a small number of agro-export companies, such as United Fruit, that have been relatively sluggish, to date, in placing their goods in Chinese markets. As is true for other Latin American nations, the perishable, labor-intensive agricultural products sold by many Central American countries simply have not been competitive against producers in China or in countries closer to China, such as the Philippines. Compounding these problems, the absence of diplomatic recognition of the PRC by most of the region's countries has complicated the process of forming business ties between agricultural and other producers in Central America and purchasers in the PRC. It has also resulted in an almost total lack of phytosanitary agreements between these countries and the PRC, effectively shutting the door on agricultural exports, even if they were otherwise possible.

Central America as a Market for Chinese Goods

Although the economies of Central America are relatively small, with low per capita earnings, these nations collectively represent a respectable-sized market for Chinese goods. Even removing Costa Rica and Panama from consideration, the remaining nations—Guatemala, Nicaragua, Honduras, El Salvador, and Belize—purchased $1.66 billion in goods from the PRC in 2007.[264] Because of the limited incomes of many Central Americans, the region is particularly attractive for cheap Chinese goods in such sectors as textiles and footwear, as well as for Chinese contraband goods, like pirated CDs and videos. Chinese motorcycles and consumer appliances are also increasingly found in the region; however, as of late 2008, little information was available on auto distributors carrying Chinese car brands.

The Nicaraguan Canal and Trans-Nicaragua Pipeline

Nicaragua's current relationship with and importance to China could be transformed dramatically by the realization of an ambitious project to construct a transoceanic canal through Nicaraguan territory. Such a canal would create a significant new alternative to the Panama Canal with respect to Chinese commerce with Brazil, Argentina, Venezuela, and the East Coast of the United States, transforming Nicaragua into an extremely important partner for China in its relationship with the Americas.

A canal through Nicaragua has been contemplated for as long as people have contemplated a canal linking the Atlantic and Pacific oceans. Although significant engineering challenges, such as removing enormous quantities of sediment from the San Juan River, have cast doubts on the project, it was revived in 2006 by then–Nicaraguan president Enrique Bolanos in a forum with Western Hemisphere defense ministers.[265] Bolanos suggested that the viability of such a project would depend on investment from banks in China and Japan.[266] Daniel Ortega, the Sandinista leader elected president of Nicaragua in 2006, has kept talk of such a canal alive by calling for it to be studied. In September 2008, the Russian government also expressed interest in supporting the construction of a canal across Nicaragua.[267]

The Nicaraguan canal project, in the form discussed by the current Sandinista government, would require an estimated $18 billion in investment. It would be able to accommodate a higher volume of traffic than the Panama Canal, including commercial ships twice the size of the largest ships currently able to use the current canal. The proposed project would be 173 miles long, transiting Nicaragua along the San Juan River, which serves as the Nicaraguan border with Costa Rica, then through Lake Nicaragua. The final section of the project, and the most difficult, would involve the construction of a channel from the western side of Lake Nicaragua to the Pacific coast. Questions of the technical feasibility of the canal notwithstanding, doubts exist as to whether the level of commerce in the foreseeable future is sufficient to support two canals in the region, given the ongoing project to widen the Panama Canal, in combination with the enormous costs of the proposed Nicaraguan canal.

Although the canal project may not be viable, the country has also been mentioned as the site of a new transcontinental road and railroad connecting Corinto on the Pacific coast to Monkey Point on the Atlantic, including modern port facilities with high-volume terminals on either side to facilitate the movement of cargo from one coast to the other.[268] From a commercial standpoint, although two canals in the region might not be viable, analysts have suggested that the region could support both an expanded Panama Canal and a trans-Nicaragua railroad and highway.

In addition to these projects, Nicaragua has been mentioned as the site of a new pipeline to move petroleum from the Atlantic to the Pacific. The pipeline would follow a route from Corinto to Monkey Point,[269] paralleling the proposed road and railroad infrastructure. This pipeline has been discussed in the context of a refinery, which potentially would be constructed with Venezuelan capital and would service the petroleum needs of Central America and, possibly, export refined petroleum products to Asia.[270]

Government and Business Infrastructures

As noted previously, the lack of formal diplomatic relations between many of the countries of Central America and the PRC has inhibited the development of a commercial and regulatory infrastructure to support the growth of commerce between China and the region. Major China-oriented trade events in the region are typically held in Panama or Costa Rica, and trade-promotion organizations from these two countries are generally the groups that lead delegations of Central Americans to events in the PRC.

The Question of Diplomatic Recognition of the PRC

Nicaragua. The 2006 election of Daniel Ortega as president of Nicaragua (for the second time) reopened the subject of Nicaragua's diplomatic recognition of the People's Republic of China. Prior to 1979, the Nicaraguan government recognized the government of the ROC as the legitimate government of China. When the socialist Sandinista Party first came to power in Nicaragua in 1979, however, it withdrew Nicaragua's recognition of the ROC and established diplomatic relations with PRC, with whom the Sandinistas were more ideologically aligned. Later, when the Sandinistas were voted out of office in 1991, the new Nicaraguan government reestablished diplomatic relations with Taiwan.[271]

Although, in previous years, Nicaragua's policy on recognition of China has changed with the government, the return of power by the Frente Sandinista de Liberación Nacional (FSLN) in 2006 has not yet been accompanied by a return to diplomatic recognition of the PRC.[272] Various members of the ruling Sandinista Party have expressed a desire to resume diplo-

matic ties with the PRC,[273] particularly in light of Costa Rica's 2007 decision to switch diplomatic recognition from Taiwan to the PRC.[274] In the
period between 1991 and 2006 (i.e., between the two periods of Sandinista
Party rule), however, Taiwan has built a web of relationships and patronage
across Nicaraguan society, including ties to the Sandinistas themselves.
Indeed, the Sandinista government's response, in part, to the change in
Costa Rica's diplomatic posture may have been to use this change to obtain
more money from Taiwan. According to one account, Sandinistas in the
Nicaraguan Congress asked the government of Taiwan to pardon
Nicaragua's $160 million external debt to Taiwan, in exchange for
Nicaragua's continuing diplomatic recognition of the ROC.[275] Taiwan, for
its part, has continued to provide generous support for the Nicaraguan government, including the donation of $750,000 to the Nicaraguan national
police for the purchase of new uniforms through 2011, as well as the sending of sixty doctors and medical technicians to provide free medical care for
thousands of Nicaraguans.[276]

Belize, El Salvador, Honduras, and Guatemala. Beyond the cases discussed above, the remaining nations of Central America continue to recognize the government of Taiwan as the legitimate government of China:
Belize, El Salvador, Honduras, and Guatemala. In general, the diplomatic
support given to the ROC by these nations has reflected the economic aid
and the network of social ties that the ROC has built in each country. In El
Salvador, for example, the government of Tony Saca has firmly supported
his government's continuing recognition of Taiwan, including a March 2006
statement in which he strongly contradicted his own vice president, Ana
Vilma de Escobar, who had discussed the possibility of switching recognition to the PRC.[277] In May 2007, the prime minister of Belize, Said Musa,
visited Taiwan and met with Taiwanese president Chen Shui-Bian, building
upon Belize's support for Taiwan in the World Health Organization (WHO)
and other international organizations.[278] In June of the same year,
Guatemalan president Oscar Berger visited Honduras, meeting with Chen
Shui-Bian; he emphasized Guatemala's desire to strengthen bilateral relations with the ROC.[279]

Prior to the emergence of an informal "truce" between China and Taiwan
in 2008, the government of the PRC had maintained an ongoing campaign of
subtle pressures and incentives to induce these Central American countries to
change their positions on the recognition of Taiwan. Although the PRC does
not openly exchange promises of aid or market access for diplomatic recognition, the inability of Central American nations to place their goods in PRC
markets is understood, in part, as a consequence of their positions on diplomatic recognition. At times, this message has been delivered in a less subtle
fashion. In August 2007, for example, the PRC sent a trade delegation to

Honduras; during the visit, its lead representative indicated that the PRC planned to invest $30 billion in Latin America in the coming years, but that it was not realistic to expect that much of it would go to Honduras, since no diplomatic relations existed between the two nations.[280]

Apart from such economic pressures and incentives, the PRC has also pursued diplomatic strategies, such as seeking to persuade the Mexican government to convince its Central American neighbors to recognize the PRC. In addition, some have also interpreted the PRC's effort, in January 1997, to obstruct the sending of a peacekeeping mission of 155 military observers to Guatemala as payback for that nation's ongoing diplomatic recognition of Taiwan.[281]

As noted previously, Costa Rica's switch of diplomatic recognition from Taiwan to the PRC in June 2007 set in motion a flurry of events, with other Central American nations publicly considering changing their own positions as well—either sincerely or in hopes of obtaining increased aid and attention from the ROC. Following a meeting with Costa Rican president Oscar Arias, Honduran president Manuel Zelaya reportedly told the PRC ambassador to Costa Rica that Honduras wished to explore commercial and diplomatic relations with the PRC.[282] Honduras subsequently announced intentions to open a trade office in the PRC.[283]

Whatever the motivations for the reactions of other Central American nations to the diplomatic switch by Costa Rica, Taiwan responded with a bout of diplomatic activity designed to shore up its relations with its remaining allies in the region through a combination of attention and economic incentives. In July 2007, Taiwanese vice president Annette Lu traveled to the Dominican Republic, Paraguay, and Guatemala to strengthen the ROC's relations with those countries, emphasizing the contribution of Taiwanese investment to the prosperity of the region, including a $250 million regional investment fund maintained by Taiwan.[284] Similarly, in August 2007, Taiwanese president Chen Shui-Bian made a state visit to Honduras to attend the sixth annual meeting of the heads of state of the Central American Isthmus and the Dominican Republic; his trip included stops in El Salvador and Santa Lucia.[285] In a May 2008 ceremony in which he was awarded by the Central American parliament, Taiwanese ambassador to Guatemala Francisco Ou pledged to continue to strengthen ties between Taiwan and Guatemala, including a new technical training center to be donated by Taiwan and set up in Guatemala, as well as the improvement of the Guatemala–El Rancho highway and the donation of equipment for infrastructure projects.[286] Taiwan has also sought to shore up its trade relationship with the countries of Central America, including the signing of a free-trade agreement with Honduras and El Salvador in May 2007.[287]

Whether or not related to the Taiwanese response, little by little, talk by Central American nations of following Costa Rica's lead and recognizing the PRC began to subside, replaced by statements affirming their diplomatic recognition of Taiwan. The August 2007 meeting of the heads of state of the Central American Isthmus and the Dominican Republic, for example, included joint statements advocating a position for Taiwan in the United Nations,[288] as well as statements of intent by Central American leaders to expand cooperation with Taiwan.[289] Similarly, despite the interest expressed by Honduran president Manuel Zelaya in developing relations with the PRC, the Honduran leader subsequently made a series of public statements in the United Nations affirming the sovereignty of the ROC and the support of Honduras for Taiwan.[290]

■ Cuba

For more than half a century, Cuba has played a pivotal role in the global struggle between the United States and outside powers, seeking to contest US dominance in the Western Hemisphere. When the communist forces led by Fidel Castro seized power in 1959, Cuba provided the Union of Soviet Socialist Republics (USSR) with an ally in the region and served as a source of inspiration and support for movements and revolutions through which the Soviet Union built new relationships across Latin America.

Although the collapse of the USSR stripped Cuba of its role as the principal agent of Soviet influence in the region, it did not eliminate its strategic relevance. In recent years, as the attention and resources of the United States have been concentrated at home and in the Middle East because of the war on terrorism, the PRC has dramatically expanded its political and economic presence in Latin America.[291] In this process, Cuba has played an important role, which in some ways resembles the role it played vis-à-vis the Soviet Union during the Cold War, but in other ways dramatically departs from it. Although Cuba possesses modest quantities of primary products important to China, including nickel, sugar, and petroleum, its value to China is dominated by two considerations. First, Cuba's geographic proximity to the United States gives it strategic value: its facilities—including Bejucal, Lourdes, and potentially Santiago de Cuba—can be used for intelligence collection. Second, Cuba is an important ideological point of reference for the Latin American left, and thus its goodwill is useful for the PRC in differentiating itself from established capitalist states such as the United States and the European Union. China's interest in continuing to rebuild its relationship with Cuba in both economic and political realms was demonstrated in the November 2008 trip to Cuba by Chinese president Hu Jintao on his way to the APEC summit in Lima, Peru. Cuba was one of only two intermediate destinations for President Hu, with the other being the nation of Costa Rica, which during the previous year had become the first nation in Central America since the end of the Cold War to diplomatically recognize the PRC. Hu's trip to Cuba also included an impressively broad range of thirty-seven commercial projects, implying a potential of $1.5 billion in new PRC investment in Cuba.[292] Despite the value of Cuba to China, the PRC remains cautious in its relationship with Cuba, reflecting such factors as Cuba's relatively small size, a desire to avoid unnecessarily provoking the United States, and uncertainty over Cuba's future after Fidel Castro's death. In the system used by China to characterize bilateral (largely economic) relationships, the PRC currently has established "strategic partnerships" or "all-around cooperative relationships" with five Latin American countries: Mexico, Argentina, Brazil, Chile, and Venezuela. In its hierarchy of diplomatic terminology, China characterizes its rapport with Cuba as a mere "traditional friendly relationship."[293]

Historical Context

Despite a shared ideological bond, relations between the communist regimes in China and Cuba have historically been characterized by distance and mistrust.[294] Although Sino-Cuban relations began well,[295] they took a turn for the worse during the Cold War due to the split between China and the Soviet Union, Cuba's principal patron.[296] The rift between the PRC and the Soviet Union was deepened by China's descent into internal turmoil with the Cultural Revolution, as well as its pursuit of detente with the United States in 1971. In addition, during this period, Cuba supported armed struggles in Ethiopia, Somalia, Zimbabwe, Angola, and Mozambique, among others, while China was on the opposite side in those fights; and, in Latin America, the PRC offended Cuba by pragmatically maintaining cordial relationships with regimes—such as those of Augusto Pinochet Ugarte's in Chile[297] and Jorge Rafael Videla's in Argentina—that had overthrown or were persecuting Cuban allies.

Despite such differences, Cuba and China pursued parallel paths in the promotion both of revolutionary movements and of the interests of developing nations, with the two nations playing important roles in the Non-Aligned Movement and maintaining low-level political and cultural contacts with each other.[298]

Beginning in the late 1980s, the collapse of the Soviet Union resulted in the evaporation of Cuba's principal economic and political support base[299] and created the conditions that drove Cuba to strengthen ties with the PRC as the sole remaining communist power.[300] Sino-Cuban ties strengthened considerably after the April–June 1989 events of Tiananmen Square, in which Cuba was one of only a handful of governments that openly backed Chinese repression of internal dissent.[301] In November 1993, Chinese president Jiang Zemin visited Cuba; President Fidel Castro of Cuba reciprocated with a trip to China in 1995.

Despite the significance of the China-Cuba rapprochement, the more important dynamic from China's perspective was arguably the silent but dramatic expansion of its economic relationship with the rest of Latin America. A later visit to China by Fidel Castro, in February 2003, may thus be considered as the beginning of the current period, in which Cuba's relationship with China is important to China, but is not its dominant relationship with the continent.[302]

The Chinese Community in Cuba

The first Chinese in Cuba can be traced to 1847, when the Spanish began to import contract laborers to work on the island's sugar plantations. Hundreds of thousands of Chinese came over through this process, largely from the province of Canton. A smaller, second wave arrived at the end of the century as well, driven by political and economic chaos in China.

As in other parts of Latin America, subsequent generations of Chinese on the island used the money that they had saved as agricultural laborers to establish small businesses, such as stores and restaurants. Unlike elsewhere in Latin America, however, the Cuban revolution of 1959 led to the government's seizure of many of these businesses and to the flight of a significant portion of the Chinese Cuban community to the United States.

The current Chinese community in Cuba is relatively small and dispersed throughout the country. Although the Chinatown district of Havana was one of the earliest such communities to be established in Latin America, and one of the largest, today it is much smaller and less vibrant, reflecting the flight of Chinese Cubans from the country since the revolution. Today, Havana's Chinatown is more of a zone maintained by the government for tourism purposes than a significant community of ethnic Chinese with potential to support the growth of Cuban commercial ties with the PRC.

China's Interest in Cuban Nickel, Sugar, and Petroleum

By contrast to nations of the Southern Cone, Cuba's principal value to the PRC is not based chiefly in its primary-product exports. Nonetheless, the island does possess nontrivial quantities of a number of goods of interest to the PRC. Cuba's exports to China in 2007 amounted to $1.11 billion, representing an increase of 110 percent over the previous year;[303] however, the nation still incurred a $60 million trade deficit with the PRC.

Central among the Cuban primary-product industries of interest to the PRC is nickel. With an estimated 800 million tons of proven reserves, Cuba is one of the largest potential sources of nickel in the world. It currently produces 75,000 tons of nickel per year, with plans to increase production to 121,000 tons per year through investment in three existing plants and construction of an additional plant in Moa, Holguín.[304] Although Cuba replaced China with Venezuela in the construction of the Holguín plant,[305] China continues to pursue projects with Cuba in the industry, including an agreement signed between Cuba and the PRC in November 2008 to construct a small refinery for nickel and cobalt to supply the minerals to China.[306] Indeed, in 2007, prior to the agreement, China purchased 37,500 tons of nickel from Cuba.[307]

Second, the PRC has an interest in Cuban sugar, as the USSR did. Approximately one-third of all Chinese sugar imports in 2004 came from Cuba, with Brazil the other principal supplier in Latin America.[308] Growing Chinese sugar demand, coupled with problems in domestic sugar production, led to a spike in sugar prices in China in 2005, and underscores the continuing importance of the commodity.[309] Sugarcane is also a potential vehicle for producing the biofuel ethanol, raising the prospect that competing demand may impair China's ability to obtain sugar from other markets.[310] Accordingly, one of the key elements of the final act of the Nineteenth Intergovernmental Commission, signed between the Chinese and Cuban governments in March 2007, was a long-term agreement for the supply of Cuban sugar to the PRC, through China National Corporation.[311] An agreement on sugar exports was the second of the two key agreements signed by Hu Jintao during his November 2008 visit to Cuba.[312]

Third, Cuba has potentially significant petroleum reserves in its territorial waters off its west coast, in the vicinity of Pinar del Rio.[313] The reserves in Cuban territory and waters are currently being developed by multiple firms, including the Chinese state enterprise Sinopec.[314] Thanks in part to Chinese investment,[315] Cuba plans to increase its oil output by 100,000 tons to 4 million tons in 2007 with the drilling of some 39 new wells.[316] Based on 2006 Cuban consumption, approximately half of this quantity may be available for export.[317] One of the agreements signed during the November 2008 trip by Hu Jintao to Cuba involved exploration for oil by Chinese companies in Cuba's exclusive economic zone off the coast of Piñar del Rio.[318]

Cuba as a Market for Chinese Goods

Unlike the situation for middle-income countries in Latin America like Argentina, Brazil, and Mexico, the limited size of the Cuban economy and the limited purchasing power of its citizens have not enabled Cuba to play a major role as a purchaser of PRC manufactured goods. Nonetheless, Cuba bought a total of $1.17 billion in goods from the PRC during 2007, representing a decrease of 7.5 percent from the previous year.[319] One of the agreements signed between China and Cuba during Hu Jintao's trip in November 2008 involved extending a new round of credits to Cuba for the purchase of Chinese goods.[320]

As part of its overall relationship, Cuba has served as an important test market for manufactured goods of higher added value, which Chinese firms eventually wish to introduce to other parts of Latin America. In 2006, for example, Cuba was the recipient of some 1,300 Chinese Yutong busses, representing the first of a total of 5,000 such vehicles to be provided by the PRC to Cuban municipalities during the coming three years.[321] Similarly, Cuba purchased 12 train engines and railcars from China in 2006 for a total of $130 million,[322] paralleling projects that it has explored with the government of Jamaica.[323] Within these larger transactions, the sale of 12 DF7G-C diesel-electric locomotives to Cuba in December 2005 paved the way for a similar sale (of 12 Chinese DF8-B locomotives) to Venezuela in December 2006,[324] although industry experts suggest that the Chinese locomotives are too far below the quality of industry-standard products to be competitive in larger markets.

Technology Cooperation

Cuba and China have not pursued large joint technology projects, such as the China-Brazil Earth Research Satellite (CBERS) project or the production of Embraer aircraft in Harbin. However, they have collaborated in biotechnology pursuits, establishing facilities in Beijing and Chanchun that leverage Cuban technology in such areas as genetically engineered proteins and monoclonal antibodies.[325] The two countries are also working together to establish a new hospital in northwest China specializing in vision, whose staff is to include fifty-two Cuban doctors.[326]

Intellectual Infrastructure

Despite its size, Cuba has a relatively strong and rapidly intellectual infrastructure for doing business with China. By contrast to other Latin American countries, however, Chinese-language and China studies programs are not typically integrated into the major Cuban universities. For example, neither FLACSO Cuba nor Universidad de Havana has a formal Chinese-language program. Rather, Cuban students typically take a series of preparatory courses in Mandarin, then travel to China to study for a period of approximately two years in a program coordinated by the Cuban Ministry of Higher Education and the Ministry of Foreign Relations.

Cuba as a Training Ground for
China's Penetration of Latin America

A little-noted phenomenon in China's relationship with Latin America is the significant number of Chinese students going to Cuba to study. As of October 2007, approximately 200 Chinese students were in Cuba.[327] As of the end of 2008, however, Cuba had agreed to permit 2,000 Chinese students to study on the island.[328] Although the numbers are modest in absolute terms, no other nation in Latin America currently hosts more than a handful of Chinese students. Although Cuba's commercial value to China may be limited, the use of Cuba as a training ground for China's relationship with Latin America makes sense from a practical standpoint. For China to develop a greater capability to do business in Latin America, or to support technical, military, political, or other forms of interaction, it requires much greater quantities of personnel with familiarity in the Spanish language and Latin American culture than it currently has. Cuba offers a relatively closed, politically controlled environment in which the PRC can send its nationals to receive the required training, while limiting the risk that they will either compromise their loyalty to the PRC or fall into activity that could damage China's image in the region.

Cuba as a Source of Ideological Legitimization
One of the important, yet intangible, ways in which the Cuba-PRC relationship benefits the PRC is that it allows China to represent itself as an ideological alternative to the United States and Western companies as it courts populist regimes in the region.

Although few of the contemporary leftist groups in Latin America are fully aligned with Cuba politically, the island remains an important symbolic point of reference in the ideological spectrum of the region. Historically, Cuba served as a home for a generation of Latin American Marxist leaders in exile from their own countries, and provided varying degrees of ideological, organizational, and material support for armed revolutionary movements across the region.[329] Although Cuba and the PRC were generally not close allies during the Cold War, the same leftist movements that revere the Cuban revolutionary movement today also give a privileged place to Mao Zedong.[330] The link helps to explain otherwise curious rhetoric, such as when newly elected Bolivian president Evo Morales, upon his visit to Beijing in January 2006, proclaimed himself a great admirer of Mao,[331] or when Hugo Chávez remarked during a visit to China in December 2004 that Simón Bolívar and Mao would have been good friends.[332]

The PRC today shares little with the legacy of Mao.[333] Maintaining a friendship with Cuba, therefore, helps contemporary Chinese leaders and businesspeople preserve some plausible revolutionary credentials as they court leftist regimes in the region, such as those of Bolivia, Ecuador, Venezuela, and Nicaragua. Being in good standing with Cuba also helps China in Africa, where Fidel Castro's regime has long-standing, personal relationships with a number of governments that the PRC is currently wooing, including those of Mozambique, Zimbabwe, and Angola,[334] the latter of which is currently the number one source of crude oil in the world for the PRC.[335]

China preserves its revolutionary credentials among the Latin American left, in part, through a combination of symbolic undertakings: high-profile visits to Cuba,[336] bilateral trade, assistance packages, and political and cultural exchanges.[337] PRC participation in the September 2006 summit of the Non-Aligned Movement in Havana, to which the ailing Fidel Castro was elected president,[338] offers an example of how even indirect associations between China and Cuba may help the former to preserve its position among the Latin American left.

Cuba as a Geographically Useful Ally

Although China emphasizes the peaceful nature of its expansion and increasing global engagement,[339] it is doubtless the job of some within the PRC to plan for the possibility of conflict with the United States. In such an undesirable eventuality, Cuba's proximity to the US mainland gives it inherent strategic military value as a base for intelligence collection and for the launching of armed forces in the opening phases of a conflict.[340] In this fashion, the presence of Cuba close to the United States mirrors the strategic vulnerability that the PRC feels at the prospect of US forces operating from Taiwan, a similar distance from the Chinese coast.[341]

Currently, China appears to be using Cuba primarily as a listening post. Reports suggest that the PRC has been operating a signal intelligence site at Bejucal, south of Havana, since 1999,[342] and is also believed to intercept US military satellite communications from a facility northeast of Santiago de Cuba.[343] In addition, the PRC may be using the facility at Lourdes, which was a Soviet collection facility during the Cold War—Cuba later converted it into a "cyber university," with 5,000 or more computers, after the Soviet Union withdrew its presence in 2001.[344]

Evidence suggests that military-to-military relations between Cuba and the PRC have strengthened in recent years and are probably at a level paralleled only by those between China and Venezuela.[345] In April 2005, Cuban defense minister Raúl Castro visited Beijing;[346] in November 2005, the chief of the general staff of the Chinese People's Liberation Army, Liang Guanglie, returned the favor, visiting Castro in Cuba.[347] Other contacts include a visit by a Cuban military delegation to Beijing in April 2006[348] and the reception of a Chinese military delegation by Raúl Castro, then acting president of Cuba, in December 2006.[349]

Cuba's Special Interest in China

Whatever Cuba's value to the PRC, Cuba arguably needs China for the economic and diplomatic survival of its regime more than China needs

Cuba.[350] Exports to the PRC, such as sugar and nickel, are one of the key mechanisms by which Cuba earns hard currency.[351] The Cuban economy also benefits from the increasing presence of Chinese businesspeople and tourists, with an estimated 10,000 visitors from the PRC to Cuba in 2006.[352] Moreover, as was true with the Soviet Union but to a lesser extent Cuba is the beneficiary of generous Chinese loans, export credits, and other forms of aid. Agreements signed during Hu Jintao's November 2004 visit to Cuba, for example, included a 10-year extension on the repayment of loans to the PRC, $12 million in donations to Cuban hospitals and schools, and the financing of a million television sets for sale in the Cuban market.[353] The PRC has also granted Cuba modest amounts of credit for the purchase of Chinese goods, such as the $6.2 million it provided in December 2005,[354] the $350 million that it provided to help Cuba rebuild its network of hospitals and clinics,[355] or the key role that the PRC played in helping Cuba to rebuild after Hurricanes Gustav, Ike, and Paloma, including 4.5 million tons of humanitarian aid provided during Hu Jintao's November 2008 visit.[356]

Beyond commerce, aid, and subsidies, China also supplies Cuba with assistance in sectors such as petroleum and agriculture,[357] and military assistance in areas such as basic equipment and training. China has not, however, offered security guarantees to the Cuban regime; it is likely that China would remain on the sidelines if the political transition following the death of Fidel Castro were to degenerate into public disorder.

■ Other Nations of the Caribbean

With a small number of exceptions involving strategic minerals, proximity to the United States, and ideological legitimation, China's relationship with the Caribbean continues to center on the recognition of Taiwan, with aid projects and diplomatic maneuvering being the key vehicles for persuasion.

The amount of attention received by the Caribbean nations in relation to their size and the economic footprint of individual countries is substantial. In January 2005, for example, China made the Caribbean the focus of its first major post-APEC diplomatic initiative, the China-Caribbean Economic and Trade Cooperation Forum,[358] featuring attendance by Chinese vice president Zeng Quinghong.[359] In September 2007, the PRC hosted the second meeting of the China-Caribbean Economic and Trade Cooperation Forum in Xiamen, China, with participation of leaders and delegations from the majority of the countries in the region with which it has diplomatic relations.[360]

Reflecting such attention, the region has very much shown itself to be "in play" in recent years with respect to its posture on recognition of Taiwan versus the PRC. Both Dominica and Grenada have switched diplomatic recognition lately from the ROC to the PRC. However, in April 2007, the small nation of St. Lucia reversed its previous recognition of the PRC, following the return to power of a government previously aligned with Taiwan.[361] In each of these cases, diplomatic pressure and financial aid by both the PRC and the ROC played significant roles.[362]

The Chinese Community in the Caribbean

As in other parts of the region, the Chinese community in the Caribbean traces its roots to immigrants who arrived in the second half of the nineteenth century to work as contract laborers in the agricultural sector. Although many of these Chinese were brought over by Spanish settlers, others were imported by the British to work in territories (for example, Guyana) and later relocated to Jamaica and other parts of the Caribbean.

In general, the Chinese Caribbean community is relatively small and not closely tied to its ethnic roots with respect to skills relevant to supporting commerce with the PRC, such as the ability to speak Mandarin.[363] After Cuba, Jamaica has the largest Chinese community in the Caribbean, with approximately 5,000 Chinese, known as *Hakka,* having immigrated from China to Jamaica between 1845 and 1884.[364] In addition, the Dominican Republic has a particularly vibrant Chinese community, including a commercial Chinatown established in the capital city, Santo Domingo, in 2006.[365]

China's Interest in Jamaican Bauxite and Other Products

Along with Cuba, Jamaica is arguably one of the PRC's closest allies in the Caribbean. Vice President Zeng Quinghong visited the island in conjunction with his trip to the China-Caribbean Economic Cooperation Conference in February 2005.[366] In January 2007, a high-ranking Chinese dignitary, Cheng Siwei, highlighted the relative importance of the country to the PRC by making it part of his regional trip, which also included Cuba and Venezuela.[367] In November 2007, Jamaican deputy prime minister Ken Baugh announced an agreement with the PRC for a new assistance package valued at $140 million, one of the largest in the region given by the PRC.[368]

In addition to its diplomatic recognition of the PRC, Jamaica is of interest to China because of its bauxite reserves. The metal is important in the fabrication of aluminum, which the PRC consumes in increasing quantities to manufacture a wide range of products. Jamaica has benefited tremendously from expanding Chinese aluminum consumption and the corresponding increase in international demand for bauxite. On the Jamaican side, 50 percent of the country's export earnings come from bauxite; demand from the PRC has contributed to record earnings for the industry.[369] The importance of bauxite has also driven Chinese interests to invest in Jamaica to establish secure sources of supply for the metal. In 2005, for example, the Chinese conglomerate Minmetals announced a joint venture with Jamaica for an aluminum bauxite extraction and processing facility in that country.[370]

Jamaican firms have followed in the footsteps of Mexican, Colombian, and other companies in leveraging the international image of Jamaican culture to market premium products to China's growing middle class. In one of the first investment initiatives to develop from the 2005 China-Caribbean Trade and Economic Cooperation Forum, the Jamaican company Coffee Mill opened a shop in the PRC selling "authentic" Jamaican Blue Mountain coffee.[371]

The Caribbean as a Market for Chinese Goods

As with Central America, because of the small size of the economies of the Caribbean, no individual country in the area has significant potential as a market for Chinese goods. Pirated Chinese goods, like CDs and DVDs, and lower-end goods, like clothing and footwear, are purchased by residents for their own use or as inputs in the enormous tourism industry that dominates the region. The economic structure of the region limits the size of the middle class, which could provide a market for more sophisticated Chinese goods (e.g., cars), while the wealthiest consumers in the Caribbean are more attracted to higher-end brand-name goods. Nonetheless, when considered as a whole, the market represented by the Caribbean is nontrivial. In 2007, for example, China sold approximately $2 billion in goods to the islands of the region, comparable to its sales to Colombia.[372]

Despite limits in the Caribbean consumer goods market, possibilities exist to employ the region as a test market for heavy Chinese goods, such as trains, as was done in Cuba. The use of Chinese companies to overhaul Jamaica's rail infrastructure was raised during the China-Caribbean Economic Cooperation Forum in 2005, and revived in May 2006,[373] although a deal in this area has not yet been realized.

Other Joint Ventures and Ties

Although the quantity of joint ventures and other projects being pursued by China in the Caribbean is relatively small, a number of projects capture the imagination. As one example, in December 2007, Mia Mottley, the deputy prime minister and minister of economic affairs and development of Barbados, indicated that the country was examining the possibility of a joint venture with China for the production of photovoltaic panels for the generation of solar electricity.[374]

Significant opportunities also exist for Sino-Caribbean cooperation with respect to tourism. The PRC has approved a number of Caribbean states as official tourist destinations, including Antigua and Barbuda, the

Bahamas, Barbados, Dominica, and Jamaica.[375] Although the volume of Chinese tourists will probably be modest compared to that from the United States and Europe, the status nonetheless conveys economic benefit on Caribbean states that recognize the PRC and lays the groundwork for expanded interaction between them and the PRC.

In the domain of military ties between the PRC and nations of the Caribbean other than Cuba, the closest relationship is arguably that between Jamaica and the PRC. Such ties include training of Jamaican soldiers by the PRC and exchanges between Chinese and Jamaican defense officials. In July 2005, for example, the vice chairman of China's Central Military Commission, Xu Caihow, traveled to Jamaica to meet with that country's chief of staff of defense forces, Hardly Macarley Lewin.[376]

Finally, although Sino-Caribbean ties remain in their infancy, communities and infrastructures are beginning to form; these will be the foundations upon which broader interactions can be built. One milestone in this process was the establishment of a Caribbean Association in Shanghai in April 2007. The group was formed with close support from the Caribbean embassies in China, with the stated purpose to "foster stronger understanding and appreciation of our Caribbean culture, strengthen Sino-Caribbean relations and serve as a support network for the Caribbean community in China."[377]

Diplomatic Recognition of the PRC

The states of the Caribbean are currently divided between those that recognize the PRC and those that maintain diplomatic relations with the ROC. As of late 2008, five Caribbean nations recognized the government of the ROC as the legitimate government of all China: Belize, Haiti, St. Kitts–Nevis, St. Vincent and the Grenadines, and St. Lucia. Nine states recognized the PRC: Antigua and Barbuda, the Bahamas, Barbados, Dominica, Grenada, Guyana, Jamaica, Suriname, and Trinidad and Tobago.[378]

Although this divide undermines the ability of Caribbean nations to speak with one voice in organizations such as the Caribbean Community (CARICOM),[379] it is not an ideological split, per se. As seen in the states of Central America as well, it reflects these states' varying responses to economic and other incentives offered by the PRC and the ROC, as interpreted through the judgments and personal relations of each country's current decisionmakers.

PRC aid to induce Caribbean states to recognize the PRC—or to reward them for having done so—is substantial. Daniel Erikson and Paul Wander (2007) point out, for example, that the PRC spent more than $140 million just in constructing or refurbishing cricket stadiums in anticipation of the 2007 World Cricket Cup—in addition to aid that paid for roads, schools, hospitals, and other infrastructure projects in the region.[380] The magnitude of the aid offered to Caribbean states by both the PRC and the ROC reflects the stakes involved for these latter countries. For the ROC, maintaining the stance of the handful of states that continue to give it diplomatic recognition is a matter of national survival, since the international legitimacy that flows from such recognition is one of the few considerations that prevent the PRC from forcibly reincorporating Taiwan into China. For the PRC, on the other hand, the continuing existence of the ROC is a profound scar in the national psyche. Reciprocally, because the nations of the Caribbean are small in terms of population and economic activities, modest amounts of aid can exert an enormous impact.

Diplomatic change in Grenada. The decision by the tiny nation of Grenada to switch its diplomatic recognition from the ROC to the PRC in 2005 illustrates both the dynamics and the potency of the contest for recognition being played out in the Caribbean. Although Grenada was one of the first nations in the region to extend diplomatic recognition to the PRC, it revoked that recognition following the events of Tiananmen Square in 1989 as an expression of its disapproval of the Chinese government's actions.[381] Nonetheless, Grenada again reversed its position, re-recognizing the PRC in January 2005.[382]

Although the aid package from the PRC that helped convince the small island nation to change its position was modest in absolute terms, it was enormously significant from the perspective of Grenada's small population,[383] bringing it, among other things, a $40 million multiuse sports stadium, which was completed in 2006.

In most of the other cases in Central America and the Caribbean, the recognition story ends there, with the establishment of diplomatic relations between the new partners and the arrival of a new aid package. In the case of Grenada, however, the story had an extra twist. In 2007, Grenada held its dedication ceremony for the stadium, with the political leadership of the island and a number of high-ranking PRC dignitaries in attendance; the Chinese construction workers who had built the stadium and the executives representing those companies were likewise there. The national police band of Grenada was present in full dress uniform, with much fanfare, to perform the national anthem for the assembled officials and guests. The band, however, made a grave error: instead of performing the national anthem of the PRC, it played the anthem of the Republic of China. The next day's press account of the event indicated that the head of the band had been relieved of his duties, pending an investigation into the incident.[384]

Diplomatic change in Dominica. Dominica is yet another Caribbean country that has switched its diplomatic recognition from Taiwan to the PRC in exchange for aid and the prospect of trade with the PRC. Dominica recognized the PRC in March 2004; since that time, it has received some $10 million in aid, including a $2.3 million primary school and a new sports stadium.[385] In total, the multiyear aid program given to the island has amounted to $112 million—equivalent to $1,600 per capita for the island's 70,000 inhabitants.[386]

Diplomatic change in the Bahamas. The Bahamas also changed its diplomatic recognition from Taiwan to the PRC, although it did so in 1997, several years prior to Grenada and Dominica. Following this alteration, the PRC logistics giant Hutchison-Whampoa invested $114 million to build a container facility in the Bahamian capital, Freeport.[387] For Hutchison, the facility is a key logistics hub for the Atlantic side of the Americas, taking in cargo from smaller container ships that come from ports on the Atlantic coast of Central and South America, or through the Panama Canal, and repackaging them into larger container ships for destinations in Europe and Asia.

In addition to Freeport, the PRC committed $1 billion for future projects in the country, including a sports complex and maritime transportation investments.[388] Today, the Bahamas stands out as a case not only of the benefits accruing to the host nation from a change in recognition, but also of the impact of such decisions on the United States. Although there is no evidence to suggest that the Hutchison facility in Freeport has been used for other than commercial purposes, it represents a major Chinese logistics operation just sixty-five miles off the US coast.

A reversal for the PRC in St. Lucia. Although Taiwan has suffered a string of diplomatic setbacks in Central America and the Caribbean in recent years, it secured one small triumph in May 2007 in the tiny Caribbean nation of St. Lucia. At that time, the island's government cut diplomatic ties with the PRC and reextended diplomatic recognition to the ROC. The change reflected the return to power by the United Workers Party (UWP) government of Sir John Compton, which had maintained diplomatic relations with the ROC while in power previously. The move thus represented a resumption of the institutional and personal relationships that had earlier existed between the ROC and the leadership elite in St. Lucia.[389]

In addition to reflecting the return to power by Prime Minister Compton and the UWP, St. Lucia's action indicated some dissatisfaction with the terms of PRC aid and discontent over a soccer stadium project. Poor planning led to construction of the stadium in a location not readily accessible to much of the island's population. Moreover, the project had been tied to the use of Chinese companies and laborers, yet was not fully funded by the PRC—forcing the government of St. Lucia to pay Chinese workers and companies out of the island's own funds to complete the stadium.

Haiti and the Chinese peacekeepers. Because, in part, of Haiti's diplomatic recognition of Taiwan and the desire of the PRC to change that position, the PRC often has been a factor in Haiti's attempts to transcend its problems and build a viable state. Indeed, Chinese scholar Shixue Jiang notes that, along with the Dominican Republic, Haiti is the focus of PRC efforts to change the diplomatic positions of those Caribbean countries continuing to recognize Taiwan.[390]

Steps taken by the PRC and Haiti to strengthen ties include the establishment of commercial affairs offices in each other's countries in 1996.[391] During the same year, however, when the United Nations was assembling the MINUSTAH peacekeeping mission in Haiti, the PRC threatened to use its veto power to block the initiative.[392] This threat and the PRC's subsequent resistance to a one-year extension of the MINUSTAH mandate[393] have been interpreted by some observers as an effort by the PRC to pressure Haiti into granting it diplomatic recognition.[394]

Despite these PRC attempts in 1996 to block the UN peacekeeping force in Haiti, two years earlier the PRC had attracted significant diplomatic attention when it sent a contingent of police to participate in this force. Sending PRC peacekeepers to Haiti was a watershed event: these were the first Chinese troops in Latin America in the modern era. The PRC has subsequently renewed its peacekeeping contingent in MINUSTAH multiple times.[395]

Beyond the presence of Chinese peacekeepers in Haiti, China has also indirectly increased its ties to Haiti through the Inter-American Development Bank, in which it became a voting member in 2008. Although China's contribution of $350 million to join the bank represents an almost minuscule number of voting shares, membership gives it a presence in day-to-day management and oversight in the institution, including the management of loans that have been made to Haiti in the past and participation in decisions on new loans.

▓ Notes

1. In 2003, China upgraded its relationship with Mexico from "all-around cooperative relationship" to "strategic partnership," reflecting the combination of political and economic importance that Mexico represents for China. "Senior Chinese Party Official Meets Mexican Senate President on Bilateral Ties." *People's Daily Online.* Beijing, China. http://english.people.com.cn. March 23, 2007. See also "Senior Chinese Party Official Meets Mexican President on Strategic Partnership." *People's Daily Online.* Beijing, China. http://english.people.com.cn. March 22, 2007.

2. According to some accounts, China has sought to convince Mexico to use its influence among Central American states to persuade those nations still recognizing the ROC to change their policy.

3. Cheng Siwei, 2005.

4. "Mexico, China to Push Forward Bilateral Investment Agreement." *People's Daily Online*. Beijing, China. http://english.people.com.cn. March 23, 2007.

5. "China, segundo socio comercial de México." *El Economista*. Mexico City, Mexico. http://www.eleconomista.com.mx. May 22, 2006.

6. "Total Import and Export Value by Country (Region) (2007/01–12)." *Ministry of Commerce*. People's Republic of China. http://english.mofcom.gov.cn. aarticle/statistic/ie/200802/20080205371690.html. February 4, 2008.

7. Ibid.

8. See, for example, Gallagher, Moreno-Brid, and Prozecanski, 2008.

9. The expansion of this strategy has been limited, however, by the relative lack of growth in the United States as Mexico's principal export market. See, for example, Carla Selman Calavaro, "Qué esperar de la economía mundial en 2007." *El Mercurio*. Santiago, Chile. http://diario.elmercurio.com. December 24, 2006.

10. Gastón Pardo, "Los Chinos en la historia de México." *Kaos en la Red*. http://www.kaosenlared.net/noticia/los-chinos-historia-de-mexico. August 23, 2008.

11. Alana Gutiérrez, "China's Economic Invasion of Mexico." *Council on Hemispheric Affairs*. http://www.mexidata.info/id636.html. October 14, 2005. See also "China, Latin America Forge Closer Links for Win-Win End (3)." *People's Daily Online*. Beijing, China. http://english.people.com.cn. October 6, 2006.

12. Mexico's relationship with China in the political realm since recognizing the PRC on February 14, 1972, has followed a relatively smooth, positive course. As Alana Gutiérrez characterizes it, "China and Mexico have set up a number of cooperative programs and two-way agreements concerning trade, technology, finance, culture, energy, shipping, tourism, telecommunications, anti-drug trafficking, agricultural cooperation, and coordination in cases of criminal jurisdiction." Gutiérrez, 2005.

13. "Derbez realizará visita a China." *El Economista*. Mexico City, Mexico. http://www.eleconomista.com.mx. February 15, 2006.

14. "Languages of Mexico." In *Ethnologue: Languages of the World*, edited by Raymond G. Gordon Jr., 15th ed. (Dallas: SIL International). Available online at http://www.ethnologue.com/. 2005.

15. Indeed, this flow was substantial enough that the two countries signed a formal accord in 1899 legalizing the immigration of Chinese to Mexico. Gutiérrez, 2006.

16. Ibid.

17. Quesada, 2006.

18. Mexicali, in Baja California, is reportedly the biggest Chinese community in the region, founded in part by Chinese who came south from the United States at the turn of the century. Although the number of Chinese in Mexicali has declined, an estimated 2,000 still live in the city. "Chinatowns in Latin America." *Answers.com*. http://www.answers.com/topic/chinatowns-in-latin-america. Accessed December 18, 2007. See also Curtis, 1995.

19. The festival is held each year in association with the Autonomous University of Tampico. See "Inauguran el Festival Cultural Chino." *El Sol de Tampico*. Tampico, Mexico. http://www.oem.com.mx/elsoldetampico/. August 29, 2007.

20. During 2006, for example, Mexico's oil reserves dropped by more than 955 million barrels, to 15.5 billion barrels, sufficient to cover approximately 9.6 years of Mexican hydrocarbon demand. See "Mexico's Oil Reserves Equivalent to 9.6 Years

of Demand: PEMEX." *People's Daily Online*. Beijing, China. http://english.people. com.cn. March 27. 2007.

21. Adam Thompson, "Energy: Oil Monopoly in Finance Trap." *Financial Times*. London, England. http://www.ft.com. May 9, 2007.

22. "Anuncio de México genera inconformidad en cumbre del Plan Puebla Panamá." *Nacion*. San José, Costa Rica. http://www.nacion.com. April 10, 2007.

23. Ibid.

24. Although Mexico is not a significant petroleum supplier to China, Chinese companies nevertheless have a presence in Mexico. China Oilfield Services, for example, signed a contract with PEMEX in December 2006 to construct and support four modular oil rigs in the Gulf of Mexico. See "China Oilfield Secures Deal in Gulf of Mexico." *Reuters*. http://www.reuters.com/. December 17, 2006. See also "COSL Wins Goimar Oil Rig Contract in Gulf of Mexico." *Interfax China*. Shanghai, China. December 21, 2006.

25. "CNODC VP Mulls Entry into US Gulf of Mexico Around 2010." *Dow Jones Energy Service*. May 5, 2008.

26. "México y China buscan más comercio agropecuario." *El Economista*. Mexico City, Mexico. http://www.eleconomista.com.mx. November 5, 2006.

27. "México podrá exportar carne de cerdo a China." *El Economista*. Mexico City, Mexico. http://www.eleconomista.com.mx. July 7, 2008.

28. "Total Import and Export Value by Country (Region) (2007/01–12)."

29. "Se suspendarán cuotas compensatorias a China." *El Economista*. Mexico City, Mexico. http://www.eleconomista.com.mx. August 29, 2007.

30. Maru Garcia, "Ropa china aniquila el comercio en Zapotanejo." *El Occidental*. Guadalajara, Mexico. http://www.oem.com.mx/eloccidental/. December 17, 2007.

31. Bussey, 2005.

32. Raúl Rodríguez Santoyo, "Debilidad del comercio mexicano frente al embate chino." *El Sol de Zacatecas*. Zacatecas, Mexico. http://www.oem.com.mx/ elsoldezacatecas/. June 19, 2007.

33. Dickerson, 2007.

34. Chinese Cars Coming to Mexico." *Business Week*. http://www. businessweek.com. November 23, 2007.

35. "China Huawei invierte 20 millones de dólares en México." *Terra*. www.terra.com. November 14, 2006.

36. "Espera México recibir hasta 900 mdd de inversions chinas." *El Sol del Bajío*. Bajío, Mexico. http://www.oem.com.mx/elsoldelbajio/. July 11, 2008.

37. In 2007, according to the Chinese Ministry of Commerce, Mexico exported $3.3 billion in goods to the PRC, while importing $11.7 billion from it—a quantity more than three times greater than the amount it exported. "Total Import and Export Value by Country (Region) (2007/01–12)."

38. Gallagher and Porzecanski, 2008.

39. Alejandro Durán, "Pide gobierno a IP hacer frente común contra amenaza china." *El Sol de México*. Mexico City, Mexico. http://www.oem.com.mx/ elsoldeMexico/. April 4, 2007.

40. "México, el pais más afectado por China e India." *El Economista*. Mexico City, Mexico. http://www.eleconomista.com.mx. September 24, 2006.

41. According to one source, NAFTA led to a tripling of the commerce between the United States and Mexico. "China, una amenaza para México: HSBC." *El Economista*. Mexico City, Mexico. http://www.eleconomista.com.mx. October 17, 2005.

42. "Desplaza China a México como proveedor de EU." *El Economista*.

Mexico City, Mexico. http://www.eleconomista.com.mx. September 3, 2007. See also "México pierde terreno en EU ante China." *El Economista*. Mexico City, Mexico. http://www.eleconomista.com.mx. November 10, 2005.

43. Ricardo Valcán, "Rápido pero sin prisa: TLC con USA." *El Comercio*. Lima, Peru. http://www.elcomercio.com.pe/ediciononline. December 10, 2006.

44. See "Mexican Business and Infrastructure 2007." *Financial Times*. London, England. http://www.ft.com. May 9, 2007.

45. "Industria textil busca impedir domino de China." *El Economista*. Mexico City, Mexico. http://www.eleconomista.com.mx. July 7, 2006.

46. "Mexican Business and Infrastructure 2007."

47. The expiration of the accord led to a flood of Chinese goods into the United States and the countries of the European Union, leading to the reestablishment of quotas and other protections by the US Department of Commerce. "Todas las miradas sobre China." *El Diario*. La Paz, Bolivia. http://eldiario.net. May 30, 2005.

48. Funakushi and Loser, 2005. See also "US Agreement with China Helps Central America," Funakuski and Loser, p. 15.

49. See, for example, Lilia González, "Industriales crean bloque contra China." *El Economista*. Mexico City, Mexico. http://www.eleconomista.com.mx. April 28, 2007.

50. Victor Manuel Chávez Ogazón, "China amenaza a la economía jalisciense." *El Occidental*. Jalisco, Mexico. http://www.oem.com.mx/eloccidental/notas/n206044.htm. March 16, 2007.

51. "Anuncia Ebrard inversión china." *El Economista*. Mexico City, Mexico. http://www.eleconomista.com.mx. October 24, 2007.

52. Because of NAFTA, in part, some 90 percent of Mexico's exports go to the United States. "China se mantiene fuerte en EU; México, detrás." *El Economista*. Mexico City, Mexico. http://www.eleconomista.com.mx. March 9, 2006. See also "México pierde terreno en EU ante China."

53. "Mexican Business and Infrastructure 2007."

54. During a weeklong export trade fair put on by the Mexican Foreign Commerce Bank (BANCOMEXT), the president of the China Auto Sales Association, Chen Xiauyu, proposed an alliance between Mexican and Chinese automakers oriented toward exporting cars to the US market. Chen gave, as part of the explanation, the superiority of Mexican technology and craftsmanship, as well as the importance of the North American Free Trade Agreement for access to the US market. "China pretende alianza automotriz con México." *El Economista*. Mexico City, Mexico. http://www.eleconomista.com.mx. November 13, 2006.

55. Jorge López Gómez, "Chinos insaciables clonan al Smart y la X5." *El Universal*. Mexico City, Mexico. http://www.eluniversal.com.mx. September 2, 2007.

56. Dickerson, 2007.

57. If the establishment of the Tijuana plant proceeds as anticipated, Zhongxing will beat its two major Chinese rivals, Chery and Geeley, in introducing a car into the US market via final assembly in Mexico. See López, 2007.

58. Dickerson, 2007.

59. Emanuel Moreno, "La empresa china Geeley se instalará en León." *El Sol del Bajío*. http://www.oem.com.mx/elsoldebajio/. July 11, 2008.

60. "El governador se reunió con inversionistas de Ningbo provincia de la República China." *El Sol del Centro*. Aguascalientes, Mexico. April 10, 2007. See also "Manifestan empresarios chinos interés por Aguascalientes." *El Sol de México*. Mexico City, Mexico. http:www.oem.com.mx/elsoldemexico/. April 10, 2007.

61. "Inversiones México-China." *Ministry of Foreign Relations. Republic of Mexico.* http://portal.sre.gob.mx/china. Accessed September 10, 2007.

62. Santoyo, "Debilidad des comercio mexicano frente al embate chino."

63. "Foro Baja California–Asia, economía, cultura y negocios." *El Sol de Tijuana.* Tijuana, Mexico. http://www.oem.com.mx/elsoldetijuana/. August 29, 2007.

64. "Inversiones México-China."

65. Bertha Becerra, "Dispuesto Calderón a comerciar con China." *El Sol de México.* Mexico City, Mexico. http://www.oem.com.mx/elsoldemexico/. July 11, 2008. See also "México es un mercado promisorio, asegura Calderón a China." *El Economista.* Mexico City, Mexico. http://eleconomista.com.mx. July 14, 2008.

66. "Internacional de Continedores Asociados de Veracruz." Hutchison Port Holdings. Official website. http://www.hph.com.hk/business/ports/america/mexico/icave.htm. Accessed September 7, 2007.

67. Becerra, 2008.

68. "Espera México recibir hasta 900 mdd de inversions chinas."

69. Manuel Lombera Martínez, "México seguirá con la negociación de TLC." *El Universal.* Mexico City, Mexico. http://www.eluniversal.com.mx. September 5, 2007.

70. Durán, 2007. See also "EEUU interpone officialmente demanda contra China en la OMC. *El Universal.* Caracas, Venezuela. http://www.eluniversal.com. April 10, 2007.

71. Frances Williams, "Abre la OMC pánel en contra de China." *El Universal.* Mexico City, Mexico. http://www.eluniversal.com.mx. September 3, 2007. See also "OMC analizará quejas ede EU y México contra China." *El Economista.* Mexico City, Mexico. http://www.eleconomista.com.mx. August 31, 2007.

72. Interview with Luis Duran, director of International Programs, FEMSA. Monterrey, Mexico. April 16, 2007.

73. "Cerveza Modelo llegará a China." *El Economista.* Mexico City, Mexico. http://www.eleconomista.com.mx. December 4, 2006. As another by-product of the same partnership, Grupo Modelo was given the right to be the exclusive distributor of the Chinese beer Tsingtao in Mexico. "Llegará a México nueva cerveza china." *El Sol de México.* Mexico City, Mexico. http://www.oem.com.mx/elsoldemexico. August 19, 2006.

74. "China versus México 2." *El Economista.* Mexico City, Mexico. http://www.eleconomista.com.mx. July 13, 2008.

75. "Inversiones México-China."

76. Manuel Lombera, "A la conquista del dragón." *El Universal.* Mexico City, Mexico. March 9, 2008. See also "Taquería El Fogoncito abre negocio en China." *Nacion.* San José, Costa Rica. http://www.nacion.com. January 26, 2007. See also "Desembarcan los tacos en China: Inauguran restaurante mexicano." *Cambio.* Sonora, Mexico. http://www.oem.com.mx.cambiosonora/. January 25, 2007.

77. "Franquicias mexicanas llegan a China." *El Economista.* Mexico City, Mexico. http://www.eleconomista.com.mx. January 14, 2007.

78. "Televisa hará telenovelas en China y venderá sus formatos de televisión." *El Comercio.* Quito, Ecuador. http://www.elcomercio.com. May 31, 2007.

79. "Los chinos tendrán su propio 'Betty la fea.'" *El País.* Cali, Colombia. http://www.elpais.com.co. July 11, 2008.

80. Interview with Luis Duran, director of International Programs, FEMSA. Monterrey, Mexico. April 16, 2007.

81. "Tequila llegará a China." *El Economista.* Mexico City, Mexico. http://www.eleconomista.com.mx. May 2, 2007.

82. Garza-Limón and Barocio, 2007. See also "Mexican Firms Need Long-Term Plans for China Market: Consultants." *People's Daily Online*. Beijing, China. http://english.people.com.cn. February 22, 2006.

83. "Destaca El País logros de Calderón en China." *El Economista*. Mexico City, Mexico. http://www.eleconomista.com.mx. July 13, 2008.

84. Becerra, 2008.

85. "Desmiente Sojo competir por el liderazgo en Sudamérica." *OEM*. http://www.oem.com.mx/oem/notas/n369220.htm. August 3, 2007.

86. "Derbez realizará visita a China."

87. In May 2006, for example, the commission conducted its second annual meeting, which advanced a collective action plan for the period 2006–2010, as well as dealing with such fields as biotechnology, nanotechnology, and academia interchanges. "Estado actual de las relaciones de cooperación México-China." *Ministry of Foreign Relations, Republic of Mexico*. Official website. http://portal.sre.gob.mx/china. Accessed September 10, 2007.

88. "México podrá exportar carne de cerdo a China."

89. "Mexico, China to Push Forward Bilateral Investment Agreement."

90. "Acuerdos en proceso de negociación entre ambos paises." *Ministry of Foreign Relations, Republic of Mexico*. Official website. http://portal.sre.gob.mx/china. Accessed September 10, 2007.

91. "Acuerdos y convenios de cooperación vigentes entre ambos países." *Ministry of Foreign Relations, Republic of Mexico*. Official website. http://portal.sre.gob.mx/china. Accessed September 10, 2007.

92. "Desmiente Sojo competir por el liderazgo en Sudamérica."

93. "Wang Jinzhen Attends China-Mexico Commerce and Investment 16th China-Mexico Entrepreneur Plenary Session." *China Council for the Promotion of International Trade*. Official website. http://english.ccpit.org/Contents/Channel_410/2007/0829/60761/con-tent_60761.htm. August 29, 2007.

94. Humberto Molina Medina noted that Mexico's spending on export promotion during 2006 was $50 million, compared to Spain's, which was $240 million during the same period. "Déficit de México con China seguirá creciendo." *El Economista*. Mexico City, Mexico. http://www.eleconomista.com.mx. November 13, 2006.

95. "Relación con China, una prioridad para Ebrard." *El Economista*. Mexico City, Mexico. http://www.eleconomista.com.mx. October 23, 2007.

96. "Ebrard firma acuerdo en China." *El Economista*. Mexico City, Mexico. http://www.eleconomista.com.mx. October 23, 2006. See also "Anuncia Ebrard inversión China."

97. "Habría Internet gratis en el DF." *El Sol de México*. April 2, 2007. See also "En 2008 la ciudad de México tendrá Internet inalámbrico gratis." *El Universal*. Caracas, Venezuela. http://www.eluniversal.com. April 3, 2007.

98. "China mira hacia el DF para inverter." *El Economista*. Mexico City, Mexico. http://www.eleconomista.com.mx. July 14, 2008.

99. "Realizará Oliva gira por China y Singapur." *El Sol de Salamanca*. Salamanca, Mexico. http://www.oem.com.mx/elsoldesalamanca/. April 9, 2007.

100. "Viajarán empresarios zacatecanos a China." *El Sol de Zacatecas*. Zacatecas, Mexico. http://www.oem.com.mx/elsoldezacatecas/. April 11, 2007.

101. The organization Mexico-ChinaBusiness.com, for example, is an association of companies dedicated to facilitating commercial transactions between Mexico and China, including offering logistics services, retail space for Mexican products in China, and support for Mexican firms seeking to identify Chinese suppliers. *Mexico-China Business*. http://www.Mexicochinabusiness.com. Accessed December 18, 2007.

102. Roberto Morales, "Bancomext abrirá otra oficina en China." *El Economista*. Mexico City, Mexico. http://www.eleconomista.com.mx. December 21, 2006.

103. See "La Expo Feria de productos mexicanos exportables a China." http:www.esmas.com/emprendedores/novedades/583880.html. January 3, 2007.

104. The center, called Cechimex, was founded by thirty-five members of the university's economics faculty. See Monica Campbell, "The National Autonomous University in Mexico Has Become the First Higher Education Institution in Latin America to Create a Center Dedicated to China Studies." *Chronicle of Higher Education* 52(38). May 26, 2006, p. A47.

105. "El Chino Mandarín está por convertirse en el 2do idioma más importante en el mundo." *El Sol de Bajío*. Bajío, Mexico. http://www.oem.com.mx/elsoldelbajio/. June 25, 2007.

106. "1st Confucius Institute Opens in Latin America." *China.org.cn*. Beijing, China. http://www.china.org.cn/english/culture/158250.htm. February 16, 2006. Now increasingly prevalent throughout Latin America and the world, Confucius Institutes play a key role not only in promoting Chinese culture, but also in providing certified professional instruction in the Mandarin language by visiting Chinese instructors. "China, Latin America Forge Closer Links for Win-Win End (4)." *People's Daily Online*. Beijing, China. http://english.people.com.cn. Accessed October 6, 2006.

107. "Antecedentes y evolución de las relaciones educativas México-China." *Embajada de Mexico en China, Secretaría de Relaciones Exteriores*. Official website. http://www.sre.gob.mx/china. Accessed December 18, 2007.

108. "Foro Baja California–Asia, economía, cultura y negocios."

109. "Turismo México-China." *Ministry of Foreign Relations, Republic of Mexico*. http://portal.sre.gob.mx/china. Accessed September 10, 2007.

110. "Aeroméxico inaugura histórico vuelo directo de América Latina a China." *Diario Financiero*. Santiago, Chile. http://www.df.cl. May 29, 2008. See also "México y China estarán conectados por vuelo directo." *Empresa Exterior*. http://www.empresaexterior.com. December 2, 2007.

111. See, for example, "México concentra mucho sus relaciones con EU." *El Sol de San Luis*. San Luis Potosí, Mexico. http://www.oem.com.mx/elsoldesanluis/. April 8, 2007.

112. Becerra, 2008.

113. "Derbez realizará visita a China."

114. "Alto funcionario chino visitará México, Venezuela, Surinam, Perú, y Samoa." *El Universal*. Caracas, Venezuela. http://www.eluniversal.com. March 12, 2007. See also "Senior Chinese Party Official Wraps Up Mexico Visit." *People's Daily Online*. Beijing, China. http://english.people.com.cn. March 26, 2007.

115. "Chinese General Meets with Mexican Secretaries of Defense, Navy." *People's Daily Online*. Beijing, China. http://english.people.com.cn. June 25, 2004.

116. Hassel Fallas, "Intel Costa Rica prevé repunte de exportaciones en este semestre." *Nacion*. San José, Costa Rica. August 22, 2008.

117. Rodrigo Quirós, "Un trato hecho con China." *Nacion*. San José, Costa Rica. http://www.nacion.com. July 13, 2007. See also "Costa Rica prepara feria commercial con China." *Nacion*. San José, Costa Rica. http://www.nacion.com. June 8, 2007.

118. "Exportadores de Costa Rica abren oficina comercial en Pekín." *Nacion*. San José, Costa Rica. http://www.nacion.com. April 24, 2007.

119. "Costa Rica prepara feria comercial con China." *La Prensa*. San Pedro Sula, Honduras. http://www.laprensahn.com. June 8, 2007.

120. "Total Import and Export Value by Country (Region) (2007/01–12)."

121. Interview with Marco Vinicio Ruiz, minister of foreign commerce. San José, Costa Rica. January 24, 2008.

122. Álvaro Murillo, "Antonio Burgués será el embajador en China." *Nacion.* San Jose, Costa Rica. July 15, 2007.

123. "Total Import and Export Value by Country (Region) (2007/01–12)."

124. "Relaciones con China abren grandes oportunidades, según expresidente del Banco Central." *Nacion.* San José, Costa Rica. http://www.nacion.com. July 25, 2007.

125. "Empresa China compró el área de hardware de IBM." *El Mercurio.* Santiago, Chile. http://diario.elmercurio.com. May 2, 2005. See also "China apuesta a ser potencia informática." *El Mercurio.* Santiago, Chile. http://diario.elmercurio. com. February 23, 2006.

126. Pragmatism and an international orientation were mentioned as driving factors in the decision by Costa Rica to recognize China by multiple senior Costa Rican leaders interviewed for this book, including Marco Vinicio Ruiz, minister of foreign commerce, January 24, 2008; Francisco Morales Hernandez, minister of labor (interviewed January 23, 2008; Edgar Ugalde, vice minister of foreign relations, San José, Costa Rica (interviewed January 22, 2008); and Ronald Espinosa Howell, assistant to the minister of international coordination, San José, Costa Rica (interviewed January 23, 2008). A similar point was made by Carlos Sojo, director of FLACSO (interviewed January 22, 2008).

127. In an interview for this book on January 24, 2008, the Costa Rican vice minister of foreign relations, Edgar Ugalde, noted that Costa Rica continues to have differences with the PRC on a range of issues, despite diplomatic recognition. A similar point was made by Carlos Sojo, director of FLACSO (interviewed January 22, 2008).

128. Interview with Marco Vinicio Ruiz, minister of foreign commerce. San José, Costa Rica. January 24, 2008.

129. The association between the recognition of China and the prior decision to move the Costa Rican embassy in Israel was made, in interviews with the author, by multiple authorities, including Edgar Ugalde, Ronald Espinosa Howell, and Carlos Sojo (for all, see note 126).

130. Interviews with Edgar Ugalde, vice minister of foreign relations, San José, Costa Rica. January 22, 2008; and Roland Espinosa Howell, assistant to the minister of international coordination, San José, Costa Rica. January 23, 2008.

131. In compliance with Costa Rican law, the diplomatic trips were recorded in the public register, but they were not announced to the press, and thus did not become a focus of public debate. Ronald Espinosa Howell, assistant to the minister of international coordination, San José, Costa Rica (interviewed January 23, 2008).

132. Fifteen million dollars of the $60 million package was a grant from the Taiwanese government, while the rest was a loan. Because of the importance of the project, President Arias devoted a portion of his news conference announcing the change in diplomatic relations to discussing plans by the Costa Rican government to complete the highway project with other funds. Correspondence with Edgar Ugalde, vice minister of foreign relations. February 6, 2008.

133. Although the Foreign Ministry traditionally prefers to serve as the single point of coordination for aid of this type, over the course of time, the individual municipalities and social groups in Costa Rica had come to coordinate directly with the Taiwanese embassy to request and negotiate individual projects. Interview with Edgar Ugalde, vice minister of foreign relations, San José, Costa Rica. January 22, 2008.

134. In July 2008, for example, a scandal emerged over funds donated by the Taiwanese to help a poor neighborhood in the capital, which were used to pay fees of consultants affiliated with government officials. "Escándalo de donación de

Taiwán pone en banquillo a ministros en Costa Rica." *Nacion*. San José, Costa Rica. http://www.nacion.com. July 29, 2008.

135. Interview with Wang Xiaoyuan, ambassador from the People's Republic of China to Costa Rica. San José, Costa Rica. January 21, 2008.

136. Interview with Wang Xiaoyuan, ambassador from the People's Republic of China to Costa Rica. San José, Costa Rica. January 21, 2008. Oscar Arias also reached out to the Chinese Costa Rican community in the months following the change in diplomatic recognition, giving a speech at a Chinese community center in Limón in October 2007. Ronald Espinosa Howell, assistant to the minister of international coordination, San José, Costa Rica (interviewed January 23, 2008).

137. Interview with Gerardo Rojas, Costa Rican Chamber of Commerce, San José, Costa Rica, January 22, 2008.

138. Interview with Marco Vinicio Ruiz, minister of foreign commerce. San Jose, Costa Rica. January 24, 2008.

139. Ronald Espinosa Howell, assistant to the minister of international coordination, San José, Costa Rica (interviewed January 23, 2008).

140. Ibid.

141. Interview with Monica Araya, president, CADEXO, San José, Costa Rica, January 21, 2008. A Taiwanese account, which is critical of Costa Rica's change in diplomatic recognition, suggested that the total aid package offered by the PRC in exchange for the switch may have amounted to $430 million. "China mira a Centroamérica para aislar a Taiwán." *El Universal*. Caracas, Venezuela. http://www.eluniversal.com. October 14, 2007.

142. Oscar Núñez Olivas, "China podrá por fin construir estadio en Costa Rica." *El Nuevo Diario*. Managua, Nicaragua. http://www.elnuevodiario.com.ni. October 18, 2008.

143. Álvaro Murillo, "China pagó ayer bonos ticos por un monto incierto." *Nacion*. San José, Costa Rica. January 24, 2008.

144. "Costa Rica y China afianzan relaciones y suscriben acuerdos de cooperación." *Nacion*. San José, Costa Rica. http://www.nacion.com. October 24, 2007. See also Álvaro Murillo, "China firma donación de $48 milliones en encuentro con Arias." *Nacion*. San José, Costa Rica. http://www.nacion.com. October 24, 2007. Also, Ronald Espinosa Howell, assistant to the minister of international coordination, San José, Costa Rica (interviewed January 23, 2008). This money was initially earmarked for upgrading a highway in San Ramon, but the funds were redirected due to the necessities identified during the period of heavy flooding. Carlos Sojo, director of FLACSO (interviewed January 22, 2008).

145. Interview with Wang Xiaoyuan, ambassador from the People's Republic of China to Costa Rica. San José, Costa Rica. January 21, 2008.

146. Persons of Chinese origin are also found among doctors, academics, businesspeople in the banana industry, and various other occupations. Interview with Wang Xiaoyuan, ambassador from the People's Republic of China to Costa Rica. San José, Costa Rica. January 21, 2008.

147. Carlos Sojo, director of FLACSO (interviewed January 22, 2008).

148. Ibid.

149. Interview with Wang Xiaoyuan, ambassador from the People's Republic of China to Costa Rica. San José, Costa Rica. January 21, 2008.

150. A number of Costa Rican congressmen of Chinese origin, for example, have come from Puenta Arenas and Guanacaste. Carlos Sojo, director of FLACSO (interviewed January 22, 2008).

151. Interview with Wang Xiaoyuan, ambassador from the People's Republic of China to Costa Rica. San José, Costa Rica. January 21, 2008. Evidence of the degree to which this community has retained its identity can be found in the fact that

the Chinese television station CCTV-4 is included as a standard channel in many cable television packages offered in San José.

152. San José was also seeking financial support from the government of China for the project. See Jairo Villegas S., "Municipio de San José impulsa crear barrio chino en capital." *Nacion.* San José, Costa Rica. January 20, 2008.

153. Álvaro Murillo, "Arias prevé aumento de exportaciones a China." *Nacion.* San José, Costa Rica. http://www.nacion.com. June 9, 2007.

154. Interview with Rodrigo Vargas, president, Café Tres Generaciones, Alajuela, Costa Rica, January 24, 2008.

155. Interview with Marco Vinicio Ruiz, minister of foreign commerce. San Jose, Costa Rica. January 24, 2008. In the domain of coffee, for example, Costa Rica is seeking niche markets in China for products that are expensive relative to many other coffees of the region, but enjoy a reputation for very high quality. Interview with Rodrigo Vargas, president, Café Tres Generaciones, Alajuela, Costa Rica, January 24, 2008.

156. Some coffee producers in the vicinity of San José, Costa Rica, sell an estimated 70 percent of their crop to Starbucks. Interview with Rodrigo Vargas, president, Café Tres Generaciones, Alajuela, Costa Rica, January 24, 2008.

157. Cinthya Arias L., "Café Britt: Desde las plantaciones ticas hast alas tazas chinas." *Enlace Mundial.* PROCOMER. September 2007, pp. 56–57.

158. Cafe Britt entered into controversy when it contracted to have a coffee mug with a Peruvian artisanal design mass-produced in China for sale in its retail outlets. Interview with Rodrigo Vargas, president, Café Tres Generaciones, Alajuela, Costa Rica, January 24, 2008.

159. Interview with Wang Xiaoyuan, ambassador from the People's Republic of China to Costa Rica. San José, Costa Rica. January 21, 2008. In exporting to China, Costa Rica faces the same Chinese phytosanitary, business, and cultural barriers that have impeded other nations of the region in their efforts to export agricultural products to the PRC. In recognition of these limitations, one of the key accords signed between China and Costa Rica during the visit by President Arias in October 2007 was a blanket phytosanitary agreement establishing basic categories and standards to facilitate transactions in agricultural goods. Beyond this blanket agreement, a specific phytosanitary agreement was signed for bananas as an "early harvest" of other agreements potentially to come, once more technical studies have been performed. Interview with Marco Vinicio Ruiz, minister of foreign commerce. San José, Costa Rica. January 24, 2008.

160. Interview with Alvaro Piedra, international marketing manager, PROCOMER, and Pedro Ramirez, coordinator for sectoral programs, PROCOMER, San José, Costa Rica, January 23, 2008.

161. Principally, such expansion would come through using existing terrain more efficiently, although territory dedicated to growing pineapples could be used to grow bananas, to some degree. Interview with Rodrigo Vargas, president, Café Tres Generaciones, Alajuela, Costa Rica, January 24, 2008.

162. Interview with Monica Araya, president, CADEXO, San José, Costa Rica, January 21, 2008.

163. Álvarez, 2006.

164. Interview with Alvaro Piedra, international marketing manager, PROCOMER, and Pedro Ramirez, coordinator for sectoral programs, PROCOMER, San José, Costa Rica, January 23, 2008.

165. Álvaro Murillo, "Contrato de $150 millones traerá camarones ticos a China." *Nación.* San José, Costa Rica. http://www.nacion.com. October 25, 2007.

166. Mauricio Soto, "Coopeindia viste al 'dragon rojo' de verde." *Enlace Mundial.* PROCOMER. http://www.procomer.com/Espanol/docs/PDF/Revistaenlace/

Revista_setiembre2007.pdf. September 2007, pp. 59–61.

167. "Costa Rica y China afianzan relaciones y suscriben acuerdos de cooperación." See also Ana Lupita Mora, "Óscar Arias quiere refinería china aquí." *Nacion.* San José, Costa Rica. http://www.nacion.com. October 20, 2007.

168. Many countries in Central America have been seeking to position themselves as the site of a new oil refinery, including Panama and Guatemala. See Juan Fernando Lara S., "Costa Rica competirá por sede de refinería regional." *Nacion.* San José, Costa Rica. http://www.nacion.com. November 22, 2006.

169. "China interesada en Costa Rica." *El Siglo.* Panama City, Panama. http://www.elsiglo.com. November 8, 2007. The agreement represented a departure from the policy of the predecessor of President Arias, Abel Pacheco, under whom the oil company Harken was expelled from the country. Carlos Sojo, director of FLACSO (interviewed January 22, 2008).

170. Juan Fernando Lara. "Costa Rica competirá por sede de refinería regional." *Nacion.* San José, Costa Rica. http://www.nacion.com. November 22, 2006.

171. "Costa Rica firma acuerdos con China." *La Prensa.* Managua, Nicaragua. http://www.laprensa.com.ni. November 17, 2008.

172. According to figures from the Chinese Ministry of Commerce, Costa Rica exported $2.31 billion to China in 2007, while importing only $567 million during the same period. "Total Import and Export Value by Country (Region) (2007/01–12)."

173. "Características del comercio exterior de China e intercambio con Costa Rica." *Enlace Mundial.* PROCOMER. http://www.procomer.com?Espanol/docs/PDF/Revistaenlace/Revista_setiembre2007.pdf. September 2007, p. 49.

174. "Empresa China compró el área de hardware de IBM." See also "China apuesta a ser potencia informática."

175. This point was made by Marco Vinicio Ruiz, minister of foreign commerce, San José, Costa Rica. January 24, 2008, as well as by Piedra and Ramirez. Interview with Alvaro Piedra, international marketing manager, PROCOMER, and Pedro Ramirez, coordinator for sectoral programs, PROCOMER, San José, Costa Rica, January 23, 2008.

176. Interview with Wang Xiaoyuan, ambassador from the People's Republic of China to Costa Rica. San José, Costa Rica. January 21, 2008.

177. Various Costa Rican experts interviewed for this book highlighted tourism as one of the most promising areas for expanding commerce with China; these experts include Monica Araya, president, CADEXO, San José, Costa Rica, January 21, 2008; and Carlos Sojo, director of FLACSO, January 22, 2008; as well as Irving Soto, Costa Rican Investment Promotion Agency (CINDE), San José, Costa Rica, January 23, 2008.

178. Interview with Irving Soto, Costa Rican Investment Promotion Agency (CINDE), San José, Costa Rica, January 23, 2008.

179. "Gross Domestic Product per Capita, Current Prices (U.S. Dollars)." *International Monetary Fund.* World Economic Outloook Database. http://www. imf.org/external/pubs/ft/weo/2007/01/data/index.aspx. April 2007.

180. By contrast to what has occurred in many other countries in the region, the expansion of Chinese goods in Costa Rica has generated relatively little backlash. In part, this reflects the relatively complementary nature of the Costa Rican and Chinese economies. When asked about China's likely use of its own companies and workers in the construction of the nation's new sports stadium, for example, Costa Rica's minister of labor, Francisco Morales, noted that the use of Chinese labor was not a major issue, given that Costa Rica itself had a net shortage of 50,000 workers in the construction sector. Interview with Francisco Morales, minister of work and social security, government of Costa Rica. San José, Costa Rica. January 23, 2008.

181. Interview with Gerardo Rojas, Costa Rican Chamber of Commerce. San José, Costa Rica, January 22, 2008.

182. Interview with Monica Araya, president, CADEXO. San José, Costa Rica, January 21, 2008.

183. Interview with Wang Xiaoyuan, ambassador from the People's Republic of China to Costa Rica. San José, Costa Rica. January 21, 2008.

184. Ibid.

185. Irene Vizcaíno, "Diputados aprueban apertura en telecomunicaciones." *Nación.* San José, Costa Rica. http://www.nacion.com. February 14, 2008.

186. Álvaro Murillo, "Gobierno se acerca a empresas chinas de telecomunicaciones." *Nacion.* San José, Costa Rica. http://www.nacion.com. October 24, 2007.

187. "Costa Rica: Declaran ganadora al 'sí' en referendo sobre CAFTA." *El Universal.* Caracas, Venezuela. http://www.eluniversal.com. October 22, 2007.

188. "Costa Rica y China afianzan relaciones y suscriben acuerdos de cooperación." See also Álvaro Murillo, "Primera estación de Arias en China: La ciudad prohibida." *Nacion.* San José, Costa Rica. http://www.nacion.com. October 22, 2007.

189. Marvin Barquero S., "Estudio recomienda iniciar negociación de TLC con China." *Nacion.* San José, Costa Rica. http://www.nacion.com. July 9, 2008.

190. Murillo, October 22, 2007.

191. The combination of strong universities and the sophistication of Costa Rican companies in the IT and biomedical sectors further creates the opportunity for technological partnerships between Costa Rican companies and Chinese partners.

192. Indeed, in discussing Costa Rica's new position, Arias himself said, "[W]e are the only country in Central America that has relations with China, and also now assured access to the US market. China can sell to this market through Costa Rica." Murillo, October 22, 2007.

193. Interview with Marco Vinicio Ruiz, minister of foreign commerce. San José, Costa Rica. January 24, 2008.

194. Interview with Francisco Morales, minister of work and social security, government of Costa Rica. San José, Costa Rica. January 23, 2008.

195. Interview with Alvaro Piedra, international marketing manager, PROCOMER, and Pedro Ramirez, coordinator for sectoral programs, PROCOMER. San José, Cosa Rica. January 23, 2008.

196. These include not only conducting market surveys, maintaining contacts, and providing information and business services, but also helping qualified small and medium-sized enterprises to become exporters, and, once ready, helping to position them in markets such as that of China. Interview with Alvaro Piedra, international marketing manager, PROCOMER, and Pedro Ramirez, coordinator for sectoral programs, PROCOMER, San José, Costa Rica, January 23, 2008.

197. "C. American Business People to Seek Opportunities in China." *People's Daily Online.* Beijing, China. http://english.people.com.cn. July 11, 2006.

198. Interview with Alvaro Piedra, international marketing manager, PROCOMER, and Pedro Ramirez, coordinator for sectoral programs, PROCOMER, San José, Costa Rica, January 23, 2008.

199. Marvin Barquero, "Empresarios viajan a explorar productos chinos." *Nacion.* San José, Costa Rica. http://www.nacion.com. April 11, 2006. See also "Más de cien empresarios centroamericanos viajarán a China en misión comercial." *Nacion.* San José, Costa Rica. http://www.nacion.com. April 6, 2006.

200. Interview with Alvaro Piedra, international marketing manager, PROCOMER, and Pedro Ramirez, coordinator for sectoral programs, PROCOMER, San José, Costa Rica, January 23, 2008. The trade fair generated an estimated $2 million in signed contracts, and an estimated total of $140 million in new business. "Genera

negocios por 140 mdd feria china en Costa Rica." *El Sol del Bajío*. Bajio, Mexico. http://www.oem.com/mx.elsoldebajio/notas/n395242.htm. August 26, 2007.

201. "Feria internacional de China para la inversión y el comercio." *Enlace Mundial*. PROCOMER. http://www.procomer.com/Espanol/docs/PDF/Revistaenlace/ Revista_setiembre2007.pdf. September 2007, p. 65.

202. Interview with Irving Soto, Costa Rican Investment Promotion Agency (CINDE), San José, Costa Rica, January 23, 2008.

203. Interview with Alvaro Piedra, international marketing manager, PRO-COMER, and Pedro Ramirez, coordinator for sectoral programs, PROCOMER, San José, Costa Rica, January 23, 2008. See also Mercedes Agüero R., "Agroindustria y turismo con mayor opción en China." *Nacion*. San José, Costa Rica. http://www. nacion.com. October 24, 2007.

204. Interview with Alvaro Piedra, international marketing manager, PRO-COMER, and Pedro Ramirez, coordinator for sectoral programs, PROCOMER, San José, Costa Rica, January 23, 2008.

205. Ibid. See also Agüero, 2007.

206. Interview with Alvaro Piedra, international marketing manager, PRO-COMER, and Pedro Ramirez, coordinator for sectoral programs, PROCOMER, San José, Costa Rica, January 23, 2008.

207. Besides facilitating contacts between Costa Rican and Chinese business-people, the PROCOMER office in Beijing conducts a range of promotional activities, such as business breakfasts and an event known as "Costa Rican Nights." Ibid.

208. Interview with Monica Araya, president, CADEXO, San José, Costa Rica, January 21, 2008.

209. Indeed, Costa Rica's ambassador to China, Antonio Burges, was the former president of CADEXO, giving him particular insight into the needs and considerations of the Costa Rican business community as they relate to his position.

210. "Costa Rica y China afianzan relaciones y suscriben acuerdos de cooperación." China Development Bank also has signed a similar agreement with Banco de Integración Centroamericano. Interview with Wang Xiaoyuan, ambassador from the People's Republic of China to Costa Rica. San José, Costa Rica. January 21, 2008.

211. Interview with Gerardo Rojas, Costa Rican Chamber of Commerce, San José, Costa Rica, January 22, 2008.

212. Interview with Irving Soto, Costa Rican Investment Promotion Agency (CINDE), San José, Costa Rica, January 23, 2008.

213. Interview with Edgar Ugalde, vice minister of foreign relations, San José, Costa Rica. January 22, 2008. Although the moratorium on new members originally expired in 2008, the member states agreed during their meeting in Sidney, Australia, in September 2008 to extend this deadline to 2010. "Los líderes cierran hasta 2010 las puertas de APEC a nuevos miembros." *El Comercio*. Quito, Ecuador. http://www.elcomercio.com. September 9, 2007.

214. Álvarez, 2006.

215. Interview with Irving Soto, Costa Rican Investment Promotion Agency (CINDE), San José, Costa Rica, January 23, 2008.

216. Ibid.

217. Interview with Wang Xiaoyuan, ambassador from the People's Republic of China to Costa Rica. San José, Costa Rica. January 21, 2008; and interview with Edgar Ugalde, vice minister of foreign relations, San José, Costa Rica. January 22, 2008.

218. Álvaro Murillo M., "Presidente Arias ya se encuentra en China." *Nacion*. San José, Costa Rica. http://www.nacion.com. October 22, 2007.

219. "Futuro embajador chino prevé fuerte comercio y cooperación con Costa Rica." *El Comercio*. Quito, Ecuador. http://www.elcomercio.com. June 18, 2007.

See also Álvaro Murillo, "Óscar Arias vende 'ideas verdes' en China." *Nacion.* San José, Costa Rica. http://www.nacion.com. October 23, 2007. Costa Rica has also established an embassy in India, in part to advance this goal. Bernal Jiménez Monge, "Diplomacia tica en el sudeste asiático." *Nacion.* San José, Costa Rica. http://www.nacion.com. June 24, 2007.

220. "Costa Rica y China afianzan relaciones y suscriben acuerdos de cooperación." See also "Una decisión correcta." *Nacion.* San José, Costa Rica. http://www.nacion.com. June 8, 2007.

221. "Destino de las exportaciones." *Ministerio de Comercio e Industrias, Viceministerio de Comercio Exterior.* Official website. http://www.mici.gob.pa/exportaciones.php. Accessed December 13, 2007.

222. Larry Rohter, "Heavy Hand of Beijing Dampens a Panama Canal Fest." *New York Times.* http://query.nytimes.com/gst/fullpage.html?res=9803EEDC 1F30F93BA3575AC-0A961958260. September 8, 1997.

223. "Normalization of China-Panama Ties Benefits Both Peoples: Li Peng." *People's Daily Online.* Beijing, China. http://english.peopledaily.com.cn. July 13, 2001.

224. Quesada, 2006.

225. Erik Jackson, "Panama's Chinese Community Celebrates a Birthday, Meets New Challenges." *Panama News* 10(9). May 9–22, 2004.

226. Ibid.

227. Lina Vega Abad, "De salsipuedes al 'barrio chino.'" *La Prensa.* Hato Pintado Panamá, República de Panamá. http://mensual.prensa.com/mensual/contenido/2003/07/20/hoy/ciudad.shtml. Accessed December 14, 2007.

228. Delfia Cortez, "Colon comienza a ventilarse." *Crítica.* Panama City, Panama. http://www.critica.com.pa. January 7, 2003.

229. As an example, it was the president of the China Association, Moisés Lou, who acted as the voice of the community when the *barrio chino* in Panama City was damaged by a serious fire in June 2007. See Juan Limachi, "Voraz incendio en Barrio Chino." *Crítica.* Panama City, Panama. http://www.critica.com.pa. June 12, 2007.

230. "Total Import and Export Value by Country (Region) (2007/01–12)."

231. "Productos Exportados en el año 2006." *Viceministerio de Comercio Exterior, Ministerio de Comercia y Industrias: Panama.* Official website. http://www.mici.gob.pa./exportaciones.php. December 2006.

232. "Total Import and Export Value by Country (Region) (2007/01–12)."

233. According to the PRC Ministry of Commerce, Chile imported $4.42 billion in goods from China, versus the $5.58 billion in goods imported by Panama. Ibid.

234. International Monetary Fund, 2006.

235. "Vienen los diablos chinos!" *Crítica.* Panama City, Panama. http://www.critica.com.pa. July 11, 2007.

236. "China COSCO se convierte en segunda mayor naviera mundial." *Empresa Exterior.* http://www.empresaexterior.com. August 29, 2005.

237. "Convenio entre AMP y China fortalecerá educación náutica." *Crítica.* http://www.critica.com.pa. October 20, 1999.

238. "Chinese Companies in Panama: COSCO." *Panda-Mart.* http://www.panda-mart.com/Project-Development/companies.htm. Accessed December 14, 2007.

239. Cortez, 2003.

240. *Kitomi.* Official Web site. http://www.kitomicorp.com. Accessed December 18, 2007.

241. Gilberto Campos. "Los productos chinos." *Nacion.* San José, Costa Rica. http://www.nacion.com. November 27, 2008.

242. Although PdVSA is not yet shipping significant quantities of petroleum to China through the canal, such nonetheless remains an important option. Currently, if Venezuela does not ship its oil through the Panama Canal, it must ship its oil by a much longer, easterly route across the Atlantic and around the Horn of Africa. Although the size of the canal prevents its use by the largest and most economical tankers, the expansion of the canal's capacity is anticipated to alleviate this problem partially, and also to reduce delays associated with the transit.

243. "China y Panamá muestran su deseo común de ampliar la cooperacion en el Canal." *Xinhua*. Beijing, China. www.spanish.xinhuanet.com. June 14, 2007.

244. "Panama Canal: A Key Latin American Project for Asia." *Latin America–Asia Review*. July 2006. p. 2.

245. "China y Panamá muestran su deseo común de ampliar la cooperacion en el Canal."

246. Manuel Luna, "Megapuerto de Farfán naufragó." *La Estrella*. Panama City, Panama. http://laestrella.com.pa. November 28, 2008.

247. The pipeline was originally constructed to support the transport of oil extracted from the North Slope oil fields of Alaska to refineries on the East Coast of the United States. Under that arrangement, oil was loaded onto tankers in Alaska, then shipped down the Pacific coast to Panama, where it was offloaded and moved through the pipeline to container facilities on the Atlantic coast. The oil was then reloaded onto tankers and shipped to US refineries, largely based in the Gulf of Mexico. When production of oil from the North Slope stopped, the pipeline fell into disuse for some time, but was briefly reopened to support the transport of Ecuadorian oil from Pacific ports across Panama, and ultimately to the same US East Coast refineries.

248. "Chávez ofrece construir una refinería y un oleoducto en Panamá." *Panda-Mart*. San José, Costa Rica. http://www.nacion.com. June 23, 2006.

249. "Chávez tienta a Panamá con plan de inversions." *Panda-Mart*. San José, Costa Rica. http://www.nacion.com. June 24, 2007.

250. Aet Elisa Tejera C., "Panamá tendrá otro canal, pero sera de petróleo." *Crítica*. Panama City, Panama. http://www.critica.com.pa. November 21, 2007.

251. Among other objectives, the exposition reportedly highlighted the advantages of the Colón duty-free zone, offering tariff-free access and an attractive strategic location to serve such markets as Venezuela and Colombia. See "Panama's Duty Free Zone Restructured to Meet Int'l Standards." *People's Daily Online*. Beijing, China. http://english.people.com.cn. November 30, 2006.

252. Iván Bautista, "Exposición commercial china reúne 100 empresas en Panamá." *EmpresaExterior*. http://www.empresaexterior.com. December 6, 2007.

253. Ibid. See also "Mañana inciará la X Exposición Económico-Comercial de China 2007 en Panamá." *Crítica*. http://www.critica.com.pa. December 5, 2007.

254. "Exposición comercial de China 2008." *La Estrella*. Panama City, Panama. http://laestrella.com.pa. November 27, 2008.

255. "Overseas Branches." *Bank of China*. Official website. http://www.boc. cn/en/common/third.jsp?category=ROOT>en>Information%20Center>BOC%20Network>Overseas%20Branches&pages=3. Accessed December 14, 2007.

256. "Panama puede pertenecer a la APEC." *Crítica*. http://www.critica. com.pa. August 19, 2005.

257. Carlos Estrada Aguilar, "Exploran entendimientos con China." *Crítica*. Panama City, Panama. http://www.critica.com.pa. October 12, 2007.

258. China y Panamá muestran su deseo común de ampliar la cooperacion en el canal."

259. "China busca incrementar comercio con Panamá." *Crítica*. Panama City, Panama. http://www.critica.com.pa. September 26, 2007.

260. Reciprocally, in October 2004, Chinese leader Jia Qinglin indicated publicly that the PRC was willing to establish state-to-state relations with Panama.
261. "Relaciones con Taíwan." *Crítica.* Panama City, Panama. http://www.critica.com.pa. June 8, 2007.
262. "Panamá mantendrá relaciones diplomáticas con Taiwán y comerciales con China." *El Nuevo Diario.* Managua, Nicaragua. http://www.elnuevodiario.com.ni. March 29, 2008.
263. "Panama's Former President Calls for Diplomatic Ties with China." *People's Daily Online.* Beijing, China. http://english.people.com.cn. June 9, 2007.
264. "Imports by Major Categories (2007/01–12)." *Ministry of Commerce of the People's Republic of China.* http://english.mofcom.gov.cn/aarticle/statistic/ie/200802/20080205372493.html. February 4, 2008.
265. "Nicaragua Considers Alternative to Panama Canal." *CNN.* http://www.cnn.com. October 19, 2006.
266. Ibid.
267. "Rusia interesada en contruir Canal Interoceánico, dice ministro." *El Nuevo Diario.* Managua, Nicaragua. http://www.elnuevodiario.com.ni. September 19, 2008.
268. "Monkey Point será puerta de Nicaragua." *El Nuevo Diario.* Managua, Nicaragua. http://www.elnuevodiario.com.ni. March 12, 2008.
269. Ibid.
270. "Venezuela ofrece poliducto a Nicaragua." *El Universal.* Caracas, Venezuela. http://www.eluniversal.com. December 17, 2006.
271. "Taiwán podría perdonar la deuda externa a Nicaragua." *Nacion.* San José, Costa Rica. http://www.nacion.com. June 26, 2007.
272. "Honduras y Nicaragua mantendrán relaciones con Taiwán." *Nacion.* San José, Costa Rica. http://www.nacion.com. June 8, 2007.
273. "Ortega busca apoyo de inversores extranjeros para crear empleos en Nicaragua." *El Universal.* Caracas, Venezuela. http://www.eluniversal.com. November 15, 2006.
274. "Nicaragua Wants More Aid from Taiwán." *CNN.* http://www.cnn.com. July 3, 2007.
275. "Taiwán podría perdonar la deuda externa a Nicaragua."
276. "Sesenta médicos de Taiwán llegarán a Nicaragua en agosto." *Los Tiempos.* Washington, DC. July 31, 2008–August 6, 2008, p. A5.
277. "Saca reitera amistad Taiwán aunque hay libertad comercio china." *Nacion.* San José, Costa Rica. http://www.nacion.com. March 31, 2006.
278. "President Chen Shui-Bian Meets Belize Prime Minister Said W. Musa." *My EGov, Republic of Taiwan.* Official website. http://english.www.gov.tw/e-Gov/index.jsp?cate-gid=14&recordid=103309. May 7, 2007.
279. "President Chen Shui-Bian Meets Guatemala President Oscar Rafael Berger Perdomo." *Office of the President, Republic of Taiwan.* Official website. http://www.president.gov.tw/en/prog/news_release/document_content.php?id=1105499445&pre_id=1105499445&g_category_number=145&category_number_2=145. June 20, 2007.
280. "Misión comercial de China busca contactos en Honduras." *El Comercio.* Quito, Ecuador. http://www.elcomercio.com. August 29, 2007
281. He Li, 2005, p. 85; and Watson, 2004.
282. "Honduras analiza relaciones diplomáticas con China." *El Universal.* Caracas, Venezuela. http://www.eluniversal.com. July 31, 2007. See also "Chen dice que Honduras puede ser amigo de Taiwán y China." *Crítica.* Panama City, Panama. http://www.critica.com.pa. August 24, 2007.

283. "Honduras puede ser amiga de Taiwán y China." *La Prensa*. San Pedro Sula, Honduras. http://www.laprensahn.com. August 23, 2007.

284. "Taiwán anima a invertir en Latinoamérica." *Nacion*. San José, Costa Rica. http://www.nacion.com. July 23, 2007.

285. "Honduras analiza relaciones diplomáticas con China."

286. M. Fernández, "Taiwán ofrece reforzar ayuda para Guatemala." *Prensa Libre*. Guatemala City, Guatemala. http://www.prensalibre.com. May 7, 2008.

287. Greta Arévalo, "Ratifican TLC entre Honduras y Taiwán." *La Jornada*. Tegucigalpa, Honduras. http://www.lajornadanet.com. July 16, 2008.

288. President Chen Shui-Bian had flown to Honduras and was present at the meeting. "Se fue Chen Shui-bian y dejó muchas promesas." *La Prensa*. San Pedro Sula, Honduras. http://www.laprensahn.com. August 25, 2007.

289. Germán Briceño, "Centroamérica advierte a Taiwán que estrechará relaciones con China." *La Prensa*. San Pedro Sula, Honduras. http://www.laprensahn.com. August 23, 2007.

290. "China se molesta con Mel." *La Prensa*. San Pedro Sula, Honduras. http://www.laprensahn.com. September 28, 2007.

291. Bilateral trade flows between the PRC and the region have increased from a level of $1.42 billion in 1989, when the Berlin Wall collapsed, to $70 billion in 2006. "Total Import and Export Value by Country (Region) (2006/01–12)."

292. "Cuba propuso a China 37 proyectos por $1,500 millones." *El Nuevo Herald*. Miami, Florida. http://elnuevoherald.com. November 23, 2008.

293. "China, Latin America Forge Closer Links for Win-Win End (3)."

294. The year 1959, when the Cuban communists consolidated power in Havana, is used as the beginning of the period of analysis because, from this point forward, both China and Cuba were governed by regimes formally proclaiming communism as their form of government. No !

295. In September 1960, before the Sino-Soviet rift, Cuba became the first country in Latin America to recognize the People's Republic of China, in lieu of the Republic of China, as the legitimate government of the mainland. Ratliff, 2006.

296. In 1960, the Soviet Union openly supported India in its brief war with China, and in 1962, then–chairman of the Chinese Communist Party Mao Zedong ridiculed Soviet president Nikita Khrushchev for capitulating to the United States during the Cuban missile crisis. Following the open ideological break, which was formalized in a series of doctrinal publications in 1963, Cuba chose a path that largely supported Soviet allies and doctrinal positions.

297. Although it was Salvador Allende's leftist regime in Chile that first recognized the PRC in 1960, the Chinese continued cordial relations with the military dictatorship of Augusto Pinochet that replaced him, while many Chilean leftists fled to Cuba. See Gabrela Donoso, "Empresarios chilenos hacen negocios en la isla." *El Nuevo Herald*. Miami, Florida. September 5, 2004.

298. These contacts included, for example, a small program in Havana helping Chinese students to learn Spanish, as well as a subsequent student exchange program between the two countries. The latter involved each country's providing a modest ten scholarships for students from the other nation to live and study in the host country. See "Bilateral Relations." *Ministry of Foreign Affairs of the People's Republic of China*. http://www.fmprc.gov.cn/eng/wjb/zzjg/ldmzs/gjlb/3488/default.htm. September 26, 2003.

299. The *CIA World Factbook*, for example, estimates that the Soviet subsidy to Cuba during this period was between $4 billion and $6 billion per year. See "Cuba." *CIA World Factbook*. https://www.cia.gov/library/publications/the-world-factbook/geos/cu.html#In-tro. Accessed December 18, 2007.

300. There were some signs of a Sino-Cuban rapprochement prior to this period, with the two nations restoring normal military relations in 1984. "Bilateral Relations." 301. Nathan, 2001. The first major diplomatic interchange between China and Cuba came almost two years after Tiananmen Square, in May 1991, when a Chinese delegation headed by the Standing Committee of the National People's Congress visited Cuba. Two months later, a Cuban delegation headed by the vice president of the Cuban Council of State paid a reciprocal visit to China. "Sino-Cuban Relations." *China Daily*. Beijing, China. http://english.people.com.cn. November 11, 2004.

302. China continues to give attention to Cuba, even as it develops its ties with the rest of Latin America. When Hu Jintao traveled to the region in conjunction with his participation in the APEC summit in Santiago, Chile, in November 2004, for example, Cuba was one of the five nations that he chose to visit. See "Foreign Minister Li Zhaoxing Comments on the Fruitful Results of President Hu Jintao's Trip to Latin America." *Ministry of Foreign Affairs of the People's Republic of China*. Official website. http://www.fmprc.gov.cn/eng/topics/huvisit/t172349.htm. November 26, 2004.

303. "Total Import and Export Value by Country (Region) (2007/01–12)."

304. "Cuba invertirá más de $300 millones en ampliar su industria del níquel." *El Universal*. Caracas, Venezuela. http://www.eluniversal.com. February 5, 2007.

305. Ibid.

306. "Cuba propuso a China 37 proyectos por $1,500 milliones."

307. "China y Cuba firman acuerdos de exportación." *La Prensa Grafica*. San Salvador, El Salvador. http://www.laprensagrafica.com. November 19, 2008.

308. See also "China's Sugar Imports Up Slightly with Price Down in 1st 7 Months." *People's Daily Online*. Beijing, China. http://english.people.com.cn. October 20, 2007.

309. "Steep Sugar Prices Lead to State Auction." *People's Daily Online*. Beijing, China. http://english.people.com.cn. December 28, 2005.

310. Indeed, Cuba itself has announced plans to increase significantly its output of ethanol, distilled from sugarcane in domestic refineries. Although the 17 Cuban distilleries currently have the capacity to produce only 180 million liters of ethanol annually, Cuba projects that ethanol output will reach 500 million liters by 2010. Andrea Rodríguez, "Cuba entra en el debate del biocombustible." *Los Tiempos*. Cochabamba, Bolivia. http://www.lostiempos.com. See also "Cuba Censures Bush over Biofuels." *People's Daily Online*. Beijing, China. http://english.people.com.cn. March 30, 2007.

311. "China agiliza agenda de cooperación en la región." *El Universal*. Caracas, Venezuela. http://www.eluniversal.com. March 28, 2007. See also "China y Cuba apuestan por más comercio." *Los Tiempos*. Cochabamba, Bolivia. http://www.lostiempos.com. March 28, 2007.

312. "China y Cuba firman acuerdos de exportación." *La Prensa Grafica*. San Salvador, El Salvador. http://www.laprensagrafica.com. November 19, 2008.

313. Analysts estimate that Cuba may have up to 1.6 billion barrels of reserves, although early exploration activities have not realized such expectations. "Caribbean Country Analysis Brief." *Energy Information Administration*. http://www.eia.doe.gov/emeu/cabs/Caribbean/Background.html. July 2006.

314. Other firms developing blocks in Cuban waters include the Canadian firms Sheritt and Peberco, the Spanish firm Repsol, the Indian firm ONGC Videsh, the Malasian firm Petronas, among others. "Cuba cifra sus esperanzas petroleras en el Golfo de México." *El Universal*. Caracas, Venezuela. http://www.eluniversal.com. March 21, 2007.

315. Venezuela is also active in helping Cuba to explore for oil in this area. See

"Venezuela to Cooperate with Cuba in Oil Exploration." *People's Daily Online.* Beijing, China. http://english.people.com.cn. August 1, 2007.

316. "Cuba to Increase Oil Output by 100,000 Tons in 2007." *Latin Petroleum Energy Daily News Summary.* http://latinpetroleum.com. March 26, 2007.

317. "Cuba aumentará producción petrolera en 700,000 barriles en 2007." *El Universal.* Caracas, Venezuela. http://www.eluniversal.com. March 25, 2007.

318. "Cuba propuso a China 37 proyectos por $1,500 milliones."

319. "Total Import and Export Value by Country (Region) (2007/01–12)."

320. "El presidente chino visita a Fidel Castro." *El Nuevo Herald.* Miami, Florida. http://www.elnuevoherald.com. November 19, 2008.

321. "Cuban Bus Drivers Cheer New Chinese Buses." *People's Daily Online.* Beijing, China. http://english.people.com.cn. January 29, 2007.

322. "Castro Appreciates Chinese Locomotives." *People's Daily Online.* Beijing, China. http://english.people.com.cn. January 18, 2007. See also "12 Chinese Locomotives Arrive in Cuba." *People's Daily Online.* Beijing, China. http://english.people.com.cn. January 10, 2007.

323. "China Jamaica Rail Talks Back on Track." *Jamaica Observer.* Kingston, Jamaica. http://www.jamaicaobserver.com. May 19, 2006.

324. "China Sells High Power Diesel Locomotives to Venezuela." *People's Daily Online.* Beijing, China. http://english.people.com.cn. December 19, 2006.

325. "Cuba propuso a China 37 proyectos por $1,500 milliones." See also "Ampliarán Cuba y China colaboración en biotecnología." *Granma.* http://www.granma.cu/. February 12, 2006.

326. "Cuba-China Medical Cooperation Boosted." *DTCuba.* http://dtcuba. com/. December 18, 2006. See also "China, Cuba Jointly Build Ophthalmic Hospital in NW China." *People's Daily Online.* Beijing, China. http://english.people.com.cn. December 8, 2007.

327. "Mil jóvenes chinos cursaran estudios de español en Cuba." *La Capital.* Rosario, Argentina. http://www.lacapital.com.ar/. October 16, 2007.

328. Anne-Marie Garcia, "Presidente chino firma docena de acuerdos en su visita a Cuba." *Nacion.* San José, Costa Rica. http://www.nacion.com. November 19, 2008.

329. These include the Fuerzas Armadas Revolucionarias de Colombia (FARC), the Movimiento Revolucionario Túpac Amaru (MRTA) in Peru, the Frente Farabundo Martí de Liberación Nacional (FMLN) in El Salvador, and the Frente Sandinista de Liberación Nacional (FSLN) in Nicaragua. Similarly, Cuban revolutionary figures such as Ernesto "Che" Guevara hold a venerated place in Latin American student and worker movements.

330. Current and historical revolutionary movements in Latin America, including the Sendero Luminoso (Shining Path) in Peru, Ejercito de Liberación Nacional (ELN) in Colombia, and FARC, employ ideological orientation and strategy that are a mixture of Cuban and Maoist ideas.

331. Andres Oppenheimer, "Leftist 'Unity' Is a Mirage in Latin America." *Miami Herald.* Miami, Florida. http://www.miamiherald.com. January 17, 2006.

332. "Chávez dice que Mao y Bolívar habrían sido buenos amigos." *El Universal.* Caracas, Venezuela. http://www.eluniversal.com. December 24, 2004.

333. See, for example, "Cuba toma distancia de modelos chino y venezolano y defiende el propio." *El Universal.* Caracas, Venezuela. http://www.eluniversal.com. March 5, 2007. Symbolic milestones in the transition of the Chinese economic system away from socialism in recent years include the opening of the banking sector to the participation of foreign institutions, tax code reform, and the passage of a law establishing legal rights in private property by the National People's Congress in March 2007. See also Adam Wolfe, "China's Priorities on Display at the National

People's Congress." *Power and National Interest Report*. http://www.pinr.com. March 21, 2007. See also "Hu Jintao, el político que echa abajo el legado de Mao Zedong." *El Commercio*. Quito, Ecuador. http://www.elcomercio.com. March 25, 2007.

334. The PRC supported the Forces of National Liberation of Angola, while Cuba supported the Popular Movement for the Liberation of Angola (MPLA), which eventually came to power.

335. Schiller, 2006b.

336. A recent example was the visit to Havana in January 2007 by Cheng Siwei, the vice chairman of the Standing Committee of China's National People's Congress. "Chinese, Cuban Senior Legislators Meet to Strengthen Bilateral Ties." *People's Daily Online*. Beijing, China. http://english.people.com.cn. January 9, 2007.

337. Chinese participation in cultural, political, and diplomatic exchanges also includes an agreement on cultural-educational exchanges signed in April 2001, including thirty scholarships for Cuban students every year. "Sino-Cuban Relations." In addition to their symbolic value, cultural exchanges play an operational role through which China can maintain a tenuous, but nonthreatening, presence in the activities of various indigenous and marginalized groups and other currents of the Latin American left.

338. "Nonaligned Movement Facing New Challenges." *People's Daily Online*. Beijing, China. http://english.people.com.cn. September 16, 2006.

339. See, for example, Suisheng Zhao, 2006.

340. As an indication of China's recognition of Cuba's strategic value, it is interesting to note that China restored military relations with Cuba in 1984, far before the resumption of regular diplomatic contacts or significant economic interactions between the two nations. "Sino-Cuban Relations."

341. Ratliff (2006:1) called this the "mirror" relationship, whereby "the United States provides sophisticated military support for the island just off China's Coast, while China, partly in response, gives similar but much more limited support to Cuba."

342. "Sino-Cuba Relations."

343. American Foreign Policy Council, *China Reform Monitor*, no. 487. March 3, 2003. http://www.afpc.org/crm/crm487.shtml. See also Alfonso, 1999. Al Santoli, ed., "China, Russia Add New Biological Weapons; China's New Electronic Intel Bases in Cuba Threaten U.S." *China Reform Monitor*, no. 217. June 28, 1999. http://www.afpc.org/crm217.htm.

344. Wines, 2001.

345. At the same time, it is important not to overemphasize Cuba's strategic value; Cuba is not the only point of Chinese presence in the Caribbean. PRC peacekeepers currently serve in Haiti, and PRC trainers work with the Jamaican armed forces. "Senior Chinese Military Leader Highlights Friendly Ties with Jamaica." *People's Daily Online*. Beijing, China. http://english.people.com.cn. July 26, 2005. In addition, the Chinese company Hutchison Port Holdings constructed and currently operates a large container port in Freeport, the Bahamas. Moreover, in the unlikely event of overt hostilities between the United States and China, the aircraft, ships, and space-based assets of the PRC would likely prove much more survivable than well-known, fixed bases lying in close proximity to major US military installations.

346. Going back even further, the PRC Ministry of Foreign Affairs lists visits (between 2000 and 2003) by three Cuban military delegations to China and four Chinese delegations to Cuba as part of what it terms "important bilateral exchanges in the military field." See "Bilateral Relations."

347. "Castro Meets Senior Chinese Military Official." *People's Daily Online*. Beijing, China. http://english.people.com.cn. November 5, 2005.

348. "Senior PLA Official Meets Cuban Guests." *People's Daily Online.* Beijing, China. http://english.people.com.cn. April 17, 2006.

349. "Cuba Willing to Strengthen Military Cooperation with China: Raúl Castro." *People's Daily Online.* Beijing, China. http://english.people.com.cn. December 5, 2006.

350. Indeed, after the collapse of the Soviet Union and prior to the consolidation of power by Hugo Chávez in Venezuela, the PRC was one of the few remaining lifelines for the regime of Fidel Castro.

351. Ironically, much of the hard currency earned from the sales of primary products to China in recent years goes to purchase foodstuffs from the United States, which has been Cuba's largest agricultural supplier since 2003. "EEUU es la principal fuente de alimentos de los cubanos." *El Universal.* Caracas, Venezuela. http://www.eluniversal.com. March 27, 2007.

352. "China y Cuba apuestan por más comercio."

353. "China, Cuba Agree to Business Deals." *NewsMax.* http://archive. newsmax.com/archives/articles/2004/11/23/231742.shtml. November 24, 2004.

354. "China Grants Cuba Credit." *Jamaica Observer.* Kingston, Jamaica. http://www.jamaicaobserver.com. December 21, 2005.

355. "Presidente chino firma docena de acuerdos en su visita a Cuba."

356. "El presidente chino visita a Fidel Castro."

357. "Cuba, China Sign Trade, Economic Cooperation Agreement." *People's Daily Online.* Beijing, China. http://english.people.com.cn. March 28, 2007.

358. *China-Caribbean Economic and Trade Cooperation Forum 2005.* Official website. http://cncforumenglish.mofcom.gov.cn/2005/index.shtml.htm. Accessed December 17, 2007.

359. "Zeng Qinghong Attends China-Caribbean Economic and Trade Cooperation Forum and Delivers Speech." *Ministry of Foreign Affairs of the People's Republic of China.* Official website. http://www.fmprc.gov.cn/eng/zxxx/t183690.htm. February 3, 2005.

360. *China-Caribbean Economic and Trade Cooperation Forum 2007.* Official website. http://cncforumenglish.mofcom.gov.cn. Accessed September 11, 2007.

361. "Tiny Nation Roars: St. Lucia Denounced by China for Ties with Taiwan." *International Herald Tribune.* London, England. http://www.iht.com. May 1, 2007.

362. "Reversal by Tiny St. Lucia Angers China." *International Herald Tribune.* London, England. www.iht.com. May 2, 2007.

363. Thus, the ability of the Chinese Caribbean community to act as a base for the expansion of commercial ties between China and the region is relatively limited.

364. "The Hakka." *Caribbean Chinese Association.* Official website. http://www.caribbeanchinese.ca/index.html. Accessed December 17, 2007. See also Marcia Davidson, "Chinese in Jamaica." http://www.jamaicans.com/culture/intro/chineseja.shtml. March 30, 1998.

365. "Los chinos celebran Fiesta de la Luna." *Diario-Libre.* Santo Domingo, Dominican Republic. http://www.diariolibre.com. October 8, 2006. See also "La cara oriental de Santo Domingo." *Diario-Libre.* Santo Domingo, Dominican Republic. http://www.diariolibre.com. September 20, 2005.

366. "Alto funcionario chino visitará México, Venezuela, Surinam, Perú, y Samoa." See also "Senior Chinese Party Official Wraps Up Mexico Visit."

367. "Senior Chinese, Venezuelan Leaders Meet to Strengthen Bilateral Ties." *People's Daily Online.* Beijing, China. http://english.people.com.cn. January 12, 2007.

368. "Jamaica to Get $140 Million in Aid from China." *Jamaica Observer.* Kingston, Jamaica. http://www.jamaicaobserver.com. November 17, 2007.

369. Julian Richardson, "Jamaica Sure to Benefit from China's Growth, Say Local Execs." *Jamaica Observer*. Kingston, Jamaica. http://www.jamaicaobserver. com. August 23, 2006.

370. During bilateral talks between Jamaica and China in 2005, agreements were signed between China Minmetals and two Jamaican organizations, the Jamaica Bauxite Institute and Jamaica Bauxite Mining, Ltd., regarding cooperation in bauxite mining and alumina production. Ibid. See also "China Minmetals Sets New Record in Trade Volume in 2005." *People's Daily Online*. Beijing, China. http://english.people.com.cn. January 19, 2006.

371. Patrick Foster, "Coffee Mill in Talks for More Shops in China." *Jamaica Observer*. Kingston, Jamaica. http://www.jamaicaobserver.com. April 19, 2006.

372. "Total Import and Export Value by Country (Region) (2007/01–12)."

373. "China, Jamaica Rail Talks Back on Track."

374. "Barbados, China Looking at Joint Solar Venture." *Jamaica Observer*. Kingston, Jamaica. http://www.jamaicaobserver.com. December 14, 2007.

375. Ronald Saunders, "China Beckons: Caricom Should Respond." *Jamaica Observer*. Kingston, Jamaica. http://www.jamaicaobserver.com. December 14, 2007.

376. "Senior Chinese Military Leader Highlights Friendly Ties with Jamaica."

377. Charmaine N. Clarke, "Caribbean Association Formed in China." *Jamaica Observer*. Kingston, Jamaica. http://www.jamaicaobserver.com. April 11, 2007.

378. Saunders, December 14, 2007.

379. Ronald Saunders, "China and Taiwan Again." *Jamaica Observer*. Kingston, Jamaica. http://www.jamaicaobserver.com. May 13, 2007.

380. Erikson and Wander, "China: Cricket 'Champion.'" *Miami Herald*. http://www.miamiherald.com. April 28, 2007.

381. He Li, 2005, p. 82.

382. "El impacto chino en América Latina." *El Diario*. La Paz, Bolivia. http://eldiario.net. March 14, 2005. Because of the change, the government of Grenada was subsequently sued for $21 million by Export-Import Bank of Taiwan, based on a loan previously provided by Taiwan to the Grenadian government. Saunders, December 14, 2007.

383. The aid package was designed, in part, to help Grenada rebuild after the damage caused by Hurricane Ivan. "El impacto chino en América Latina."

384. "Taiwan Anthem Played for China Officials." *CBS News*. "Dominica and China Mark Second Anniversary of Diplomatic Relations." *Caribbean Net News*. http://www.caribbeannetnews.com/. March 24, 2006.

385. "Dominica and China Mark Second Anniversary of Diplomatic Relations." *Caribbean Net News*. http://www.caribbeannetnews.com/. March 24, 2006.

386. Mosher, 2006.

387. "China Targets Caribbean Trade." *CNN*. http://www.cnn.com/. February 19, 2005. See also "Freeport Container Port." Hutchison Port Holdings. Official website. http://www.hph.com.hk/. Accessed October 15, 2007.

388. "China Targets Caribbean Trade."

389. Saunders, December 14, 2007.

390. Shixue Jiang, 2008a, p. 37.

391. He Li, 2005, p. 82.

392. Ibid.

393. The PRC sought to renew the mandate of MINUSTAH for only three months. Ultimately, a compromise renewal period of eight months was agreed to.

394. Jubany and Poon, 2006.

395. "China, Latin America Forge Closer Links for Win-Win End (3)."

7
Considering
Latin America's Future

———————————◼———————————

CHINA'S RELATIONSHIP WITH LATIN AMERICA PROFOUNDLY impacts the region and the United States' relationship to the region. These impacts may be understood in terms of the dynamics of a complex, highly interconnected system. Although the Chinese government doubtlessly has strategic plans and goals with respect to Latin America, its actions also respond to each country's evolving conditions and to the opportunities and threats presented by those conditions. Similarly, governments, businesses, and other actors in Latin America operate and plan domestically based on the changing opportunities and threats presented by the PRC. The actions of each entity change the landscape of interactions for all the rest.

At a macro level, as well, virtually all government and commercial deals impact the calculations of other players and, thus, influence the events that follow. Costa Rica's diplomatic recognition of the PRC, for example, led to quid pro quo gestures by the Chinese to expand contacts with Costa Rican coffee growers and open up their markets to Costa Rican coffee. Although seemingly innocuous, that chain of events could help to determine whether Costa Rica, rather than Colombia or Ecuador, develops the market infrastructure to become the dominant actor in regional coffee exports to Asia. Similarly, a deal to construct a petroleum refinery in Costa Rica for exporting petroleum to China will impact the viability of a parallel refinery under study for Panama, with long-term implications concerning who gains the value added by the refining process and who gets the petroleum.

The emergence of centers or markets involving China can also be understood in complexity terms. Agreements between governments or corporations change the playing field and the calculations of other actors. Chinese purchases of products from a particular group of exporters, for example, may lead to increased commercial activity in the previously sleepy town where those goods were brought to market. The new activity, in turn, may draw in local producers to supply the market, opening the door for the emergence of secondary businesses, from hotels and restaurants to logistics and other services. Such commerce, and the increased revenue from it, may lead the national or local government to enhance roadways and other infrastructure. The area's growth may also have the effect of attracting other purchasers, Chinese and otherwise, and other suppliers, consolidating the emergence of that district as a major commercial hub.

In examining how the new patterns of commerce involving the PRC will unfold, physical infrastructure is also important. The successful realization of the Manta-Manaus-Belém corridor project, for example, could help make Ecuador the new point of access for Chinese commerce with the vast markets of Brazil. The new flow of goods through this corridor would then impact the viability of plans to upgrade other routes to the Brazilian market, such as the highway corridors connecting Brazil to the Peruvian ports of Paita and Ilo, or a range of other projects contemplated under the Initiative for the Integration of Regional Infrastructure (IIRSA), which have not yet been funded.

Just as the Manta-Manaus-Belém corridor would transform the port of Manta, prospective new highway routes connecting Brazil to the Peruvian ports of Paita and Ilo would transform the economy of the surrounding region, giving rise to a flood of secondary industries to provide logistical, transportation, security, packaging, and information technology services, and even restaurants and hotels to support the newly emergent Pacific commercial hub. The realization of one, or both, of these routes would create a viable alternative to the transport of goods overland to Brazil's east coast and their shipment across the Atlantic Ocean and around the Horn of Africa to China. Either project would, thus, have significant consequences for the development of Brazil's interior, including the growing industrial city of Manaus, as well as the trade throughput of Peru.

While it is important to recognize at the outset that many of the specific impacts of China on the region are contingent on and, in turn, affect other developments, it is possible to identify some long-term trends. And although one cannot know for a certainty the path that particular countries or projects will take as a consequence of their interactions with China, one may identify a number of developments:

1. Latin America's economic performance will increasingly be tied to the PRC.
2. Chinese communities and corporations will grow in significance in the domestic politics of Latin America.

3. Latin America will grow in consequence as a technology partner for the PRC.
4. The landscape of Latin American ports will be transformed, with new roles for previously low-volume ports and the expansion of existing deepwater ports on the Pacific coast.
5. Major Latin American cities in Pacific-facing countries will become hubs for companies and organizations doing business with China.
6. The expansion of commerce with China will bring fresh forms of interaction between Chinese and Latin American organized crime.
7. The United States will find its ability to conduct operations in the hemisphere such as counterdrug and law enforcement activities ever more constrained by the Chinese presence.
8. US military planners will, increasingly, have to take the Chinese presence into account, including planning for an expanded Chinese ability to collect information and disrupt US military operations in the hemisphere in the event of war.

■ Latin America's Economic Health Increasingly Tied to China

The commercial bonds between the PRC and Latin America are increasingly binding the economic health of Latin America to the economic performance of China, the actions of its government, and the behavior of its corporations. During the past fifteen years, China has evolved from a position of virtual irrelevance as a trading partner to one of the major suppliers and customers for many Latin American countries. In 2007, for example, China became the number one export customer for Chile[1] and the number two customer for Peru behind the United States.[2] The Asian giant continues to be among the top five partners in bilateral trade for Argentina, Brazil, and Mexico, among others. Even beyond direct trade relationships, the growing weight of China in the global economy impacts the region's economic performance through commodity prices. Because of the expanding portion of worldwide commodity markets represented by the PRC, Chinese actions in these markets are increasingly important in determining commodity prices and, thus, ultimately, the revenues and profits of Latin American commodity producers. As the global recession spread in 2008, a recurring theme in Latin America was how badly decreased Chinese demand for commodities would hurt the price and volume of Latin American exports.

For Chile, mining is the country's major export sector; copper represented $32 billion of $37 billion in Chilean mining exports in 2006. China is the world's largest importer of copper and the principal customer for

Chilean copper exports. Actions by the Chinese government to manage demand affect global copper prices and, thus, Chilean revenues.[3]

The impact of Chinese iron purchases on Brazil parallels the impact of China's copper demand on Chile. China is the world's largest iron importer;[4] its weight in the market was acknowledged in 2006, when, for the first time, a Chinese purchaser, Baosteel, took the lead in negotiating the supply price for iron ore with a Brazilian counterpart, Companhia Vale do Rio Doce (CVRD).[5] In the iron industry, the price agreed to in the lead negotiation, by tradition, becomes the standard for the rest of the industry, with significant impacts on the balance sheets of both producers and consumers.

The position of China with respect to Argentine soy exports resembles its position vis-à-vis copper in Chile and iron in Brazil. In 2006, the PRC was the primary export market for Argentine soy and for sunflower and other oilseed products, accounting for 73.2 percent of all Argentine exports of these goods.[6] The record value of the 2007 Argentine harvest, some $4 billion, was ascribed in part to high Chinese demand for these products.[7] In consequence of such interconnectedness, a decision in August 2007 by Chinese authorities to delay 150,000 tons of soy shipments over a phytosanitary issue caused significant financial damage to Argentina and led to a major trade dispute between the Argentine and Chinese governments.[8]

In the petroleum sector, Chinese demand, in combination with US oil imports,[9] played an important role in increasing international oil prices to more than $140 per barrel. High prices, in turn, have dramatically increased state revenues for such oil-producing countries in Latin America as Venezuela and Ecuador and have helped to sustain the populist politics of those countries even though, thus far, very little oil from these nations has been sold directly to China. Moreover, Chinese companies are increasingly important players in the ability of Venezuela and Ecuador to extract their oil wealth. In Venezuela, Chinese companies have a significant presence in mature oil fields (like Intercampo and Junin-4), as well as in the exploration and development of vast potential reserves in the Orinoco belt.[10] China's contribution of $8 billion in loans to Venezuela's Heavy Investment Fund played an important role in helping the Venezuelan government remain solvent. Chinese capital and companies will also be critical in the construction of a fleet of tankers to transport Venezuelan oil to China and in the construction of new refineries in China itself to process the unique, heavy form of Venezuelan oil found in Orinoco.[11] In Ecuador, China's $1.42 billion purchase of the oil fields and petroleum pipeline assets of the Canadian firm EnCana in 2006 to form the Andes Petroleum consortium[12] makes Andes one of the most important oil producers in the country, while Chinese companies are also positioned to play an important role in virtually all of the country's new petroleum products, from the new Ishpingo-Tambococha-Tiputini (ITT) oil fields[13] to the contemplated $6 billion refinery in Manabí.[14]

The weight of China as an investor in Latin America was also increased by the creation of a $200 billion sovereign wealth fund in September 2007, and the associated establishment of the China Investment Corporation to run it.[15] Although it is doubtful that the fund will be used for risky transactions, such as the purchase of mines and oil fields in Latin America, the sheer size of the fund creates a state of affairs in which decisions by Chinese fund managers could have significant influence in the valuation of Latin American assets across a range of commodity sectors. Indeed, the global financial crisis that began in 2008 has made China even more important as a source of investment and financial liquidity.

■ The Importance of Chinese Communities and Entities in Latin American Politics

The impact of China on Latin America is not limited to issues of economics. As China develops business and government relationships in the region, the influence of Chinese ethnic communities, businesses, and organizations in the Latin American political space will continue to grow. An increasing quantity of Chinese businesspeople, government representatives, academics, and others will travel to the region in the coming years. Chinese governmental organizations, corporations, and financial institutions will set up more representative offices in Latin America. Chinese tourism to Latin America will grow, as the PRC declares an expanding number of Latin American countries as "official tourist destinations," allowing its citizens to travel there. The addition of new direct flights and China-oriented tourist infrastructure in the region will further encourage Chinese to travel to Latin America for both tourism and business puposes. The number of Chinese corporations operating in Latin America will continue to rise, from CNPC and Sinopec, to ZTE and Huawei in the telecom sector, to Hutchison-Whampoa in logistics, to COSCO in shipping, to China Development Bank in finance; and from China Minmetals, Chinalco, and Baosteel, to Shougang and Shandong Luneng in mining, to Haier in consumer appliances. Signs of the increasing role of Chinese entities and ethnic Chinese communities in the Latin American political space can already be seen in a number of countries, in both positive and negative ways.

In Peru, the Chinese firm Shougang, which operates a mine near the southern town of Marcona, has been embroiled in labor disputes and battles with regulatory agencies since purchasing the mine from the Peruvian government in 1993. Shougang has experienced an average of one to two strikes a year, with four strikes in 2006 alone,[16] and has been repeatedly fined or publicly challenged by the government over alleged environmental abuses and failure to make promised investments in the mine.

Chinese companies in Latin America find themselves caught up in tax disputes with the government and in labor disputes with local workers. On the government front, for example, the Chinese company CNPC clashed with the Venezuelan government over $11 million in back taxes allegedly owed by the company.[17] In the labor domain, in May 2008, local workers in the Anaco gas project shut down the operation of twenty-seven out of thirty-seven CNPC drilling rigs in the zone in a protest over alleged violations of their work contract.[18]

Chinese petroleum companies operating in the remote jungle region in northeast Ecuador have become embroiled in multiple conflicts with indigenous groups and other activists. One cycle of conflict began in July 2007, producing thirty-one injuries over eight days of unrest in the department of Orellana, when protests against the Chinese oil firm Petroriental turned violent.[19] Violence resumed a month later, and involved peasants throwing dynamite at soldiers[20] and sabotage of the Petroriental pipeline near the town of Dayuma.[21] By November 2007, the government was forced to declare a state of emergency in the region. Nor were the outbreaks of violence in Orellana unprecedented. In a prior incident in November 2006, activists in Tarapoa had seized a Chinese-operated oil field, taking thirty hostages and forcing a significant reduction in production.[22]

In addition to Chinese corporations, Chinese ethnic communities across Latin America are increasingly becoming a topic of attention in local politics. In part, this is because these communities are linked to the expansion of commercial ties to the PRC, either through commerce or by association in the eyes of the surrounding community. In many cases, the goods sold by ethnic Chinese shopkeepers in local communities are the most tangible symbols of the expansion of Chinese imports into an area. Further, the Chinese community is often perceived as culturally and linguistically distinct from the surrounding community, reinforcing its association with new merchandise or services that compete with established businesses or otherwise threaten the status quo. One example in which such a combination gave rise to ethnic tensions is the highly publicized strike by a group of Argentine truck drivers against Chinese shop owners in June 2006, involving allegations that truck drivers had been badly treated by the shop owners,[23] but also reflecting tensions between Chinese shopkeepers and other sectors of Argentine society. As noted previously, in a much more serious incident, in November 2004, Chinese shopkeepers in the Venezuelan province of Carabobo were violently attacked by local mobs, and their stores broken into and looted, when they closed their stores in solidarity with a broader national strike against the regime of Hugo Chávez. The event prompted an urgent request by the Chinese embassy in Venezuela for the Venezuelan authorities to do more to ensure their safety.[24]

Although incidents such as those described in the previous paragraphs have thus far been relatively rare, they are likely to occur with more frequency in the coming years with the simultaneous growth of Chinese commerce and of Chinese Latino communities in the region.

■ Technology Partners

The PRC, commonly associated with cheap, low-quality goods, is seeking aggressively to expand the technological sophistication and diversity of its production base. Latin America is a logical partner in this endeavor for a number of reasons. First, bargain-hunting Latin American consumers make the region an attractive place for Chinese firms looking to enter a new sector on the basis of cost competition, then leveraging their position in the market to improve quality and efficiency. In addition to selling their manufactured goods in the region, the Chinese would like to develop production and development partnerships with Latin American firms to improve their own technical capabilities. In March 2007, Chinese investors from Ningbo expressed interest in jointly building an automotive industrial park in Aguascalientes, Mexico; their interest was based on a desire to work with their Mexican partner to improve Chinese automotive-production capabilities.[25] In another instance, one motive for the partnership between China Aircraft Industries Corporation (CAIC) II and the Brazilian aircraft maker Embraer was, arguably, to develop CAIC II's capabilities in support of China's strategic goal to manufacture large aircraft.[26] Likewise, the partnership between CNPC and the Brazilian state firm Petrobras was partly motivated by CNPC's desire to learn from Brazilians in areas such as deepwater drilling.[27]

An increasing number of projects in recent years have also involved cooperation between Latin American and Chinese entities in the space sector. China is part of the Asia-Pacific Space Cooperation Organization; it has signed space cooperation agreements with Argentina and Brazil, and exchanged personnel in the field with Peru and Chile.[28] Although the PRC's collaboration in this area has been principally with partners in the more developed countries of the Southern Cone, China has pursued an important joint venture with Venezuela in the development, launch, and operation of the Simón Bolívar satellite.[29] Sino–Latin American teamwork has emcompassed a range of projects, from the China-Brazil Earth Resource Satellite (CBERS) program, to work with Argentina's San Juan University on a laser-based satellite range-finder, to the PRC's efforts to participate in satellite projects with both Argentina and Chile.[30]

Another technology-cooperation arena with significant potential for expansion is nuclear power. In 2004, China expressed interest in teaming with the Argentine nuclear agency, CONEA, on the design and development of a medium-sized nuclear reactor that could be marketed to other Latin American countries.[31] Similarly, as Brazil and Argentina expand their nuclear power industry in the coming years, and as Chile explores the possibility of building nuclear power plants,[32] China has among the broadest and most current experience in designing and constructing new nuclear reactors.

Although much of China's technology collaboration is focused on the larger, more developed countries, such as Mexico, Brazil, Chile, and Argentina, this is not exclusively so. As noted previously, China has, for example, entered into a series of exchanges and medical technology agreements with Cuba, including the exchange of doctors and the development of gene technology capabilities.[33]

In a number of technology areas, such as aerospace, biotechnology, and nuclear power, the United States is likely to look nervously upon Chinese technology partnerships. In the aerospace domain, for example, some will question whether China's ultimate goal in partnering with Latin American firms is not simply a commercial one, but the advancement of military capabilities. In a world in which high technology is the defining element of weapon systems and of commercial competitiveness, separating Chinese motivations in seeking to acquire valuable technology capabilities is an impossible, if not meaningless, task. Whatever China's motivations, with the exception of companies that employ special US-licensed defense technologies, the United States probably can do little, contractually, to block technology partnerships between Latin America and the PRC. Nonetheless, the issue is almost certain to become a regular fixture of analysis and discussion for the US national security establishment as it follows China's evolving relationship with Latin America.

■ The Transformation of Latin American Ports

In addition to its other impacts, the growth of Latin America's commerce with China is driving an expansion and modernization of the Pacific port infrastructure that carries that commerce. As the commercial throughput between Latin America and Asia increases, established deepwater ports (as well as smaller facilities) in strategic locations are being transformed. Channels are being dredged. New loading cranes are being brought in. Roads and other infrastructure are being expanded. Logistics operations and service companies are emerging to leverage these fresh opportunities. The trend is driven by anticipated commercial openings and pragmatic efforts by governments and investors to resolve bottlenecks, and is likely to accelerate in the coming years.[34]

The transformation of the region's ports can be found along the entire length of Latin America's Pacific coastline. In Mexico, ports like Michoacán and Ensenada (where the Chinese firm Hutchison has a commercial presence) have benefited significantly from the country's expanding bilateral trade with Asia. Further to the south, the $5.25 billion project to expand the Panama Canal (to be completed in 2014) not only will transform Pacific port infrastructure in that country, but also will likely generate significant additional commerce in other ports by increasing the volume of traffic able to pass through the canal for other destinations.[35]

In Colombia, plans are under way to increase significantly the capabilities of the (previously dilapidated) port of Buenaventura, including addition of loading cranes, expansion of the port itself, dredging of the access channel to permit larger ships, and improvement of the highway leading into and out of the port.[36] These improvements promise to transform Buenaventura into a modern gateway for Colombia, oriented toward China and the rest of Asia. More distant projects under discussion, such as modernization of the port of Cupica, in Antioquia, suggest that the work in Buenaventura is only the beginning.

Moving south from Colombia to Ecuador, a consortium led by the Chinese firm Hutchison has been engaged in a project to expand the port of Manta and link it to the neighboring airport, which the Ecuadorian government wishes to transform into a new hub airport for flights between Asia and South America.[37] The possibility exists of linking the modernized port and airport to a new, multimodal transport corridor spanning the continent from Manta to Manaus, in Brazil, as well as to a new, international airport.

In Peru, virtually the entire Pacific port infrastructure is experiencing a boom. Peru's principal port, Callo, has seen an explosion of commerce, with throughput by weight increasing almost 29 percent from 2006 to 2008 alone, forcing Peru to open up part of the port area to a commercial concession to attract the $1.5 billion in improvements required just to keep up with demand.[38] Similarly, in Paita, the port that is the site of the northern route for the interoceanic highway, volume has doubled in the past decade.

In addition to such projects, interoceanic corridors being constructed from the Brazilian Amazon to the Peruvian ports of Parta and Ilo, and the proposed Tacna-to–Santa Cruz route, each contemplate a significant investment to expand and modernize what historically has been a relatively small port, with the ultimate aim of linking it to raw material markets in Brazil.[39] Additionally, the Peruvian port of Ilo has been mentioned as one of the possible beneficiaries of yet another contemplated interoceanic highway passing through the remote province of Madre de Dios[40] linking the Brazilian state of Mato Grosso to the Pacific.[41]

Like its northern neighbors, Chile is the focus of numerous contemplated infrastructure projects. As an example, the ports of Arica and Iquique, in the north, will be connected to the Brazilian port of Santos through a new, $600 million highway development announced in December 2007 by the presidents of Chile, Brazil, and Bolivia, to be completed by the first quarter of 2009.[42] This corridor could make the two ports more viable outlets for Brazilian and Argentine exports, as well as serving as points of entry for Chinese products destined for those markets. The port of Iquique is also the site of a booming free-trade zone that serves as a point of entry for products coming from Asia to a variety of South American markets.[43] Iquique has also been mentioned as part of an improved transit corridor connecting it to the Argentine province of Salta, while the Chilean port of Antofagasta is one element in a contemplated infrastructure improvement plan that would link it to the Argentine province of Mendoza and, from there, to the consumer market of the greater Buenos Aires region.[44]

For all of these Pacific coast ports, the expansion of throughput, the construction of new facilities, and the growth of supporting industries will create a range of challenges that will greatly tax the resources of local governments. Among other considerations, the expansion is likely to strain severely the existing infrastructures for water, electricity, police, fire, and other services. Furthermore, costly demands to support the new growth may, initially, increase more rapidly than local governments can fully realize compensating increases in tax receipts from port operations.[45]

The expansion of Pacific port cities is also likely to impact the economies throughout the countries in which they are located. The growth of jobs in port areas is likely to attract people from other parts of the country, creating "urban fringe" areas, with associated challenges for law enforcement, schools, hospitals, and other community services. As suggested previously, growth of the Chinese communities in these areas and the movement of ethnic Chinese into activities associated with the expanding Asian commerce are likely to exacerbate ethnic tensions, creating even more challenges for law enforcement and service providers, who must develop skills to deal with communities that may have a different culture and a different language than the majority population has.

In the political arena, the growth of Pacific port cities will create new interests and new players at both the local and national levels. Commercial entities operating in these areas, and generating significant revenue from their activities, are likely to seek infrastructure improvements or regulatory changes to improve the efficiency and profitability of their operations. National elites, however, may be hard-pressed to accommodate these demands, particularly if established coalitions perceive that they are divert-ing resources and influence away from traditional uses.[46]

■ Pacific-Facing Countries as Hubs for Commerce with Asia

In addition to the transformation of Pacific coast ports, the increasing vol-ume of commerce with Asia will dramatically impact major Latin American cities in Pacific-facing countries. Not all of these cities will benefit equally; it is likely that the biggest winners will be modern capital cities near the Pacific, such as, Santiago, Lima, and San José, with possible secondary development for other capital cities, like Managua, or major centers, like Guayaquil and Cali.

For each of these cities, it is likely that the synergy between govern-ment agencies, multinational corporations, and supporting technology, edu-cation, and service sectors will attract Chinese firms wishing to establish local headquarters for their operations in the region. The existence of estab-lished Chinese communities in cities like Lima, San José, and Guayaquil may complement the business case for locating corporate operations there, due to presence of Chinese speakers and a service industry familiar with Chinese culture and business practices. In a manner similar to the dynamics of port cities, the growth of a core of companies and organizations in these capital cities dedicated to commerce between China and Latin America, in turn, may give rise to such secondary industries as information technology, consulting services, legal services, language schools, and educational insti-tutions. The net effect will be to give a new economic vibrancy to these Latin American cities.

■ New Patterns for Organized Crime

An important dimension of the expanding ties between China and Latin America is the proliferation of governmental, commercial, and human inter-actions between the two. Unfortunately, these interactions are likely, as well, to create incentives and opportunities for a corresponding increase in criminal activity. Such expansion is likely to flow from several changes: growth of new commercial activities, such as trans-Pacific logistics and port operations, will generate fresh sources of revenue to be contested by Latin American and Chinese criminal organizations; fresh flows of people and goods will create opportunities to conduct illicit activities within the shad-ow of legitimate commerce; expansion of air and maritime traffic between the two regions,[47] for example, will spawn more opportunities for human trafficking and narcotics shipments; and expansion of banking ties between the two regions will lead to innovative infrastructures for money laundering and financial crime.

Preliminary indications of the new patterns of criminal activity are already beginning to emerge. Oscar Naranjo, head of the Colombian national police, for example, notes that increasing activity of Chinese mafias in narcotrafficking and in casinos and other gambling organizations in Colombia has "set off alarms." Among other examples, Naranjo points to the high-profile case of Zhenli Ye Gon, the Chinese pharmaceutical company that was producing precursor chemicals for synthetic drugs.[48] Several studies note activity by the Chinese organizations Fuk Ching, Flying Dragons, and Tai Chen, and by other Chinese criminal groups in the triborder area between Paraguay, Brazil, and Argentina.[49]

Another prominent dimension of the emerging criminal relationships between China and Latin America is the expansion of human trafficking. Countries in the Andean region and Central America form part of a transit zone for Chinese immigrants bound for the United States. Chinese immigrants are brought to Pacific-facing countries such as Colombia and Ecuador, where they are provided with false documents and smuggled overland through Central America, or transported by other means to the United States. The number of Chinese detained by authorities in Colombia and Ecuador has increased significantly, for example, since each eliminated visa requirements for persons traveling from China. Similarly, authorities in Costa Rica, Panama, and Colombia registered an increase of 2,500 percent in illegal Chinese immigration from 2005 to 2006.[50] In Costa Rica, which is part of the transit zone, an estimated 5,000 Chinese immigrants are illegally in the country.[51] In Bolivia in 2006, a scandal came to light involving the Chinese mafia organization Red Dragon. In the affair, 16 Bolivian congressmen and 12 former congressmen were accused of accepting bribes to help secure visas for prospective Chinese immigrants en route to the United States.[52]

Press accounts involving the detention of Chinese immigrants across Latin America are likewise becoming increasingly commonplace. In April 2007, for example, thirty-one Chinese immigrants were captured in the Venezuelan city of Puerto Ordaz and deported to Guyana.[53] During the same month, sixty-five Chinese immigrants were detained off the coast of Manta, Ecuador,[54] while another sixty-five were detained off the coast of Costa Rica.[55] In Bolivia, some twenty-five illegal Chinese immigrants were arrested in February 2007.[56]

The problem of illegal Chinese immigration is becoming so great that it is overwhelming the resources of local authorities. In Colombia, for example, some 180 Chinese remained in the country awaiting deportation, because the authorities lacked the funds to purchase plane tickets to return them to China.[57]

In general, it is likely that human smuggling and other activities by Chinese criminal organizations in Latin America will take advantage of the existence and relative isolation of Chinese Latin American communities to hide and provide temporary work and shelter to immigrants in transit, just as Chinese criminal organizations in the past have used flows of new Chinese immigrants and have thrived in the relative insularity of Chinese enclaves. Unfortunately, any association between Chinese communities and organized crime is likely to compound problems that exist between Chinese Latin Americans and surrounding communities.

As ties between China and Latin America expand, collaboration and competition between criminal organizations will evolve in difficult-to-predict ways.[58] It is possible that the entry of Chinese criminal organizations into Latin America will challenge the existing balance of power, and will give rise to novel forms of collaboration as well as power struggles between Chinese and Latin American criminal groups, from narcotraffickers, to guerillas, to maras and other groups. In each of these cases, one consequence is likely to be an increase in violence as power relationships are resolved. Even more worrisome is the possibility that collaboration between Chinese and Latin American criminal entities could involve terrorist organizations operating in areas such as the triborder region between Brazil, Argentina, and Paraguay. However, little concrete evidence has yet emerged of such three-way collaboration involving global terrorism. Whatever the ultimate outcome, the interactions between Chinese and Latin American criminal groups are likely to fuel police and security challenges that, in turn, will play a significant role in the agendas of local and national governments and, perhaps, in the discourse of those governments with the United States.

■ Increasing Constraints for US Operations in the Hemisphere

Growing ties between Latin America and the PRC not only will affect the region itself, but will also increasingly affect the US relationship to the region. One of the most striking examples of this phenomenon is the annual high-level consultation meetings between the United States and China regarding Latin America. The April 2006 visit to China by US deputy assistant secretary of state Tom Shannon was the first time that a major US State Department official had traveled to China to talk solely about Latin America;[59] this was an implicit recognition that the PRC has come to occupy a seat at the table with respect to regional affairs.[60] Subsequent meetings between Secretary of State Shannon and his Chinese counterparts took place in Washington, D.C., in 2007, and again in Beijing in 2008.

In the political realm, the impact of China is principally felt in two ways: through its existence as an alternative trading partner, ally, and source of capital, and through its influence on Latin America's willingness to cooperate with the United States. Cooperation with the United States ranges from participation in multinational initiatives, such as the Free Trade Area of the Americas, to the "Washington Consensus," which posits a Western-style model of free trade and fiscal responsibility as the path to development. Indeed, as noted in Chapter 3, for Latin Americans who do not wish to follow a US-style political or economic path, China ostensibly suggests an alternative model for how a country can achieve sustained economic development without political liberalization or adherence to human rights.

The effect of China as an "alternative" for Latin America also has shaped the region's willingness to cooperate with the United States in the security realm. When the US Congress passed the American Servicemen's Protection Act in 2002, demanding that nations receiving military assistance from the United States exempt US soldiers from compulsory criminal jurisdiction of the International Court of Justice, eleven countries in Latin America refused to comply[61] and were consequently cut off from participation in the International Military Education and Training (IMET) program.[62] The existence of China as another source of officer exchanges and professional military education undercut the punitive impact of the aid cutoff. A number of Latin American nations, including key US allies, such as Chile, began to expand military-to-military contacts with China, in part to compensate for programs with the United States that had been lost.[63] US military leaders, such as the then–commander of the US Southern Command, General Bantz Craddock, expressed concern over the loss of contact with a generation of Latin American officers, particularly in light of evidence that China and other countries were entering the vacuum created by the cutoff in US assistance.[64] In November 2004, key Latin American militaries were exempted from provisions of the act. In the end, thus, the availability of China as an alternative partner for Latin American militaries forced the United States to drop its demands and deal with the nations of the region on their terms.

■ The Impact of China's Presence on US Agencies

In addition to the impact of China as an alternative ally and commercial partner for Latin America, the physical presence of the PRC in the hemisphere presents a number of challenges, both for US organizations and agencies that work in the hemisphere and for those groups whose job is to plan for a broad range of military contingencies.

In the domain of counternarcotics operations and other actions against organized crime, US agencies such as the Drug Enforcement Administration (DEA) and the Federal Bureau of Investigation (FBI) cooperating with their counterparts in Latin America must take into account PRC business personnel and companies. This work includes following money trails that lead to Chinese corporations and financial institutions. While it is possible to pursue investigations in Chinese communities in Latin America and to secure the cooperation of Chinese banks and companies in reviewing financial records, the combination of linguistic differences, mistrust, and other factors can seriously hamper the process.

The Chinese involvement in Latin America, furthermore, presents US military planners with a range of difficult considerations and challenges, should the United States and the PRC ever go to war. While a conflict with China is neither desirable nor inevitable, as the PRC emerges as a global power, US military planners must consider the possibility of such a conflict and how it might play out.[65]

First, through their presence in the hemisphere, the Chinese have ongoing opportunities to gain insights into US military capabilities, doctrine, and training. At the strategic and operational levels, such insights are accrued as officers from China and from Latin American nations participate in exchanges with each other's militaries. At the tactical level, the PRC gains information from training programs or intelligence-sharing relationships that Latin American countries may have had previously with the United States. When Venezuela expelled US Special Operations Forces (SOF) trainers from the country after the failed attempt to oust the government of Hugo Chávez in April 2002, for example, the Venezuelans immediately brought in Chinese military trainers to replace the US ones. The new trainers were able to observe Venezuelan soldiers closely, and thus to understand the content and effectiveness of their US training.

In addition to general opportunities to learn US doctrine and tactics, the Chinese political and commercial presence in the region proliferates opportunities for the PRC to collect information on, and potentially disrupt, US forces or interests. In December 2007, seventy Chinese with improper visas were detained by Brazilian authorities in the São Paulo headquarters of the Chinese telecom company Huawei.[66] Although the event did not necessarily involve espionage, it illustrates how the growing Chinese commercial infrastructure in the region immensely simplifies challenges of cover, logistics, and resources for Chinese intelligence or military personnel who wish to operate in the hemisphere.[67]

The Chinese presence in Latin America is also significant to the United States in military terms because, in the undesirable event of a global war, the Western Hemisphere remains important to the United States. In the preparations for a major conflict, logistics and support operations will be conducted at US ports and associated military bases and supply facilities. In this context, the facilities that the Chinese are believed to operate near the US mainland, including those in Bejucal, Lourdes, and possibly Santiago, Cuba, are potentially useful sites for collecting intelligence on the activity of US forces. Similarly, the commercial container facility operated by the Chinese firm Hutchison on Grand Bahama Island, just sixty-five miles off the Florida coast,[68] is attractive real estate for launching and recovering covert Chinese intelligence-collection and intelligence-disruption operations. In order to be close to US customers, new Chinese factories in the Mexican maquiladora sector may be located close to the US border and US military facilities, such as naval bases in San Diego. Similarly, the infrastructure of Chinese companies operating in the Panama Canal zone, such as the China Overseas Shipping Company (COSCO) and Hutchison-Whampoa could be used by China to identify US warships, submarines, and other forces passing from the Atlantic to the Pacific during the run-up to a conflict.

In contrast to the strategic situation at the end of the twentieth century, the growing Chinese presence in Latin America implies that the Western Hemisphere cannot be considered a US sanctuary in a future conflict with the PRC and that the United States will be forced to devote significant resources to protecting its operations there, as well as in the Asian theater of operations.

■ The Issue of Comparative Advantage Revisited

The interactions between China and Latin America touched upon in this book suggest that, in the current global context, comparative advantage, driven by the logic of profit and return on investment, is a powerful dynamic that is accelerating Latin America's increasing specialization in primary products and agricultural goods, while the PRC leverages its manufacturing edge.

The cases examined by this book suggest that comparative advantage has produced important benefits for Latin American economies in the short term: high commodity prices and increased demand for goods have created record profits for the region's primary-products and agricultural industries, and likewise generated a flow of new capital into those sectors to expand their capacity.[69] We have seen that specialization achieved by comparative advantage is not a preexisting condition, but is produced by competition, either fair or unfair, that accompanies the new trade relationship—in which the gains of the winners and the more diffuse benefits to society are attained through the destruction of existing businesses and the displacement of existing workers.

Comparative advantage is a dynamic phenomenon that must be evaluated, in part, by the effects incurred by pursuing it. While, in the short term,

Latin America may have a comparative advantage in primary products, for example, with the PRC having a comparative advantage in manufacturing, the value added to primary-product industries, and the proportion of that added value flowing to the workers, tend to be lower over the long term than those for manufacturing. In short, while such a pattern may produce more wealth and optimize the allocation of resources globally, it will do so, in part, by propagating income inequality and a lack of well-paying jobs throughout Latin America.[70] Moreover, as Francisco González has pointed out, while some Latin American countries are currently reaping benefits from the commodity boom produced by Chinese demand, China's deliberate effort to move up the value-added chain into manufacturing and high technology implies that this demand and its benefits may not be lasting.[71] Finally, as demonstrated by the global recession that began in 2008, Chinese demand alone is not sufficient to maintain high global commodity prices; countries whose economies depend too much on commodity exports may find themselves vulnerable when global commodity prices fall.

The cases discussed in this book suggest that such considerations as free-trade agreements, political orientation, and government and business infrastructures help to shape in what sectors, and in what forms, the dynamics of comparative advantage are realized. An empirical study by the World Bank found a correlation between competition between Chinese and locally manufactured goods and a tendency to pass legislation to protect local markets.[72]

Further, Chinese initiatives to move up the manufacturing value-added chain into such sectors as computers, cars, and aircraft, while Latin America undergoes a process of progressive deindustrialization, illustrate that comparative advantage is a dynamic process whose evolution is virtually always shaped by political and social actors in the nations involved. As Robert Devlin notes, it may be useful to interpret China's economic surge as a wake-up call for Latin America to diversify and upgrade its exports so as to achieve "growth, economic development, and poverty reduction in an era of globalization."[73]

Finally, Chinese initiatives to build final-assembly facilities in places like the maquiladora sector of Mexico illustrate that regulatory structures (e.g., trade agreements), as well as intangible considerations (e.g., differential access to intellectual property in different countries), complement production costs in understanding the complexities of comparative advantage.

Unfortunately, the implications of the comparative advantage model for Latin America are no more promising now than they were when US purchases of the region's primary products drove the dynamics of comparative advantage a half century ago. Then, as now, economies specializing in primary-product exports have suffered when global conditions change, causing a fall in the demand for the commodities being exported, as well as a corresponding fall in their prices. Moreover, then, as now, the actor with the comparative advantage in manufacturing proved much more adept than its Latin American counterpart in leveraging that advantage to increase the value generated by the economic activities of the society as a whole. Today, as then, in some cases the windfall from Latin America's primary-product export boom is flowing into the hands of large private or commercial interests, augmenting the traditional problem of inequality suffered by the region. In other cases, the windfall is being captured by populist regimes, none of which have yet demonstrated the ability to use those resources in an efficient manner to transform their societies in a way that generates more wealth for all.

It is undeniable that current market dynamics are helping to fuel the growth of new infrastructures, including the expansion of Pacific ports, power facilities, gas lines, and rail and highway connections; these dynamics are lowering transaction costs and making it more economically attractive for actors in the region to take part in dealings that will generate value. However, only a limited amount of new infrastructure investment is coming from the Chinese themselves. Growing Chinese ownership of the means of production in key sectors, from mining to petroleum to agriculture, suggests that one consequence of this investment is that, as also happened a half century ago, the goods themselves will flow out of the region, while very little of the associated value added generated by transactions will be realized by the companies or the people of Latin America.

Finally, the economic displacements in Latin American manufacturing and the political responses to Chinese companies and to Chinese Latin American communities touched upon by this book serve as reminders that the economic processes shaped by comparative advantage have powerful social repercussions that can also affect nations' prospects for development.

■ Conclusion

During more than four years of closely following Latin America's unfolding relationship with China, I have been repeatedly struck by the impression that the mixture of illusions, plans, hopes, and fears that arise out of that relationship are as powerful in their impact on the region as are the deals and events themselves. The region's growing commercial and political relationship with China is changing realities for Latin Americans, but, perhaps more important for a region that celebrates the magical realism of Gabriel García Márquez and the romanticized revolutionism of Ché Guevara, the greatest impact of China will come from what it leads the region to dream, and what Latin America finds when it awakens.

China's engagement with Latin America generates a complex mixture of opportunities and threats for the region's countries as well as for the United States. In states such as Venezuela and Ecuador, Chinese commodity purchases and investments help to sustain the viability of regimes pursuing antimarket, anti–United States agendas, even while the policy volatility and administrative inefficiency of those same regimes privately frustrate and concern the Chinese. In other nations, such as Chile, Peru, and Costa Rica, commerce with the PRC contributes to the success of regimes pursuing policies that leverage market mechanisms, respect contracts and private property, and reinforce existing institutions and democratic processes.

Scholars such as Cynthia Watson argue that distance and cultural barriers may limit how quickly the ties develop between the PRC and Latin America;[74] what is clear, however, is that engagement with China is transforming the region. Competition from China is putting some local manufacturers and artisans out of business, even while consumers are benefiting from cheaper goods, allowing them, in some cases, to buy such products as appliances, motorcycles, and cars that were otherwise out of their reach. New globalized production operations and supply chains are also emerging in which Latin America plays an important role as a partner to China. In most of the region, primary-product sectors are expanding, driven by a sustained period of high demand and high prices. What is not clear, however, is the long-term impact of this boom on income inequality, given that such industries usually reward those who own the land and capital. The long-term effect on corruption is also unclear, since primary-product industries such as petroleum and mining generally involve large state-owned companies or bureaucracies that decide which interests have access to the country's mineral wealth. Perhaps most importantly, the impact of China on the ability of the region to achieve sustainable growth with fair wages is equally unclear. China is currently moving into higher value–added sectors, such as the production of autos and computers, raising questions as to what avenues will remain open to Latin American countries to achieve economic diversity and well-paid employment in the years to come.

Opportunities exist for the United States and the PRC to collaborate on shared interests that also serve the interests of Latin America. For both the United States and the PRC, for example, the region is a valuable supplier and an important customer. Although China's sales to and purchases from the region differ somewhat from those of the United States, both countries have a vested interest in the region's continuing stability and the functioning of its commercial infrastructure. In this context, they have a shared interest in working with Latin American countries to overcome political crises and maintain a secure environment for commerce; doing so includes assisting nations in the control of crime and other forms of violence and in the improvement of institutions and bureaucracies. Such assistance also logically extends to working with nations of the region to help them strengthen predictability and efficiency in the administration and enforcement of contracts and property rights.

In his visit to China in April 2006, Assistant Secretary of State Tom Shannon discussed the shared interests of China and the United States in Latin America, as well as the creation of mechanisms for more effectively pursuing these interests together and for avoiding sources of misunderstanding.[75] Two outcomes of the Shannon visit were a plan for a regular series of coordinating meetings between China and the United States to discuss Latin America, and the establishment of institutional mechanisms to exchange data on topics of interest in the region.[76] It will be important in the coming years for the United States and China to continue to build on the process initiated by that visit, including better delineating their shared interests in Latin America and specifically how to advance them, in coordination with individual nations and multilateral institutions in the region. Maintaining this process after the upcoming political change in the United States and through the eventual leadership succession in China will also be challenging.

Perhaps most importantly, however, both the United States and China must avoid encouraging political change or administrative actions in any country that benefit the commercial interests of one party over another but ultimately undermine the stability, institutional health, and economic performance of the region as a whole. In Venezuela, for example, the policies of the Chávez regime have been beneficial to Chinese companies in the short term, but have also given rise to a cycle of unpredictability, particularism, and administrative inefficiency that may ultimately render the country incapable of having a productive commercial relationship with any party. But, lest anyone derive a sense of moral superiority from such an outcome, it is important to recall the previous situation, in which Western companies had legally, financially, and administratively achieved a lock on the resources of such countries as Venezuela and Ecuador, paved the way for the current state of affairs of anticapitalistic pronouncements by, and administrative chaos in, certain nations.

In addition to improving coordination with the PRC in the region, the United States will be well served to increase substantially its engagements with the individual nations of Latin America, to help them to bolster their ability to secure solid commercial deals with China on equitable terms. The "institution-building" approach that the United States has used in other areas, such as counternarcotics programs, can be similarly applied to help countries in the negotiation of free-trade agreements with China and in planning major infrastructure projects. Similarly, the United States can work with Latin American governments and multilateral institutions to build or strengthen programs that leverage revenues from expanded primary-product sales and apply them in a way that positions the region to develop sustainable, competitive industries. In this fashion, the United States can begin to build new forms of partnership with Latin America, in which all players collaborate to realize the opportunities offered by expanded commerce with China, while mitigating the tensions, social dislocations, and sources of misunderstanding that such interactions generate.

▧ Notes

1. Eduardo Olivares. "China es mayor destino de exportaciones tras el TLC." *El Mercurio.* Santiago, Chile. http://diario.elmercurio.com. April 18, 2007.
2. "Exportación a Estados Unidos pierde ritmo." *El Comercio.* Lima, Peru. September 26, 2007, p. B2.
3. Sociedad Nacional de Mineria, "Principales Exportaciones Mineras (2006–2007)." *Portal Minera Sonami.* http://www.portalsonami.cl/01_exportaciones_mensual.htm. Accessed December 7, 2007. In the numerous articles about copper that appear in the Chilean financial press, fluctuations in the international copper price are routinely tied to ongoing Chinese decisions about where and how much copper to purchase to meet its domestic demand. See, for example, Daniel Hynes, "Las existencias de cobre volverán a subir." *Diario Financiero.* Santiago, Chile. http://www.df.cl. November 30, 2007. See also "Cobre enfrenta scenario de nuevos y graduals decensos." *Diario Financiero.* Santiago, Chile. http://www.df.cl. November 26, 2007. See also Paula Carrasco S., "Cobre baja de los US$3 dispués de ocho meses y tipo de cambio se dispara." *Diario Financiero.* Santiago, Chile. http://www.df.cl. November 22, 2007.
4. "China podría agotar su minas de oro en seis años." *Diario Financiero.* Santiago, Chile. http://www.df.cl. December 7, 2007.
5. In previous years, Japanese steelmakers, because of their dominant market position, had played this lead role. For the industry to accept Baosteel as leader in its negotiation with its Brazilian counterpart, CVRD, illustrated the new influence that the Chinese have in the global steel industry, as consumers of some 38 percent of the world's rolled steel.
6. "China, principal comprador de oleaginosas argentinas." *Diario El Dia.* La Plata, Argentina. http://www.eldia.com.ar. July 10, 2007.
7. Matías Longoni. "Otra récord para la soja y el trigo: La cosecha vale US$4.000 milliones más." *Clarín.* Buenos Aires, Argentina. http://www.clarin.com. August 31, 2007.
8. "Bajan el tono a la controversia comercial con China." *La Nacion.* Buenos Aires, Argentina. http://www.lanacion.com.ar. August 29, 2007. Similarly, an action by the PRC in 2004, blocking twenty-three Brazilian companies from exporting soy products to China for two months, caused an estimated $1 billion in losses for the Brazilian soy industry. Luis Waldmann, "Brazil: China Lifts Soy Ban." *Brazzil Magazine.* http://www.brazzil.com. June 2004.
9. Chinese petroleum imports are projected to rise from 1.5 million barrels per day in 2000 to 9.4 million barrels per day in 2025, at the same time that US imports are projected to rise from 10.85 million barrels per day to 19.70 million barrels per day. Toro Hardy, "Petróleo: Estados Unidos, China, y Venezuela." *El Universal.* Caracas, Venezuela. http://www.eluniversal.com. September 29, 2005.
10. "Venezuela Looks to Tar Deposits to Supply Surging Global Energy Needs." *Latin Petroleum Magazine.* www.latinpetroleum.com. May 30, 2006.
11. "Venezuela y China concretan acuerdos para impulsar integración estratégica." *El Universal.* Caracas, Venezuela. http://www.eluniversal.com. March 26, 2007.

12. "China CNPC preocupada e interesada por Ecuador." *El Universal.* Caracas, Venezuela. http://www.eluniversal.com. June 1, 2006.

13. The area, referred to as the ITT blocks, will require $3 to $5 billion in investments to develop if the government decides to go ahead with the project, which includes activities in environmentally sensitive areas designated as Yasuni National Park. See "Empresas de once países están interesadas en explotar el ITT." *El Comercio.* Quito, Ecuador. http://www.elcomercio.com. April 13, 2007; and "PdVSA Estudia Asociaciones con Ecuador en yacimientos de ITT." *El Universal.* Caracas, Venezuela. http://www.eluniversal.com. April 17, 2007.

14. "Sinopec y Petroecuador firman acuerdo para explotar el yacimiento Ishpingo-Tambococha-Tiputini." *El Comercio.* Quito, Ecuador. http://www. elcomercio.com. March 26, 2007.

15. The fund was initially capitalized with an unprecedented $200 billion from Chinese foreign-exchange reserves, with the mission to identify opportunities for new Chinese investments. "China reducirá reservas en dólares y tambalea la divisa estadounidense." *Diario Financiero.* Santiago, Chile. http://www.df.cl. November 8, 2007.

16. Emmott, 2005.

17. Peter Millard, "Venezuela Tax Office Fines CNPC $11 M in Industry Audit." *Wall Street Journal.* http://www.wsjonline.com/americas. September 7, 2006.

18. "Conflicto laboral amenaza proyecto de gas en Anaco." *El Universal.* Caracas, Venezuela. http://www.eluniversal.com. May 22, 2008.

19. "Protestas contra Petroriental dejan 31 heridas en ocho días." *El Comercio.* Quito, Ecuador. http://www.elcomercio.com. July 4, 2007.

20. "Campesinos armados de Ecuador buscan paralizar actividad de petrolera china." *El Universal.* Caracas, Venezuela. http://www.eluniversal.com. July 23, 2007.

21. "Petroriental denuncia atentado en oleoducto en China." *El Universal.* Caracas, Venezuela. http://www.eluniversal.com. July 21, 2007.

22. In the incident, indigenous activists seized control of an oil field operated by the Chinese-controlled consortium Andes Petroleum. The activists took some 30 Chinese oil field workers hostage, shut down power, and caused output from the field to fall from 42,000 to 14,000 barrels per day during the occupation. "Petrolera china dice que incidents en Amazonia no afectarán sus intereses en Latinoamérica." *El Comercio.* Quito, Ecuador. http://www.elcomercio.com. November 14, 2006. See also Juliette Kerr, "Protests Against Chinese Company's Oil Operations End in Ecuador." *Global Insight Daily Analysis.* http://www.uofaweb.ualberta.ca/ chinainstitute/. November 13, 2006.

23. "Los camioneros ratifican el boicot a los súper y autoservicios chinos." *Clarín.* Buenos Aires, Argentina. http://www.clarin.com. June 26, 2006.

24. Yolanda Ojeda Reyes, "Ciudanos chinos reciben protección." *El Universal.* Caracas, Venezuela. http://www.eluniversal.com. November 11, 2004.

25. "El governador se reunió con inversionistas de Ningbo provincia de la República China." *El Sol del Centro.* Aguascalientes, Mexico. April 10, 2007. See also "Manifestan empresarios chinos interés por Aguascalientes." *El Sol de Mexico.* Mexico City, Mexico. http:www.oem.com.mx/elsoldemexico/. April 10, 2007.

26. "Chinese Military Company Delivers 144 Planes in 2005." *People's Daily Online.* Beijing, China. http://english.people.com.cn. January 11, 2006.

27. "Brazil's Petrobras Eyes Partnerships with Chinese Oil Firms." *Xinhua.* http://www.uofaweb.ualberta.ca/chinainstitute/. September 10, 2006.

28. "China Signs 16 Int'l Space Cooperation Agreements, Memorandums in Five Years." *People's Daily Online*. Beijing, China. http://english.people.com.cn. October 12, 2006.

29. Alfonso Daniels, "Venezuela Joins Space Club Nations." *BBC Radio World Service*. http://news.bbc.co.uk/1/hi/world/americas/7697130.stm. October 29, 2008.

30. Patricio González Cabrera, "Defensa sondea 25 empresas para construir el nuevo satélite chileno." *El Mercurio*. Santiago, Chile. http://diario.elmercurio.com. April 18, 2007.

31. "Argentina explora cooperación con China en material nuclear." *El Universal*. Caracas, Venezuela. http://www.eluniversal.com. October 23, 2004.

32. Andrea Henriquez, "¿Chile Nuclear?" *BBC Mundo*. http://news.bbc.co.uk/hi/spanish/latin_america/newsid_7119000/7119847.stm. November 19, 2007. See also "REFILE-Chile's Nuclear Decision to Take Years." *Reuters*. http://www.alertnet.org/thenews/newsdesk/N25388579.htm. September 25, 2007.

33. "Ampliarán Cuba y China colaboración en biotecnología." *Granma*. Havana, Cuba. http://www.granma.cu/ February 12, 2006.

34. Although much of the commercial demand and capital transforming Latin America's Pacific ports will come from China, some will also come from India, Japan, and other Asian nations, which are also likely to expand their commerce with Latin America during this period.

35. "Panama Canal: A Key Latin American Project for Asia." *Latin America–Asia Review*. July 2006. p. 2.

36. Written correspondence with Pablo Echavarría Toro, former Colombian ambassador to the People's Republic of China. November 16, 2008.

37. "Ecuador ofrece a China el aeropuerto de Manta." *El Comercio*. Quito, Ecuador. http://www.elcomercio.com/solo_texto_search.asp?id_noticia=100599&anio=2007&mes=11&dia=30. November 30, 2007.

38. Chauvin, 2006, p. 32.

39. "Congress Passes Bill to Build Tacna Megaport—Bolivia, Peru." *Business News Americas*. http://www.bnamericas.com. February 27, 2006.

40. Part of the perceived benefit of such a route would be to increase the reliability of commercial flows between Brazil and nations of the Pacific by circumventing Bolivia entirely, thus avoiding roads or rail lines that could be blocked during (the frequent) periods of political unrest in Bolivia. Sources interviewed for this book suggested, however, that the viability of the project is unclear, due to a lack of funds by the Peruvian government to invest in a route through the Andes and the unwillingness of Brazil to invest in a major infrastructure project in Peru.

41. The Peruvian cities of Matarani and Marcona have also been mentioned as part of this corridor. See Guthrie and Preston, 2007.

42. Vaca, 2007. See also "Empresas chinas quieren invertir en corredor bioceánico Chile-Brasil." *Diario Financiero*. Santiago, Chile. http://www.df.cl. November 6, 2006.

43. "What Is ZOFRI?" Official website of the Zona Franca de Iquique S.A. http://www.zofri.com/info_corporativa/i_index.html. Accessed December 30, 2008.

44. Interview with Ernesto Fernandez Taboda, executive director of the Sino-Argentine Chamber of Production, Industry, and Commerce. Buenos Aires. November 7, 2007.

45. The creation of free-trade zones and other incentives to attract investment in these port complexes is likely to complicate matters further by, in the short term, lowering rents collected from the new tenants.

46. In some, but not all, cases, these coalitions are also likely to be politically

left of center, encompassing important social sectors, like organized labor, thus making it even more difficult politically to increase resources flowing to corporations and new elites in prosperous urban areas.

47. See, for example, the October 2006 announcement by Mexico City mayor Marcielo Ebrard that his government was working with his counterpart in China to establish direct flights between Mexico City and Beijing. "Anuncia Ebrard inversión china." *El Economista.* Mexico City, Mexico. http://www.eleconomista.com.mx. October 24, 2007.

48. "Denuncian mafias en América Latina." *El Universal.* Caracas, Venezuela. http://www.eluniversal.com. August 1, 2007.

49. See Tokatlian, 2008, p. 88; Hudson, 2003; Kenny, 2006.

50. José Meléndez, "La mafia china aumenta el tráfico de personas en AL." *El Universal.* Mexico City, Mexico. http://www.eluniversal.com.mx. May 10, 2007.

51. Interview with Ana Duran Salvatierra, vice minister of government and police, San José, Costa Rica, January 24, 2008. According to one estimate, approximately 5,000 undocumented Chinese immigrants are believed to be in Costa Rica.

52. "Con trabajo en equipo se destapó el caso de las visas." *La Razón.* La Paz, Bolivia. http://www.la-razon.com. December 13, 2006.

53. Sailú Urribarrí Núñez, "Desmantelan banda que traía ilegalmente chinos." *El Universal.* Caracas, Venezuela. http://www.eluniversal.com. April 20, 2007.

54. "Los emigrantes chinos, con rumbo al Perú." *El Comercio.* Guayaquil, Ecuador. http://www.elcomercio.com. April 18, 2007.

55. "Llegan a costa costarricense 61 inmigrantes dejados a la deriva." *Nacion.* San José, Costa Rica. http://www.nacion.com. April 23, 2007.

56. "Descubren asiáticos con estadía irregular en el país." *Los Tiempos.* Cochabamba, Bolivia. http://www.lostiempos.com. February 2, 2007.

57. "Otro grupo de chinos trató de utilizar a Colombia como trampolín para llegar ilegalmente a E.U." *El Tiempo.* Bogotá, Colombia. http://www.eltiempo.com. May 11, 2007.

58. Currently, some analysts speculate that the PRC government itself has restrained the triads and other Chinese criminal organizations from more aggressively entering Latin America, in order to avoid offending diplomatic sensitivities.

59. Luis Ramirez, "US Watching China's Growing Influence in Latin America." *VOA News.* http://www.voanews.com. April 19, 2006.

60. "China y EEUU abordan diálogo estratégico sobre Latinoamérica." *El Universal.* Caracas, Venezuela. http://www.eluniversal.com. April 11, 2006. See also "EE.UU y China hablan de A. Latina." *BBC Mundo.* Washington, DC. http://www.bbcmundo.com. April 14, 2006.

61. Chirinos, 2006.

62. Gertz, 2006.

63. "China Training Latin American Military, Says U.S. General." *CNN.* http://www.cnn.com. March 14, 2006.

64. Gertz, 2006.

65. As Tokatlian argues, "[T]he substantive issues of most concern to Latin America require cooperative approaches," 2008, p. 79.

66. "Police Raid Huawei Offices in Brazil." *Light Reading.* http://www.lightreading.com/document.asp?doc_id=140867. December 7, 2007.

67. In contemplating the chance that China could use its corporate presence in Latin America against the United States in time of war, the key consideration is not whether Chinese firms with a commercial presence in Latin America (such as Hutchison, Huawei, and ZTE) are under the operational control of the People's

Liberation Army. What is most salient is that companies with headquarters in China, including Shanghai and Hong Kong, as well as Beijing, are far easier for the Chinese government to work with than companies without such ties. Executives of these companies may share a common language and be accessible through personal or institutional ties; moreover, by contrast to other companies, Chinese companies based in or having a significant operating presence in the PRC may be more susceptible to regulatory and other forms of pressure from the Chinese government. Beyond pressure, in times of war, even the bonds of Chinese patriotism may play a role.

68. "Freeport Container Port." Hutchison Port Holdings. Official website. http://www.hph.com.hk/business/ports/america/bahamas.htm. Accessed October 15, 2007.

69. See González, 2008.

70. Colburn, 2008.

71. González, 2008, p. 163.

72. Facchini, Olearreaga, Silva, and Willman, 2007.

73. Devlin, 2008, p. 123.

74. Watson, 2008, p. 69.

75. "China y EEUU abordan diálogo estratégico sobre Latinoamérica."

76. Ibid. See also "EE.UU y China hablan de A. Latina."

Bibliography

Agostin, Manuel R., Pablo Rodas Martini, and Neantra Saavedra-Rivanro. "The Emergence of China: A View from Central America." *Inter-American Development Bank*. Economic and Sector Study Series. Document No. RE2-04-006. October 2004.

Agüero, Mercedes R. "Agroindustria y turismo con mayor opción en China." *Nacion*. San José, Costa Rica. http://www.nacion.com. October 24, 2007.

Alfonso, Pablo. "China Installs Two Communication Bases in Cuba." *El Nuevo Herald*. Miami, Florida. June 24, 1999.

"Alto funcionario chino visitará México, Venezuela, Surinam, Perú, y Samoa." *El Universal*. Caracas, Venezuela. http://www.eluniversal.com. March 12, 2007.

Álvarez Araya, Óscar. "En el siglo del Pacífico." *Nacion*. San José, Costa Rica. http://www.nacion.com. April 3, 2006.

Alvaro, Mercedes. "Ecuador's President Seeks Stronger Ties with China." Dow Jones Emerging Markets Report. http://www.uofaweb.ualberta.ca/chinainstitute/. March 29, 2007.

"Anuncia Ebrard inversión china." *El Economista*. Mexico City, Mexico. http://www.eleconomista.com.mx. October 24, 2007.

"Argentina explora cooperación con China en material nuclear." *El Universal*. Caracas, Venezuela. http://www.eluniversal.com. October 23, 2004.

Arostegui, Martin. "Chávez: Venezuela to Launch Defense Satellite." *Washington Times*. Washington, DC. http://www.washingtontimes.com. September 12, 2007.

Arriagada, Genaro. "Petropolitics in Latin America: A Review of Energy Policy and Regional Relations." Andean Working Paper. Washington DC: Inter-American Dialogue, December 2006, p. 11.

Artaza, Mario Ignacio. "Hay oro en aquellas colinas." *Biblioteca del Congreso Nacional del Chile*. http://asiapacifico.bcn.cl/columnas/hay-oro-en-aquellas-colinas. December 3, 2007a.

———. "No estamos de brazos cruzados con China." *Biblioteca del Congreso Nacional del Chile*. http://asiapacifico.bcn.cl/columnas/no-estamos-de-brazos-cruzados-con-china. December 28, 2007b.

———. "Noviembre se escribe C-H-I-N-A." *El Mostrador*. November 2, 2007c.

———. "Vámosnos al Chancho con China." *CHICIT*. October 2007d.

"Bachelet inaugura primera cumbre empresarial China–América Latina." *Xinhua*

News. Beijing, China. http://www.spanish.xinhuanet.com/spanish/2007-11/28/content_532647.htm. November 28, 2007.

Barrionuevo, Alexi. "To Fortify China, Soybean Harvest Grows in Brazil." *New York Times.* New York, New York. www.nytimes.com. April 6, 2007.

Becerra, Bertha. "Dispuesto Calderón a comerciar con China." *El Sol de México.* Mexico City, Mexico. http://www.oem.com.mx/elsoldemexico/. July 11, 2008.

"Bilateral Relations." *Ministry of Foreign Affairs of the People's Republic of China.* http://www.fmprc.gov.cn/eng/wjb/zzjg/ldmzs/gjlb/3488/default.htm. September 26, 2003.

Blázquez-Lidoy, Jorge, Javier Rodríguez, and Javier Santiso. *Angel or Devil? Chinese Trade Impacts on Latin America.* Paris: OECD Development Center, 2006.

"Bolivia-Estadísticas Económicas: Sector Exportaciones (2006)." *Instituto Nacional de Estadística: Bolivia.* http://www.ine.gov.bo. Accessed December 26, 2007.

"Brazil Gets Port on Pacific Coast and China Becomes Much Closer." *Brazzil Magazine.* http://www.brazzilmag.com. December 17, 2007.

"Brazil's Petrobras Eyes Partnerships with Chinese Oil Firms." *Xinhua.* http://www.uofaweb.ualberta.ca/chinainstitute/. September 10, 2006.

Bussey, Jane. "China's New World Trade Coveted, Feared." *Miami Herald.* Miami, Florida. http://www.miamiherald.com. September 26, 2005.

Camel Anderson, Eduardo. "Tecnología China apoyará las telecomunicaciones locales." *El Universal.* Caracas, Venezuela. http://www.eluniversal.com. February 20, 2007.

Cardozo, Gustavo A. "China y Argentina en la politica bilateral, 1989–2006." *Observatorio de la Economía y la Sociedad de China,* no. 1. January 2007. http://www.eumed.net/rev/china/.

Castro, Lucio, Marcelo Olarreaga, and Daniel Saslavsky. "The Impact of China and India on Argentina's Manufacturing Employment." Working Paper No. 4153. World Bank. March 2007.

CEPAL. *Oportunidades en la relación económica y comercial entre China y Mexico.* Comisión para America Latina y el Caribe (CEPAL). Mexico City: United Nations, 2007.

Cesarin, Sergio. "The Relationship Between China and Latin America: Realities and Trends." In *Enter the Dragon: China's Presence in Latin America.* Cynthia Aranson, Mark Mohr, and Riordan Roett, eds. Washington, DC: Woodrow Wilson International Center for Scholars, 2008, pp. 17–25. www.wilsoncenter.org.

Chauvin, Lucien. "Hierro Peru: China's Footprint in the Andes." *China Dialogue.* www.chinadialogue.net. December 1, 2006.

Cheng, Joseph Y. S. "Latin America in China's Contemporary Foreign Policy." *Journal of Contemporary Asia* 36(4). 2006, pp. 500–528.

"China apoya inclusion de Ecuador a APEC." *El Comercio.* Quito, Ecuador. http://www.elcomercio.com.ec. March 28, 2007.

"China apuesta a ser potencia informática." *El Mercurio.* Santiago, Chile. http://diario.elmercurio.com. February 23, 2006.

"China CNPC preocupada e interesada por Ecuador." *El Universal.* Caracas, Venezuela. http://www.eluniversal.com. June 1, 2006.

"China donó US$100.000 a Perú para retirar minas de frontera con Ecuador." *Diario Financiero.* Santiago, Chile. http://www.df.cl. July 24, 2008.

"China estima que inversión en el país llegará a $2.000 millones." *El Universal.* Caracas, Venezuela. http://www.eluniversal.com. March 30, 2007.

"China Fishery Acquires New Plant in Peru's Largest Fishing Port." *China Fishery Group Ltd.* Press release. http://www.chinafisherygroup.com/newsroom)_press.htm. October 10, 2007.

"China Forecast to Be Brazil's Top Trade Partner." *China Daily.* Beijing, China. www.chinadaily.com.cn. July 10, 2008.

"China, fundamental para desarrollo de AL." *El Economista.* Mexico City, Mexico. http://www.eleconomista.com.mx. July 6, 2006.

"China in Latin America: Trade, Not Military Involvement." *Latin America–Asia Review.* July 2006.

"China, Jamaica Rail Talks Back on Track." *Jamaica Observer.* Kingston, Jamaica. http://www.jamaicaobserver.com. May 19, 2006.

"China, Latin America Forge Closer Links for Win-Win End (1)." *People's Daily Online.* Beijing, China. http://english.people.com.cn. October 6, 2006.

"China, Latin America Forge Closer Links for Win-Win End (3)." *People's Daily Online.* Beijing, China. http://english.people.com.cn. October 6, 2006.

"China, Latin America Forge Closer Links for Win-Win End (4)." *People's Daily Online.* Beijing, China. http://english.people.com.cn. Accessed October 6, 2006.

"China Leaving Imprint on Latin American Energy." *Alexander's Oil and Gas Connections* 12(9). May 12, 2007.

"China Minmetals hará uso de su opción por mina Gaby." *Portal Minero.* http://www.portalminero.com. March 30, 2007.

"China promete negocios por casi US$20 mil millones en diez años." *Clarín.* Buenos Aires, Argentina. http://www.clarin.com. November 17, 2004.

"China Signs 16 Int'l Space Cooperation Agreements, Memorandums in Five Years." *People's Daily Online.* Beijing, China. http://english.people.com.cn. October 12, 2006.

"China's NPC Consolidates Strategic Alliance with Brazil." *People's Daily Online.* Beijing, China. http://english.people.com.cn. September 4, 2006.

"China Targets Caribbean Trade." *CNN.* http://www.cnn.com/. February 19, 2005.

"China, Uruguay to Upgrade Parliamentary Cooperation." *China View.* http://chinaview.com. January 8, 2007.

"China Wins Heavy Oil Area in Venezuela." *Alexander's Gas and Oil Connections* 11(21). November 9, 2006.

"China y Cuba apuestan por más comercio." *Los Tiempos.* Cochabamba, Bolivia. http://www.lostiempos.com. March 28, 2007.

"China y EEUU abordan diálogo estratégico sobre Latinoamérica." *El Universal.* Caracas, Venezuela. http://www.eluniversal.com.

"China y Panamá muestran su deseo común de ampliar la cooperacion en el canal." *Xinhua.* Beijing, China. www.spanish.xinhuanet.com. June 14, 2007.

"Chinese, Argentine Vice Presidents Hold Talks." *People's Daily Online.* Beijing, China. http://english.people.com.cn. October 26, 2006.

"Chinese Soybean Farmers Battered by Low Import Prices." *People's Daily Online.* Beijing, China. http://english.people.com.cn. December 1, 2006.

Chirinos, Carlos. "EE.UU: Alarma por China en A. Latina." *BBCMundo.com.* Washington, DC. March 15, 2006.

"CNPC Says Oil Discovered in Peru's Northern Jungle: Ministry." *Platts Commodity News.* http://www.uofaweb.ualberta.ca/chinainstitute. March 29, 2007.

Colburn, Forrest D. "Asia Looms over Latin America." *Dissent.* Winter 2008, pp. 9–12.

"Comercio con China creció 641% en una década." *Diario Financiero*. Santiago, Chile. http://www.df.cl. June 25, 2007.

"¿Cómo vive la comunidad asiática en Uruguay?" *Espectador*. Montevideo, Uruguay. http://www.espectador.com. November 7, 2007.

"Compañía china confirmó emprendimiento automotor en Uruguay." *Espectador*. Montevideo, Uruguay. http://www.espectador.com. July 17, 2007.

"Congress Passes Bill to Build Tacna Megaport: Bolivia, Peru." *Business News Americas*. http://www.bnamericas.com. February 27, 2006.

"Contact Us." *Huawei*. Official website. http://www.huawei.com/about/-officeList.do#Chile. Accessed December 30, 2007.

"Correa hace más ofertas a China." *El Universo*. Guayaquil, Ecuador. http://www.eluniverso.com. November 22, 2007.

"Correa le propone a China que Manta sea su ruta de comercio." *El Universo*. Guayaquil, Ecuador. http://www.eluniverso.com. November 23, 2007.

Cortez, Delfia. "Colon comienza a ventilarse." *Crítica*. Panama City, Panama. http://www.critica.com.pa. January 7, 2003.

"Costa Rica y China afianzan relaciones y suscriben acuerdos de cooperación." *Nacion*. San José, Costa Rica. http://www.nacion.com. October 24, 2007.

Cravino, Javier, Daniel Lederman, and Marcelo Olarreaga. "Foreign Direct Investment in Latin America During the Emergence of China and India." Working Paper No. 4360. World Bank. September 2007a.

———. "Substitution Between Foreign Capital in China and India and the Rest of the World and Latin America: Much Ado About Nothing?" Working Paper No. 4361. World Bank. September 2007b.

"Cuba-China Relations." *Cuba Facts*, no. 21. May 2006. Institute for Cuban and Cuban American Studies, University of Miami.

"Cuba propuso a China 37 proyectos por $1,500 millones." *El Nuevo Herald*. Miami, Florida. http://elnuevoherald.com. November 23, 2008.

Curtis, James R. "Mexicali's Chinatown." *Geographical Review* 85(3). July 1995, pp. 335–348.

"Derbez realizará visita a China." *El Economista*. Mexico City, Mexico. http://www.eleconomista.com.mx. February 15, 2006.

"Desmiente Sojo competir por el liderazgo en Sudamérica." *OEM*. http://www.oem.com.mx/oem/notas/n369220.htm. August 3, 2007.

Devlin, Robert. "China's Economic Rise." In *China's Expansion into the Western Hemisphere*. Riordan Roett and Guadalupe Paz, eds. Washington, DC: Brookings Institution Press, 2008, pp. 111–147.

Devlin, Robert, Antoni Estevadeordal, and Andrés Rodríguez-Clare. *The Emergence of China: Opportunities and Challenges for Latin America and the Caribbean*. Cambridge, MA: Harvard University Press, 2006.

Díaz, Claudio. "Frente a Frente con el gran dragón de Oriente." *El Sur*. Concepción, Chile. http://www.elsur.cl/edicion_hoy/secciones/ver_suple.php?dia=11330604-00&id=2380. November 27, 2005.

Díaz, Paola. "Chile y China entran de lleno en trativas sobre capítulos de servicios e inversiones." *Diario Financiero*. Santiago, Chile. http://www.df.cl. April 23, 2007.

Dickerson, Marla. "Mexican Retailer, Partner to Build Cars." *Los Angeles Times*. Los Angeles, California. http://www.latimes.com. November 23, 2007.

Domínguez, Jorge I. *China's Relations with Latin America: Shared Gains, Asymmetric Hopes*. Working Paper. Washington, DC: Inter-American Dialogue, June 2006.

Dreyer, June Teufel. "The China Connection." China–Latin America Task Force. Center for Hemispheric Policy, University of Miami, Coral Gables, Florida. http://www6.miami.edu/UMH/CDA/UMH_Main/0,1770,45362-1;55907-2;512-19-3,00.html. November 8, 2006a.

———. "From China with Love." *Brown Journal of World Affairs* 12(2). Winter/Spring 2006b.

Dunbaugh, Kerry, and Mark P. Sullivan. "China's Growing Interest in Latin America." Congressional Research Service Report for Congress, no. RS22119. April 20, 2005.

Duran, Alejandro. "Pide Gobierno a IP hacer frente común amenaza China." *El Sol de México*. Mexico City, Mexico. http://www.oem.com.mx/elsoldemexico/. April 4, 2007.

Dutta, Manoranjan. *China's Industrial Revolution and Economic Presence*. Saddle Brook, NJ: World Scientific, 2006.

ECLAC. *Foreign Investment in Latin America and the Caribbean, 2003*. Report. United Nations. www.eclac.cl. May 2004.

ECLAC. *Latin America and the Caribbean in the World Economy 2005–2006*. Report. United Nations. www.eclac.cl. October 2006.

"Ecuador busca ampliar exportaciones bananeras a China." *El Universo*. Guayaquil, Ecador. http://www.eluniverso.com. April 4, 2007.

"Ecuador-China relaciones comerciales." Unpublished background paper. Ministerio de Relaciones Exteriores. July 10, 2007.

"EE.UU y China hablan de A. Latina." *BBC Mundo*. Washington, DC. http://www.bbcmundo.com. April 14, 2006.

"Eje Manta-Manaos, alter nativa al Canal de Panamá para desarrollo de Amazonía." *El Comercio*. Quito, Ecuador. http://www.elcomercio.com. May 6, 2007.

"El bloque 15 decendió al ritmo de Petroecuador en producción." *El Comercio*. Quito, Ecuador. http://www.elcomercio.com. October 25, 2006.

"El chino mandarín está de moda." *El Mercurio*. Santiago, Chile. http://diario.elmercurio.com. April 15, 2006.

"El impacto chino en América Latina." *El Diario*. La Paz, Bolivia. http://eldiario.net. March 14, 2005.

"El Perú destacó durante una semana en la televisión china." *El Comercio*. Lima, Peru. http://www.elcomercio.com.pe/ediciononline. August 6, 2006.

"El presidente chino visita a Fidel Castro." *El Nuevo Herald*. Miami, Florida. http://www.elnuevoherald.com. November 19, 2008.

Ellis, R. Evan. "Acogiendo a los dragones." *Air and Space Power Journal en Español*. Third Semester, 2007.

———. *U.S. National Security Implications of Chinese Involvement in Latin America*. Carlisle Barracks, PA: US Army War College Strategic Studies Institute. https://www.strategicstudiesinstitute.army.mil/index.cfm. June 2005.

Emmott, Robin. "Peru Miners Feel Oppressed by China's Shougang." *Mines and Communities*. http://www.minesandcommunities.org/Action/press686.htm. July 21, 2005.

"Empresa china compró el área de hardware de IBM." *El Mercurio*. Santiago, Chile. http://diario.elmercurio.com. May 2, 2005.

"Empresas chinas quieren invertir en corredor bioceánico Chile-Brasil." *Diario Financiero*. Santiago, Chile. http://www.df.cl. November 6, 2006.

"En Cali, foro ministerial de los países del Pacífico." *El País*. Cali, Colombia. http://www.elpais.com.co. January 23, 2007.

Erikson, Daniel. "A Dragon in the Andes? China, Venezuela, and U.S. Energy Security." *Military Review*. July–August 2006, pp. 83–89.

Erikson, Daniel, and Paul Wander. "China: Cricket 'Champion.'" *Miami Herald*. http://www.miamiherald.com. April 28, 2007.

"Espera México recibir hasta 900 mdd de inversions chinas." *El Sol del Bajío*. Bajío, Mexico. http://www.oem.com.mx/elsoldelbajio/. July 11, 2008.

Facchini, Giovanni, Marcielo Olearreaga, Peri Silva, and Gerald Willman. "Substitutability and Trade Policy: Latin America's Trade Policy and Imports from China and India." Working Paper No. 4188. World Bank. April 2007.

Farrell, Diana, Ulrich A. Gersch, and Elizabeth Stephenson. "The Value of China's Emerging Middle Class." *McKinsey Quarterly*. http://www.mckinseyquarterly.com. June 2006.

Ferrari, Céar. "China, Colombia y Perú: Impactos sobre crecimiento e ingreso." *Latin American Trade Network*, no. 25. April 2007.

"Foro Baja California–Asia, economía, cultura y negocios." *El Sol de Tijuana*. Tijuana, Mexico. http://www.oem.com.mx/elsoldetijuana/. August 29, 2007.

Frank, Andre Gunder. *Capitalism and Underdevelopment in Latin America*, 3rd ed. London: Penguin Books, 1971.

Franko, Patrice M. *The Puzzle of Latin American Economic Development*, 3rd ed. Boulder, CO: Rowman & Littlefield, 2007.

"Freeport Container Port." Hutchison Port Holdings. Official website. http://www.hph.com.hk/. Accessed October 15, 2007.

"Full Text: China's Space Activities in 2006." *People's Daily Online*. Beijing, China. http://english.people.com.cn. October 12, 2006.

Funakushi, Tomoe, and Claudio Loser. "China's Rising Economic Presence in Latin America." Report. Washington DC: Inter-American Dialogue, July 2005.

Gallagher, Kevin, Juan Carlos Moreno-Brid, and Roberto Porzecanski. "The Dynamism of Mexican Exports: Lost in (Chinese) Translation?" *World Development* 36(8). August 2008, pp. 1365–1380.

Gallagher, Kevin, and Roberto Porzecanski. "China Matters: China's Economic Impact in Latin America." *Latin American Research Review* 43(1). 2008.

"García dice que la carretera interoceánica es la obra más importante de la región." *Terra*. http://actualidad.terra.es. Madrid, Spain. July 13, 2007.

Garza-Limón, Cecilia, and Raúl Rodríguez Barocio. "Two Notes on the Need for a China Policy in Mexico." China–Latin America Task Force. Center for Hemispheric Policy, University of Miami, Coral Gables, Florida. http://www6.miami.edu/-UMH/CDA/UMH_Main/0,1770,45362-1;55907-2;51219-3,00.html. April 26, 2007.

Gertz, Bill. "Chinese Military Trains in West." *Washington Times*. Washington, DC. http://www.washingtontimes.com. March 15, 2006.

González, Francisco E. "Latin America in the Economic Equation—Winners and Losers: What Can Losers Do?" In *China's Expansion into the Western Hemisphere*. Riordan Roett and Guadalupe Paz, eds. Washington, DC: Brookings Institution Press, 2008, pp. 148–169.

"Grandes empresas chinas invertirán en Bolivia." *Portal Minero*. http://www.portalminero.com. January 10, 2006.

"Gross Domestic Product per Capita, Current Prices (U.S. Dollars)." *International Monetary Fund*. World Economic Outloook Database. http://www.imf.org/external/pubs/ft/weo/2007/01/data/index.aspx. April 2007.

Guo, Rongxing. *How the Chinese Economy Works*, 2nd ed. New York: Palgrave Macmillan, 2007.

Guthrie, Amy, and Susan H. Preston. "Feeding a Dragon." *Latin Finance.* http://www.latinfinance.com. August 1, 2007.

Guthrie, Doug. *China and Globalization.* New York: Routledge, 2006.

Gutiérrez, Alana. "China's Economic Invasion of Mexico." *Council on Hemispheric Affairs.* http://www.mexidata.info/id636.html. October 14, 2005.

Gutiérrez Guerrero, Aleyda. "Cumple promesa a su padre." *Cambio de Michocán.* Sonora, Mexico. http://www.cambiodemichoacan.com.mx. March 6, 2006.

Hago, Washington. "Ecuatorianos y chinos en una relación que viene de siglos." *Aniversario de las Relaciones Diplomáticas entre la República Popular China y la República del Ecuador.* Guayaquil, Ecuador: Diseño y Diagramación, 2005, p. 64.

Hanratty, Dannin M., and Sandra W. Meditz, eds. *Paraguay: A Country Study.* Washington, DC: Government Publications Office for the Library of Congress, 1988.

Hardy, Toro. "Petróleo: Estados Unidos, China, y Venezuela." *El Universal.* Caracas, Venezuela. http://www.el-universal.com. September 29, 2005.

Hawksley, Humphrey. "China's New Latin American Revolution." *Financial Times.* http://www.ft.com. April 4, 2006.

He, Li. "China-Taiwan Rivalry in Latin America and Its Implications." In *Enter the Dragon? China's Presence in Latin America.* Cynthia Aranson, Mark Mohr, and Riordan Roett, eds. Washington, DC: Woodrow Wilson International Center for Scholars, 2008, pp. 53–58. www.wilsoncenter.org.

———. "Red Star over Latin America." *NACLA Report on the Americas.* September/October 2007, pp. 23–27.

———. "Rivalry Between Taiwan and the PRC in Latin America." *Journal of Chinese Political Science* 10(2). Fall 2005.

Henriquez, Andrea. "¿Chile Nuclear?" *BBCMundo.com.* http://news.bbc.co.uk/hi/spanish/latin_america/newsid_7119000/7119847.stm. November 19, 2007.

Hirst, Monica. "A South-South Perspective." In *China's Expansion into the Western Hemisphere.* Riordan Roett and Guadalupe Paz, eds. Washington, DC: Brookings Institution Press, 2008, pp. 90–108.

Ho Choon Seng, "China Fishery Group Limited: Raising the Stakes in Fishmeal Processing; CIMB." *World Press.* http://sgmarkettalk.worldpress.com/2007/10/16/china-fishery-group-limited-raising-the-stakes-in-fishmealprocessing-cimb. October 17, 2007.

"Honduras analiza relaciones diplomáticas con China." *El Universal.* Caracas, Venezuela. http://www.eluniversal.com. July 31, 2007.

Hudson, Rex. *Terrorist and Organized Crime Groups in the Tri-Border Area (TBA) of South America.* Report. Washington, DC: Federal Research Division, Library of Congress. www.loclgov/rr/frd/pdf-files/TerrOrgCrime_TBA.pdf. 2003.

Hulse, Janie. "China's Expansion into and U.S. Withdrawal from Argentina's Telecommunications and Space Industries and the Implications for U.S. National Security." Carlisle Barracks, PA: US Army War College Strategic Studies Institute, September 2007. http://www.StrategicStudiesInstitute.Army.mil.

"Imports by Major Categories (2007/01–12)." *Ministry of Commerce of the People's Republic of China.* http://english.mofcom.gov.cn/aarticle/statistic/ie/200802/20080205372493.html. February 4, 2008.

"Intercambio comercial del país, por año, según región y país seleccionado (miles $US): Período 1994; al último dato disponible." *Republica Oriental de Uruguay. Instituto Nacional de Estadistica.* http://www.ine.gub.uy/economia/externo.htm. Accessed December 29, 2007.

International Monetary Fund. *World Economic Outlook Database*. September 2006.

"Interview: China, Uruguay Committed to World Peace, Development; Uruguayan Parliament Speaker." *People's Daily Online*. Beijing, China. http://english.people.com.cn. January 19, 2007.

"Inversiones México-China." *Ministry of Foreign Relations. Republic of Mexico*. http://portal.sre.gob.mx/china. Accessed September 10, 2007.

"Is the Chinese Model Gaining Political and Economic Influence in Latin America?" White Paper. Washington, DC: Hudson Institute, March 2007.

"ITT: Utopía camina hacia la realidad." *Boletín: Dirección de Comunicación Social, Ministerio de Energia y Minas, Republica del Ecuador*, no. 182. www.menergia.gov.ec. July 3, 2007.

Jasmine Geffner, Xinyue. "La economía peruana y la china son complementarias." *El Comercio*. Lima, Peru. http://www.elcomercio.com.pe/ediciononline. March 28, 2007.

Jenkins, Rhys, and Enrique Dussel Peters. *The Impact of China on Latin America and the Caribbean*. Beijing: DFID, 2006.

Jenkins, Rhys, Enrique Dussel Peters, and Mauricio Mesquita-Moreira. "The Impact of China on Latin America and the Caribbean." *World Development* 36(2). February 2008, pp. 235–253.

Jiang, Shixue. "The Chinese Foreign Policy Perspective." In *China's Expansion into the Western Hemisphere*. Riordan Roett and Guadalupe Paz, eds. Washington, DC: Brookings Institution Press, 2008a, pp. 27–43.

———. "Three Factors in the Recent Development of Sino–Latin American Relations." In *Enter the Dragon? China's Presence in Latin America*. Cynthia Aranson, Mark Mohr, and Riordan Roett, eds. Washington, DC: Woodrow Wilson International Center for Scholars, 2008b, pp. 43–54. www.wilsoncenter.org.

Jubany, Florencia, and Daniel Poon. "Recent Chinese Engagement in Latin America and the Caribbean: A Canadian Perspective." *FOCAL*. www.focal.ca/pdf/china_lat-am.pdf. March 2006.

Kenny, Alejandro. "China's Presence in Latin America: A View on Security from the Southern Cone." *Military Review*. September–October 2006, pp. 60–66.

Kurlantzick, Joshua. "China's Latin Leap Forward." *World Policy Journal* 23(3). Fall 2006, pp. 33–41.

"La alternativa para explotar el ITT avanza." *El Comercio*. Quito, Ecuador. http://www.elcomercio.com. July 9, 2007.

Lafargue, Francois. "China's Strategies in Latin America." *Military Review*. May–June 2006, pp. 80–84.

"Latinoamérica es objectivo de autos chinos." *Nacion*. San José, Costa Rica. http://www.nacion.com. July 16, 2007.

Lederman, Daniel, and William F. Maloney. *Natural Resources: Neither Curse nor Destiny*. Daniel Lederman and William F. Maloney, eds. Palo Alto, CA: Stanford University Press, 2007.

Lederman, Daniel, Marcelo Olarreaga, and Isidro Soloaga. "The Growth of China and India in World Trade: Opportunity or Threat for Latin America and the Caribbean?" Working Paper No. 4320. World Bank. August 2007a.

Lederman, Daniel, Marcelo Olarreaga, and Eliana Rubiano. "Specialization and Adjustment During the Growth of China and India: The Latin American Experience?" Working Paper No. 4318. World Bank. August 2007b.

Liu, John. "Huawei and ZTE Gain in Developing World." *International Herald Tribune*. London, England. http://www.iht.com. December 18, 2006.

Liu Yuquin. "Fortalecer la cooperación amistosa binacional y crear juntos una nueva perspectiva más brillante." *25 Aniversario de las Relaciones Diplomáticas entre la República Popular China y la República del Ecuador.* Quito, Ecuador: Diseño y Diagramación. 2006.

Lo, Chi. *Understanding China's Growth.* New York: Palgrave Macmillan, 2007.

Logan, Sam, and Ben Bain. "China Entices S. America with Investment." *ISN Security Watch.* http://www.isn.ethz.ch/news/sw/details_print.cfm?id=12337. August 4, 2005.

López-Córdova, J. Ernesto, Alejandro Micco, and Danielken Molina. "How Sensitive Are American Exports to Chinese Competition in the U.S. Market?" Working Paper No. 4497. World Bank. January 2008.

Lopez Gomez, Jorge. "Chinos insaciables clonan al Smart y la x 5." *El Universal.* Mexico City, Mexico. http://www.eluniversal.com.mx. September 2, 2007.

Lora, Eduardo. "Should Latin America Fear China?" Working Paper No. 531. Washington, DC: Inter-American Development Bank. 2007.

"Los emigrantes chinos, con rumbo al Perú." *El Comercio.* Guayaquil, Ecuador. http://www.elcomercio.com. April 18, 2007.

Loser, Claudio. "The Growing Economic Presence of China in Latin America." Working Paper for the University of Miami Center for Hemispheric Policy, China–Latin America Task Force. Coral Gables, Florida. http://www6.miami. edu/hemispheric-policy/LoserFinalDraft1.pdf. December 15, 2006.

———. "China's Rising Economic Presence in Latin America." Working Paper. Washington, DC: Inter-American Dialogue. July 2005.

"Los nuevos herederos del dragón." *Asociación Peruano-Chino.* http://www. apochi.com. October 29, 2005.

Lozada, Carlos. "Evolucion y potencíal de los productos agrícolas de exportación." Presentation for Semana de Comercio Exterior (SCEX) 2007. *Asociación de Exportadores.* http://www.adexperu.org.pe/informacion.htm. October 18, 2007.

Maciel, Rodrigo. "The Economic Relationship Between China and Brazil." In *Enter the Dragon? China's Presence in Latin America.* Cynthia Aranson, Mark Mohr, and Riordan Roett, eds. Washington, DC: Woodrow Wilson International Center for Scholars, 2008, pp. 27–41. www.wilsoncenter.org.

"Main Indicators of Foreign Trade and Economy (2007/01–12)." *Ministry of Commerce. People's Republic of China.* http://english.mofcom.gov.cn/aarticle/ statistic/iein-dicators/200802/20080205371703.html. February 4, 2007.

Mastel, Greg. *The Rise of the Chinese Economy.* Armonk, NY: M. E. Sharpe, 1997.

McGregor, James. *One Billion Customers.* New York: Free Press, 2005.

"Mercosur trabado por las estrategias de sus socios." *El País.* http://www.elpais. com.uy. Montevideo, Uruguay. December 20, 2007.

Mesquita-Moreira, Mauricio. "Fear of China: Is There a Future for Manufacturing in Latin America?" *World Development* 35(3). March 2007, pp. 355–376.

"Mexican Business and Infrastructure 2007." *Financial Times.* London, England. http://www.ft.com. May 9, 2007.

"Mexico, China to Push Forward Bilateral Investment Agreement." *People's Daily Online.* Beijing, China. http://english.people.com.cn. March 23, 2007.

"México pierde terreno en EU ante China." *El Economista.* Mexico City, Mexico. http://www.eleconomista.com.mx. November 10, 2005.

"México podrá exportar carne de cerdo a China." *El Economista.* Mexico City, Mexico. http://www.eleconomista.com.mx. July 7, 2008.

Montalva, Juan Diego, and Patricio Navia. "Chile and China: Building Relations Beyond Trade?" Working Paper for the University of Miami Center for

Hemispheric Policy, China–Latin America Task Force. Coral Gables, Florida. http://www6.miami.edu/UMH/CDA/UMH_Main/0,1770,45362-1;55907-2;5121-9-3,00.html. March 6, 2007.

Mosher, Steven W. "Red China on the March." *National Review*. http://www. nationalreview.com. February 14, 2006.

Murillo, Álvaro. "Primera estación de Arias en China: La ciudad prohibida." *Nacion*. San José, Costa Rica. http://www.nacion.com. October 22, 2007.

Namur, Paula. "China se convierte por primera vez en el principal exportador del mundo." *Diario Financiero*. Santiago, Chile. http://www.financiero.cl. October 24, 2007.

Nathan, Andrew J. "The Tiananmen Papers." *Foreign Affairs* 80(1). January/ February 2001.

Naughton, Barry. *The Chinese Economy: Transitions and Growth*. Cambridge, MA: MIT Press, 2007.

Ojeda Reyes, Yolanda. "Ciudanos chinos reciben protección." *El Universal*. Caracas, Venezuela. http://www.eluniversal.com. November 11, 2004.

Olivares C. Eduardo. "China es mayor destino de exportaciones tras el TLC." *El Mercurio*. Santiago, Chile. http://diario.elmercurio.com. April 18, 2007.

Oppenheimer, Andrés. *Cuentos chinos*. Buenos Aires, Argentina: Editorial Sudamerica, 2005.

O'Quinn, Robert P. *Overview of the Chinese Economy*. Joint Economic Committee (JEC) Study. Washington DC: Government Printing Office. July 2005.

Palacios, Luisa. "Latin America as China's Energy Supplier." In *China's Expansion into the Western Hemisphere*. Riordan Roett and Guadalupe Paz, eds. Washington, DC: Brookings Institution Press, 2008, pp. 170–189.

Paus, Eva. *Inversión extranjera, desarrollo y globalización*. San José, Costa Rica: Palgrave Macmillan, 2007.

Pei, Minxin. *China's Trapped Transition: The Limits of Developmental Autocracy*. Cambridge, MA: Harvard University Press, 2006.

"Perfil de los cooperantes: Republica Popular de China." *Instituto Ecuatoriano de Cooperacion Internacional (INECI)*. http://www.mmrree.gov.ec/ineci/perfiles/ china.asp. Accessed December 28, 2007.

"Perfil País." *Centro de Promoción Bolivia (CEPROBOL)*. La Paz, Bolivia. http://www.ceprobol.gov.bo/ppais.aspx. Accessed December 26, 2007.

"Peru." Country Analysis Brief. Energy Information Administration. http://www.eia. doe.gov. Updated June 2008.

"Petrobras Delays Pipeline Construction as Sinopec Raises Cost." *Alexander's Gas and Oil Connections* 10(14). http://www.gasandoil.com/. July 20, 2005.

"Petróleo y sector financiero Ecuador en mira de empresas chinas." *Nacion*. San José, Costa Rica. http://www.nacion.com. April 5, 2006.

"Petrolera China desestima que protesta en Tarapoa haya afectado sus intereses." *El Universo*. Guayaquil, Ecuador. http://www.eluniverso.com/. November 14, 2006.

"Petrolera china negocia contratos en Venezuela." *Diario Financiero*. Santiago, Chile. http://www.diario-financiero.cl. June 29, 2007.

"Petrolera sinopec negocia extracciones en la faja." *El Universal*. Caracas, Venezuela. http://www.eluniversal.com. June 29, 2007.

"Police Raid Huawei Offices in Brazil." *Light Reading*. http://www.lightreading. com/document.asp?doc_id=140867. December 7, 2007.

"Por fin: Interoceánica norte en marcha." *Carretera Interoceánico*. http://www. carreterainteroceanica.com/modules/news/article.php?storyid=4. May 6, 2006.

Population Division, Department of Economic and Social Affairs, United Nations Secretariat. *World Population Prospects: The 2004 Revision and World Urbanization Prospects.* http://esa.un.org/unpp.

———. *World Urbanization Prospects: The 2001 Revision, Data Tables and Highlights.* (ESA/P/WP.173). March 20, 2002.

Population Reference Bureau. *2001 World Population Data Sheet.* Washington, DC: Population Reference Bureau, 2001.

Prebisch, Raul. "The Latin American Periphery in the Global System of Capitalism." *UNCLA Review*, no. 13. April 1981.

"Prepared Statement of the Honorable Dan Burton, a Representative in Congress from the State of Indiana, and Chairman, Subcommittee on the Western Hemisphere." Transcript for the Record. 109th Congress, 2nd Session. http://foreignaffairs.house.gov/archives/whhear.htm. April 6, 2005.

"Presidente chino firma docena de acuerdos en su visita a Cuba." *Nacion.* San José, Costa Rica. http://www.nacion.com. November 19, 2008.

"Primer semestre 2007 principales productos de Chile a China." *China Customs.* Commercial Office. Beijing, China. August 2007.

"Producirán camiones chinos en Venezuela." *El Universal.* Caracas, Venezuela. http://www.eluniversal.com. October 29, 2007.

"Protestas contra Petroriental dejan 31 heridas en ocho días." *El Comercio.* Quito, Ecuador. http://www.elcomercio.com. July 4, 2007.

"Proyecto eje multimodal Manta-Manaus." Comision Especial Interinstitucional del Proyecto del Puerto de Teransferencia Interacional de Carga del Ecuador en el Puerto de Manta. http://www.puertodetransferencia.gov.ec/manaus. Accessed December 22, 2008.

Quesada, Charo. "Latinos from the Far East." *IDB América.* http://www.iadb.org/idbamerica/index.cfm?thisid=3961. March 2006.

Ratliff, William. "Mirroring Taiwan: China and Cuba." *China Brief* 6(10). Jamestown Foundation. May 10, 2006.

"Relaciones bilaterales de comercio Colombia–Republica Popular China." *Ministerio de Comercio, Industria y Turismo.* http://www.mincomercio.gov.co. Accessed August 11, 2007.

"Reversal by Tiny St. Lucia Angers China." *International Herald Tribune.* London, England. www.iht.com. May 2, 2007.

Reyes Matta, Fernando. "Chile-China: La fuerza de los acuerdos regionales." *Diario Financiero.* Santiago, Chile. http://www.df.cl. September 4, 2007.

Rodríguez Santoyo, Raúl. "Debilidad del comercio mexican frente al embate chino." *El Sol de Zacatecas.* Zacatecas, Mexico. http://www.oem.com.mx/elsoldezacatecas/. June 19, 2007.

"Satélite chino-brasileño es una super herramienta de control de la Amazonía." *Nacion.* San José, Costa Rica. http://www.nacion.com. September 27, 2007.

Saunders, Ronald. "China and Taiwan Again." *Jamaica Observer.* Kingston, Jamaica. http://www.jamaicaobserver.com. May 13, 2007.

———. "China Beckons: Caricom Should Respond." *Jamaica Observer.* Kingston, Jamaica. http://www.jamaicaobserver.com. December 14, 2007.

Schiller, Ben. "The Axis of Oil: China and Venezuela." *Open Democracy.* http://www.opendemocracy.net/globalization-corporations/china_venezuela_33-19.jsp. February 3, 2006a.

———. "China's African Encounter." *China Dialogue.* http://www.chinadialogue.net/article/show/single/en/515-China-s-African-encounter. November 6, 2006b.

Scobell, Andrew, and Larry Wortzel. "Introduction." In *Civil-Military Change in China: Elites, Institutes and Ideas After the 16th Party Congress.* Andrew

Scobell and Larry Wortzel, eds. Carlisle Barracks, PA: Army War College Strategic Studies Institute, September 2004, pp. 1–10.

"Secuestran a un piloto y dos técnicos petroleros en el Chocó." *Radio Caracol*. http://www.caracol.com.co/nota.asp?id=318540. August 9, 2006.

"Se estableció el Comité Empresarial Perú-China ProInversión y Consejo Chino de Promoción del Comercio Internacional (CCPIT) lo presiden." *ProInversion* 2(18). http://www.proinversion.gob.pe/RepositorioAPS/0/0/JER/NEWS LETTER/octubre/Nota4.htm. October 2006.

"Senior Chinese Military Leader Highlights Friendly Ties with Jamaica." *People's Daily Online*. Beijing, China. http://english.people.com.cn. July 26, 2005.

"Senior Chinese Party Official Meets with Venezuelan President." *People's Daily Online*. Caracas, Venezuela. http://english.peopledaily.com.cn/. March 27, 2007.

"Senior Chinese Party Official Wraps Up Mexico Visit." *People's Daily Online*. Beijing, China. http://english.people.com.cn. March 26, 2007.

"Shengli Oíl decidió apostar por Bolivia con gas natural." *Los Tiempos*. Cochabamba, Bolivia. http://www.lostiempos.com. October 21, 2004.

"Sino-Cuban Relations." *China Daily*. Beijing, China. http://english.people.com.cn. November 11, 2004.

Siwei, Cheng. "Bright Prospects for China–Latin America and the Caribbean Cooperation." Speech before the Organization of American States. Washington, DC. http://www.oas.org/speeches/speech.asp?sCodigo=05-0273.

Soler, Enrique. "Chile y su inserción en el Asia Pacífico." *La Razón*. La Paz, Bolivia. http://www.la-razon.com. April 15, 2007.

Stallings, Barbara. "The U.S.–China–Latin America Triangle: Implications for the Future." In *China's Expansion into the Western Hemisphere*. Riordan Roett and Guadalupe Paz, eds. Washington, DC: Brookings Institution Press, 2008, pp. 239–259.

Stewart, Marcio. "Latin American Logistics Infrastructure: A Strategic Concern for the Chinese." *Tendencias: Infoamericas*. http://www.infoamericas.com. December 2006.

"Taiwan Anthem Played for China Officials." *CBS News*. http://www.cbsnews.com/stories/2007/02/04/world/printable2429938.shtml. February 4, 2007.

"Taiwán podría perdonar la deuda externa a Nicaragua." *Nacion*. San José, Costa Rica. http://www.nacion.com. June 26, 2007.

"Taiwán promueve con 250 millones dólares inversiones en Paraguay." *Nacion*. San José, Costa Rica. http://www.nacion.com. May 6, 2006.

"Taquería El Fogoncito abre negocio en China." *Nacion*. San José, Costa Rica. http://www.nacion.com. January 26, 2007.

"Televisa hará telenovelas en China y venderá sus formatos de televisión." *El Comercio*. Quito, Ecuador. http://www.elcomercio.com. May 31, 2007.

"Tequila llegará a China." *El Economista*. Mexico City, Mexico. http://www.el-economista.com.mx. May 2, 2007.

"The Economy of Heat." *The Economist*. http://www.economist.com/specialreports/displaystory.cfm?story_id=89-52496. April 12, 2007.

"TIDE toma las riendas del puerto." *El Comercio*. Quito, Ecuador. http://www.el-comercio.com. February 2, 2007.

"Tiny Nation Roars: St. Lucia Denounced by China for Ties with Taiwan." *International Herald Tribune*. http://www.iht.com. May 1, 2007.

"TLC con China cumple un año con un aumento de 100% en las exportaciones." *Diario Financiero*. Santiago, Chile. http://www.df.cl. October 1, 2007.

Tokatlian, Juan Gabriel. "A View from Latin America." In *China's Expansion into the Western Hemisphere*. Riordan Roett and Guadalupe Paz, eds. Washington, DC: Brookings Institution Press, 2008, pp. 59–89.

"Total Import and Export Value by Country (Region) (2006/1–12)." *Ministry of Commerce*. People's Republic of China. http://english.mofcom.gov.cn.aarticle/statistic/ie/200712/20071205267122.html. February 6, 2007.

"Total Import and Export Value by Country (Region) (2007/01–12)." *Ministry of Commerce*. People's Republic of China. http://english.mofcom.gov.cn.aarticle/statistic/ie/200802/20080205371690.html. February 4, 2008.

"Tras TLC con China, Perú negocia con Corea y Japón." *El Universo*. Guayaquil, Ecuador. http://www.eluniverso.com. November 18, 2008.

"Tratados bilaterales: Republica Popular de China." *Ministerio de Relaciones Exteriores. República Argentina*. http://www.mrecic.gov.ar/. Accessed January 1, 2008.

"Tratados y convenios internacionales." *Ministerio de Relaciones Exteriores. Republica Oriental del Uruguay*. http://www.mrree.gub.uy/Tratados/MenuInicial/busqueda/Pais/PaisConsul.asp. Accessed December 29, 2007.

Trinh, Tamara, Silja Voss, and Steffen Dyck. "China's Commodity Hunger." Deutsche Bank Research. Report. Frankfurt, Germany. http://www.chinatrade-information.net/chinas-commodity-hunger. June 13, 2006.

"Turismo México-China." *Ministry of Foreign Relations. Republic of Mexico*. http://portal.sre.gob.mx/china. Accessed September 10, 2007.

"Un dragón en la puerta." *La Razón*. La Paz, Bolivia. http://www.la-razon.com. August 13, 2006.

"Un gran estadio nacional." *Nacion*. San José, Costa Rica. January 20, 2008.

"Un megapuerta en Tacna." *La Razón*. La Paz, Bolivia. http://www.la-razon.com. September 3, 2006.

"US Agreement with China Helps Central America." *Latin America–Asia Review*. December 2005, p. 15.

"US-China Trade Relations." *U.S.-China Business Council*. http://www.uschina.org/info/forecast/2007/trade-relations.html. February 2007.

"USD 15 milliones se invirtieron en el puerto de Manta en 7 meses." *El Comercio*. Quito, Ecuador. http://www.elcomercio.com. October 19, 2007.

US Department of Agriculture. World Agricultural Supply and Demand Estimates, market year 1999/00. 2000.

Vaca, Mery. "Acuerdan un corredor interoceánico." *BBCMundo*. http://news.bbc.co.uk. December 17, 2007.

Veillette, Connie. *Plan Colombia: A Progress Report*. CRS Report for Congress. Congressional Research Service. Report RL32774. February 2005.

"Venezuela Aims to Tap Chinese Market." *Business Monitor International*. http://www.businessmonitor.com. February 26, 2007.

Venezuela: Country Analysis Briefs. Energy Information Administration. http://www.eia.doe.gov. September 2006.

"Venezuela Maps Out Plan for Chinese Oil Investment." *Reuters*. http://www.reuters.com. March 28, 2007.

"Venezuela y China concretan acuerdos para impulsar integración estratégica." *El Universal*. Caracas, Venezuela. http://www.eluniversal.com. March 26, 2007.

"Venezuela y China crean fondo estratégico y firman 5 acuerdos." *El Universal*. Caracas, Venezuela. http://www.eluniversal.com. March 27, 2007.

"Venezuela y China inician fábrica de teléfonos celulares." *El Universal*. Caracas, Venezuela. http://www.eluniversal.com. November 15, 2006.

Watson, Cynthia A. "U.S. Responses to China's Growing Interests in Latin America: Dawning Recognition of a Changing Hemisphere." In *Enter the Dragon?*

China's Presence in Latin America. Cynthia Aranson, Mark Mohr, and Riordan Roett, eds. Washington, DC: Woodrow Wilson International Center for Scholars, 2008, pp. 65–71. www.wilsoncenter.org.

———. "A Warming Friendship: Part II of a Two-Part Series on China, Taiwan, and Latin America." *China Brief.* Jamestown Foundation. 2004.

Wines, Michael. "Russia Closing Two Major Posts for Snooping, One in Cuba." *New York Times.* October 18, 2001, p. A9.

Wise, Carol, and Cinthia Quiliconi. "China's Surge in Latin American Markets: Policy Challenges and Responses." *Politics and Policy,* no. 1. 2007, pp. 410–438.

Wolf, Charles, Jr., K. C. Yeh, and Benjamin Zycher. *Fault Lines in China's Economic Terrain.* Santa Monica, CA: Rand, 2003.

Xiang Lanxin. "An Alternative Chinese View." In *China's Expansion into the Western Hemisphere.* Riordan Roett and Guadalupe Paz, eds. Washington, DC: Brookings Institution Press, 2008a, pp. 44–58.

———. "A Geopolitical Perspective on Sino–Latin American Relations." In *Enter the Dragon? China's Presence in Latin America.* Cynthia Aranson, Mark Mohr, and Riordan Roett, eds. Washington, DC: Woodrow Wilson International Center for Scholars, 2008b, pp. 59–64. www.wilsoncenter.org.

Zambrano Castillo, Guido. "Análisis político económico." *Inteligencia Estratégica,* no. 106. June 1–15, 2007. Corporación de Información Liderazgo y Desarrollo Internacional (CILDI). Quito, Ecuador.

———. *La colombianizacion de Ecuador: Peligros y asechanzas de fuerzas corruptoras colombianas.* Quito, Ecuador: Corporación de Información, Liderazgo y Desarrollo Ecuatoriano, 2006.

Zhang, Xueyuan, and Patrick Reinmoeller. "Foreign Firms in China: Success by Strategic Choices." In *The Chinese Economy in the 21st Century.* Barbara Krug and Hans Hendrischke, eds. Northhampton, MA: Edward Elgar Publishing, 2007, pp. 42–70.

Zhao, Suisheng. "China's National Security Strategy and Diplomatic Engagement." China–Latin America Task Force. University of Miami Center for Hemispheric Policy. http://www6.miami.edu/UMH/CDA/UMH_Main/0,1770,45362-1;51219-3,00.html. December 12, 2006.

———. "China's Pragmatic Nationalism: Is It Manageable?" *Washington Quarterly* 29(1). Winter 2005–2006, p. 139.

Zhao Xuemei. "Comercio e inversiones de China con América Latina." Presentation to the Medellín Chamber of Commerce for Antioquia. Medellín, Colombia. August 10, 2007.

Zheng Bijian. "China's Peaceful Rise and New Role of Asia." *China Forum.* Autumn 2005, p. 3.

Index

Agency for Investment and Export Promotion (Brazil), 59

Agriculture: Chinese crisis in, 10, 11, 12; export-oriented, 26; industrial contamination of land and, 12. *See also* individual countries

Air China, 60, 96*n242*

Albuquerque, Francisco Roberto de, 97*n257*

Aleman, Hector, 225

Alencar, José, 61

Alexandria Fishing Company (Peru), 152

Allende, Salvador, 35, 148, 265*n297*

Alternative Boliviariana de las Americas (ALBA), 17, 170*n32*

American Servicemen's Protection Act (2002), 91*n126*, 284

Andean Trade Preferences Drug Enforcement Act (ATPDEA), 165, 186*n265*

Andes Petroleum (Ecuador), 128, 179*n155*

Antigua: tourism in, 245

Argentina, 62–75; agricultural exports, 12, 25, 62, 65–66, 274; agricultural strike in, 62, 63, 65; Asia studies programs in, 74; auto/motorcycle sales, 68; banking sector in, 73, 74; business infrastructure in, 72–74; business presence in China, 73; Chinese community in, 63–65; consumer goods imports, 68; customs restrictions on China products, 69, 70; economic collapse in, 26; economic

diversification in, 65, 175*n97*; electronics industry, 68; export promotion by, 73; exports to India, 98*n276*; failure of Chinese investments to materialize, 70; fashion industry in, 67; free-trade zone in, 68; gas exports, 40; government infrastructure in, 72–74; high costs of transporting goods to China, 70–71; historical context in evolution of relations with China, 63; human rights issues in, 63; infrastructure projects in, 70–71; intellectual infrastructure, 74; investment in, 66; leather goods exports, 66; livestock production, 65, 66; logistics infrastructure in, 63; low-end inexpensive imports, 68; manufactured imports in, 62; as market for Chinese goods, 68–70; middle class in, 68; military cooperation with China, 63, 74–75; mining sector, 67, 99*n301*; nuclear power in, 72; petroleum industry in, 66–67; petroleum reserves in, 99*n292*; political relations with China, 74–75; premium product exports, 67; pressure to erect trade barriers in, 69; primary product exports, 224; recognition of China, 63; sophisticated product exports, 67; space technology collaboration with United States, 101*n346*; space technology in, 57; as "strategic partner," 17, 62, 74, 175*n97*, 200; strong military ties with United States, 75;

technology industry, 71–72; telecommunications industry in, 63, 69; tourism in, 64, 65, 72; trade deficits in, 62; trade tensions with China, 62, 69, 75; transportation industry, 68–69; Unión de Residentes Taiwaneses Justicialistas in, 64; visits from Chinese leaders, 63, 66, 70, 72, 75; winemaking in, 68

Arias, Oscar, 215, 216, 218, 219, 220, 222, 223–224, 235, 256n132, 257n136, 258n159, 259n169, 260n192

Arias, Rodrigo, 223–224

Asia-Pacific Economic Cooperation (APEC), 26, 34, 46, 63, 136, 148, 155, 156, 157, 165, 166, 168, 201, 214, 223, 229, 236

Association of China-Bolivia Friendship, 146

Association of Southeast Asian Nations (ASEAN), 84n2

Astori, Danilo, 76, 103n393

Australia: mining exports, 51; uranium exports, 58

Bachelet, Michelle, 40, 43, 47, 48

Bahamas: Tiananmen Square crisis, 248; tourism in, 246

Banco Azteca (Mexico), 204

Banco Cathay, 223

Banco de Brazil, 59, 60

Banco de Chile, 45

Banco de Inversión y Comercio Exterior (Argentina), 74

Banco de Latin America Nacio de Peru (BNP), 155

Banco Nacional of Costa Rica, 222

Bancosur, 17

Banking, 3

Bank of China, 96n236

Baosteel (China), 51, 274, 291n3

Barbados: tourism in, 246

Barco, Virgilia, 158

Baugh, Ken, 244–245

Beijing Consensus, 28

Belize: low-end inexpensive imports, 232; recognition of Taiwan by, 15, 234

Berger, Oscar, 234

Betancur, Belisario, 158

BHP Billiton (Colombia), 161

Bitar, Sergio, 46

Bolanos, Enrique, 232

Bolívar, Simón, 30

Bolivia, 137–147; agricultural production, 185n262; Asia studies programs in, 145–146; auto/motorcycle imports, 143; business infrastructure, 144–145; business presence in China, 144–145; Chinese caution in, 137; Chinese community, 138; conservative military regimes in, 138; consumer electronics imports, 143; contraband goods in, 143; expansion of exports to China by, 186n265; free-trade zones in, 143; government infrastructure, 144–145; historical context in evolution of relations with China, 138; informal sector in, 142, 143; infrastructure projects in, 143–144; intellectual infrastructure, 145–146; joint oil exploration in, 139; low-end inexpensive imports, 142, 143; as market for Chinese goods, 142–143; military cooperation with China, 146–147; mining exports, 12, 141–142; nationalization of hydrocarbons sector, 137, 139, 140; non-Asian exports, 145; partnership with Venezuela in petroleum sector, 140; per capita income, 195n446; petroleum exports, 138–141, 184n240; political relations with China, 146–147; political stability in, 183n225; populist regime in, 17; primary product exports, 137, 183n222; private sector in, 145; purge of military leadership in, 147; recognition of China, 138; Red Dragon group in, 138; secession issues in, 137; as source of resistance to US domination, 137; stagnating export situation in, 142; telecommunications sector in, 137, 143; uncertain political stability in, 137, 144; visits from Chinese leaders, 138

Bolivian Association for Friendship with China, 146

Bolivian Institute of Foreign Commerce (IBCE), 145

Bolivian Institute of Foreign Trade, 142

Bonelli, Enrique, 80
Brazil, 49–62; agricultural exports, 12, 25, 50–51, 92n142; aircraft industry in, 57; Asia studies programs in, 60; banking sector in, 59, 60; business presence in China, 57, 59, 60; Chinese community in, 49–50, 60, 91n138; commercial competition with China, 49; commercial infrastructure in, 59; difficulties in transporting oil to China, 93n169; economic diversification in, 57, 59, 175n97; effect of high costs of transporting goods to China, 52, 55; energy production in, 56; export promotion agencies, 59; free-trade zone in, 54, 55; government/business infrastructure in, 58–60; High Level Commission in, 59; historical context in evolution of relations with China, 49; industrial imports, 54, 55; infrastructure deficiencies for agricultural commerce, 50–51; infrastructure investment in, 94n195; infrastructure projects in, 55–56; intellectual infrastructure in, 60; issues in export transportation infrastructure, 191n375; as largest Latin American exporter to China, 49; logistics services, 60; low-end inexpensive imports in, 54, 55; as market for Chinese goods, 54–55; meat product exports, 53; military cooperation with China, 61–62; mining exports, 12, 51–52, 274; multicultural society in, 50; need for transportation infrastructure projects in, 51; nuclear industry, 58; petroleum exports, 12, 52–53; petroleum industry in, 93n168; political relations with China, 61–62; primary product exports, 49, 224; recognition of China by, 49; regional leadership role, 49; responsibility of China in loss of exports to Chile and United States, 91n135; sophisticated product imports, 54, 55; space technology in, 57; as "strategic partner," 17, 49, 61, 175n97, 200; technology projects in, 57–58; telecommunications industry in, 54, 55, 100n321; trade deficit with China, 54; trade infrastructure, 53;

uranium deposits, 58; visits from Chinese leaders, 61; wood product exports, 53; Workers' Party in, 61; in World Trade Organization, 49
Brazil-China Business Council, 60
Brazil-China Chamber of Commerce, 60
Bridas (Argentina), 67
Burges, Antonio, 214, 261n209
Bustamante, Victor, 157

Cabanillas, Mercedes, 156
Café Britt, 115, 218, 258n158
Cai Runguo, 123
Calderón, Felipe, 204, 207, 210, 213
Camara de Industria, Comercio, Servicios y Turismo de Santa Cruz (Bolivia), 145
Canada: oil reserves in, 111, 169n22; petroleum projects with China, 111
Cansing Group (Ecuador), 129
Cantrell (Mexico), 202
Cao Gangchuan, 48, 61, 62, 75, 97n257, 136, 147, 157, 168, 197n487
Capital: crises, 110; formation, 10; global investment, 26; goods, 10, 11, 20n18; investment, 1, 19n6, 26, 28; limited, 28; movement, 26; projects, 29
Caribbean: China's quest to isolate Taiwan and, 14–15; Chinese community in, 244; free entry to US markets, 199; issue of recognition in, 246–249; joint ventures in, 245–246; lack of logistics for large quantity exports to China, 14, 15; limited middle class in, 245; low-end inexpensive imports, 245; as market for Chinese goods, 245; market proximity to United States, 199; relations with China, 243–249; strategic geographic positions, 199; substantial aid from China to, 243; tourism in, 245; visits from Chinese leaders, 244–245
Caribbean Community (CARICOM), 246
Caribbean Development Bank (CDB), 3, 8n16
Carmona, Pedro, 122
Castro, Fidel, 236, 237, 238, 241, 242, 269n350

Castro, Raúl, 242
Central America: China's quest to isolate Taiwan and, 14–15; free entry to US markets, 199; inability to place products in Chinese markets, 234; lack of governmental and commercial infrastructure for relations with China, 230; lack of logistics for large quantity exports to China, 14–15; as market for Chinese goods, 200; market proximity to United States, 199; primary-product economies in, 230; remittances from United States, 230; small middle class in, 15; strategic geographic position, 199; subtle pressures by China for recognition, 234, 235
Central America Free Trade Agreement (CAFTA), 220, 221, 230
Central American-China Friendship Federation, 81
Centro de Promoción Bolivia (CEPROBOL), 145
Centro Energético de las Américas (CELA), 228
Chamber of Exporters of Costa Rica (CADEXO), 214
Changquing Petroleum Exploration Bureau (China), 127
Chávez, Hugo, 17, 22n58, 22n64, 29, 30, 107, 108, 109, 110, 112, 114, 121, 122, 174n84, 175n91, 175n97, 228, 241, 269n350, 276
Cheng Siwei, 106n453, 268n336
Chen Shui-Bian, 234, 235, 265n288
Cheyre, Juan, 48
Chiabra, Roberto, 157
Chile, 34–48; ability to deliver agricultural exports quickly, 86n41; accords with United States, 34; advantageous geographical location, 34; agricultural exports, 25, 38–39; agro-industrial sector, 38; Asian studies programs in, 46; banking sector in, 45; business presence in China, 34, 38, 39, 43–45, 45; business presence in Shanghai, 89n86; Chinese community in, 35–36; commercial/bureaucratic infrastructure in, 34; as commercial nexus between Asia and United States, 41–43; competency of

bureaucracy in, 43; disputes with China over fishing, 38, 47; domestic sensitivity to use of nuclear power in, 87n62; fishing industry, 38–39; focus on US and EU partners for nuclear power, 41; free-trade agreements with China, 34, 84n3; free-trade zones in, 41; governmental/business infrastructure, 42, 43–45; government support to exporters in, 38; historical context in evolution of relations with China, 35; intellectual infrastructure in, 45–47; interest in integrated supply chains in, 37–38; leading destination for Chinese products, 39, 40; limited agricultural exports, 34; as market for Chinese goods, 39–40; membership in Asia-Pacific Economic Cooperation, 34; middle class in, 39; military cooperation with China, 47–48, 91n126; mining exports, 12, 34, 36–38, 45, 273; nuclear energy in, 87n62; Partido Por Latin America Democracia in, 47; political relations with China, 47–48; preferential treatment to exports from China to, 88n71; premium product exports, 13; primary product exports, 34, 37; pro-trade political culture in, 40; recognition of China by, 35, 47; representation in Shanghai and Hong Kong, 43, 44; strategic relationship with United States, 48; support for China in World Trade Organization, 35; total exports to China, 31n11; transport infrastructure, 38; visits from Chinese leaders, 26, 35, 47; vulnerable energy supply in, 40; winemaking in, 13, 39, 45, 86n42
Chile-China Economic Cooperation Forum, 44
China: agricultural exports, 12, 86n41; as alternative to US dominance in Latin America, 28–30; antidumping investigations against, 69; attempts to isolate Taiwan, 14–15; attempts to use Chinese labor and companies for work in Latin America, 56, 99n304; auto/motorcycle exports, 204; auto/motorcycle production, 39, 54,

68, 83–84, 116, 132, 153, 164, 207; in Caribbean Development Bank, 8*n16*; collaboration with India on Latin American acquisitions, 193*n421*; competition with United States, 16–17; computer industry, 116, 132, 210; computer production, 207, 214; contributions to UN peacekeeping forces, 48; crisis in agricultural production in, 10, 11; Cultural Revolution in, 237; demand for iron and steel, 51, 52; direct contracts with agricultural growers, 65; diversification of exports by, 39, 40; economic growth in, 9, 24, 30*n5*; effects of future relations with Latin America, 271–291; electronics industry, 68; employment of nuclear power in, 40, 41; expansion of exports across range of sectors, 2; expansion of ties with Latin America, 1–7; export competition with Latin America, 6; food product imports in, 11, 12; geopolitical ambitions of, 1; hurdles to doing business with, 23; importance of diplomatic recognition to, 2; imports of agricultural goods, 10; industrial development in, 19*n6*; industrial expansion in, 10, 11; informal "truce" with Taiwan, 234; infrastructure investment in Brazil, 94*n195*; in Inter-American Development Bank, 8*n16*; interest in Latin America, 9–19; interest in populist regimes, 29; interim product imports, 20*n18*; level of savings by Chinese population, 10; low consumption of goods in, 10; low-end inexpensive exports, 2, 54, 55; manufacturing partnerships, 165; in manufacturing value-added chain, 199, 256; markets for Latin American goods in, 24; migration in, 20*n24*; need for primary products from Latin America, 9–13; need to import foodstuffs, 50–51; new middle class in, 24, 215, 218; nuclear energy in, 87*n62*; observer status in Organization of American States, 200; opening of banking sector to foreign institutions, 267*n333*; opportunities for collaboration with United States, 289; "peaceful rising" of, 16; personal relationships in business, 23; petroleum consumption in, 11, 20*n14,* 112; petroleum imports, 11, 52–53, 66–67, 110–115, 126–128, 138–141, 148, 149–150, 159–160, 202–203, 291*n9*; petroleum projects in Canada, 111; population's interest in foreign goods, 209; pragmatism in diplomatic relations, 35; premium product imports, 162, 218, 258*n155*; price competition with, 1; primary product imports, 24, 25, 183*n222,* 209; private property rights, 267*n333*; promotion of revolutionary movements by, 237; provision of technology by, 29; rapproachment with Taiwan, 82; responsibility in loss of Brazilian exports to Chile and United States, 91*n135*; rising prosperity and consumer imports, 11, 12, 13, 20*n18,* 20*n21,* 24, 39; rural to urban employment patterns, 11–12; share of US textile market for, 206; sophisticated product exports, 2, 54, 55, 209; "strategic partnerships" with, 17, 49, 61, 62, 74, 107, 199; strategy of "going out" by, 11; support for anti-US regimes by, 29; support for populist regimes, 17; tax code reform in, 267*n333*; technology partnerships with Latin America, 273, 277–278; telecommunications production, 40, 69; Three Gorges Dam, 57; Tiananmen Square crisis, 17, 63, 237, 247, 266*n301*; trade surpluses in, 10; trade tensions with Argentina, 62, 69; use of comparative advantage by, 5–7; visits from Latin American leaders, 3, 47, 61, 69, 75, 76, 80, 97*n257,* 108, 109, 121, 123, 124, 132, 133, 136, 137, 138, 146, 148, 156, 157, 158, 164, 165, 166, 167, 183*n226,* 204, 210, 211, 213, 218, 223–224, 237, 238, 266*n301*; wine market in, 13, 39, 45, 68, 77, 86*n44*; wish to avoid tension with United States, 16, 22*n58*

China, business presence: in Argentina, 69, 102*n363*; in Bolivia, 144–145; in

Brazil, 60; in Chile, 37, 44, 45; in Ecuador, 124, 126, 127, 177n119; in Mexico, 206; in Panama, 225; in Peru, 151, 154–155; in Venezuela, 116–118

China-Argentina relations, 62–75; agricultural, 62, 65–66; auto/motorcycle sales, 68; bilateral trade, 62; electronics, 68; government/business infrastructures, 72–74; historical context in evolution of relations, 63; intellectual infrastructure, 74; investment projects, 66; military cooperation, 63, 74–75; mining, 67; petroleum agreements, 66–67; phytosanitary agreements, 66, 72; political relations, 74–75; technology cooperation, 71–72; telecommunications, 69; trade tensions, 62, 75

China Beneficence, 125

China-Bolivia relations, 137–147; government/business infrastructure, 144–145; historical context in evolution of relations, 138; intellectual infrastructure, 145–146; military cooperation, 146–147; mining, 141–142; political relations, 146–147; telecommunications projects, 137

China-Brazil Earth Research Satellite (CBERS), 57–58

China-Brazil High Level Committee on Consultation and Cooperation, 61

China-Brazil relations, 49–62; agricultural, 91n142; agricultural exports, 50–51; auto/motorcycle sales, 54; China-Brazil Earth Research Satellite project, 57–58; Chinese exports, 54–55; free-trade areas and, 55; historical context, 49; infrastructure projects, 55–56; intellectual infrastructure, 60; investments in timberland, 53; iron and steel interests, 51–52; military cooperation, 61–62; mining interests, 51–52; nuclear power projects, 58; petroleum agreements, 52–53; phytosanitary agreements, 53; political relations, 61–62; space technology, 57; strategic dialogues of, 58, 59; student exchanges, 62; technology cooperation, 57–58; telecommunications industry, 54; tensions over use of Chinese companies/labor for projects in, 56; transportation projects, 55, 56

China-Caribbean Economic and Trade Cooperation Forum, 243

China-Caribbean Economic and Trade Summit (2005), 109

China-Caribbean relations, 243–249; centered on issue of recognition, 243; mining, 244–245

China-Caribbean Trade and Economic Cooperation forum, 213

China–Central American relations: question of recognition and, 233–236

China-Chile Free Trade Agreement (2005), 84n5

China-Chile relations, 34–48; agricultural, 38–39; cooperation in nuclear industry, 40–41; fishing, 38–39; free-trade agreements, 34, 39, 42; historical context, 35; intellectual infrastructure, 45–47; military, 91n126; military cooperation, 47–48; mining, 85n27; mining interests, 36–38, 45; political relations, 47–48; student exchange programs, 46

China-Colombia relations: agricultural, 160, 161–162; business infrastructure, 165–167; government infrastructure, 165–167; infrastructure projects, 162–163; intellectual infrastructure, 167; investment protection agreements, 168; manufacturing partnerships, 165; military cooperation, 167–168, 197n487; mining, 160–161; petroleum agreements, 159–160; phytosanitary agreements, 161; political relations, 167–168; student exchange programs, 168

China–Costa Rica Chamber of Commerce and Industry, 222

China–Costa Rican relations, 214–224; government/business infrastructure, 221–223; intellectual infrastructure, 223; phytosanitary agreements, 218, 258n159; production chains in, 221; tourism, 220

China-Cuba relations: caution in, 237; historical context in evolution of relations, 237–238; ideological legitimization and, 241–242; intellectual infrastructure, 240; military cooperation, 268*n340,* 268*n346;* rapprochement in, 237–238; strategic value of Cuba in, 236, 237; student exchanges, 240–241, 268*n336;* technology cooperation, 240

China Development Bank, 29, 45, 60, 74, 110, 120, 151, 155, 169*n15,* 172*n50,* 222, 261*n210*

China-Ecuador Society, 125, 135

China-Ecuador relations, 122–137; agricultural, 129, 130, 131; expansion of presence in Ecuador, 134–135; government/business infrastructure, 135; historical context in evolution of relations, 123–124; intellectual infrastructure, 135–136; military cooperation, 136–137; mining, 129; petroleum agreements, 126–128; phytosanitary agreements, 131; political relations, 136–137

China Education Expo, 73

China Fishery Group, 152

China International Trust and Investment Corporation (CITIC), 41

China Investment Corporation (CIC), 27

China–Latin America Business Summit (2007), 119

Chinalco (China), 151

China Metallurgical Construction, 51

China Metallurgical Group, 115

China-Mexico relations, 200–214; cooperative projects in, 250*n9;* global production chains in, 206; historical context in evolution of relations, 201; intellectual infrastructure, 212–213; military cooperation, 213–214; phytosanitary agreements, 210; political relations, 200, 213–214; reciprocal protection of investments in, 210

China-Mexico relations, and NAFTA: agricultural, 203; competitive/complementary manufacturing status, 205–208; government/busisiness infrastructure, 210–212

China Minmetals, 11, 20*n20,* 37, 38, 51, 86*n35,* 129, 151, 245, 270*n370*

China National Astronomical Observatories (NAOC), 72

China National Offshore Development Corporation (CNODC), 53, 67, 150, 203

China National Petroleum Corporation (CNPC), 11, 29, 66, 111, 128, 159, 170*n26,* 170*n36,* 202, 219

China Ocean Shipping Company (COSCO), 224, 227

China Ordins, 86*n35*

China-Panama relations, 224–230; agricultural, 226; government/business infrastructure, 229; historical context in evolution of relations, 224–225; infrastructure projects, 227–228

China-Paraguay Chamber of Commerce, 81

China-Paraguay Friendship Society, 81

China-Paraguay relations, 81–84; historical context in evolution of relations, 81; military cooperation, 84; political relations, 84

China-Peru relations, 147–157; agricultural, 151–152; free-trade agreements, 155; government/business infrastructure, 154–155; historical context in evolution of relations, 148–149; infrastructure projects, 153; intellectual infrastructure, 155–156; military cooperation, 156–157; mining, 148, 150–151; petroleum agreements, 148, 149–150; political relations, 156–157

China Petroleum and Chemical Corporation (CPCC), 170*n36*

China Shipbuilding Industry Corporation (CSIC), 172*n49*

China Sonangol firm, 66

China State Shipbuilding Corporation (CSSC), 172*n49*

China Trade Exposition, 229

China-Uruguay relations, 75–80; agricultural, 75, 76, 77, 79; government/business infrastructure, 79; historical context in evolution of relations, 76; industrial, 76; manufacturing, 77; military cooperation, 80; political relations, 80

China-Venezuela relations, 107–122; auto/motorcycle sales, 116; Center of Technology Innovation for, 174*n87;* commercial infrastructure projects,

108; government/business infrastructure, 119–120; High-Level Mixed Commission, 119, 173*n64*; historical context in evolution of relations, 108–109; intellectual infrastructure, 120–121; military, 102*n375*; military cooperation, 121–122; mining, 115; petrochemical industry, 115; petroleum agreements, 110–115; political, 121–122; social projects, 120; technology cooperation, 118–119; telecommunications, 116, 117

Chinese Aircraft Industry Corporation (CAICII), 57

Chinese communities: in Bolivia, 138; in Brazil, 49–50; in Caribbean, 244; in Chile, 35–36; in Colombia, 158–159; in Costa Rica, 217, 257*n146*, 257*n150*; in Cuba, 238; in Dominican Republic, 244; in Ecuador, 124–126, 135, 177*n127*, 180*n178*; in Jamaica, 244; in Mexicali, 250*n18*; in Mexico, 202; in Panama, 225–226, 262*n229*; in Paraguay, 81–82; in Peru, 149; significance in domestic politics of Latin America, 272, 275–277; in Uruguay, 76–77; in Venezuela, 109, 169*n11*, 169*n13*

Chinese Council for the Promotion of International Trade (CCPIT), 27, 59, 135, 154, 211, 222

Chinese-language programs, 2, 3, 30*n1*, 30*n2*, 45, 46, 73, 74, 80, 120, 121, 136, 146, 156, 167, 182*n210*, 209, 212, 223, 240, 255*n106*

Chinese State Commission for Reform and Development, 118

Chiriboga, Galo, 127

Choquehuanca, David, 137, 146

City Group (China), 120

Claro, Ricardo, 34, 45, 85*n8*

CODELCO (Chile), 36, 37, 38, 43, 44, 86*n35*, 89*n86*

Codina, Rodolfo, 48

Coimbol (Bolivia), 142

Colombia, 157–167; agricultural competition with other Latin American countries, 161; agricultural exports, 160, 161–162; Asian studies programs in, 167; as assembly platform for Chinese goods, 165; auto/motorcycle imports, 164; business infrastructure, 165–167; business presence in China, 166; Chinese community in, 158–159; coffee production in, 162; consumer goods imports, 164; contraband goods in, 163; decline in petroleum production in, 193*n413*; Ejercito de Liberación Nacional in, 267*n330*; Fuerzas Armadas Revolucionarias de Colombia in, 267*n329*; government infrastructure, 165–167; "Head of the Serpent" in, 193*n410*; historical context in evolution of relations with China, 158; history of criminality in, 157, 161, 163; illegal immigration in, 193*n410*; infrastructure projects, 162–163; intellectual infrastructure, 167; lack of development of coast infrastructure, 157; legal infrastructure in, 166; light manufactured imports, 164; limited relations with China, 157; low-end inexpensive imports, 163; as market for Chinese goods, 163–165; military cooperation with China, 167–168, 197*n487*; mining exports, 160–161, 194*n426*; modest petroleum industry in, 159–160; Multi-Fiber Agreement and, 163; paramilitary and guerrilla groups in, 163; per capita income, 195*n446*; petroleum agreements, 159–160; political relations with China, 167–168; poor relations with Venezuela, 118; premium product exports, 13, 162; recognition of China, 158; relations with United States, 157, 158, 162, 167–168, 197*n480*; state of transition in, 158; student exchange programs with China, 168; support for membership in Asia-Pacific Economic Cooperation, 166; tariffs on some Chinese imports, 163; telecommunications in, 164; trade deficit with China, 195*n447*; uranium deposits in, 58, 161; visits from Chinese leaders, 158

Colombian National Association of Coffee Growers, 162

Colombian National Council for Economic and Social Policy (CONPES), 163

Comisión Nacional de Energía Atómica (Argentina), 72

Commission to Promote Exports and Tourism (PromPeru), 154

Compañía Anónima de Administración y Fomento Eléctrico (Venezuela), 117

Compañía Anónima Nacional Teléfonos de Venezuela (CANTV), 117, 174n79

Compañía General de Minería de Venezuela (CVG), 117

Compañia Sudamericana de Vapores (Chile), 45, 85n8

Comparative advantage, 5–7, 286–288

Comphania Vale do Rio Doce (Brazil), 51, 52, 274

Compton, John, 248

Conde, Felipe, 157

Confucius Institutes, 3, 46, 74, 104n421, 212, 255n106

ConocoPhillips, 111

Contraband goods, 1, 14, 21n38, 78, 116, 131, 143, 163, 173n63, 173n64, 227

Copaco Company (Paraguay), 83

Copyright infringements, 209

Corporación Andino de Fomento (Brazil), 3, 94n197

Corporation for the Promotion of Exports (Ecuador), 135

Correa Delgado, Rafael, 29, 123, 132, 133, 134, 136, 178n144, 182n205

Costa Rica, 214–224; agricultural exports, 217–219, 258n159; application for Asia-Pacific Economic Cooperation membership, 223; Asia studies programs in, 2, 209, 212, 223; as assembly platform, 221; auto/motorcycle imports, 220; bid for seat on UN Security Council, 224; biotechnology industry in, 221; business infrastructure, 221–223; change in policy on Taiwan, 3; Chinese community in, 217, 257n146, 257n150; as commercial nexus between Asia and United States, 41–43; computer production, 214; consumer goods imports, 220; financial infrastructure, 222; free-trade agreements, 221; government infrastructure, 221–223; high wages in, 218; historical context in evolution of relations with China, 215; inability to increase agricultural exports, 218; information technology in, 260n191; information technology industry in, 214; information technology sector in, 219; intellectual infrastructure, 223; low-end inexpensive imports, 220; as market for Chinese goods, 220; oil refining in, 219; per capita income in, 220; petroleum exports, 219; political relations with China, 223–224; positive trade balance in, 219; premium product, 13; premium product exports, 13, 215, 218, 258n155; recognition of China, 82, 215, 223–224, 256n126, 271; recognition of China by, 24, 214; shifting recognition from Taiwan, 215–217; switches recognition from Taiwan, 214; telecommunications in, 220; tourism in, 214–215, 220; trade disputes with European Union, 218; trade promotion in, 222; value-added sectors, 221; visits from Chinese leaders, 214, 219, 221

Costa Rican Chamber of Exporters (CRECEX), 222

Craddock, Bantz, 284

Crime: drug, 128, 162; drug trafficking, 82, 282; human smuggling, 138, 225, 282; organized, 118, 273, 281–283

Crown American Investment Corporation, 83

Cuba, 236–243; Chinese community in, 238; ethanol production, 266n310; exports to China, 238–239; geographic value to China, 236; historical context in evolution of relations with China, 237–238; as ideological point of reference for leftist Latin America, 236; intellectual infrastructure, 240; interest in relations with China, 242–243; joint biotechnology projects, 240; limited purchasing power of, 239; as market for Chinese

goods, 239–240; mining sector, 238–239; oil reserves in, 266n313; petroleum reserves, 239; pivotal role in struggle against US hegemony, 236; primary product industries in, 238–239; promotion of revolutionary movements by, 237, 241; recognition of China, 265n295; role in strategic presence of China in Latin America, 236; as Russian ally in region, 236; as source of ideological legitimization, 241–242; sugar exports, 239, 243; support for leftist movements in Africa, 237; trade deficit with China, 238; as training ground for Chinese penetration of Latin America, 240–241; use as listening post by China, 242; visits from Chinese leaders, 236, 237, 266n301, 266n302, 268n336, 268n346
Cultural: cooperation, 121; friendship associations, 35; programs, 3

Dell Computer Company, 214
Deng Xiaoping, 17
Derbez, Luis, 210
Development: comparative advantage and, 5–7; fuel, 25–28; manufacturing, 4; mutual, 6; social, 26, 134
Diaz, Alejo, 80
Dominica: diplomatic change in, 247–248; recognition of China, 243; tourism in, 246
Dominican Republic: Chinese community in, 244; recognition of Taiwan by, 15; visits by Taiwanese leaders, 235
Duran, Sixto, 124

Eastern Petrogas (China), 140
Ebrard, Marcelo, 206, 211
Economic: diversification, 30n3; diversity, 32n33; dominance, 1
Economic Commission for Latin America and the Caribbean, 39
Ecopetrol (Colombia), 160
Ecopetrol (Ecuador), 177n132
Ecuador, 122–137; agricultural exports, 129, 130, 131; agricultural production in, 180n170; alternative fuel crops in, 130; alternatives to bonds

with United States, 136; anti-US policy in, 3; Asia studies programs in, 135, 136; auto/motorcycle imports, 132; banking sector in, 135; business infrastructure, 135; business presence in China, 124, 177n119, 181n205; Chinese community in, 124–126, 135, 177n127, 180n178; Chinese fixed investment in, 29, 123; as commercial nexus between Asia and United States, 41–43; consumer imports, 132; contraband markets in, 131; disputes over oil production in Yasuni National Park, 127, 178n138; environmental disagreements in, 178n144; fishing industry, 124, 130; as gateway to other Latin American markets, 132; government infrastructure, 135; historical context in evolution of relations with China, 123–124; hydroelectric development in, 134; imports of value-added products, 132; informal sector in, 131; infrastructure projects in, 132–134; institutional unpredictability in, 123; intellectual infrastructure, 135–136; lack of diversified export sector, 129; large input of capital into, 123; low-end inexpensive imports, 131; Manta-Manaus-Belém corridor project, 133, 134; as market for Chinese goods, 131–132; military cooperation with, 136–137; mining exports, 129; mining industry in, 179n157; niche industries in, 130; oil reserves in, 126; petroleum exports, 12, 126–128; political relations with China, 136–137; populist regime in, 17; primary product exports, 129; private sector in, 135; projects expanding Chinese presence in, 134–135; recognition of China, 123, 124; relations with United States, 130; removal of Occidental Petroleum, 127; social development projects, 134; sophisticated product exports, 130; state control and taxation of oil companies, 128; tourism, 182n209; uneven progress in projects, 122, 123; unpredictability as oil supplier, 53; uranium deposits, 58;

visits from Chinese leaders, 124, 136; war with Peru, 179n159
Ecuador–China Chamber of Commerce, 125, 135
Ecuadorian Institute for International Cooperation (INECI), 134
Ejercito de Liberación Nacional (ELN), 267n330
El Consejo Mexicano de Comercio Exterior, 211
El Niño effect, 152
El Salvador: free-trade agreement with Taiwan, 235; Frente Farabundo Martí de Liberación Nacional in, 267n329; low-end inexpensive imports, 232; recognition of Taiwan by, 15, 234; visits by Taiwanese leaders, 235
Embraco (Brazil), 57
Embraer (Brazil), 57, 59
Enarsa (Argentina), 66
Enbridge (Canada), 111
EnCana (Canada), 122, 126, 128, 274
Endara Galimany, Guerrmo, 230
Energía Argentina Sociedad Anónima, 67
Escobar, Ana Vilma de, 234
Espinosa Howell, Ronald, 256n126
Expo China trade fair, 44
ExxonMobil, 108, 111, 114

Fernandez, Heber, 80
Flores, Cilia, 176n101
Foreign policy: anti-US, 17; and Taiwan, 3
Fox, Vicente, 210, 213
Free Trade Area of the Americas, 284
Frei, Eduardo, 47
Frente Farabundo Martí de Liberación Nacional (FMLN), 267n329
Frente Sandinista de Liberación Nacional (FSLN), 233, 267n329
Fuentes, Bulmaro, 212
Fuerzas Armadas Revolucionarias de Colombia (FARC), 267n329
Fujimori, Alberto, 148, 149, 184n241
Fundación Exportar (Argentina), 73

Garcia, Alan, 148, 153, 156
García Belaúnde, José Antonio, 155
Garré, Nilda, 75
Gerdau (Brazil), 51

Giant Engine Company (China), 207
Glassven (Venezuela), 115
Global Banana Congress, 129
Gomes de Mattos, Roberto, 61
Great Wall Motor Company (China), 39
Grenada: diplomatic change in, 247; lawsuit from Export-Import Bank of Taiwan, 270n382; recognition of China, 243
Group of Eight (G-8), 49
Group of Seventy-Seven (G-77), 17
Grupo FEMSA (Mexico), 208, 209
Grupo Interbank (Peru), 155
Grupo Modelo (Mexico), 201, 208, 209, 253n73
Grupo Socoma (Argentina), 68
Grupo Terno (Ecuador), 132
Grupo Wong (Ecuador), 124, 135
Guatemala: Chinese efforts to obstruct sending of peacekeeping mission to, 235; low-end inexpensive imports, 232; recognition of Taiwan by, 15; visits by Taiwanese leaders, 235
Guevara, Ernesto "Che," 267n329
Gutierrez, Lucio, 125

Haier (China), 54, 116, 143
Hainan Airlines (China), 57
Haiti: Chinese peacekeepers in, 249, 268n345; recognition of Taiwan by, 15
Heavy Industry Fund, 29, 109–110, 115, 120, 121, 174n80, 274
Herrera Campins, Luis, 108
Hewlett-Packard Corporation, 214
Hilton quota, 66
Honduras: free-trade agreement with Taiwan, 235; low-end inexpensive imports, 232; opening of trade office in China by, 235; recognition of Taiwan by, 15; visits from Chinese leaders, 27
Hong Kong Bank of China (HSBC), 223
Huawei Company (China), 40, 54, 63, 69, 73, 83, 94n188, 117, 118, 143, 164, 204, 275
Hu Jintao, 17, 26, 35, 47, 61, 63, 66, 70, 72, 75, 82, 94n195, 136, 156, 157, 165, 201, 213, 214, 219, 221, 236, 237, 239, 243, 266n302
Hutchison-Whampoa (China), 100n321,

132, 133, 180n180, 181n191, 208, 224, 225, 227, 229, 248, 268n345

Import substitution industrialization, 30n3

India: collaboration with China on Latin American acquisitions, 193n421; economic growth in, 24, 25; imports from Argentina, 98n276; Latin America/China competition for markets, 31n13; mining exports, 51; oil imports from Venezuela, 170n32; primary product imports, 25

Indonesia: petroleum exports to China, 11

Industry and Commerce Bank of China (ICBC), 74

Initiative for the Integration of Regional Infrastructure (IIRSA), 272

Institutions: financial, 17, 73, 74; global, 16; international, 8n16, 49; lending, 26; multilateral, 3, 22n55; political, 17; supranational, 3

Instituto Costarricense de Electricidad (Costa Rica), 220

Inter-American Development Bank (IADB), 3, 8n16, 17, 200, 213–214, 249

International Court of Justice, 284

International Monetary Fund, 6

Investigaciones Aplicadas Sociedad del Estado (Argentina), 71, 72

Investment: capital, 1, 19n6, 26, 28; commodity fund, 27; to control commodities and resources, 27; in dollar-denominated assets, 32n29; domestic, 19n6; energy sector, 27; expectations and realities, 2, 3; final-assembly facilities, 27, 31n24, 199; fixed, 123; foreign direct, 19n6, 26, 31n16, 31n21, 137; in fuel development, 25–28; identifying opportunities for, 27; infrastructure, 3, 7, 26, 27, 94n195; in mines, 27; in telecommunications, 26; Western, 29

Iran: petroleum exports to China, 11

Itaú (Brazil), 59

Izurieta, Oscar, 48

Jamaica: Chinese community in, 244; military cooperation with China, 246, 268n345; mining exports,

244–245, 270n370; rail infrastructure, 245; tourism in, 246

Jarrin, Oswaldo, 136

Jiangxi Copper Corporation (China), 151

Jiang Zemin, 17, 35, 63, 76, 109, 138, 149, 158, 237

Jindal (India), 141

Jin Yan Mining (China), 115

Kirchner, Cristina Fernández de, 75

Kirchner, Nestor, 69, 75

Labor: inexpensive, 6, 79, 104n409, 130; price differentials, 205

Lacalle, Luis Alberto de, 76

Land: speculation, 12; suitable for cultivation, 11, 20n23

Lang Chao (China), 116, 117

Latin America: Chinese-language programs in, 2, 3, 45, 46, 73, 74, 80, 120, 121, 136, 146, 156, 167, 209, 212; consumer goods exports, 2, 24; damage to domestic manufacturing due to imports, 13; debt crises, 26; decrease in Western investment in, 26; "deindustrialization" in, 6; development of manufacturing industries in, 4; economic performance tied to China, 272, 273–275; effect of participation in global economic relations in development, 5–7; effects of future relations with China, 271–291; energy sector investment in, 27; expansion of ties with China, 1–7; export competition with China, 6; export-led growth hopes in, 24–25; increased crime in, 26; infrastructures, 6; interaction of Chinese and Latin American organized crime, 273, 281–283; interest in China, 23–30; investment by China in fuel development in, 25–28; low-end inexpensive imports in, 14; as market for Chinese goods, 13–14; in "middle income" category, 14; mining exports, 12; political economy of, 30n3; premium product exports, 2; pressures to restrict or place tariffs on Chinese imports, 13; primary product exports, 2, 3, 6; reasons for Chinese interest in, 9–19; significance of Chinese communities on domestic politics in, 272, 275–277; sophisticated product imports in, 14; as source of primary products, 9–13; as technology partner for China, 273, 277–278; transformation of ports in, 273, 278–281; use of comparative advantage by, 5–7; visits from Chinese leaders, 3. *See also* individual countries

Latin America–China Business Summit, 45

Latin America–East Asia Cooperation forum (FOCALAE), 60

Latin American Parliament, 3

Le Kequiang, 19

Lenovo (China), 116, 207, 210, 214, 215, 219

Lewin, Hardly Macarley, 246

Liang Guanglie, 48, 75, 80, 136, 157, 242

Li Changchun, 113, 134, 136, 156, 172n50, 175n101, 213

Li Peng, 109, 148, 225

Li Zhaoxing, 155

Lou, Moisés, 262n229

Lu, Annette, 82, 235

Lugo, Fernando, 82, 84

Lukoil (Russia), 111

Luksic, Andronico, 34, 39, 45

Lula da Silva, Luiz Inácio, 61, 134

Macri, Mauricio, 73

Mahuad, Jamil, 124

Ma Jing-jeou, 82

Manta-Manaus-Belém corridor, 133, 134, 228–229, 272

Mao Zedong, 17, 30, 138, 241, 265n296

Market(s): commodity, 273; contraband goods, 1, 14, 78, 116, 131, 143, 163, 173n63, 173n64; domestic, 66; economy, 70; export, 1; foreign, 10; informal, 14, 116, 131, 142, 143; international, 25; niche, 215, 218, 258n155; targeting, 59; traditional, 1, 13

Mercosur (Southern Common Market), 54, 55, 68, 78, 93n186, 100n316, 104n409

Mesa Gisbert, Carlos, 137, 139, 140

Mexican Committee of Foreign Trade, 211

Mexican Foreign Commerce Bank (BANCOMEXT), 211, 212, 252n54

Mexico, 200–214; agricultural exports, 203; Asian studies programs in, 212–213; attempts to eliminate barriers to entry of agricultural products to China, 203; auto/motorcycle assembly in, 207; auto/motorcycle imports, 204; banking sector in, 212; beer production in, 13, 39; business infrastructure, 210–212; business presence in China, 201, 208–210; Chinese community in, 202, 250n18; competition with Chinese manufactured goods, 200–201, 205–208; competitive advantage in, 201, 211; consumer credit infrastructure in, 204; consumption rather than export of primary products, 200; decline in oil reserves, 202, 250n20; desire to demonstrate independence from United States, 213–214; drops objections to Chinese membership in World Trade Organization, 204; economic diversification in, 175n97; evolution of economic relationship to partnership status, 201, 205–208; final-assembly plants in, 206, 208, 252n57; global-supply-chain partnership with China, 207; government infrastructure, 210–212; high costs of transporting goods to China value-added manufacturing sector in, 201; historical context in evolution of relations with China, 201; intellectual infrastructure, 212–213; leadership role in region, 200; legal infrastructure, 210; low-end inexpensive imports, 204; manufacturing sector, 205; maquiladora sector in, 205, 206, 207; as market for Chinese goods, 203–204; market proximity to United States, 199; military cooperation with China, 213–214; Multi-Fiber Agreement and, 205–206; petroleum exports, 202–203; political relations with China, 200, 213–214, 250n9; port infrastructure in, 210; premium product exports, 13; pressure on by China to convince Central America for recognition of, 235, 249n2; private sector trade promotion in,

210–211; prohibitions on foreign investment in, 202; provision of support for China in United Nations, 200; recognition of China by, 97*n263*, 200, 201, 250*n9*; reduction of petroleum export commitment, 202, 203; request from industry for government protection against Chinese goods, 206; sale of manufactured goods to United States, 205; sophisticated product imports/exports, 209; strategic geographic position, 199; as "strategic partner," 17, 175*n97*, 200, 249*n1*; tariff-free access to US markets, 199, 201, 205; telecommunications in, 209; tense economic relations with China, 200; tourism in, 213; trade balances, 200, 204; trade deficit with China, 251*n37*; trade promotion by regional governments, 211; trade promotion in, 254*n94*; visits from Chinese leaders, 201, 213

Mexico-China Permanent Binational Commission, 210
Mexico-China Plenary Reunion (2007), 210
Migration, in China, 20*n24*
Monroe Doctrine, 17
Morales, Evo, 30, 137, 138, 139, 140, 146, 147, 183*n226*, 184*n242*, 241
Morales Hernandez, Francisco, 221, 256*n126*, 259*n180*
Moreno, Luis Alberto, 8*n16*
Mottley, Mia, 245
Movimiento Revolucionario Túpac Amaru (MRTA), 267*n329*
Movistar-Teléfonica (Venezuela), 117
Multi-Fiber Agreement, 163, 205, 206
Multilateralism, 16
Musa, Said, 234

Navarro, Samuel, 230
Nicaragua: Frente Sandinista de Liberación Nacional in, 267*n329*; low-end inexpensive imports, 232; recognition of China and Taiwan in, 15, 233–234; Sandinista Party in, 233, 234; trans-Nicaragua pipeline, 232–233; transoceanic canal in, 232–233

Nineteenth Intergovernmental Commission (2007), 239
Noboa, Gustavo, 124
Noboa Group (Ecuador), 129
Non-Aligned Movement, 237, 242
Norasia Shipping (Hong Kong), 45
North American Free Trade Agreement (NAFTA), 201, 205, 206, 251*n41*, 252*n52*, 252*n54*
Northern Peru Copper (Canada), 151

Occidental Petroleum (United States), 127, 179*n155*
Oil and Natural Gas Corporation (India), 111
Oman: petroleum exports to China, 11
Organization of American States (OAS), 3, 200, 213–214; Chinese observer status in, 17, 200
Ortega, Daniel, 232, 233
Ospina, Carlos, 197*n487*

Pacheco, Abel, 259*n169*
Pacific Basin Forum, 166
Panama, 224–230; agricultural exports, 226; alternatives to Panama Canal, 228–229; auto/motorcycle imports, 226; banking sector in, 229; business infrastructure, 229; business presence in China, 225; Chinese community in, 225–226, 262*n229*; consumption of goods/services in support of Canal traffic, 227; contraband goods in, 227; disagreements over recognition of China, 229–230; duty-free zones, 263*n251*; financial sector in, 229; free-trade zone in, 227; government infrastructure, 229; historical context in evolution of relations with China, 224–225; importance of Panama Canal for relations with China, 224, 227; infrastructure projects in, 227–228; low-end inexpensive imports, 226; as market for Chinese goods, 226–227; modernization/expansion of Panama Canal, 224, 227; per capita income in, 226; recognition of Taiwan by, 15, 225, 226; return of sovereignty of Panama Canal to, 225; Revolutionary

Democratic Party in, 230; Solidarity
Party in, 230; trans-Panama pipeline,
228; well-developed administrative
infrastructure for Canal, 229
Panama Canal: alternatives to, 228–229,
232–233; importance of in relations
with China, 224, 227; modernization
and expansion of, 224, 227; return of
sovereignty to Panama, 225
Paraguay, 81–84; agricultural exports,
83; Chinese community in, 81–82;
Colorado Party in, 81; historical context in evolution of relations with
China, 81; isolationist foreign policy
in, 81; lack of access to seacoast, 81;
as market for Chinese goods, 83–84;
military cooperation with China, 84;
nonrecognition of China by, 82–83;
political relations with China, 84;
recognition of Taiwan by, 15, 76, 83;
visits by Taiwanese leaders, 235
Paz Zamora, Jaime, 138, 184n241
Peirano, Miguel, 69
People's Republic of China (PRC). See
China
Perez, Ernesto, 230
Pérez Villamil, Ximena, 45
Peru, 147–157; agricultural exports, 12,
25, 151–152; agricultural technology
in, 152; Asia studies programs in,
155–156; auto/motorcycle imports,
153; banking sector in, 155; business
infrastructure, 154–155; business
presence in China, 154–155; Chinese
community in, 149; Chinese investment in, 27; as commercial nexus
between Asia and United States,
41–43; commodity trade in, 155;
decline in petroleum production in,
150; El Niño effect on fishing industry, 152; failure of China to fulfill
investment promises in, 151; favorable geographic position, 148; fishing industry in, 38, 148, 151; free-
trade agreements with China, 155;
government disputes with Chinese
companies on environmental issues,
150–151; government infrastructure,
154–155; historical context in evolution of relations with China,
148–149; infrastructure projects in,

153; intellectual infrastructure,
155–156; as market for Chinese
goods, 152–153; market orientation,
148; military cooperation with
China, 156–157; mining exports, 12,
148, 150–151; Movimiento
Revolucionario Túpac Amaru in,
267n329; offices in Shanghai and
Hong Kong, 154; petroleum exports,
148, 149–150; political relations
with China, 156–157; premium product imports, 152–153; recognition of
China, 98n263, 148; Sendero
Luminoso in, 267n330; support for
Chinese control of Tibet, 157;
tourism in, 192n391; trade infra-
structure in, 155; trade surplus in,
148; visits from Chinese leaders,
148, 149, 156, 157; war with
Ecuador, 179n159
Peru-Brazil Interoceanic corridor,
228–229
Peru-China Chamber of Commerce,
154, 155
Peru Copper (Canada), 151
Peruvian Association of Exporters
(ADEX), 152
Petrobas (Brazil), 52, 53, 59, 127,
172n55
Petrocaribbe, 17
PetroCaribe, 170n32
Petrochina, 53
Petroecuador, 127, 177n135
Petroleos de Venezuela Sociedad
Anonima (PdVSA), 112, 114, 117,
127, 170n26, 170n29, 170n32,
172n49, 172n55, 263n242
Petróleos Mexicanos (PEMEX), 202,
251n24
Petropars (Iran), 111
Petroriental (China), 128, 276
Petrosur, 17
Pinochet Ugarte, Augusto, 35, 85n10,
237, 265n297
Plan Colombia, 197n480
Plan Puebla Panama, 202
PlusPetrol Norte (Argentina), 150
Ponce Lerou, Enrique, 34, 38, 45
PRC. See China
ProChile, 43, 73
Proexport (Colombia), 161

ProMexico, 211

Qiao Qingchen, 80

Recession, global, 9, 28, 51, 52, 62, 65, 207, 273, 274
Red Dragon group, 138
Reform: institutional, 28
Repsol YPF (Spain), 67, 128
Republic of China. *See* Taiwan
Rights: human, 28, 63, 85*n10*; intellectual property, 14; property, 12, 267*n333*; third world, 146
Rodriguez Lara, Guillermo, 124
Rodriguez Veltze, Eduardo, 137, 139, 140
Roldós Aguilera, Jaime, 124

Saca, Tony, 234
St. Kitts and Nevis: recognition of Taiwan by, 15
St. Lucia: recognition of Taiwan, 244, 248; visits by Taiwanese leaders, 235
St. Vincent and the Grenadines: recognition of Taiwan by, 15
Samper, Ernesto, 158
Sanchez de Lozada, Gonzalo, 137, 140
Sanguinetti, Julio Maria, 76
San Miguel, Walker, 147
Santos, Juan Manuel, 168
Sarabia Vilches, Aldo, 48
Scioli, Osvaldo, 75
Sector, informal: Chinese goods in, 14, 116; migration and, 20*n24*
Semana de Comercia Exterior 2007, 152
Sendero Luminoso (Peru), 267*n330*
Serra, José, 61
Service companies, 2
Shandong Gold Mining (China), 115
Shandong Luneng (China), 137, 141
Shanghai Federation of Commerce and Industry Business Encounter, 44
Shannon, Tom, 283, 290
Shengli Oil (China), 137, 139
Shougang (China), 51, 275
Shougang Hierro Peru, 150
"Simon Bolívar" satellite, 118–119, 122, 174*n87*, 277
Sino-Argentine Chamber of Commerce, 73
Sinochem Internacional (China), 86*n35*
Sino-Chilean free-trade agreement, 42

Sino-Chilean FTA, 34
Sinopec (China), 56, 111, 127, 139, 239
Sino-Venezuelan Agricultural Investment Company, 120
Sister-city agreements, 3, 42
Society for the Promotion of Industry (Chile), 44
Sojo, Carlos, 256*n126*, 256*n127*, 259*n177*
Sol del Oriente (Ecuador), 124, 135
Solo, Eduardo, 210
South American Regional Infrastructure Integration Initiative (IIRSA), 55–56
Southern Cone countries: agricultural exports by, 33; effect of Andes mountains on commerce with China, 33; middle income levels in, 33; resistance to expansion of trade with China in, 33. *See also* individual countries
Stagno, Bruno, 216, 223–224
Starbucks, 115, 162, 218, 258*n156*
Strategic partnership status, 17, 49, 61, 62, 74, 175*n97*
Stroessner, Alfredo, 81

Taina, Jorge, 75
Taiwan: activities to shore up relations with allies in Central America, 235; diplomatic isolation of, 14–15; rapproachment with China, 82, 234; recognition of, 14–15, 82, 199, 234; recognition of by Caribbean nations, 15; recognition of in Central America, 14–15; support for in United Nations, 236
Technology: agricultural, 152; biological, 71, 72; centrifuge, 58; computer, 84; cooperation in, 216; information, 82, 214, 219, 221, 260*n191*; nuclear, 58, 71; photo-imaging, 58; public-security, 78; space, 57–58, 71; transfer, 174*n85*
Teixeira, Alessandro, 59
Telecommunications: in Argentina, 63, 69; in Bolivia, 137; in Brazil, 54, 55; in Colombia, 164; in Costa Rica, 220; investment in, 26; in Mexico, 209; satellites, 29; in Uruguay, 78; in Venezuela, 108, 117
Telefónica (Brazil), 55
Toledo, Alejandro, 156
Torrijos, Martin, 230

Trade: balances, 200, 214, 219; bilateral, 35, 42, 62, 107, 147, 200, 214, 224, 234, 265n291; commodity, 155; complimentary/competitive effect, 1, 205; deficits, 54, 62, 195n447, 204; delegations, 211, 215; disputes, 218; fairs, 2, 25, 43, 59, 60, 79, 119, 222; globalization of, 205; infrastructures, 53, 155; international, 10; mercantilist, 28; preferential access, 15; promotion, 43, 59, 79, 145, 154, 161, 210–211, 222; relationships, 23, 30n3; specialization, 6
Transparency, 28

Ugalde, Edgar, 256n126, 256n127
United Nations: support for Taiwan in, 236
United Nations Conference on Trade and Development (UNCTAD), 17
United Nations Security Council: Chilean request for seat on, 35
United Nations Stabilization Mission in Haiti (MINUSTAH), 48
United States: accords with Chile, 34; agricultural supplies to Cuba from, 269n351; Chinese competition with, 16–17; complaints against China in World Trade Organization, 13, 14; consultative meetings with China, 283, 284; dominance in Latin America by, 28–30; drops objection to Chinese membership in Inter-American Development Bank, 8n16; Drug Enforcement administration, 284; future relations with Latin America constrained by Chinese presence, 273, 283–284; grain embargo against South America, 92n142; independence from political influence of, 1; issues in oil commitments from Venezuela, 110–115; Latin American rebellions against trade relations with, 23; military planning and Chinese presence in hemisphere, 273, 283–284; military ties with Argentina, 75; opportunities for collaboration with China, 289; primary product imports, 25; relations with Colombia, 157, 158, 162, 167–168, 197n480; tariffs on Latin American goods, 186n265

Uribe, Alvaro, 30, 160, 161, 164, 165, 166, 167
Uruguay, 75–80; agricultural exports, 75, 76, 77; Asia studies programs in, 79–80; business infrastructure, 79; business presence in China, 68, 79; Chinese community in, 76–77, 79–80; contraband goods in, 78; delegate offices in Shanghai and Hong Kong, 79; exports to European markets, 77; government infrastructure, 79; historical context in evolution of relations with China, 76; industrial exports, 76; intellectual infrastructure, 79–80; interest in integrated supply chains, 79; joint manufacturing enterprises in, 104n409; low-end inexpensive imports, 77; manufacturing sector in, 77; as market for Chinese goods, 77–78; middle class in, 77; military cooperation with, 80; as official tourist destination, 105n421; political relations with China, 80; as production/distribution hub, 78–79; public-security project, 78; recognition of China, 76; sophisticated product imports, 77, 78; tariff-free exports to Brazil, 93n186, 100n316; telecommunications industry in, 78; tourism in, 80; visits from Chinese leaders, 76, 80; winemaking in, 77
US International Military Education and Training programs, 91n126

Vanco Comercio Exterior de Venezuela (BANCOEX), 119, 120
Varela, Juan Carlos, 229–230
Vargas, Wilfredo, 147
Vásquez, Tabaré, 76, 80
Venezuela, 107–122; anti-US policy in, 3, 22n64; arms imports from Russia, 176n109; Asia studies program in, 120, 121; asset-seizure of Exxon-Mobil in, 108, 114; avoidance of dependence on United States, 110; bid for UN Security Council membership, 121; business infrastructure, 119–120; business presence in China, 119, 120, 175n92; capital crisis in, 110; chemical production, 173n57; Chinese community in, 109, 169n11, 169n13;

Chinese investment in, 31*n21*; choice of Russian military equipment over Chinese, 122; computer assembly plants in, 29, 116; consumer electronics imports, 116; contraband goods in, 116, 173*n63*, 173*n64*; difficulty in accessing foreign currency, 116; financial limits on importing ability, 116; former alignment with United States, 108; free-trade zones in, 116, 117; government infrastructure, 119–120; Heavy Industry Fund in, 29, 109–110, 115, 120, 121, 274; historical context in evolution of relations with China, 108–109; hostility to foreign investment in, 110; informal sector in, 116; infrastructure projects in, 118; infrastructure subsidies in, 116; intellectual infrastructure, 120–121; issues in financing commitments, 110, 112, 113; lack of banking infrastructure in, 120; lack of stable judiciary in, 108; low-end inexpensive imports, 116; as market for Chinese goods, 116–118; military cooperation with China, 102*n375*, 121–122; mining exports, 115; Movimiento del Quinto Republica in, 175*n101*; nationalization of petroleum industry in, 29; nationalization of Western companies by, 108; national rail system in, 174*n84*; oil exploration assistance to Cuba, 266*n315*; oil reserves in, 12, 108, 111; petrochemical industry, 115; petroleum drilling equipment imports, 171*n37*; petroleum exports, 12, 170*n32*; petroleum industry, 108; political relations with China, 121–122; poor relations with Colombia, 118; populist regime in, 17; premium product exports, 115; private sector trade initiatives, 119, 120; problems in oil production, 112, 113, 114; railroad system modernization in, 118; rum production in, 115; "Simon Bolívar" satellite, 118–119, 122, 174*n87*, 277; sophisticated product imports, 116; as "strategic partner," 17, 107, 175*n97*, 200; technology projects, 118–119; telecommunications industry in, 108, 117, 174*n81*; uncertainty over ability to deliver promised oil exports, 53, 169*n19*, 172*n56*; use of China as counterweight to United States by, 109; visits from Chinese leaders, 108, 109, 121, 172*n50*

Venezuelan Foundation for the Development of Agriculture, Fishing, and Forestry (FONDAFA), 120

Venturelli, Jose, 35

Vergara, Angel, 48

Videla, Jorge Rafael, 237

Viegas Gilho, José, 62

Vinicio Ruiz, Marco, 24, 216, 256*n126*, 258*n155*, 258*n159*

Vivo (Brazil), 55

Wagner, Allan, 157

Wang Jinzhen, 27

Wang Qi Shan, 211

Wang Xiaoyuan, 216, 258*n159*, 261*n210*

War of the Pacific (1879), 36, 184*n240*

Washington Consensus, 28, 284

Wen Jiabao, 12, 27

Wong, Segundo, 129

World Bank, 6

World Health Organization (WHO), 234

World Trade Organization (WTO), 21*n42*; antidumping charges in, 70; Brazil in, 49; Chilean support for China in, 35

Wu Bangguo, 47, 61, 80

Xi'an Phoenix Aircraft Corporation (China), 69

Xi Jinping, 17

Xu Caihou, 214, 246

Xu Qiliang, 48

Yacimientos Petrolíferos Fiscales Bolivianos (YPFB), 139

Yang Jiechi, 61, 156, 230

Yang Shangkun, 76, 138

Yunnan Copper Company (China), 38

Zelaya, Manuel, 235, 236

Zhang Tuo, 109, 121, 138

Zheng He, 16

Zheng Quinghong, 61, 75, 109, 121, 156, 213, 243, 244–245

Zijin Mining Group (China), 151

ZTE Company (China), 40, 54, 55, 63, 69, 117, 118, 143, 165, 204, 211, 275

About the Book

WITH CHINA ON THE MINDS OF MANY IN LATIN AMERICA—FROM politicians and union leaders to people on the street, from business students to senior bankers—a number of important questions arise. Why, for example, is China so rapidly expanding its ties with the region? What is the nature of the new connection and how will it affect institutions, economic structures, politics, and society? R. Evan Ellis provides a comprehensive look at the character and impact of the developing PRC–Latin America relationship.

Ellis examines how the relationship has taken on distinct characteristics in various subregions, considering the role of supplier-and-market countries such as Argentina and Brazil, China's cautious dance with populism as it seeks access to Andean oil, and the dominance of the Taiwan issue in China's dealings with Central America and the Caribbean. He also addresses the unique case of Cuba. Not least, his work sheds light on the implications of the China–Latin America relationship for conventional wisdom regarding globalization, development, and the links between economics and politics.

R. Evan Ellis is professor at the Center for Hemispheric Defense Studies, where he focuses on Chinese initiatives in Latin America, populism in the Andes, and other Latin American security issues.